NORAGAMI
STRAY GOD

ADACHITOKA

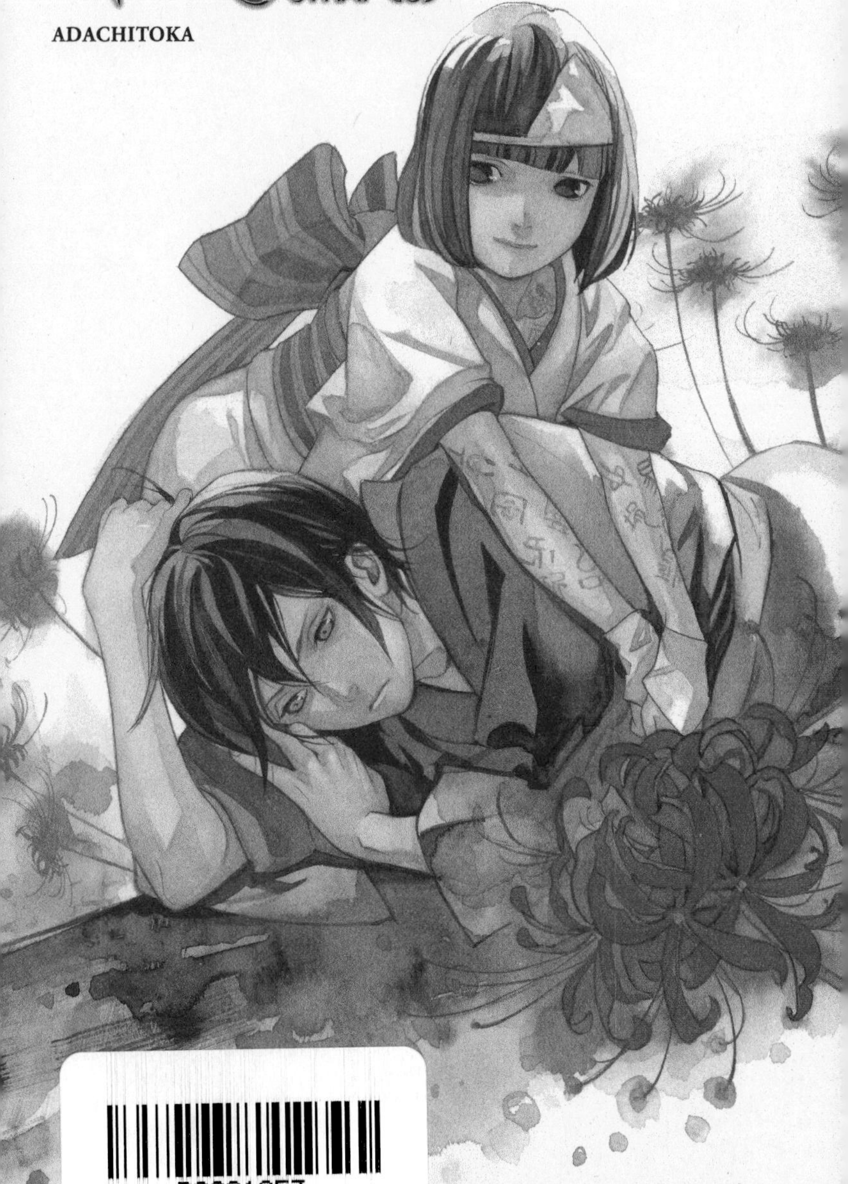

CHAPTER 12: TO CUT, OR NOT TO CUT   5

CHAPTER 13: SIGNS   51

CHAPTER 14: HER MEMORIES   97

CHAPTER 15: THAT WHICH WITHERS AWAY   143

Characters

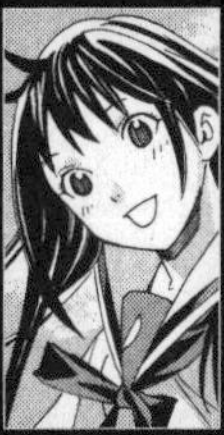

HIYORI IKI

A middle school student who has become half ayakashi.

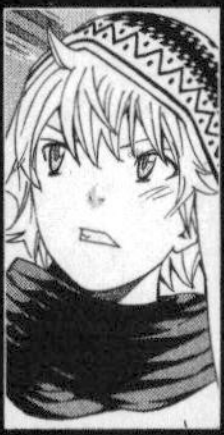

YUKINÉ

Yato's shinki who turns into a sword.

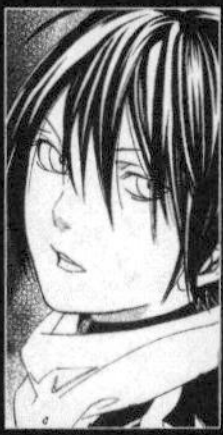

YATO

A minor deity who always wears a sweatsuit.

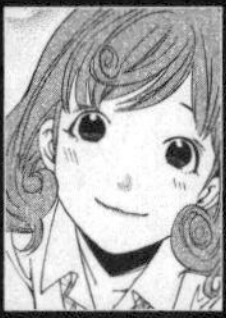

KOFUKU

A goddess of poverty who calls herself Ebisu after the god of fortune.

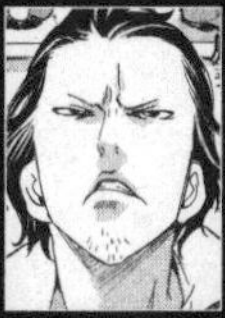

DAIKOKU

Kofuku's shinki who summons storms.

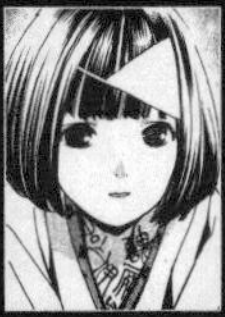

STRAY

A shinki who serves an unspecified number of deities

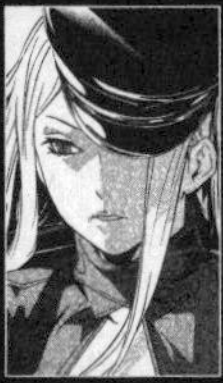

BISHA-MONTEN

A powerful warrior god who seeks vengeance on Yato.

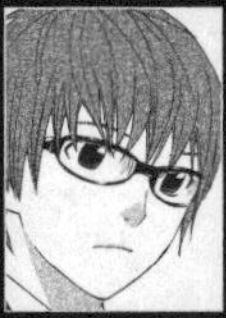

KAZUMA

A navigational shinki who serves as guide to Bishamon.

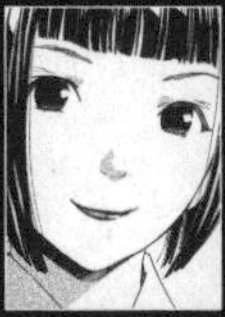

MAYU

Formerly Yato's shinki, now Tenjin's shinki.

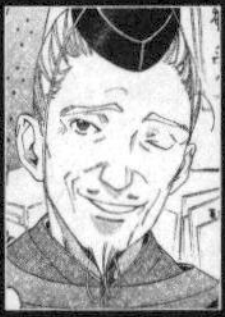

TENJIN

The God of Learning, Sugawara no Michizane.

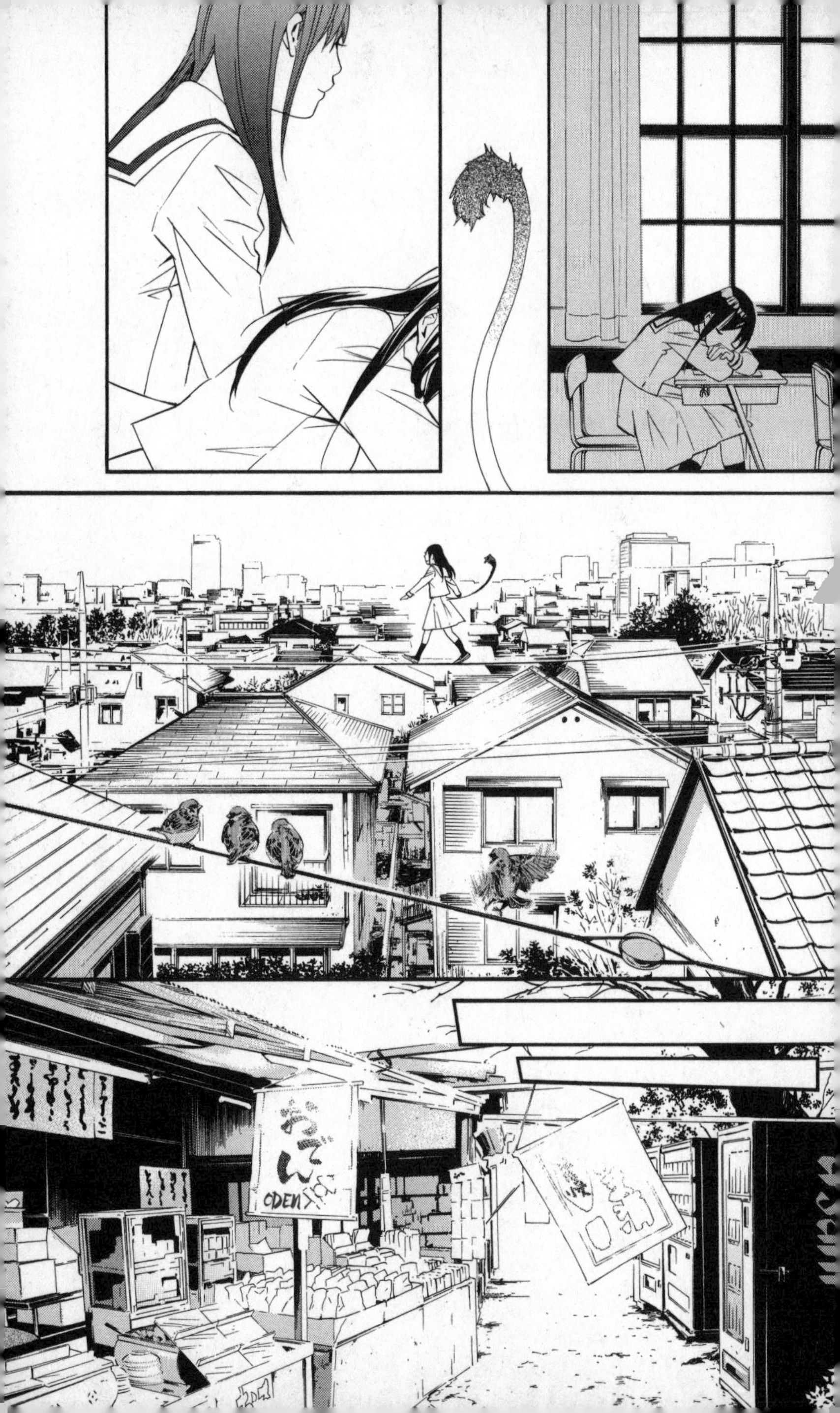
おでん
ODEN

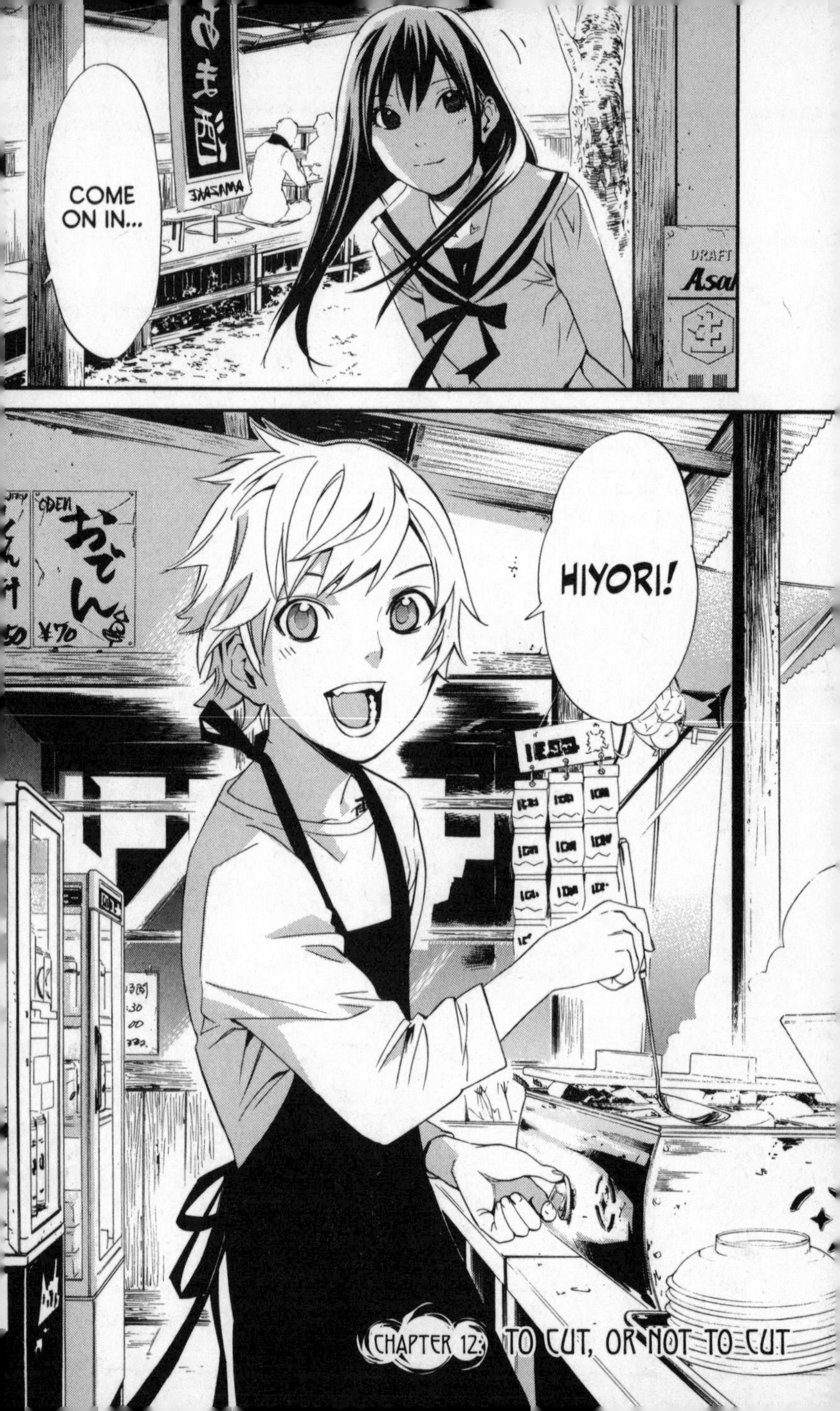
COME ON IN...
DRAFT
ODEN
¥70
HIYORI!
CHAPTER 12: TO CUT, OR NOT TO CUT

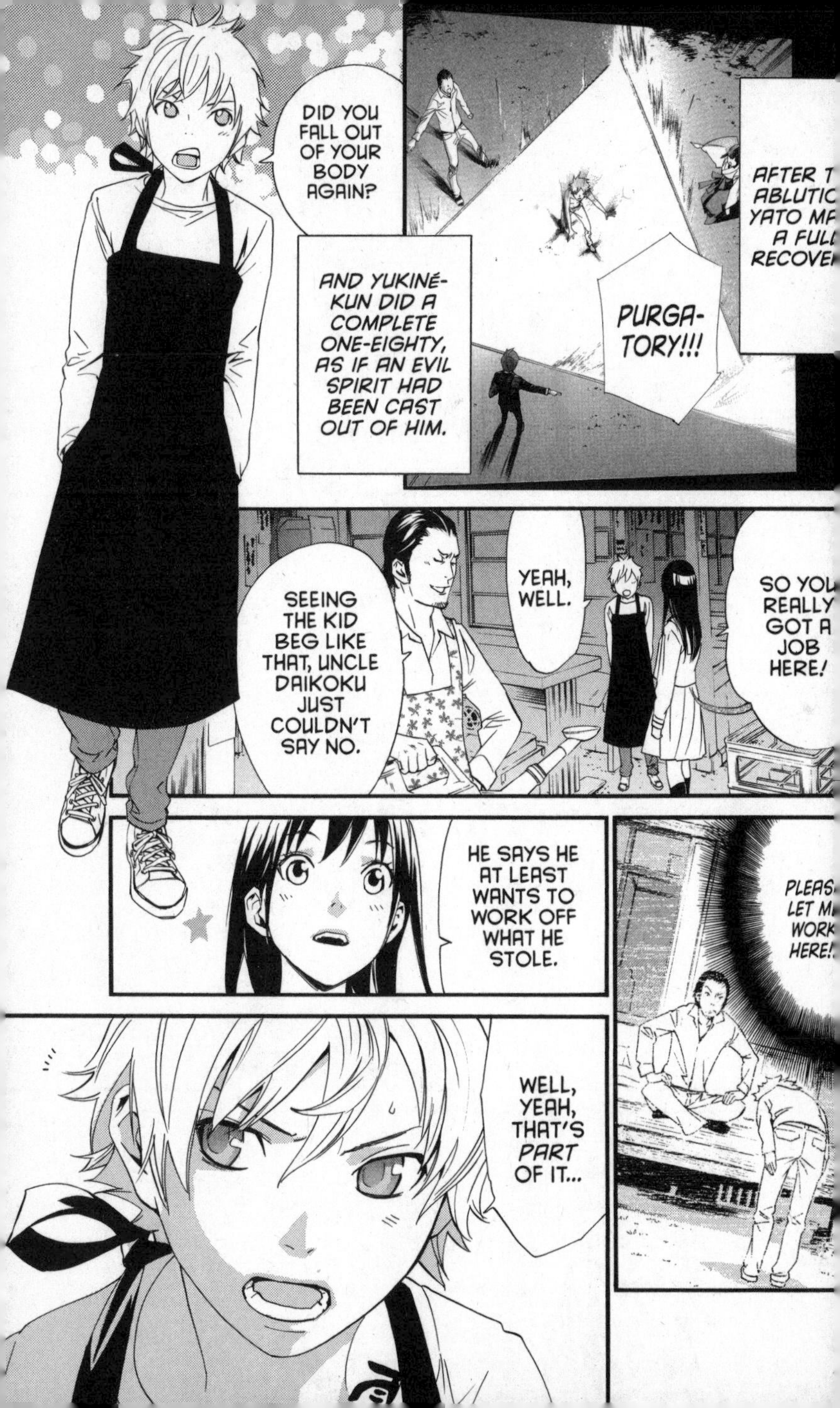

AFTER T ABLUTIC YATO MA A FULL RECOVEI
PURGA-TORY!!!
AND YUKINÉ-KUN DID A COMPLETE ONE-EIGHTY, AS IF AN EVIL SPIRIT HAD BEEN CAST OUT OF HIM.
DID YOU FALL OUT OF YOUR BODY AGAIN?
SO YOU REALLY GOT A JOB HERE!
YEAH, WELL.
SEEING THE KID BEG LIKE THAT, UNCLE DAIKOKU JUST COULDN'T SAY NO.
PLEAS LET MI WORK HERE!
HE SAYS HE AT LEAST WANTS TO WORK OFF WHAT HE STOLE.
WELL, YEAH, THAT'S *PART* OF IT...

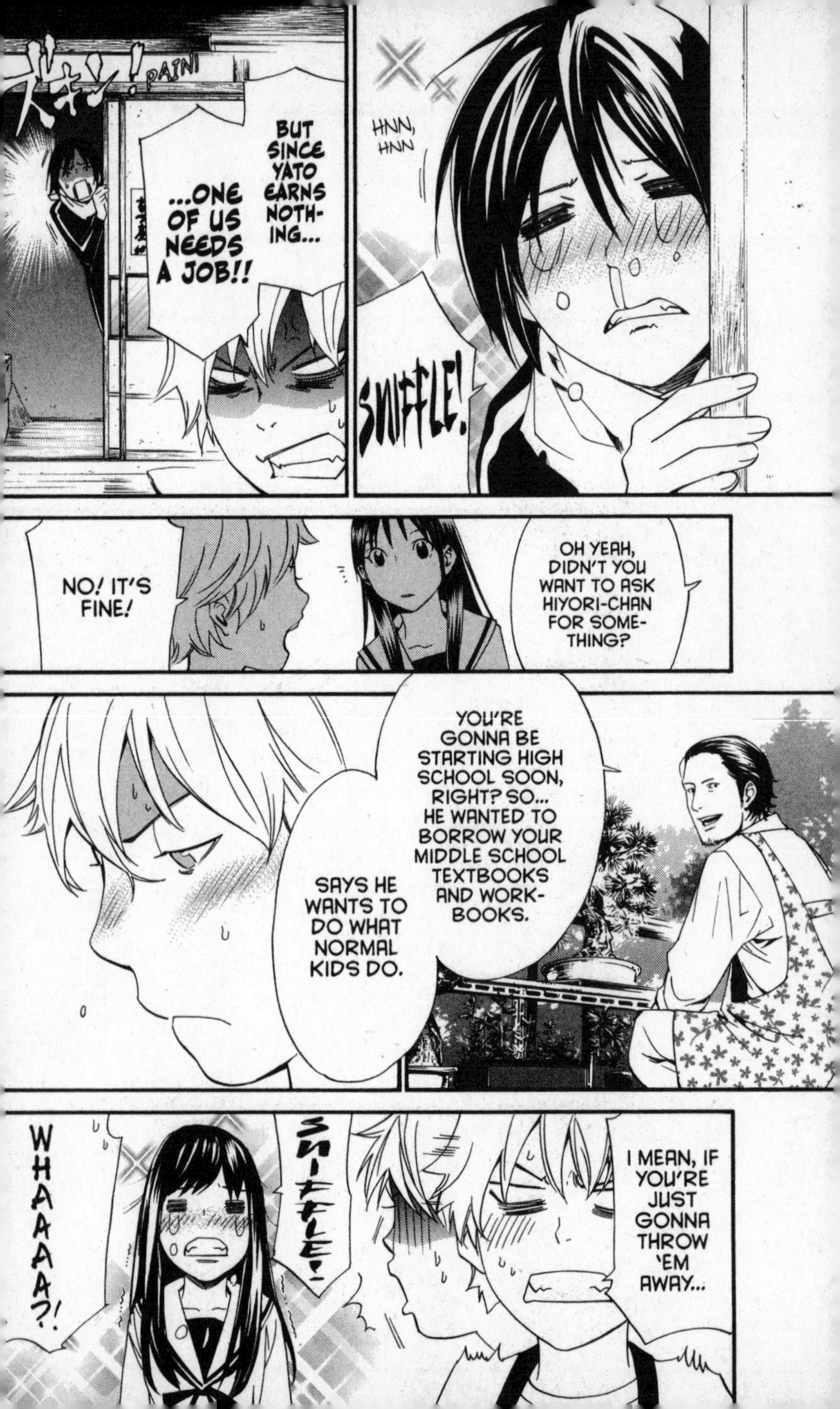
HNN, HNN
SNIFFLE!
BUT SINCE YATO EARNS NOTHING...
...ONE OF US NEEDS A JOB!!
PAIN!
OH YEAH, DIDN'T YOU WANT TO ASK HIYORI-CHAN FOR SOMETHING?
NO! IT'S FINE!
YOU'RE GONNA BE STARTING HIGH SCHOOL SOON, RIGHT? SO... HE WANTED TO BORROW YOUR MIDDLE SCHOOL TEXTBOOKS AND WORKBOOKS.
SAYS HE WANTS TO DO WHAT NORMAL KIDS DO.
I MEAN, IF YOU'RE JUST GONNA THROW 'EM AWAY...
SNIFFLE!
WHAAAAA?!

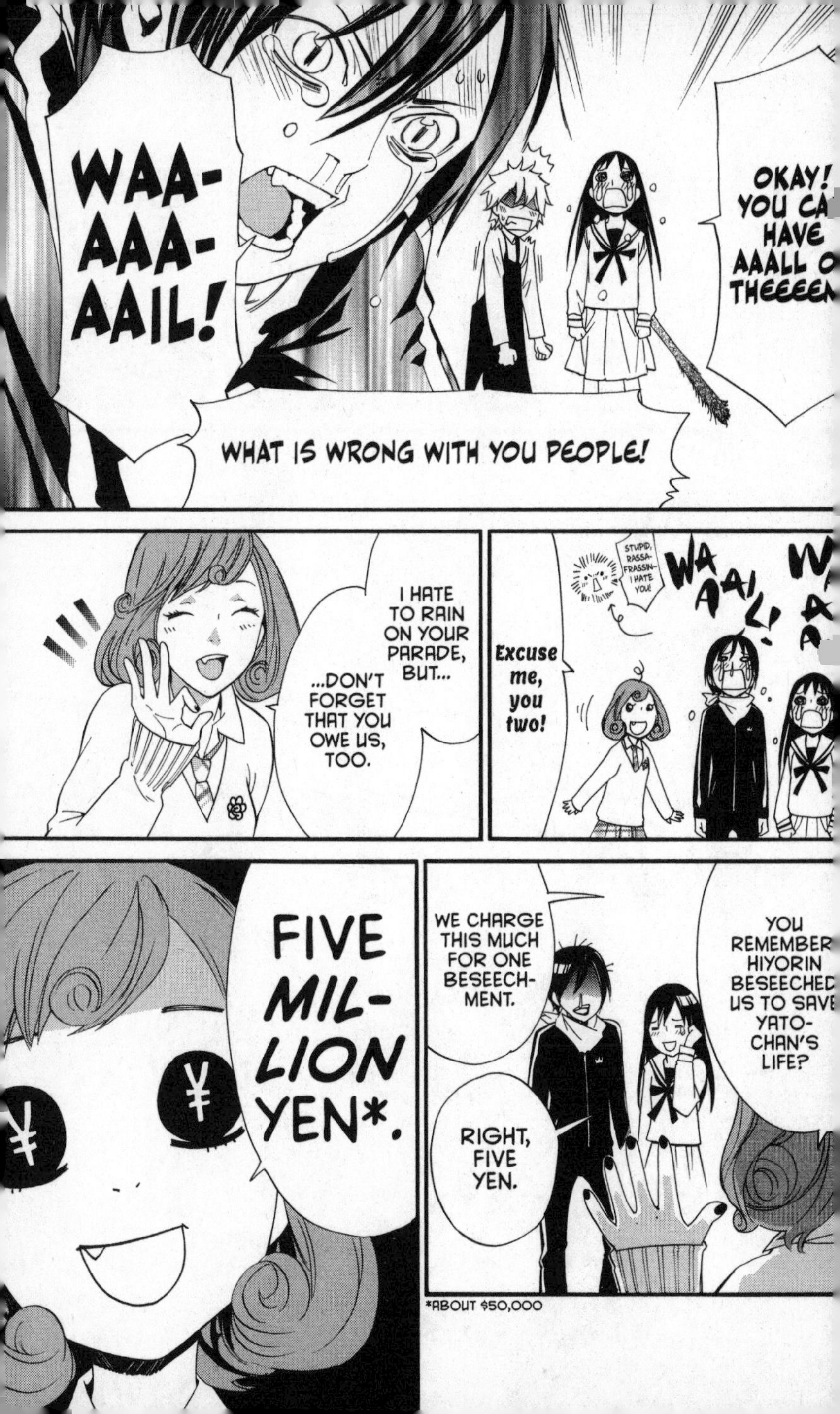
OKAY! YOU CA HAVE AAALL O THEEEEN
WAA-AAA-AAIL!
WHAT IS WRONG WITH YOU PEOPLE!
WA AAI L!
STUPID, RASSA-FRASSIN- I HATE YOU!
Excuse me, you two!
I HATE TO RAIN ON YOUR PARADE, BUT...
...DON'T FORGET THAT YOU OWE US, TOO.
YOU REMEMBER HIYORIN BESEECHED US TO SAVE YATO-CHAN'S LIFE?
WE CHARGE THIS MUCH FOR ONE BESEECHMENT.
RIGHT, FIVE YEN.
FIVE MILLION YEN*.
*ABOUT $50,000

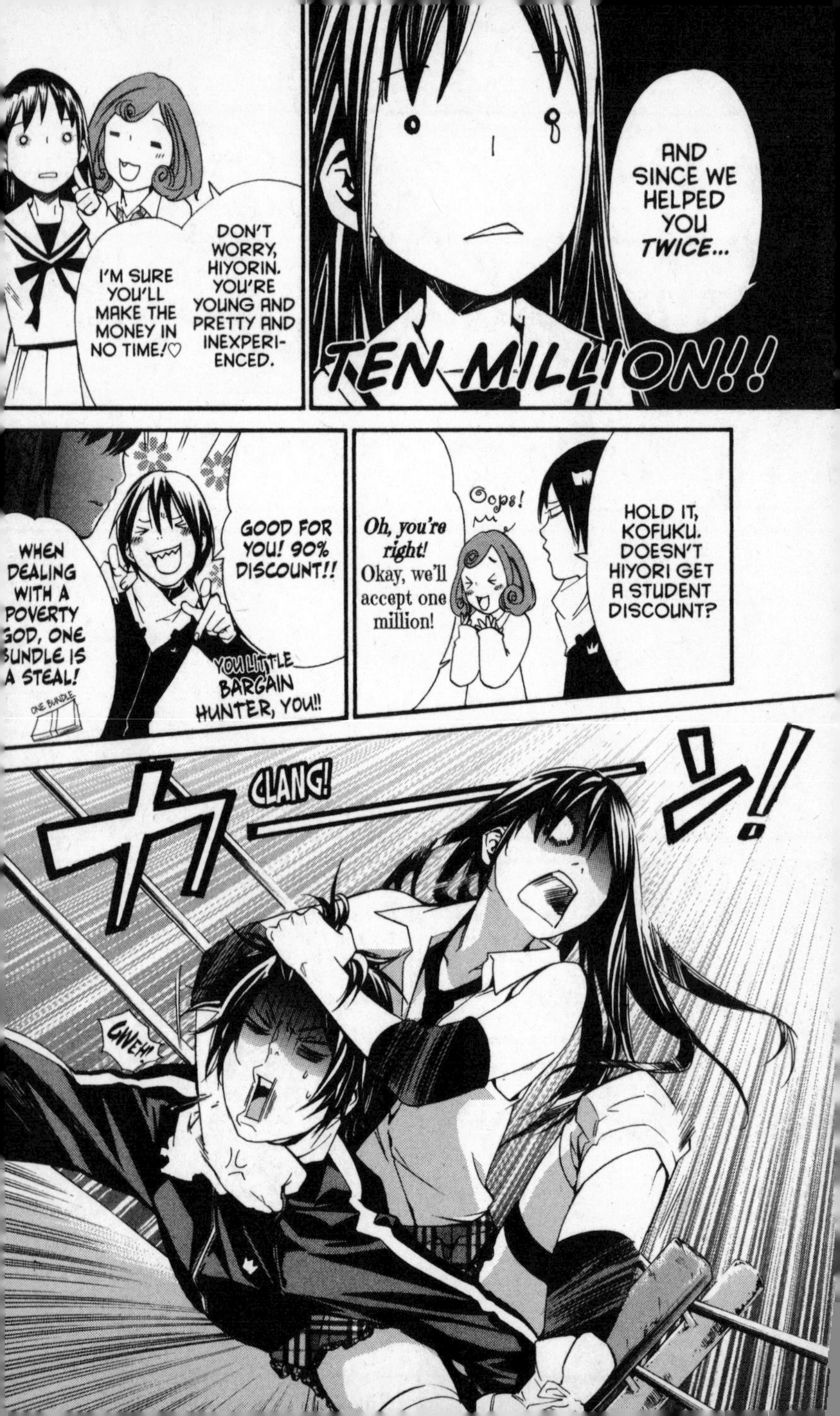
AND SINCE WE HELPED YOU TWICE...
TEN MILLION!!
DON'T WORRY, HIYORIN. YOU'RE YOUNG AND PRETTY AND INEXPERIENCED.
I'M SURE YOU'LL MAKE THE MONEY IN NO TIME!♡
HOLD IT, KOFUKU. DOESN'T HIYORI GET A STUDENT DISCOUNT?
Oops!
Oh, you're right! Okay, we'll accept one million!
GOOD FOR YOU! 90% DISCOUNT!!
YOU LITTLE BARGAIN HUNTER, YOU!!
WHEN DEALING WITH A POVERTY GOD, ONE BUNDLE IS A STEAL!
ONE BUNDLE
CLANG!
GWEH!

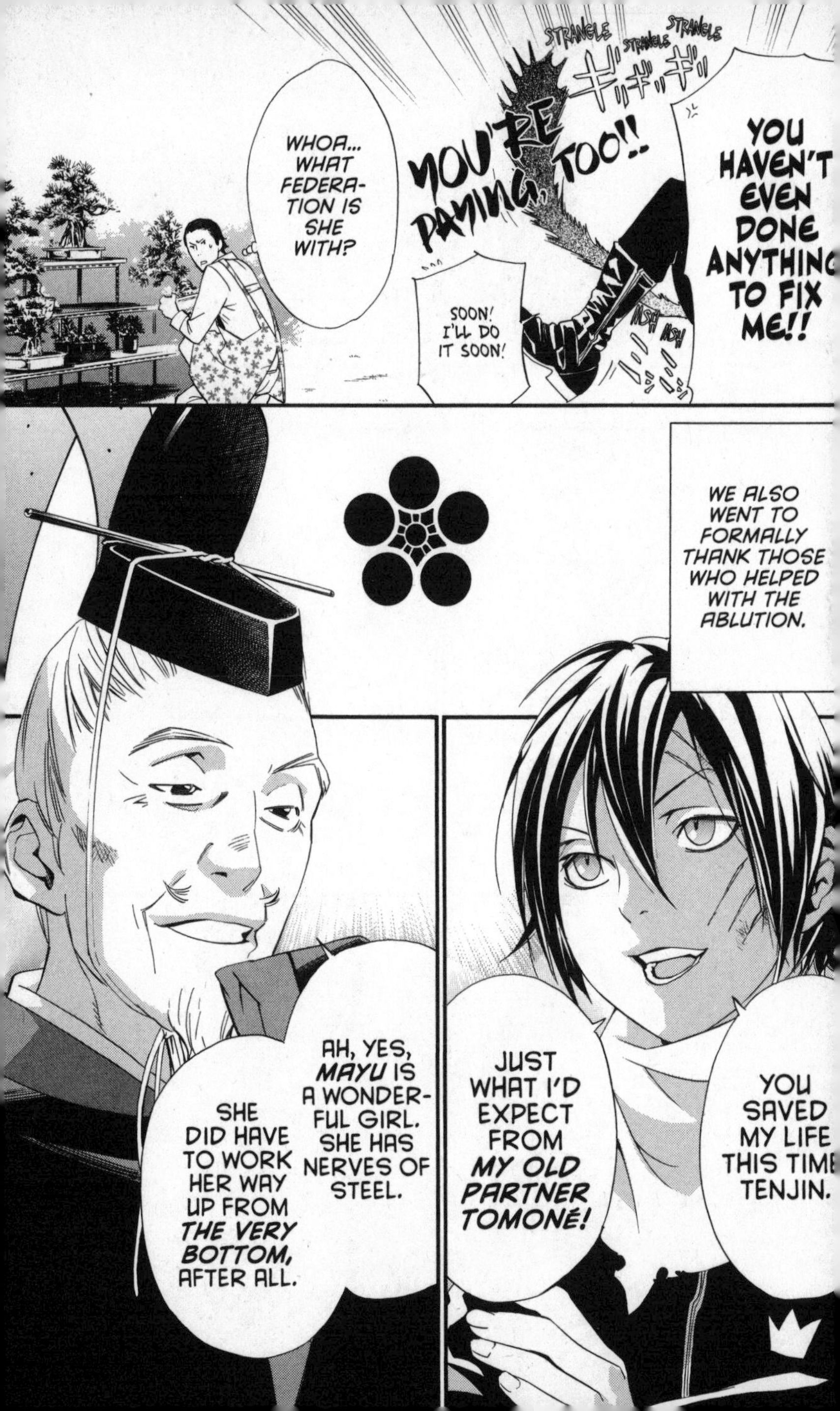

YOU HAVEN'T EVEN DONE ANYTHING TO FIX ME!!
STRANGLE STRANGLE STRANGLE
YOU'RE PAYING, TOO!!
SOON! I'LL DO IT SOON!
WHOA... WHAT FEDERATION IS SHE WITH?
WE ALSO WENT TO FORMALLY THANK THOSE WHO HELPED WITH THE ABLUTION.
YOU SAVED MY LIFE THIS TIME, TENJIN.
JUST WHAT I'D EXPECT FROM *MY OLD PARTNER TOMONÉ!*
AH, YES, *MAYU* IS A WONDERFUL GIRL. SHE HAS NERVES OF STEEL.
SHE DID HAVE TO WORK HER WAY UP FROM *THE VERY BOTTOM,* AFTER ALL.

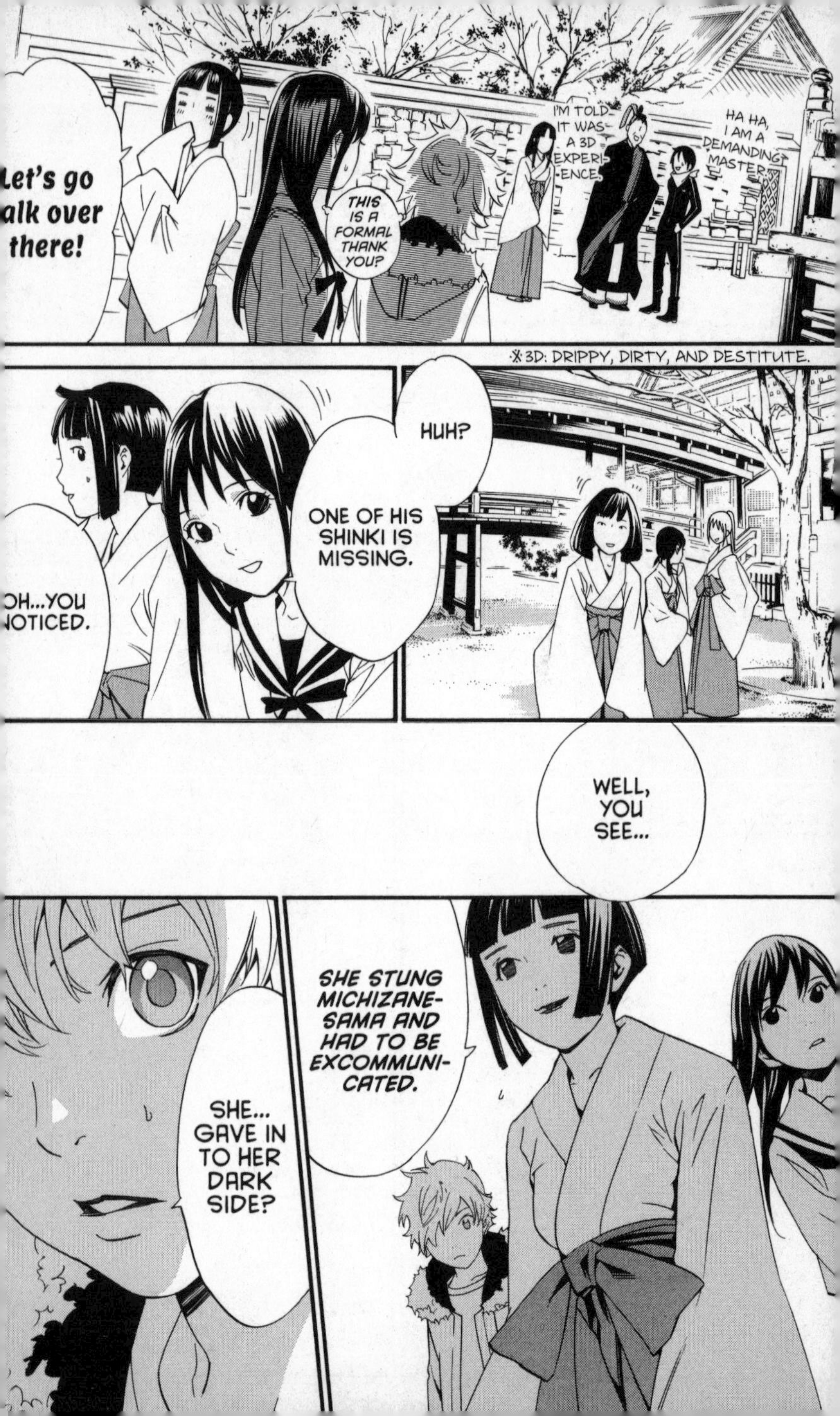
HA HA, I AM A DEMANDING MASTER.
I'M TOLD IT WAS A 3D EXPERIENCE.
THIS IS A FORMAL THANK YOU?
Let's go alk over there!
※3D: DRIPPY, DIRTY, AND DESTITUTE.
HUH?
ONE OF HIS SHINKI IS MISSING.
OH...YOU NOTICED.
WELL, YOU SEE...
SHE STUNG MICHIZANE-SAMA AND HAD TO BE EXCOMMUNICATED.
SHE... GAVE IN TO HER DARK SIDE?

WHAT HAPPENED TO YOU, YUKINÉ-KUN... IT'S VERY CONTAGIOUS.
JUST SEEING SOMEONE IN THAT STATE IS ENOUGH TO INFLUENCE ONE OF US.
I WANT TO BE A SCHOOLTEACHER WHEN I GROW UP.
MINAMI ELEMENTARY 1ST GRADE, HARUKA SAKAKI
AND SO...
I want to get into music school!!
Please let us all get accepted into the same high school!!
Akina Makoto Yūri
May my daughter Hanano grow into a fine woman!
SHE KIND OF...SLIT HER WRIST.

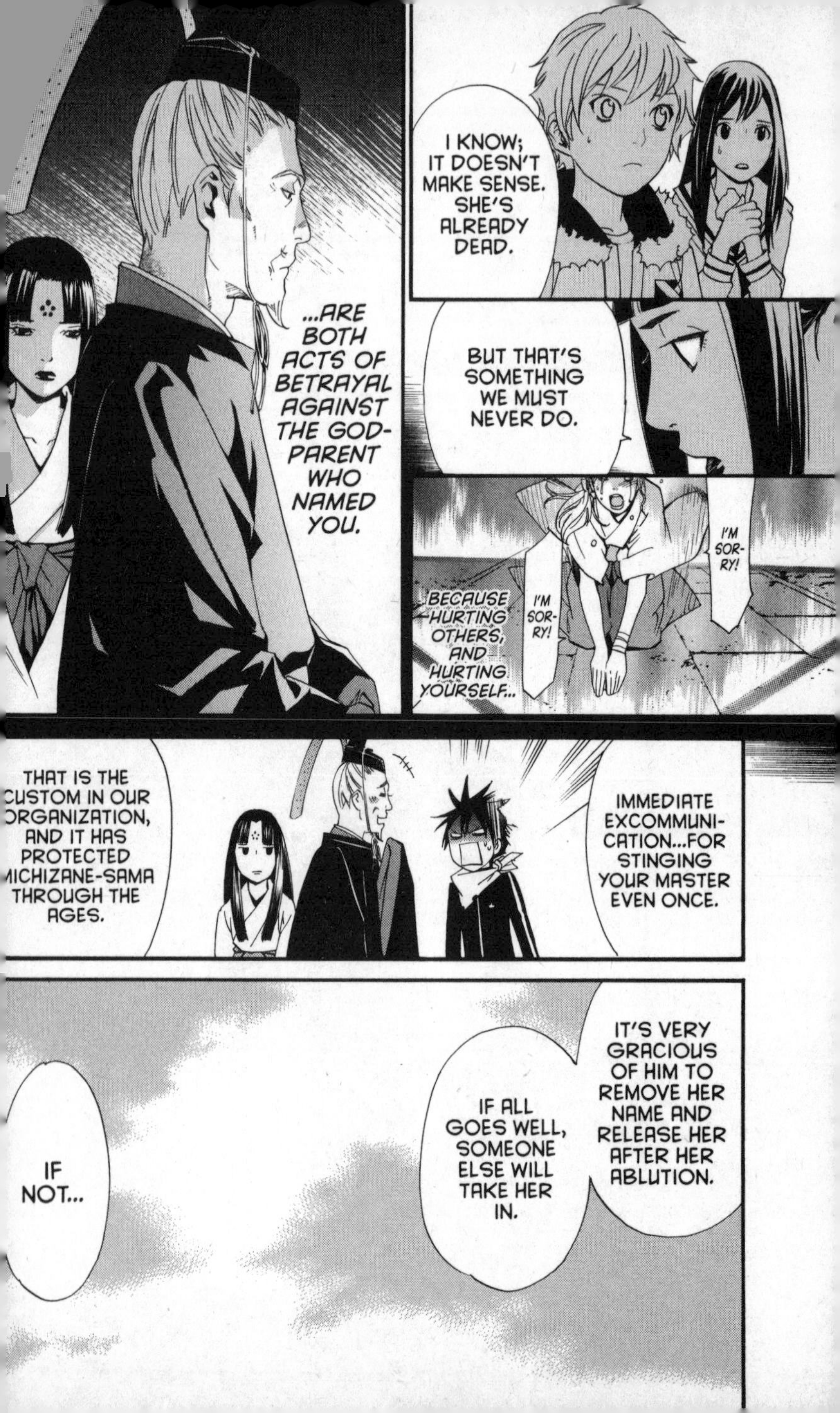
I KNOW; IT DOESN'T MAKE SENSE. SHE'S ALREADY DEAD.
BUT THAT'S SOMETHING WE MUST NEVER DO.
I'M SOR-RY!
BECAUSE HURTING OTHERS, AND HURTING YOURSELF...
I'M SOR-RY!
...ARE BOTH ACTS OF BETRAYAL AGAINST THE GOD-PARENT WHO NAMED YOU.
IMMEDIATE EXCOMMUNI-CATION...FOR STINGING YOUR MASTER EVEN ONCE.
THAT IS THE CUSTOM IN OUR RGANIZATION, AND IT HAS PROTECTED ICHIZANE-SAMA THROUGH THE AGES.
IT'S VERY GRACIOUS OF HIM TO REMOVE HER NAME AND RELEASE HER AFTER HER ABLUTION.
IF ALL GOES WELL, SOMEONE ELSE WILL TAKE HER IN.
IF NOT...

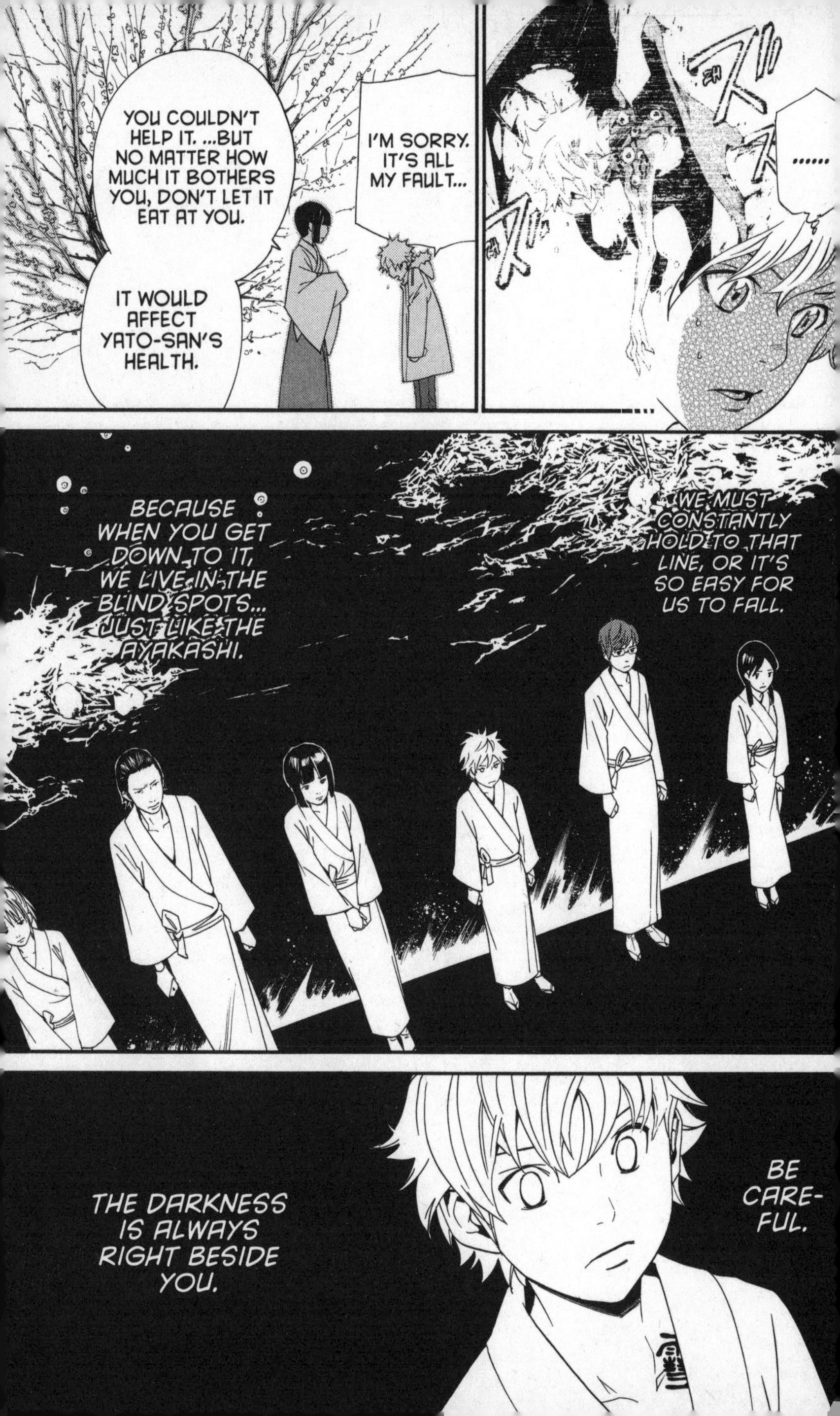
ZU
ZU
......
ZU
I'M SORRY. IT'S ALL MY FAULT...
YOU COULDN'T HELP IT. ...BUT NO MATTER HOW MUCH IT BOTHERS YOU, DON'T LET IT EAT AT YOU.
IT WOULD AFFECT YATO-SAN'S HEALTH.
WE MUST CONSTANTLY HOLD TO THAT LINE, OR IT'S SO EASY FOR US TO FALL.
BECAUSE WHEN YOU GET DOWN TO IT, WE LIVE IN THE BLIND SPOTS... JUST LIKE THE AYAKASHI.
BE CARE-FUL.
THE DARKNESS IS ALWAYS RIGHT BESIDE YOU.

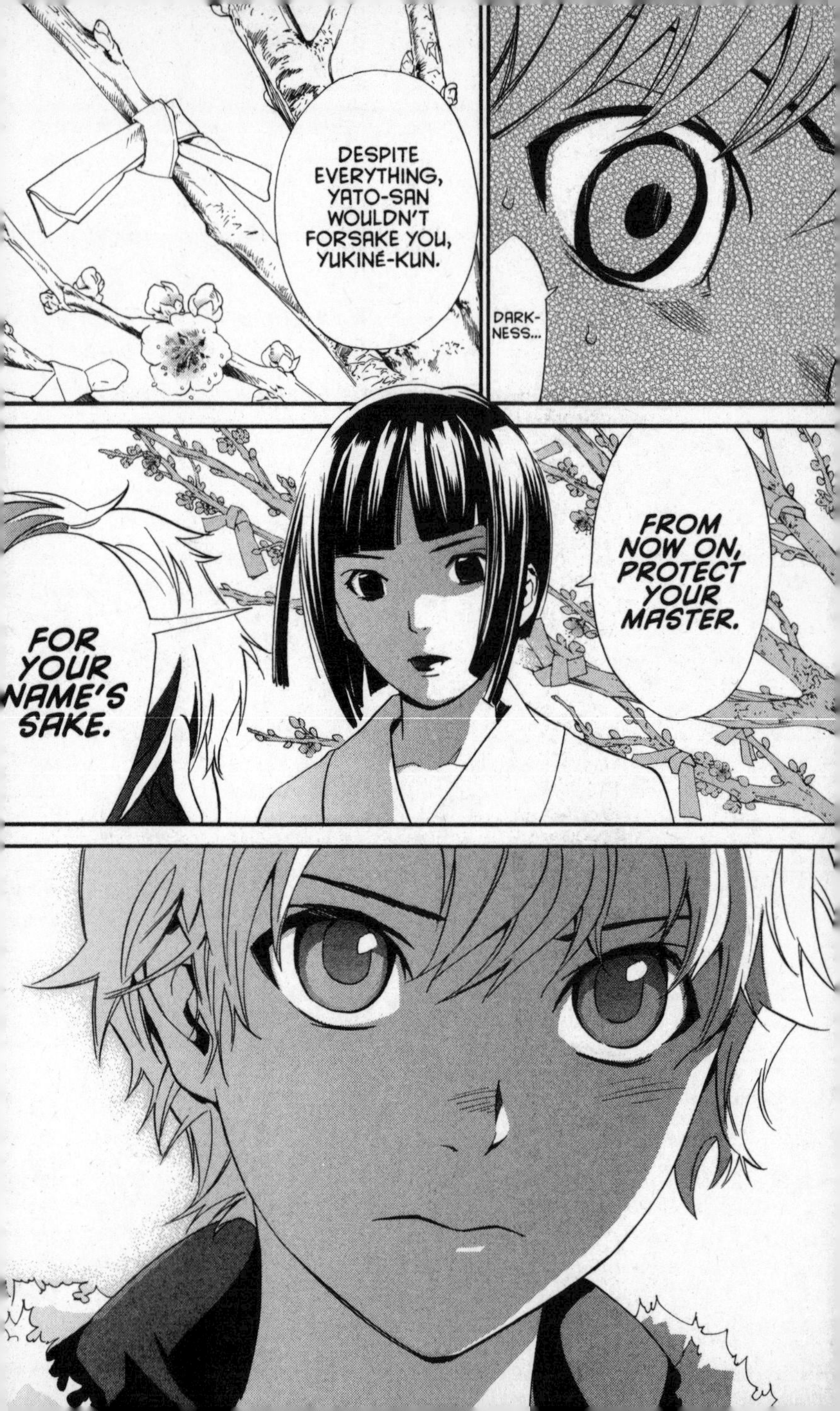
DARK-NESS...
DESPITE EVERYTHING, YATO-SAN WOULDN'T FORSAKE YOU, YUKINÉ-KUN.
FROM NOW ON, PROTECT YOUR MASTER.
FOR YOUR NAME'S SAKE.

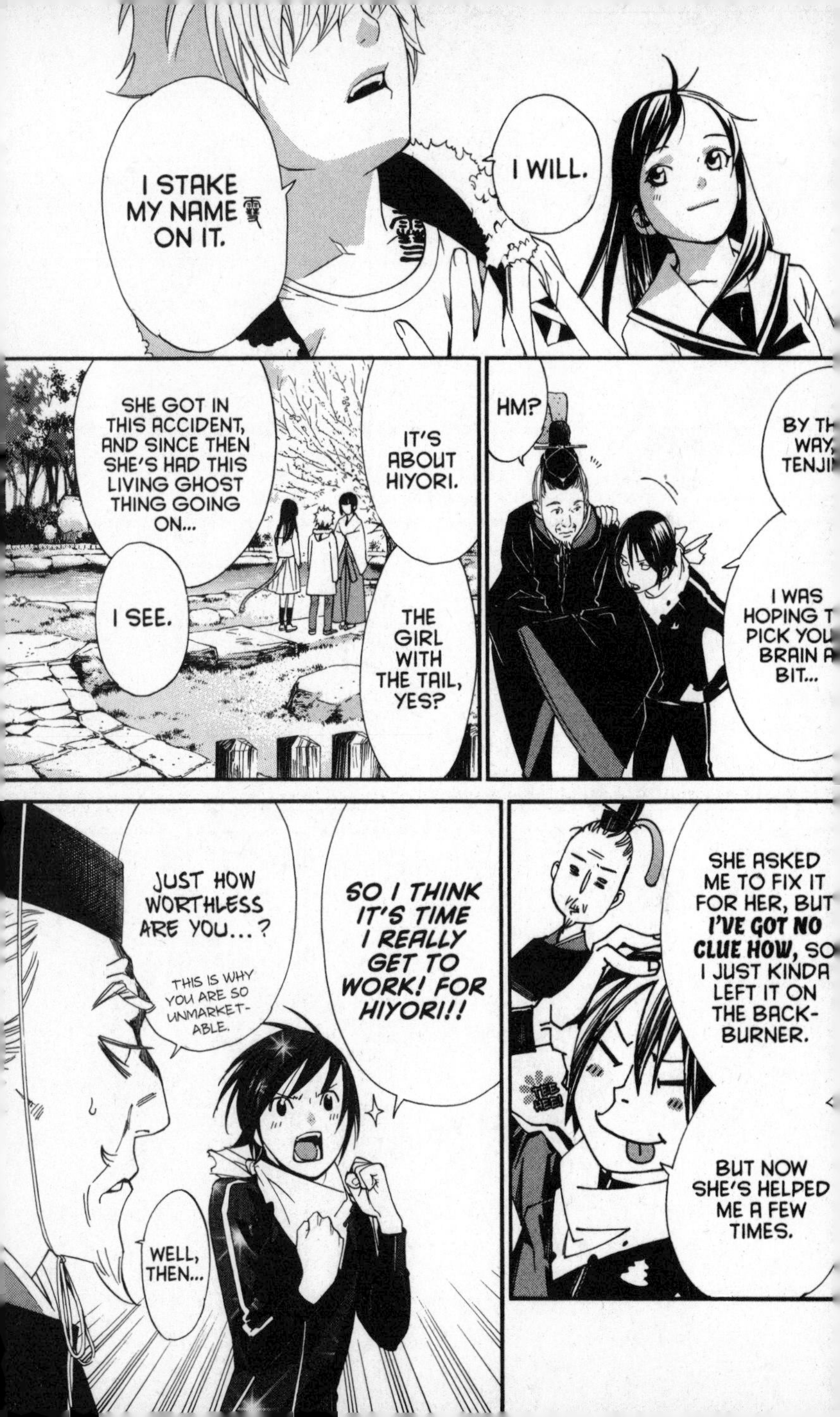
I WILL.
I STAKE MY NAME ON IT.
BY TH WAY, TENJI
HM?
I WAS HOPING T PICK YOU BRAIN A BIT...
IT'S ABOUT HIYORI.
THE GIRL WITH THE TAIL, YES?
SHE GOT IN THIS ACCIDENT, AND SINCE THEN SHE'S HAD THIS LIVING GHOST THING GOING ON...
I SEE.
SHE ASKED ME TO FIX IT FOR HER, BUT **I'VE GOT NO CLUE HOW,** SO I JUST KINDA LEFT IT ON THE BACK-BURNER.
TEE HEE!
BUT NOW SHE'S HELPED ME A FEW TIMES.
WELL, THEN...
SO I THINK IT'S TIME I REALLY GET TO WORK! FOR HIYORI!!
JUST HOW WORTHLESS ARE YOU...?
THIS IS WHY YOU ARE SO UNMARKETABLE.

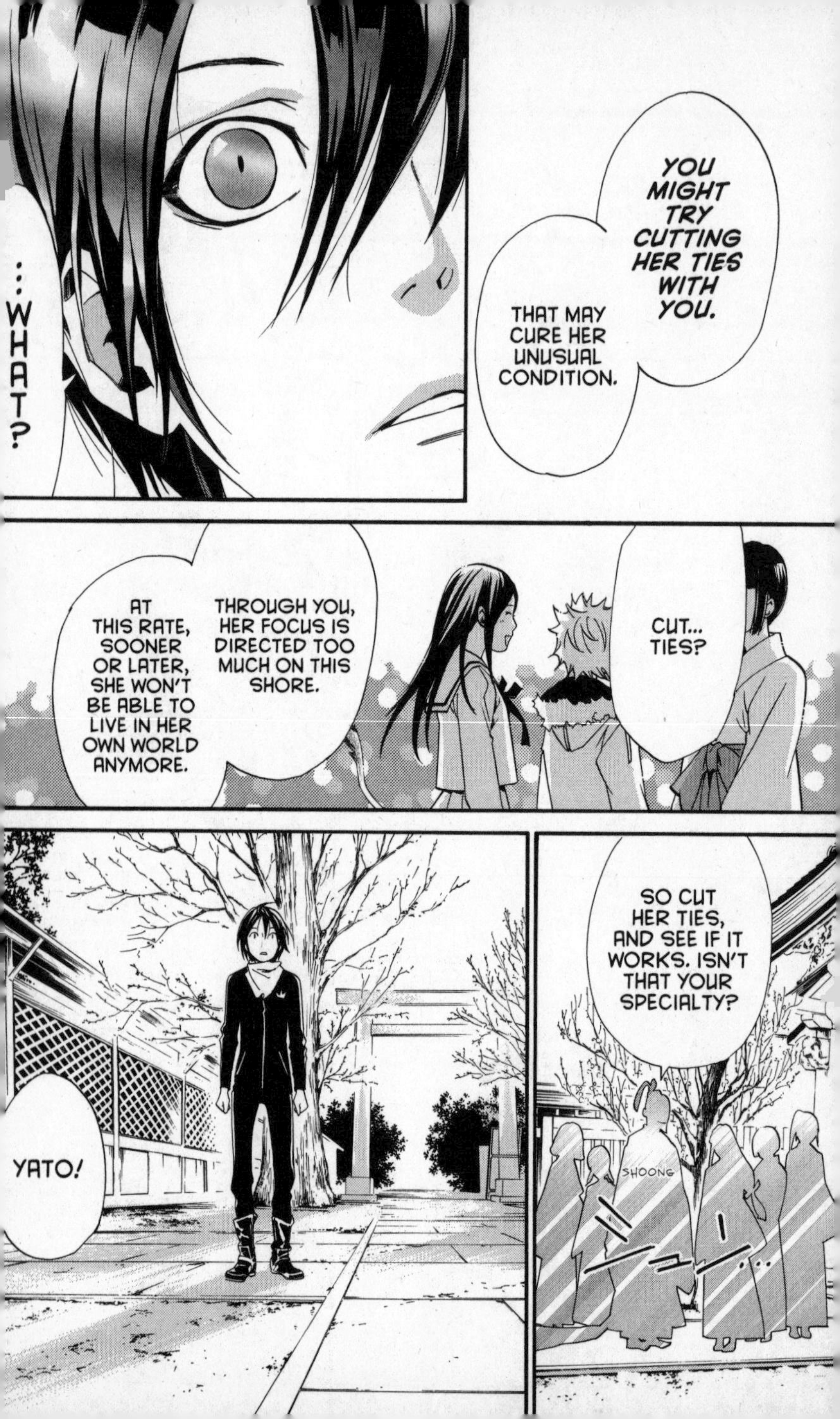
YOU MIGHT TRY CUTTING HER TIES WITH YOU.
THAT MAY CURE HER UNUSUAL CONDITION.
...WHAT?
CUT... TIES?
THROUGH YOU, HER FOCUS IS DIRECTED TOO MUCH ON THIS SHORE.
AT THIS RATE, SOONER OR LATER, SHE WON'T BE ABLE TO LIVE IN HER OWN WORLD ANYMORE.
SO CUT HER TIES, AND SEE IF IT WORKS. ISN'T THAT YOUR SPECIALTY?
SHOONG
YATO!

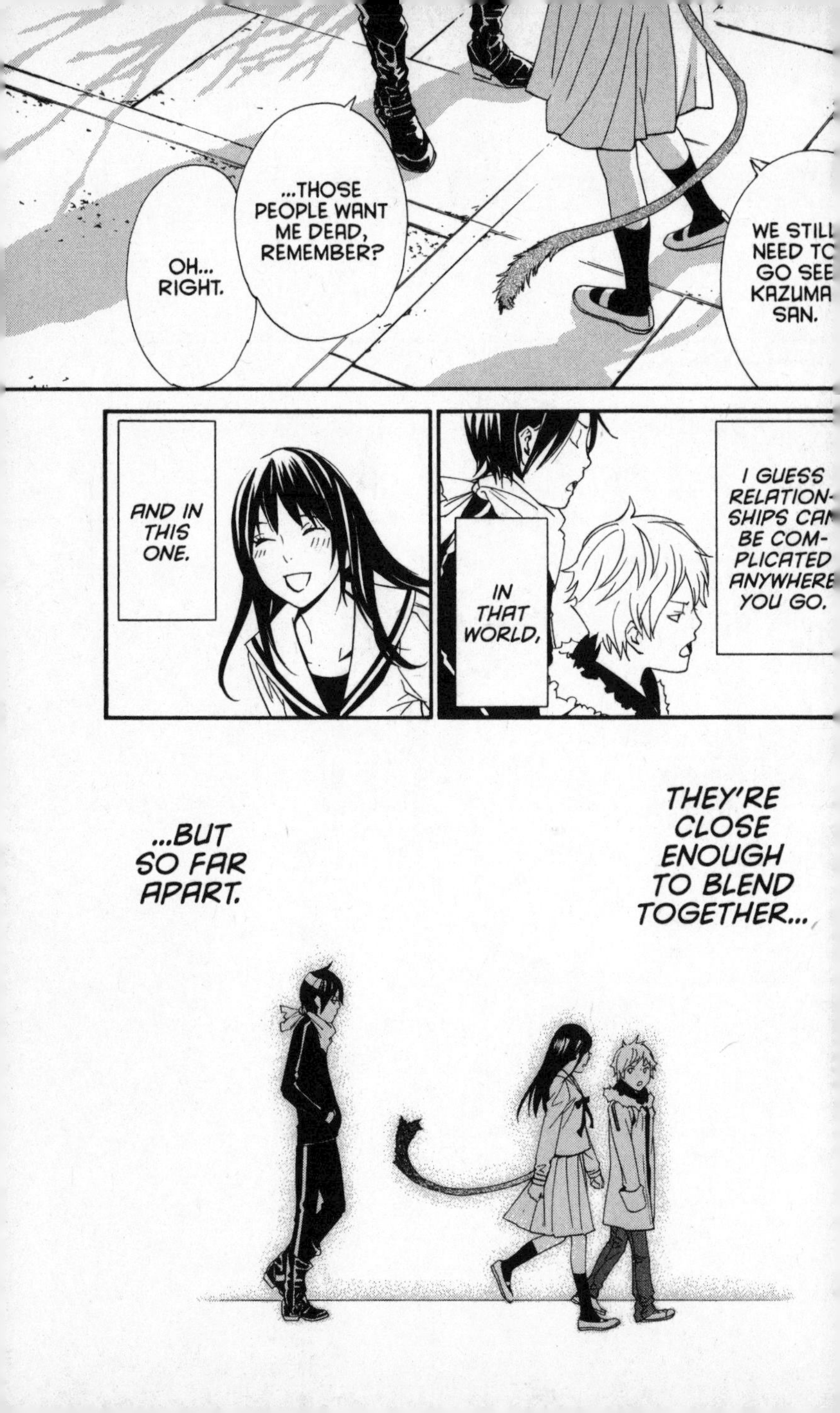
WE STILL NEED TO GO SEE KAZUMA SAN.
...THOSE PEOPLE WANT ME DEAD, REMEMBER?
OH... RIGHT.
I GUESS RELATION-SHIPS CAN BE COM-PLICATED ANYWHERE YOU GO.
IN THAT WORLD,
AND IN THIS ONE.
THEY'RE CLOSE ENOUGH TO BLEND TOGETHER...
...BUT SO FAR APART.

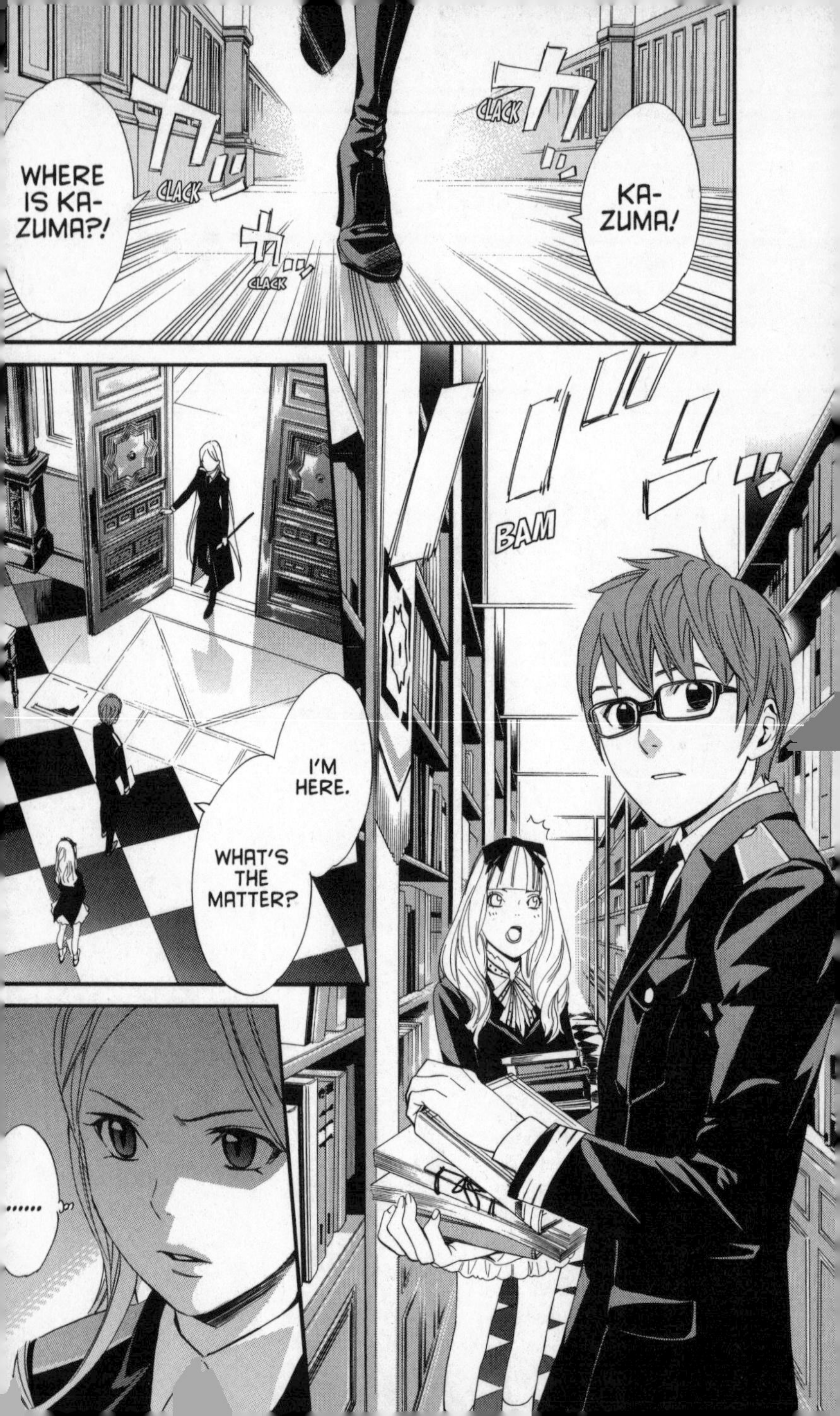

CLACK
KA-ZUMA!
WHERE IS KA-ZUMA?!
CLACK
CLACK
BAM
I'M HERE.
WHAT'S THE MATTER?
......

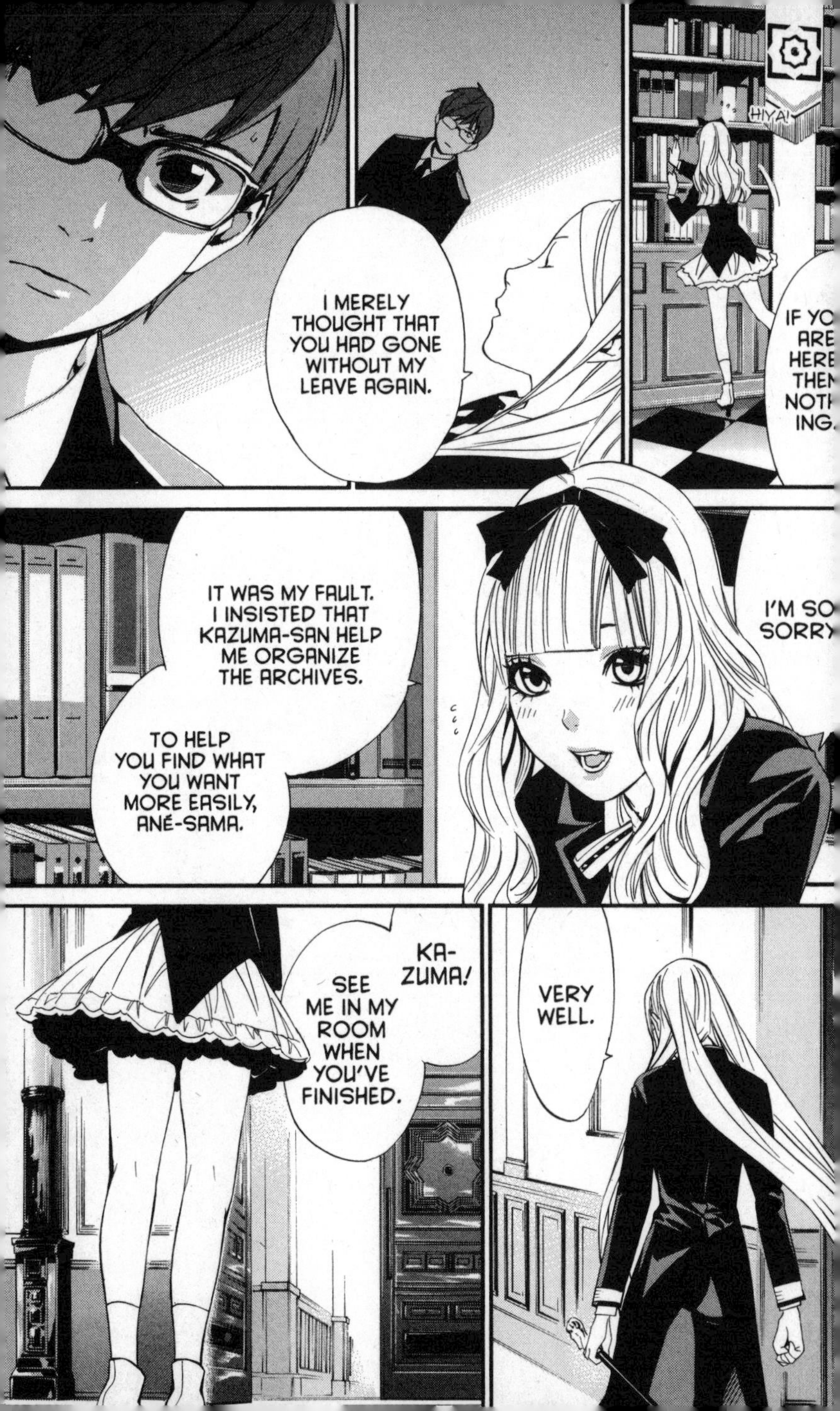

HIYA!
IF YO ARE HERE THEN NOTH ING.
I MERELY THOUGHT THAT YOU HAD GONE WITHOUT MY LEAVE AGAIN.
I'M SO SORRY
IT WAS MY FAULT. I INSISTED THAT KAZUMA-SAN HELP ME ORGANIZE THE ARCHIVES.
TO HELP YOU FIND WHAT YOU WANT MORE EASILY, ANÉ-SAMA.
VERY WELL.
KA-ZUMA!
SEE ME IN MY ROOM WHEN YOU'VE FINISHED.

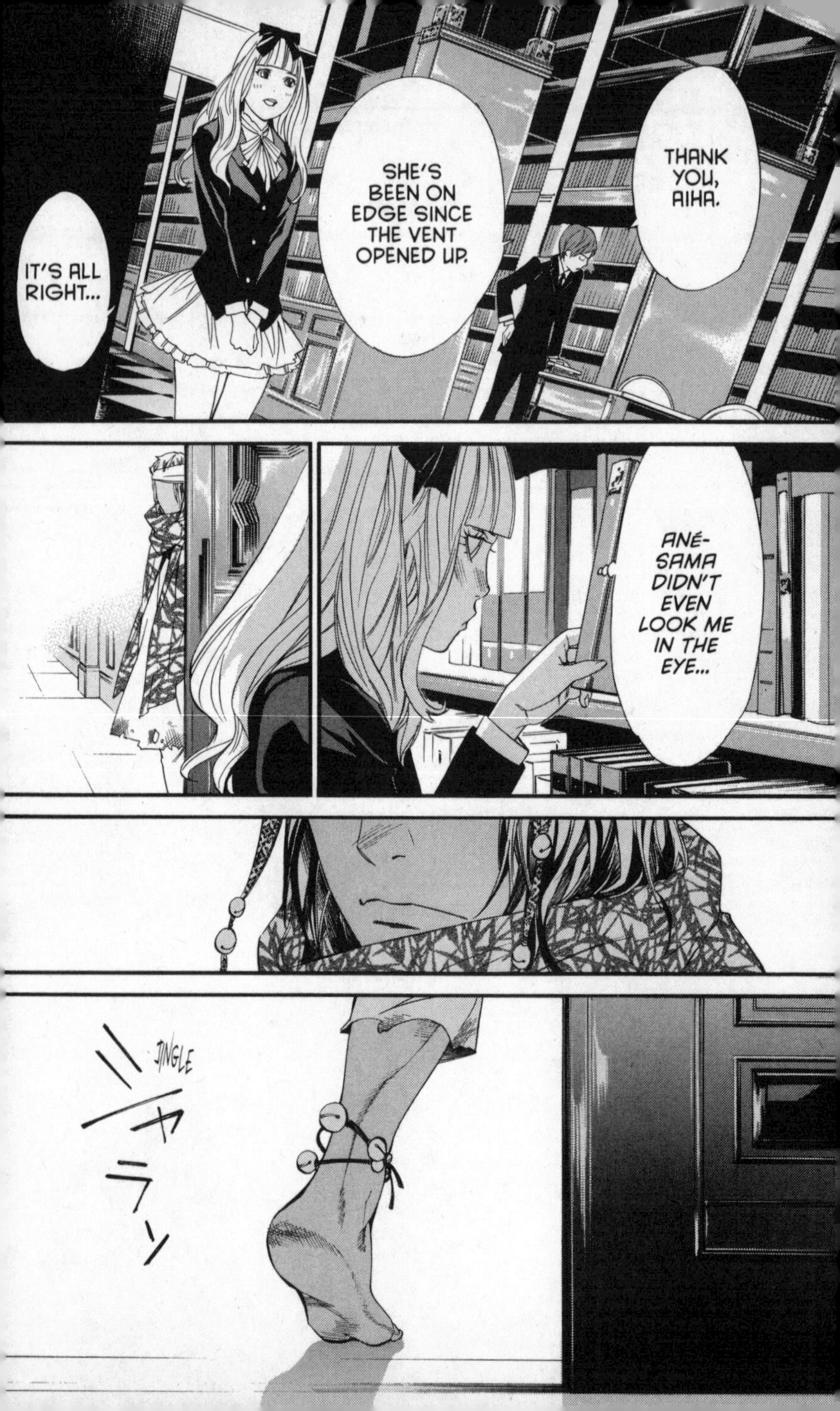
THANK YOU, AIHA.
SHE'S BEEN ON EDGE SINCE THE VENT OPENED UP.
IT'S ALL RIGHT...
ANÉ-SAMA DIDN'T EVEN LOOK ME IN THE EYE...
JINGLE
シャラン

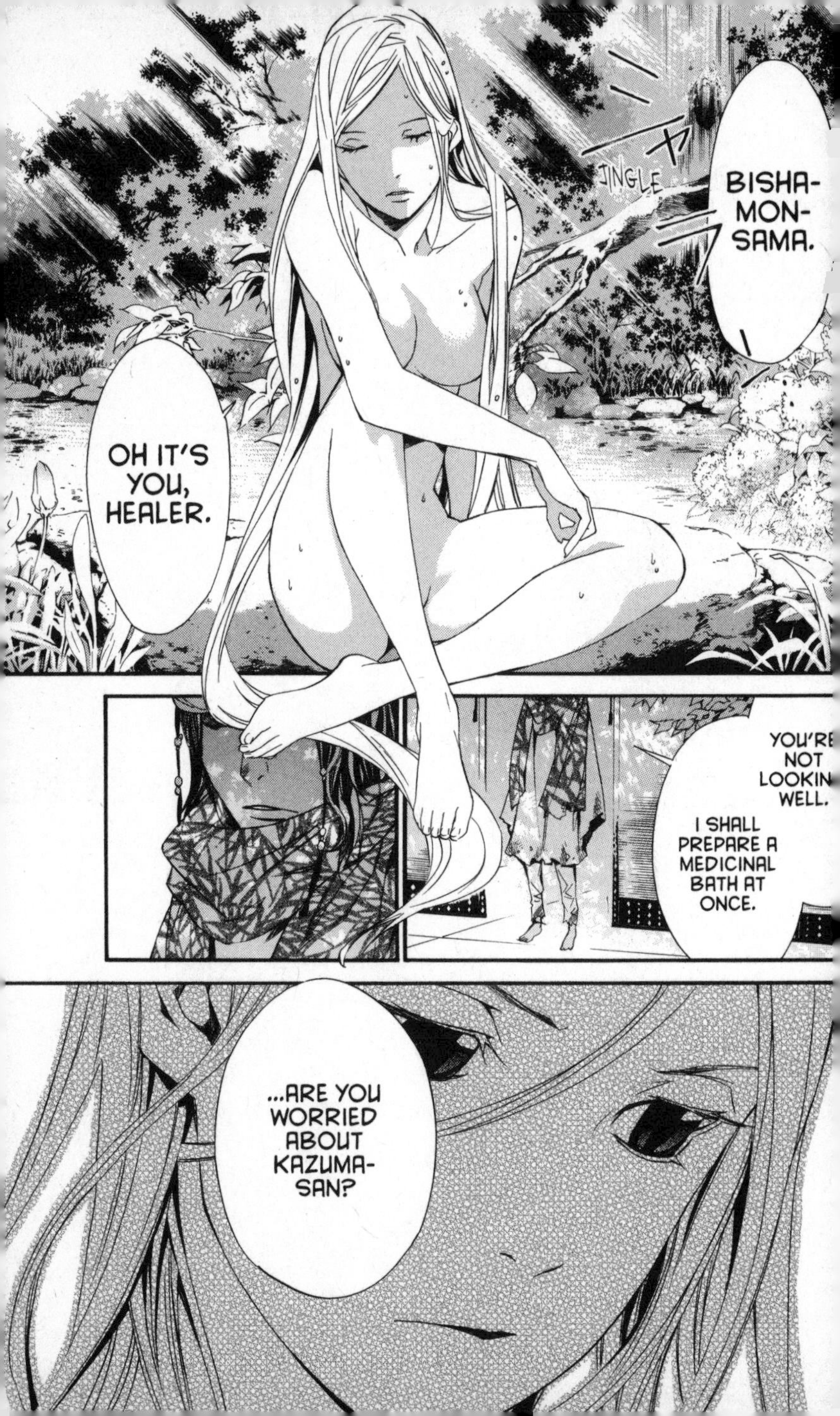
JINGLE
BISHA-MON-SAMA.
OH IT'S YOU, HEALER.
YOU'RE NOT LOOKIN WELL.
I SHALL PREPARE A MEDICINAL BATH AT ONCE.
...ARE YOU WORRIED ABOUT KAZUMA-SAN?

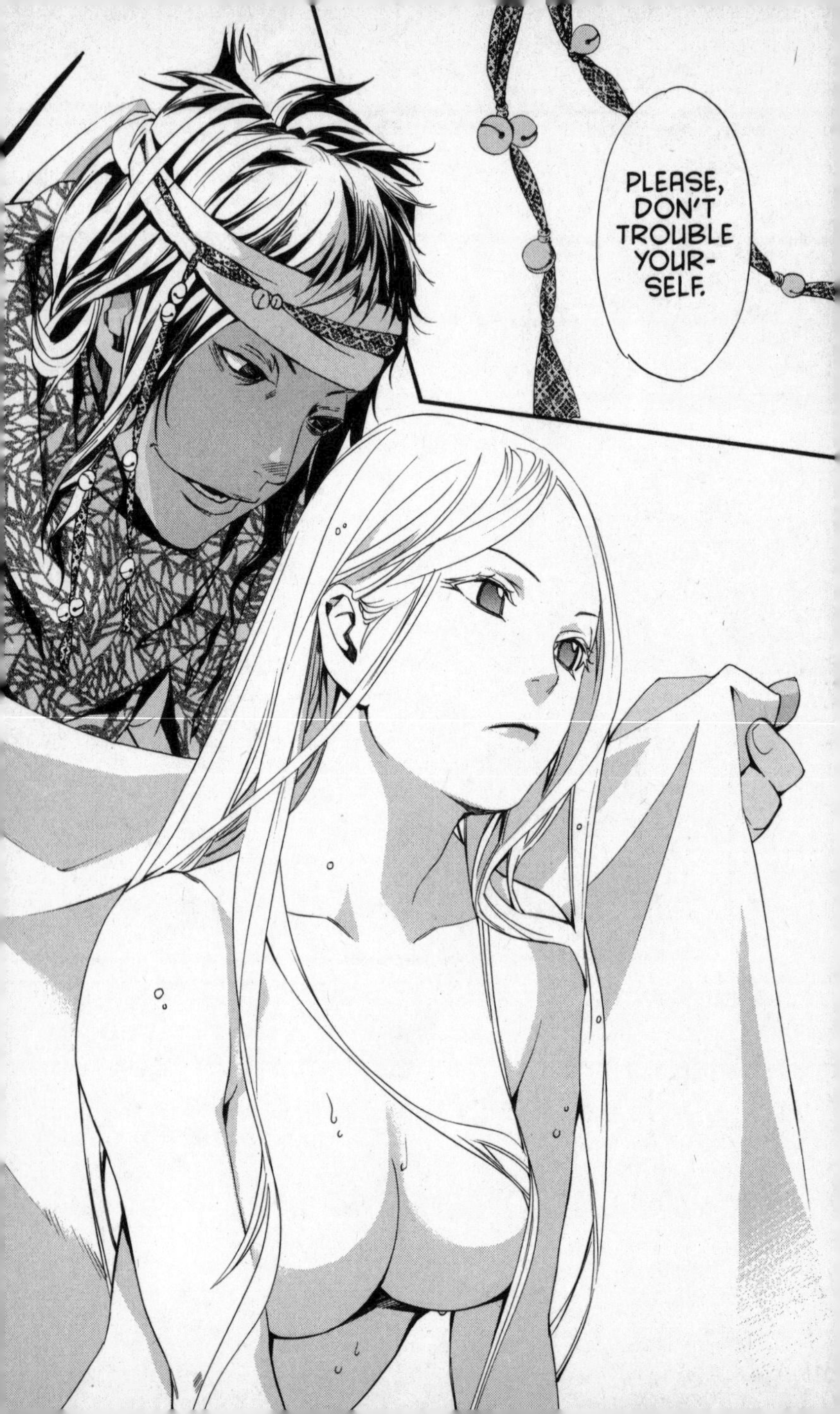
PLEASE, DON'T TROUBLE YOUR-SELF.

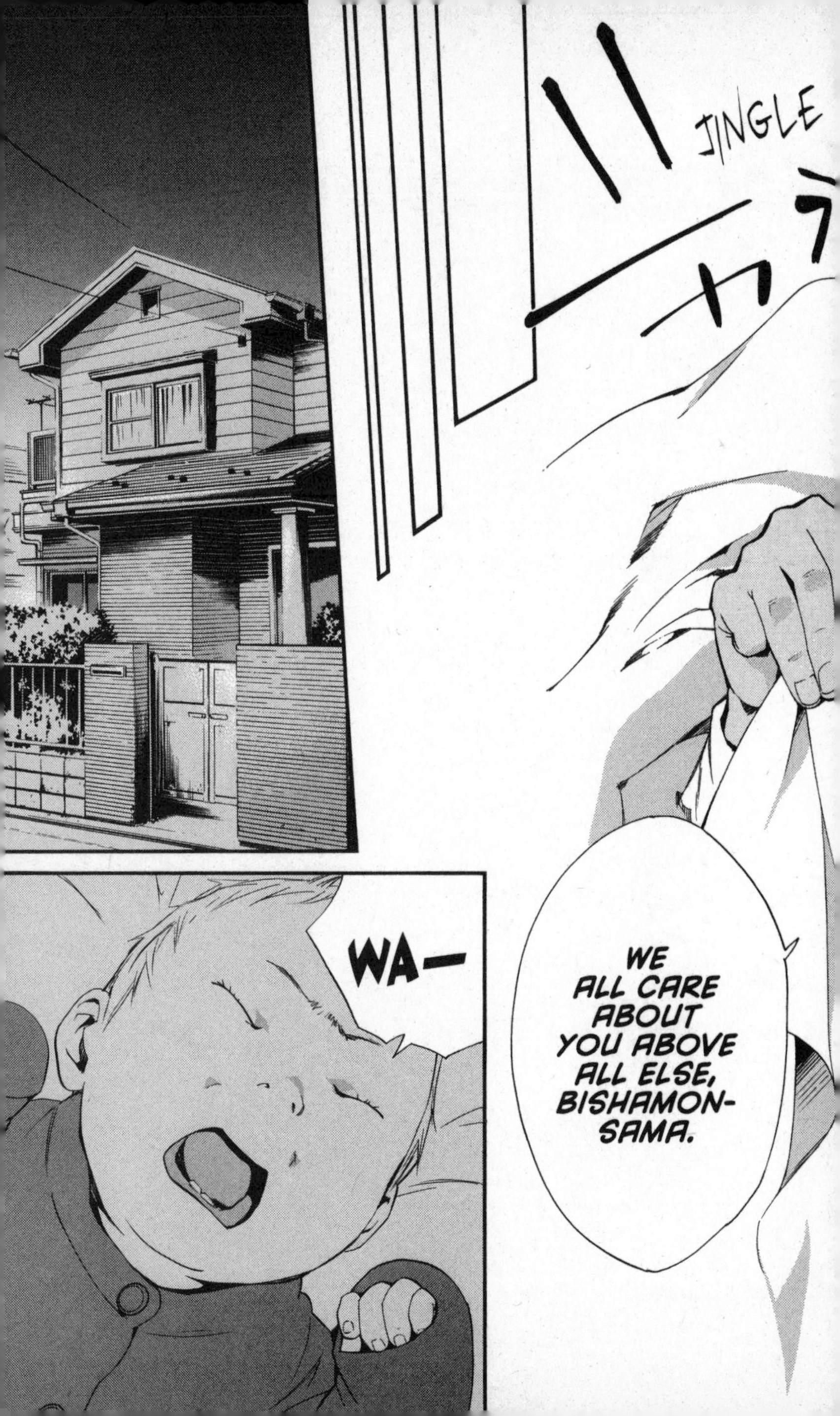
JINGLE
WE ALL CARE ABOUT YOU ABOVE ALL ELSE, BISHAMON-SAMA.
WA—

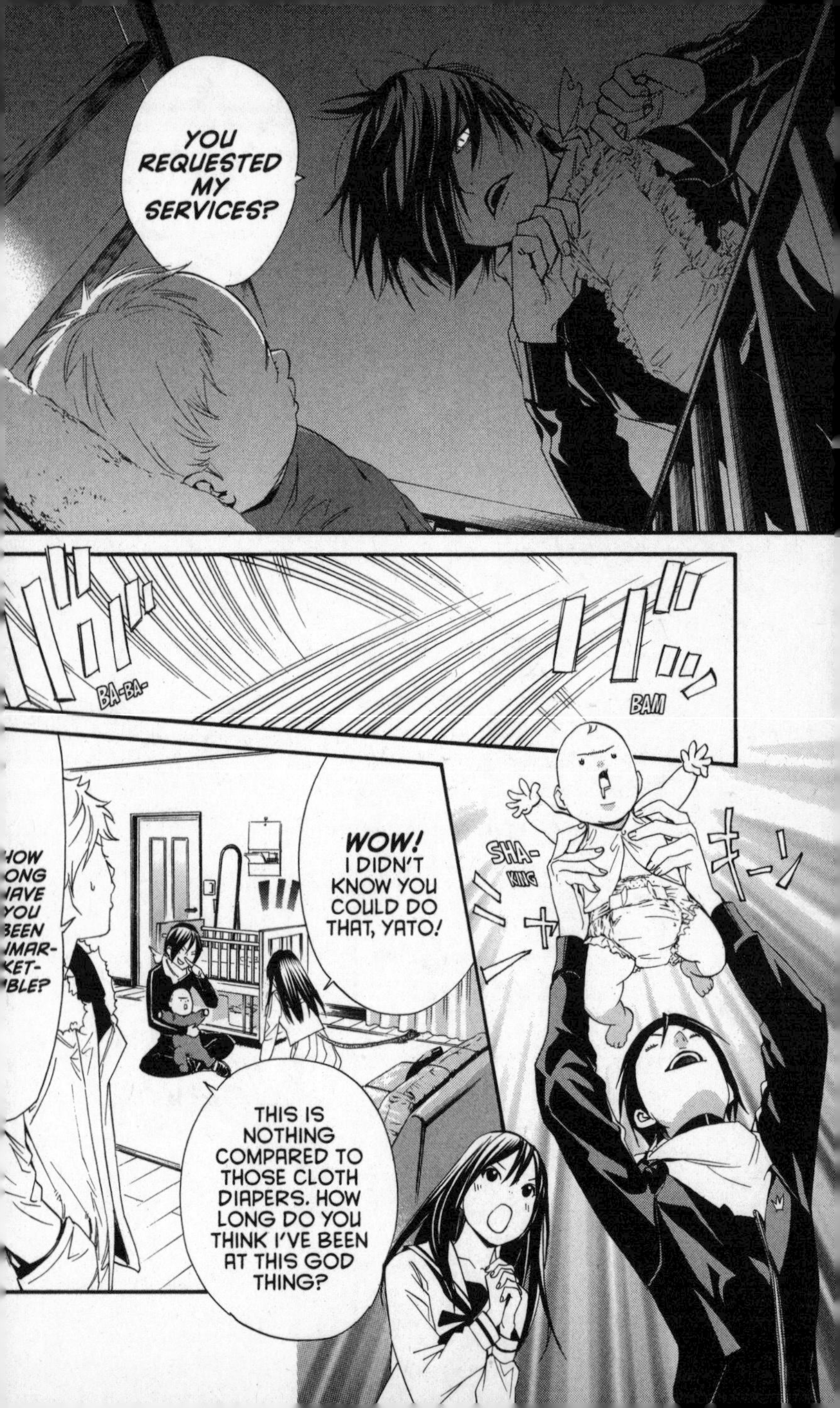
YOU REQUESTED MY SERVICES?
BAM
BA-BA-
SHA-KING
WOW! I DIDN'T KNOW YOU COULD DO THAT, YATO!
THIS IS NOTHING COMPARED TO THOSE CLOTH DIAPERS. HOW LONG DO YOU THINK I'VE BEEN AT THIS GOD THING?
OW ONG AVE YOU EEN MAR-KET-BLE?

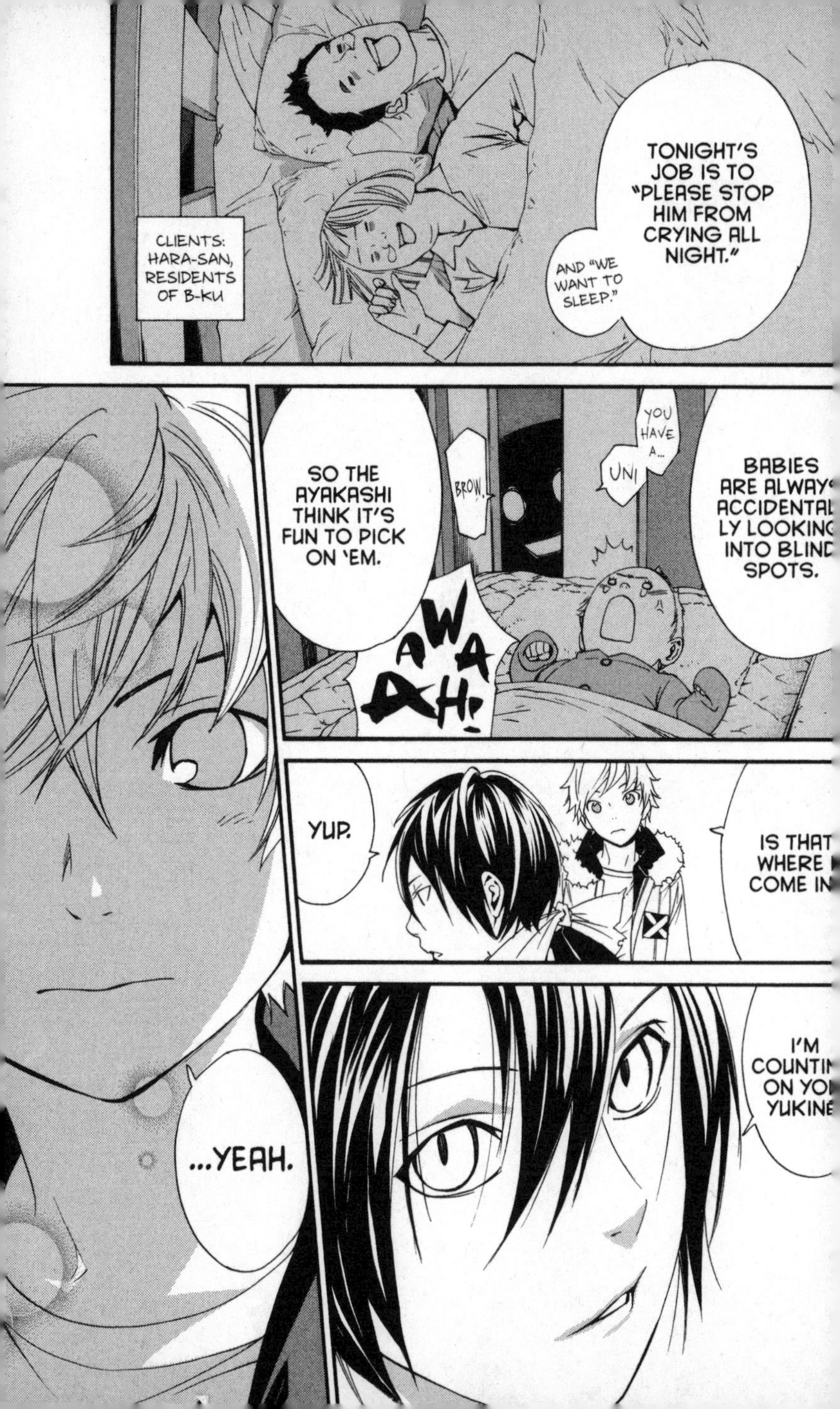
TONIGHT'S JOB IS TO "PLEASE STOP HIM FROM CRYING ALL NIGHT."
AND "WE WANT TO SLEEP."
CLIENTS: HARA-SAN, RESIDENTS OF B-KU
BABIES ARE ALWAY ACCIDENTAL LY LOOKIN INTO BLIN SPOTS.
YOU HAVE A...
UNI
BROW
SO THE AYAKASHI THINK IT'S FUN TO PICK ON 'EM.
WAAAH!
IS THAT WHERE COME IN
YUP.
I'M COUNTIN ON YO YUKINE
...YEAH.

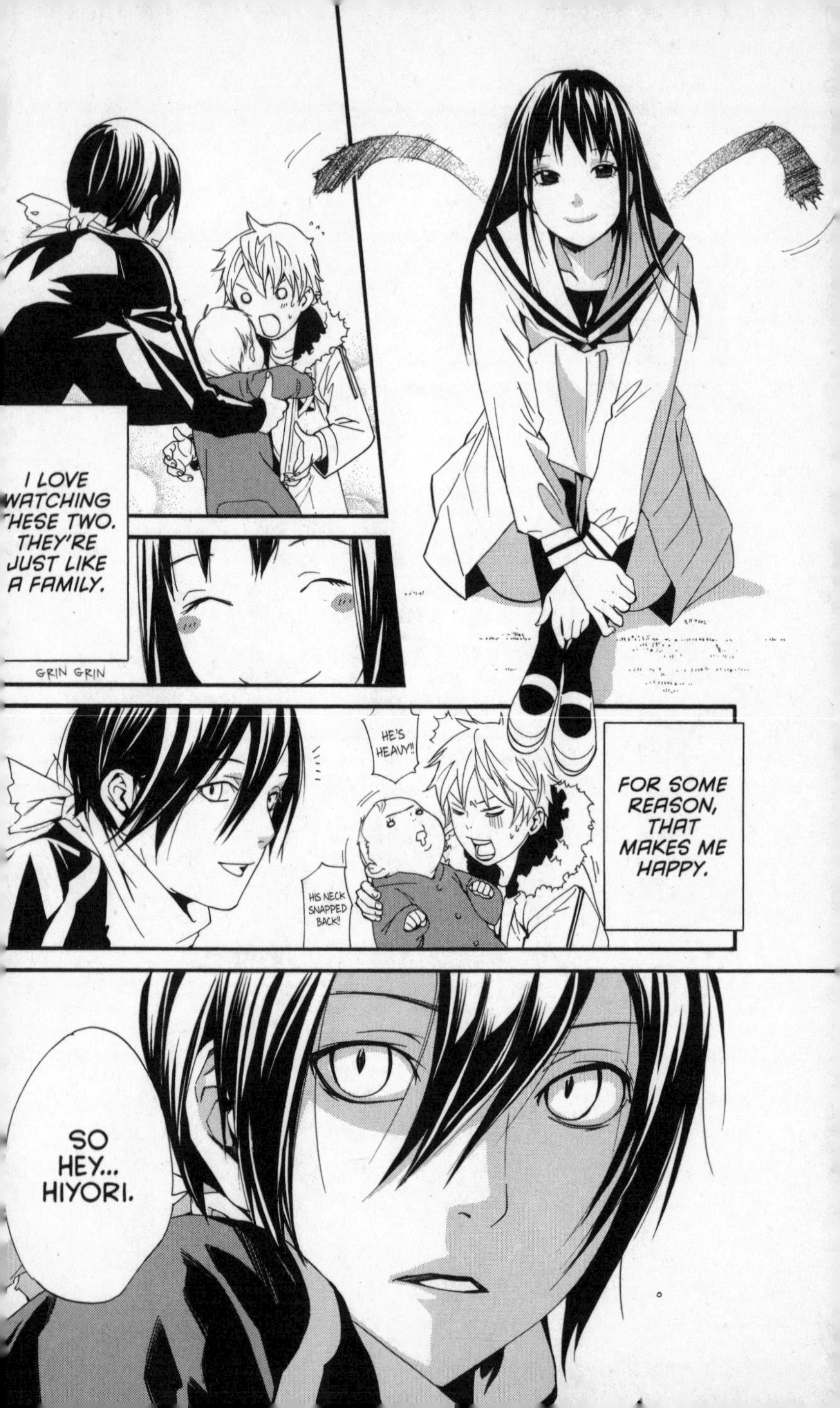
I LOVE WATCHING THESE TWO. THEY'RE JUST LIKE A FAMILY.
GRIN GRIN
FOR SOME REASON, THAT MAKES ME HAPPY.
HE'S HEAVY!!
HIS NECK SNAPPED BACK!!
SO HEY... HIYORI.

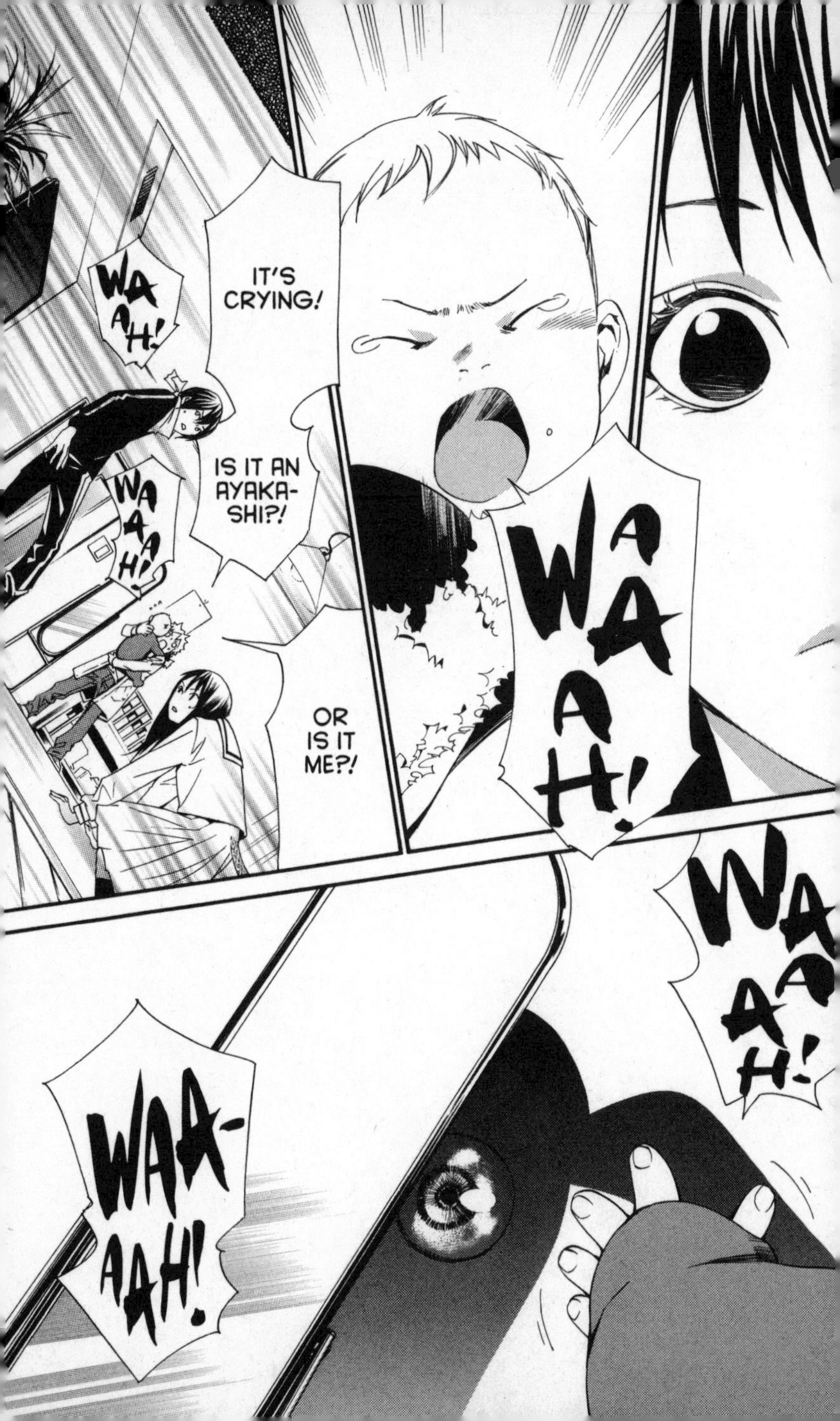
WAAAH!
WAAH!
IT'S CRYING!
WAAAH!
IS IT AN AYAKA-SHI?!
OR IS IT ME?!
WAAAH!
WAA-AAH!

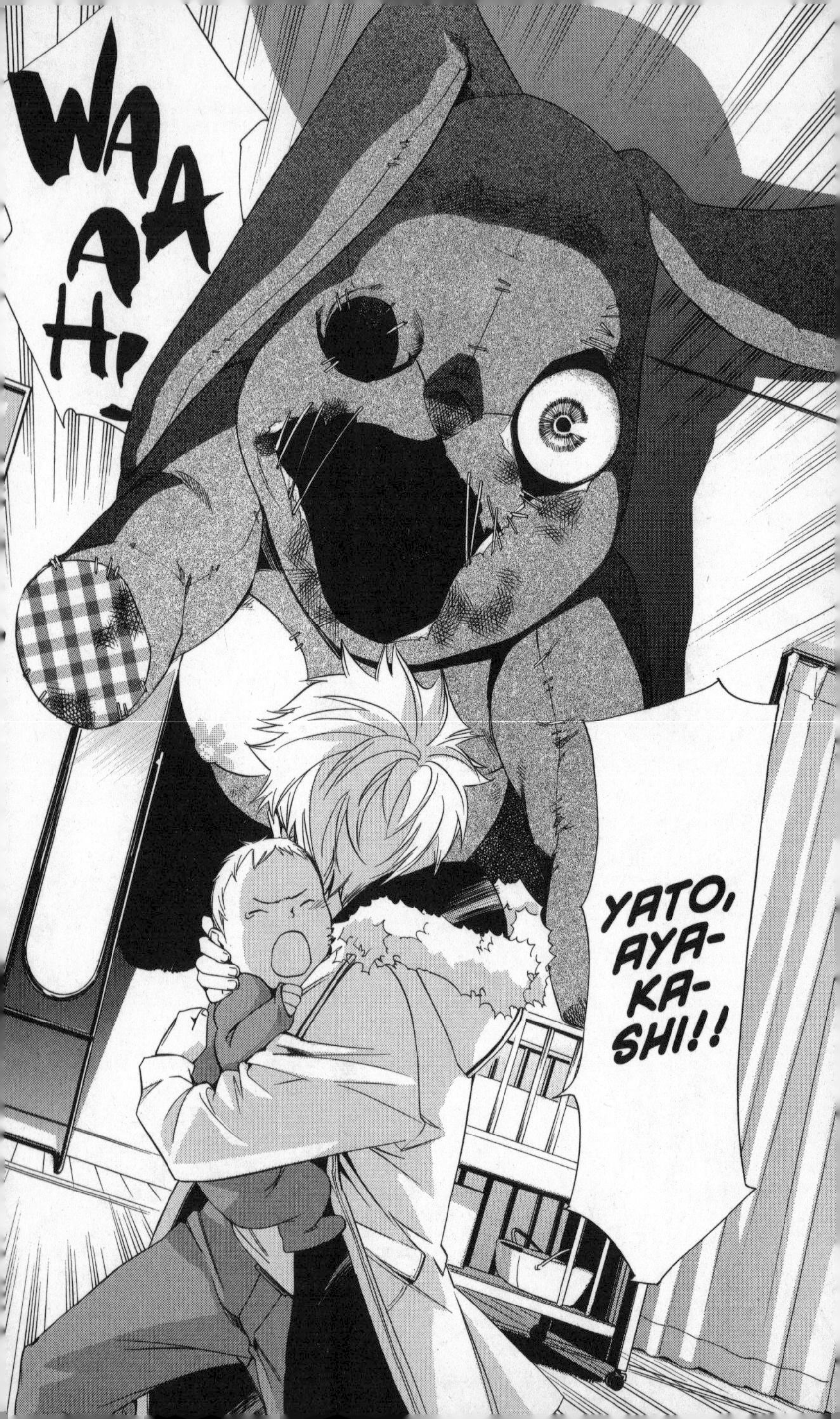
WAAAAH!
YATO! AYAKASHI!!

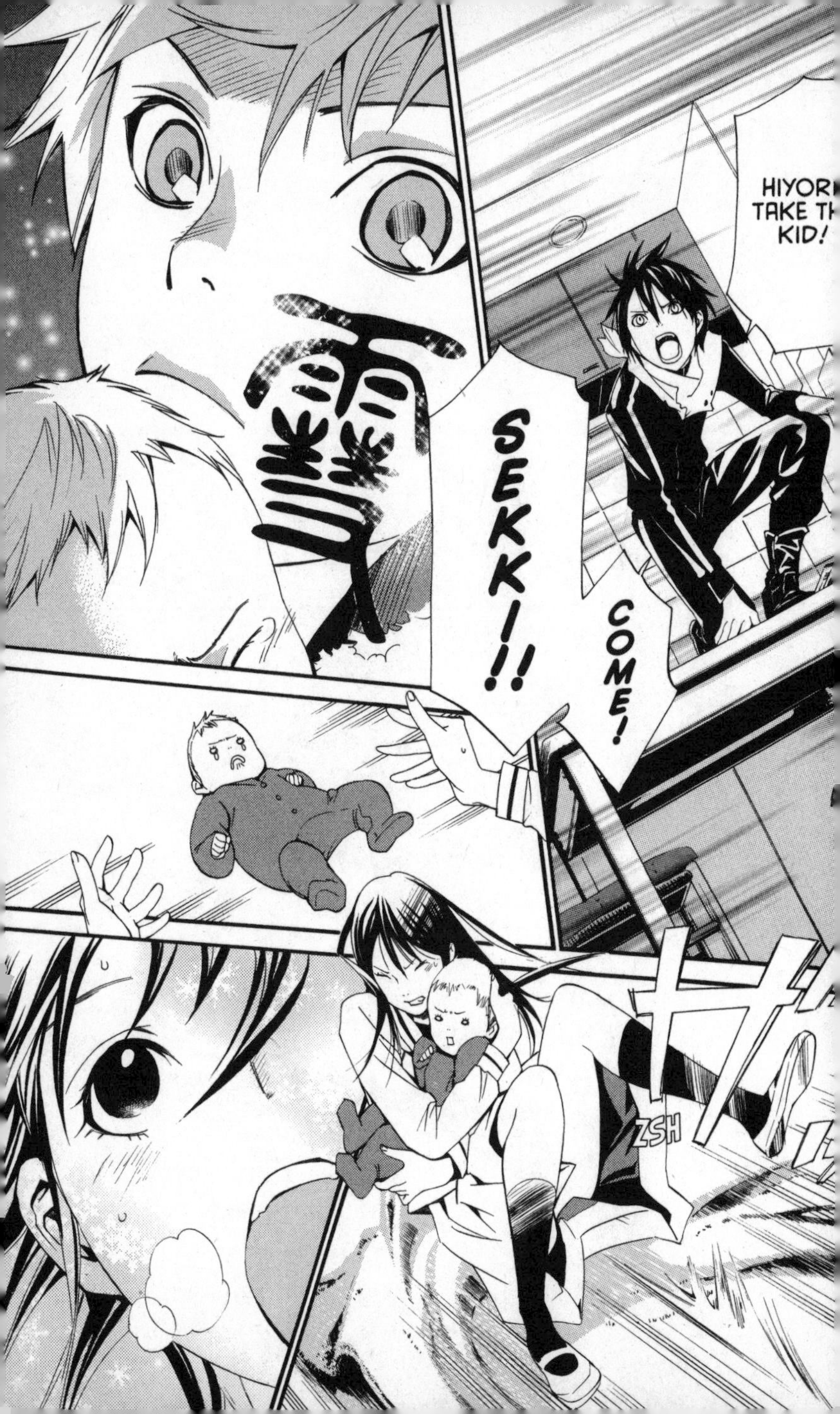
HIYORI TAKE TH KID!
SEKKI!!
COME!
ZSH

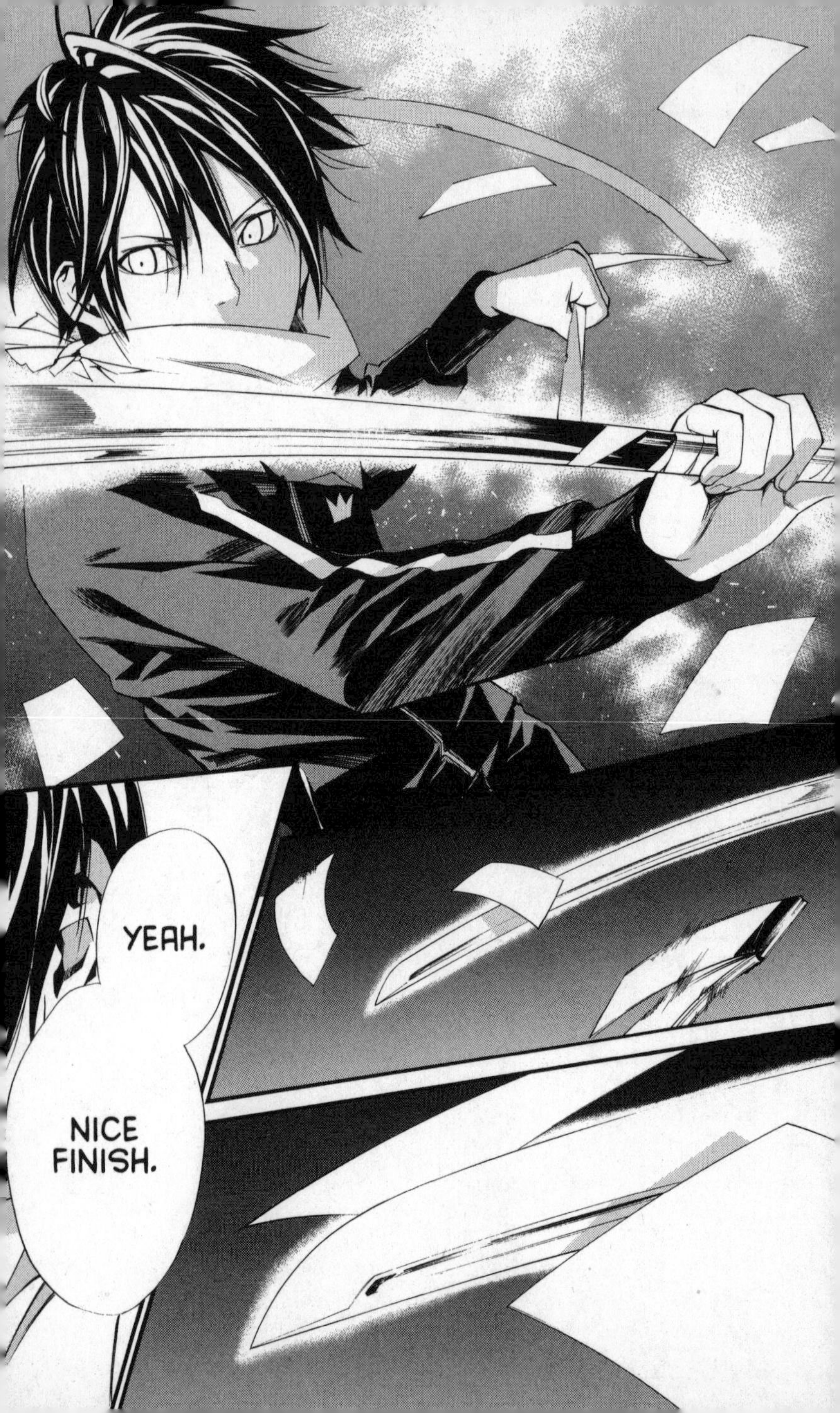
YEAH.
NICE FINISH.

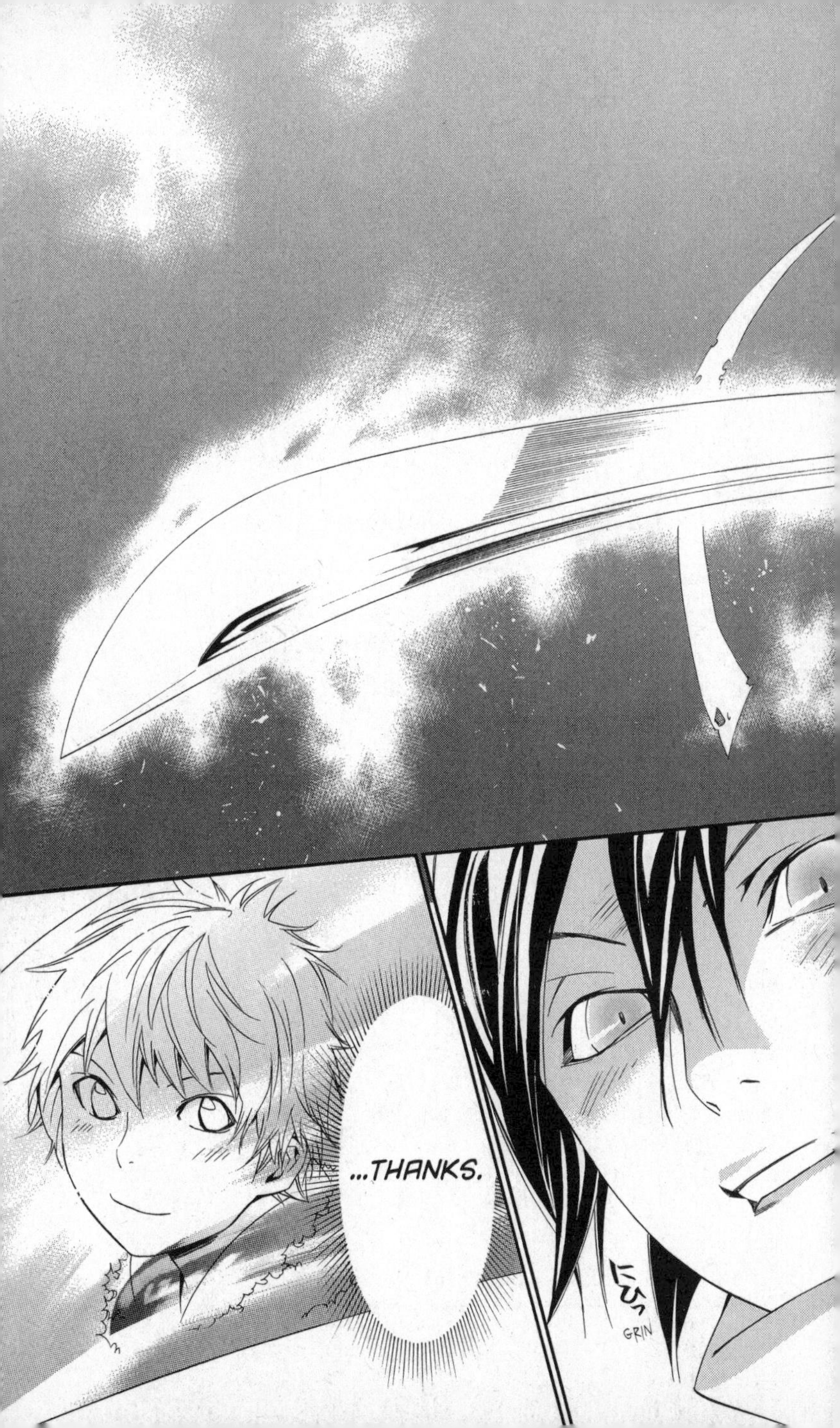
...THANKS.
GRIN

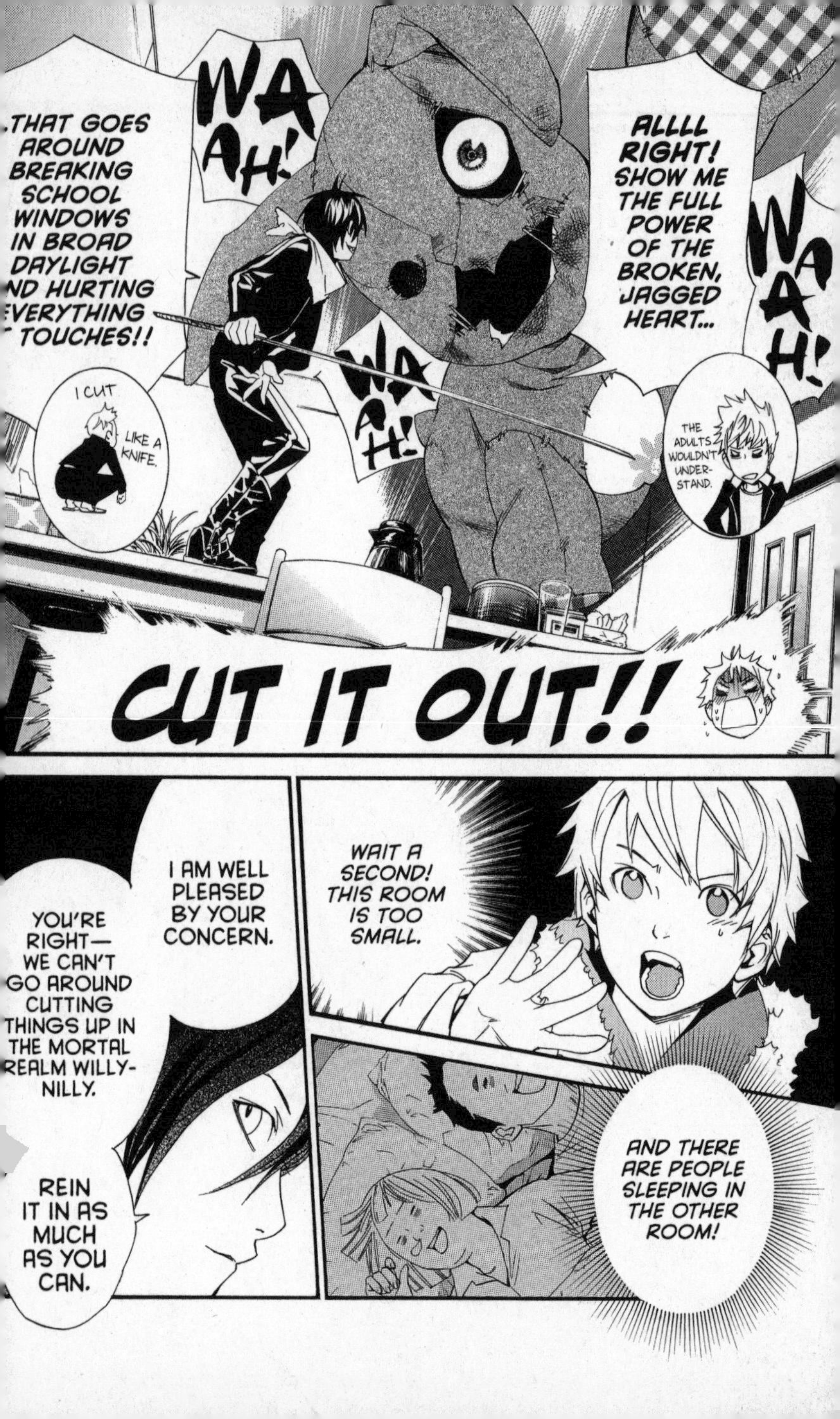

ALLLL RIGHT! SHOW ME THE FULL POWER OF THE BROKEN, JAGGED HEART...
WAAAH!
THE ADULTS WOULDN'T UNDERSTAND.
WAAH!
.THAT GOES AROUND BREAKING SCHOOL WINDOWS IN BROAD DAYLIGHT ND HURTING EVERYTHING TOUCHES!!
WA AH!
I CUT LIKE A KNIFE.
CUT IT OUT!!
WAIT A SECOND! THIS ROOM IS TOO SMALL.
AND THERE ARE PEOPLE SLEEPING IN THE OTHER ROOM!
I AM WELL PLEASED BY YOUR CONCERN.
YOU'RE RIGHT— WE CAN'T GO AROUND CUTTING THINGS UP IN THE MORTAL REALM WILLY-NILLY.
REIN IT IN AS MUCH AS YOU CAN.

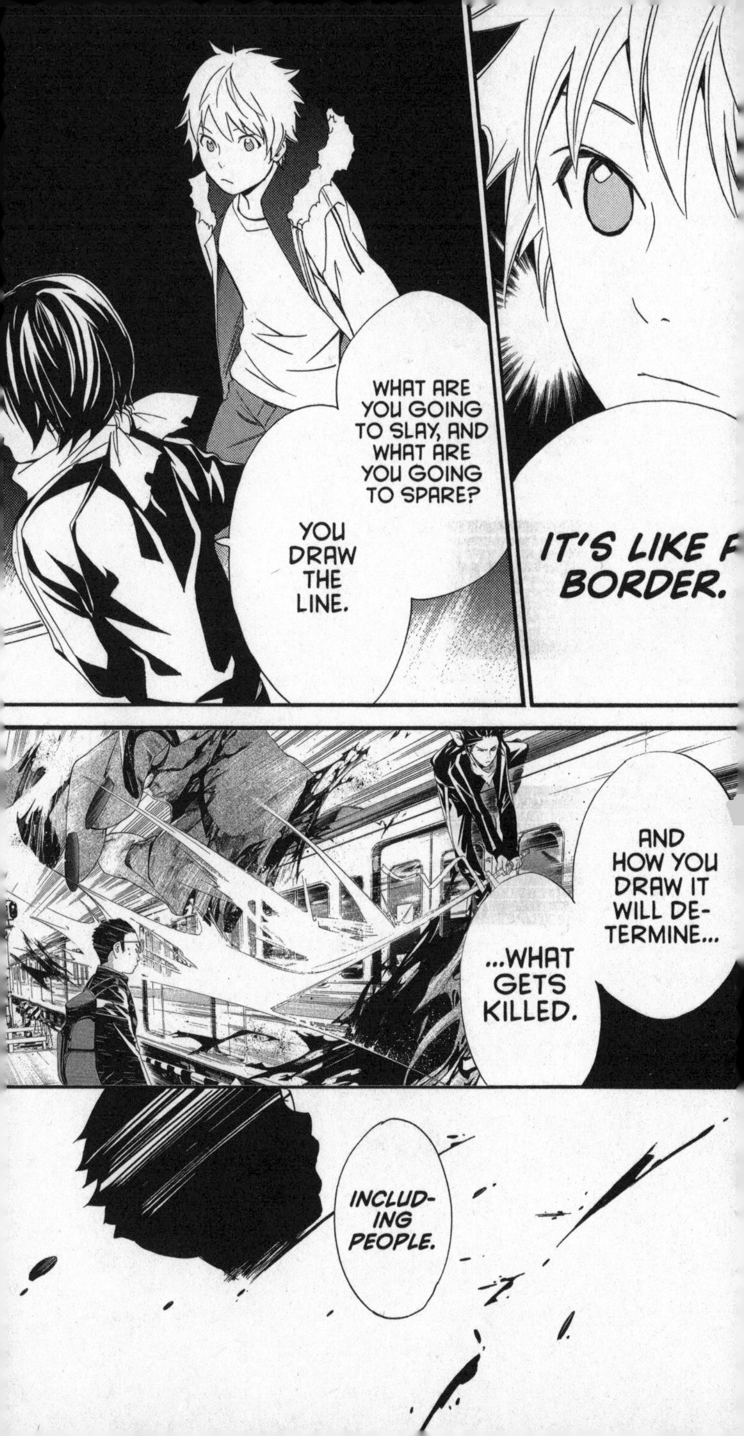
IT'S LIKE
BORDER.
WHAT ARE YOU GOING TO SLAY, AND WHAT ARE YOU GOING TO SPARE?
YOU DRAW THE LINE.
AND HOW YOU DRAW IT WILL DE-TERMINE...
...WHAT GETS KILLED.
INCLUD-ING PEOPLE.

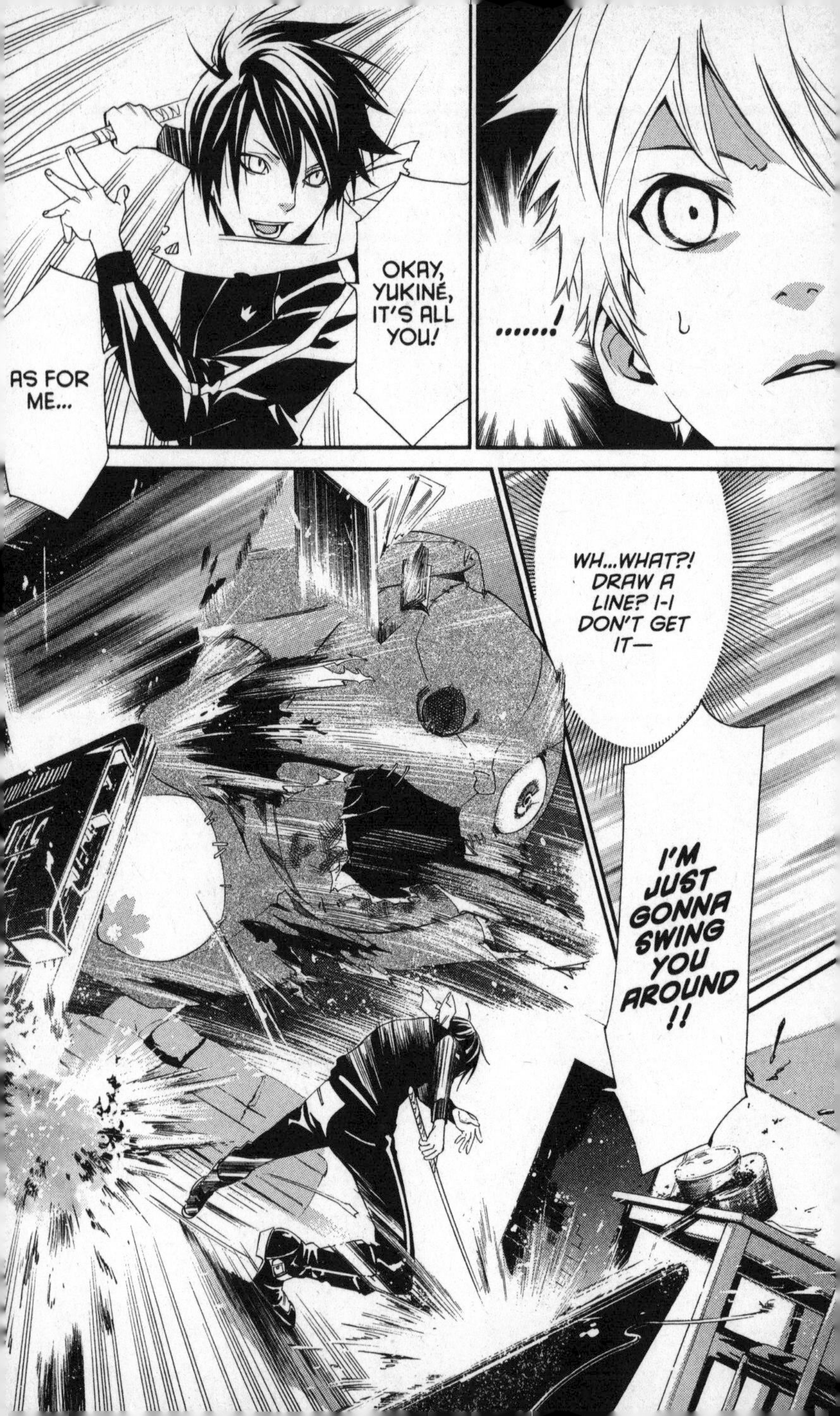

......!
OKAY, YUKINÉ, IT'S ALL YOU!
AS FOR ME...
WH...WHAT?! DRAW A LINE? I-I DON'T GET IT—
I'M JUST GONNA SWING YOU AROUND!!

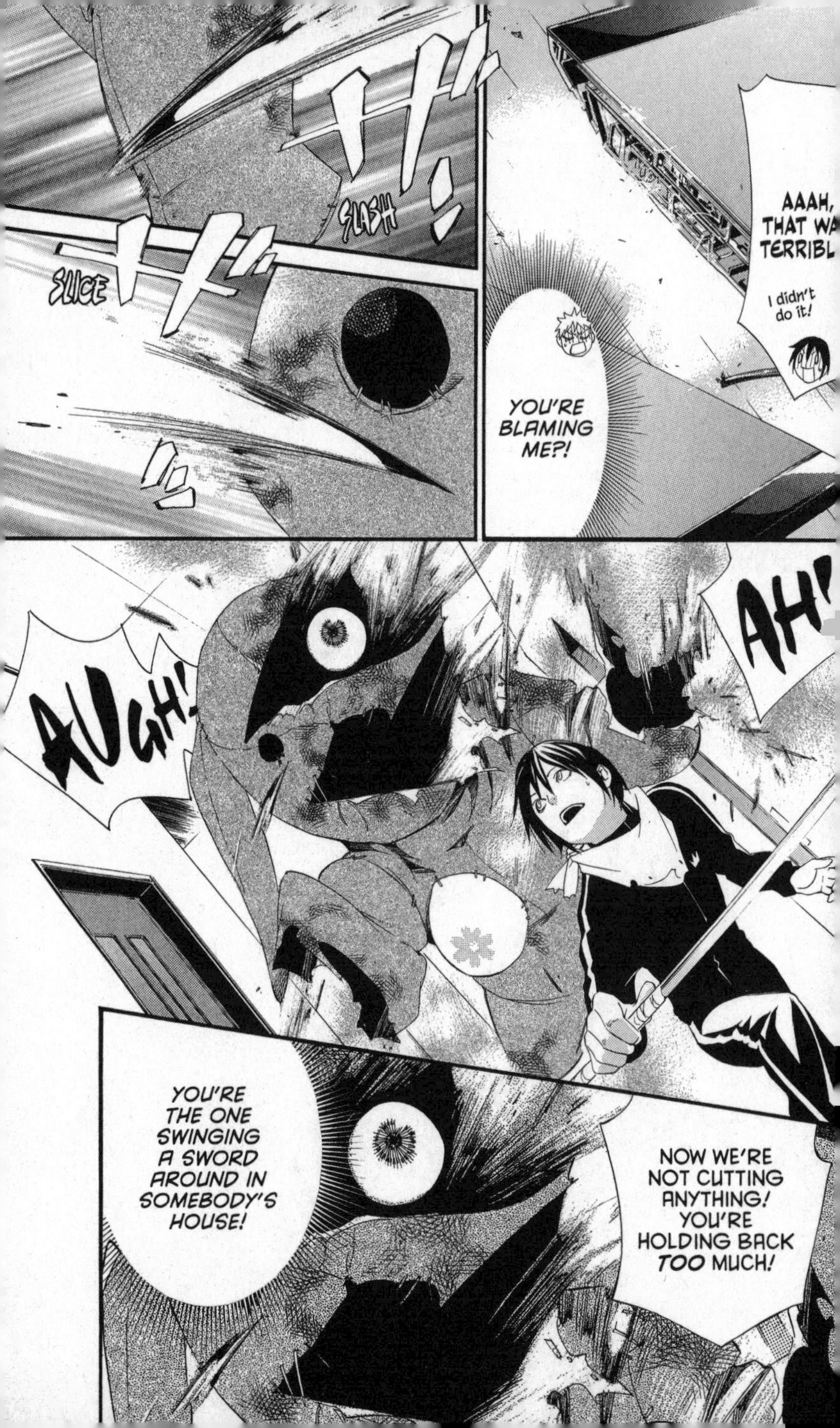
AAAH, THAT WA TERRIBL
I didn't do it!
YOU'RE BLAMING ME?!
SLASH
SLICE
AH
AUGH!
NOW WE'RE NOT CUTTING ANYTHING! YOU'RE HOLDING BACK *TOO* MUCH!
YOU'RE THE ONE SWINGING A SWORD AROUND IN SOMEBODY'S HOUSE!

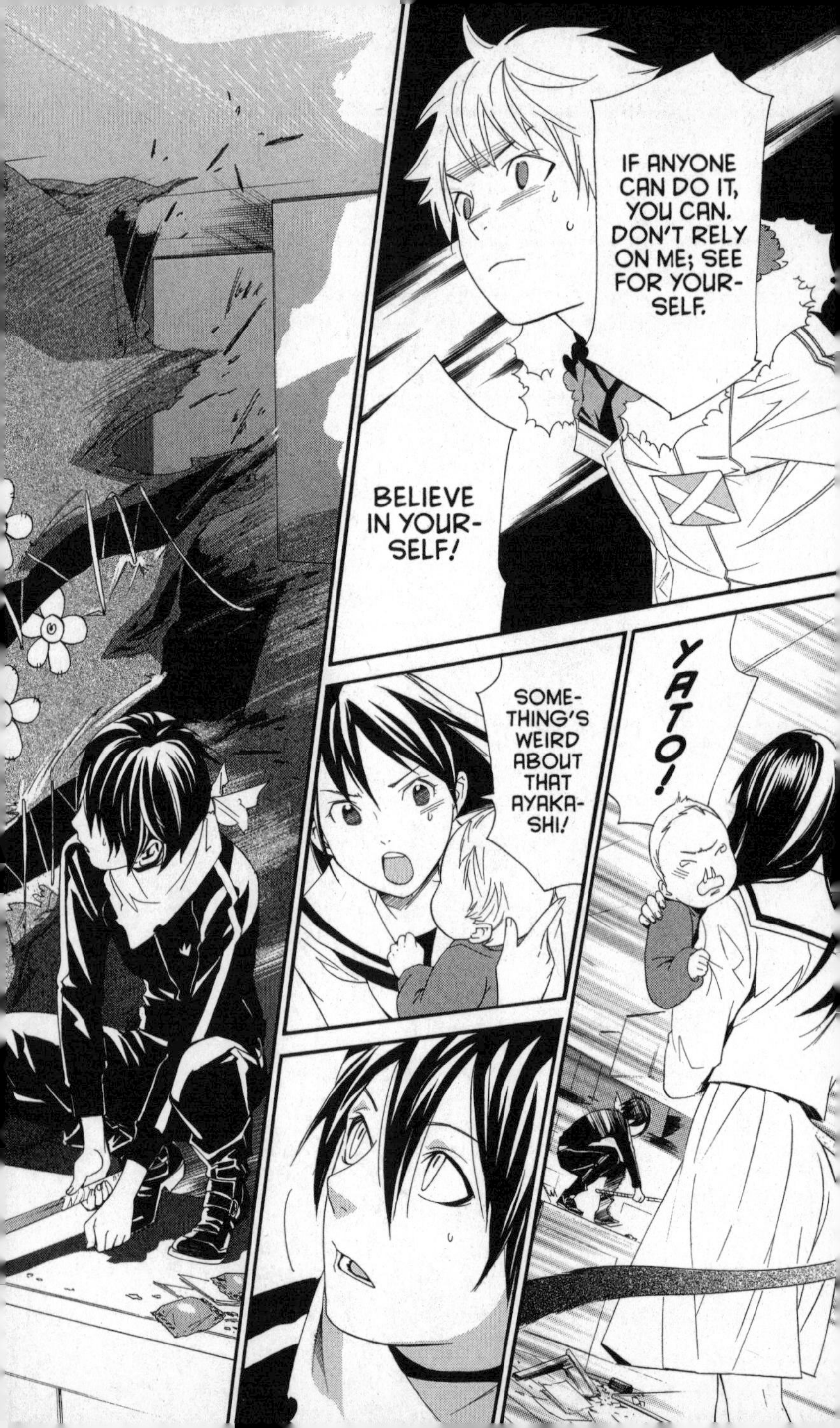
IF ANYONE CAN DO IT, YOU CAN. DON'T RELY ON ME; SEE FOR YOUR-SELF.
BELIEVE IN YOUR-SELF!
YATO!
SOME-THING'S WEIRD ABOUT THAT AYAKA-SHI!

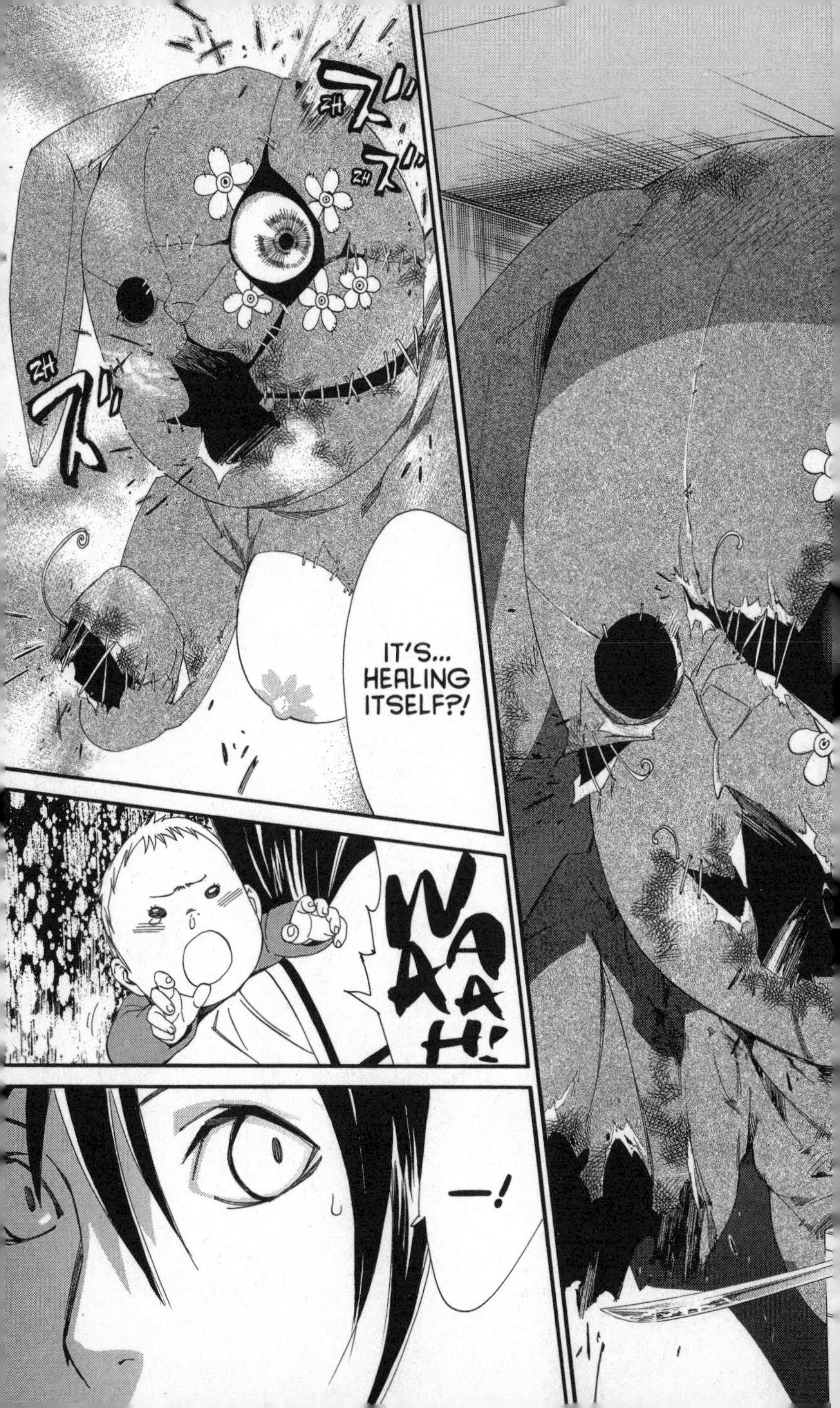
ZH
ZH
ZH
IT'S... HEALING ITSELF?!
WAAAH!
—!

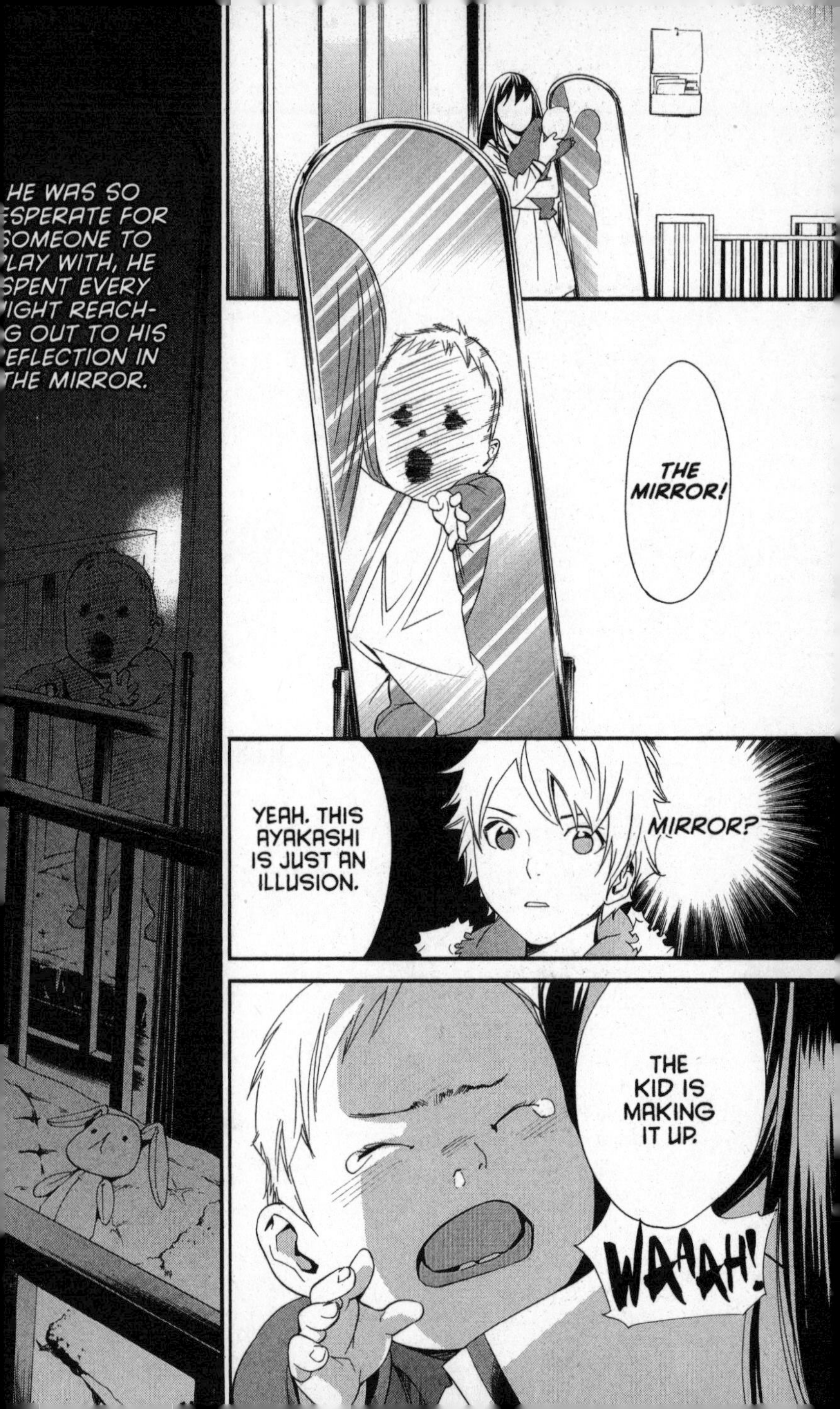
THE MIRROR!
MIRROR?
YEAH. THIS AYAKASHI IS JUST AN ILLUSION.
THE KID IS MAKING IT UP.
WAAAH!
HE WAS SO ESPERATE FOR SOMEONE TO LAY WITH, HE SPENT EVERY IGHT REACH- G OUT TO HIS EFLECTION IN THE MIRROR.

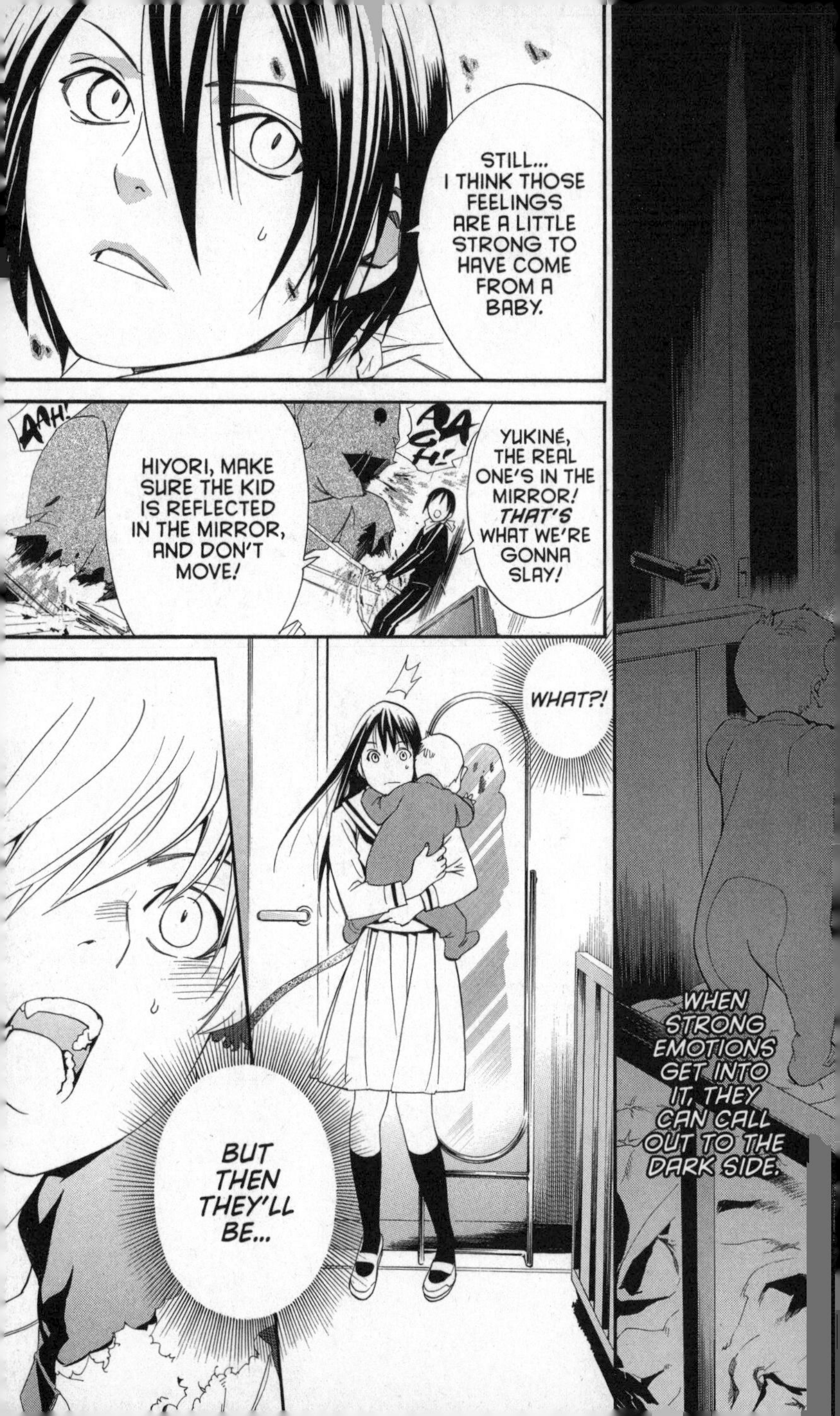
WHEN STRONG EMOTIONS GET INTO IT, THEY CAN CALL OUT TO THE DARK SIDE.
STILL... I THINK THOSE FEELINGS ARE A LITTLE STRONG TO HAVE COME FROM A BABY.
YUKINÉ, THE REAL ONE'S IN THE MIRROR! THAT'S WHAT WE'RE GONNA SLAY!
AAGH!
HIYORI, MAKE SURE THE KID IS REFLECTED IN THE MIRROR, AND DON'T MOVE!
AAH!
WHAT?!
BUT THEN THEY'LL BE...

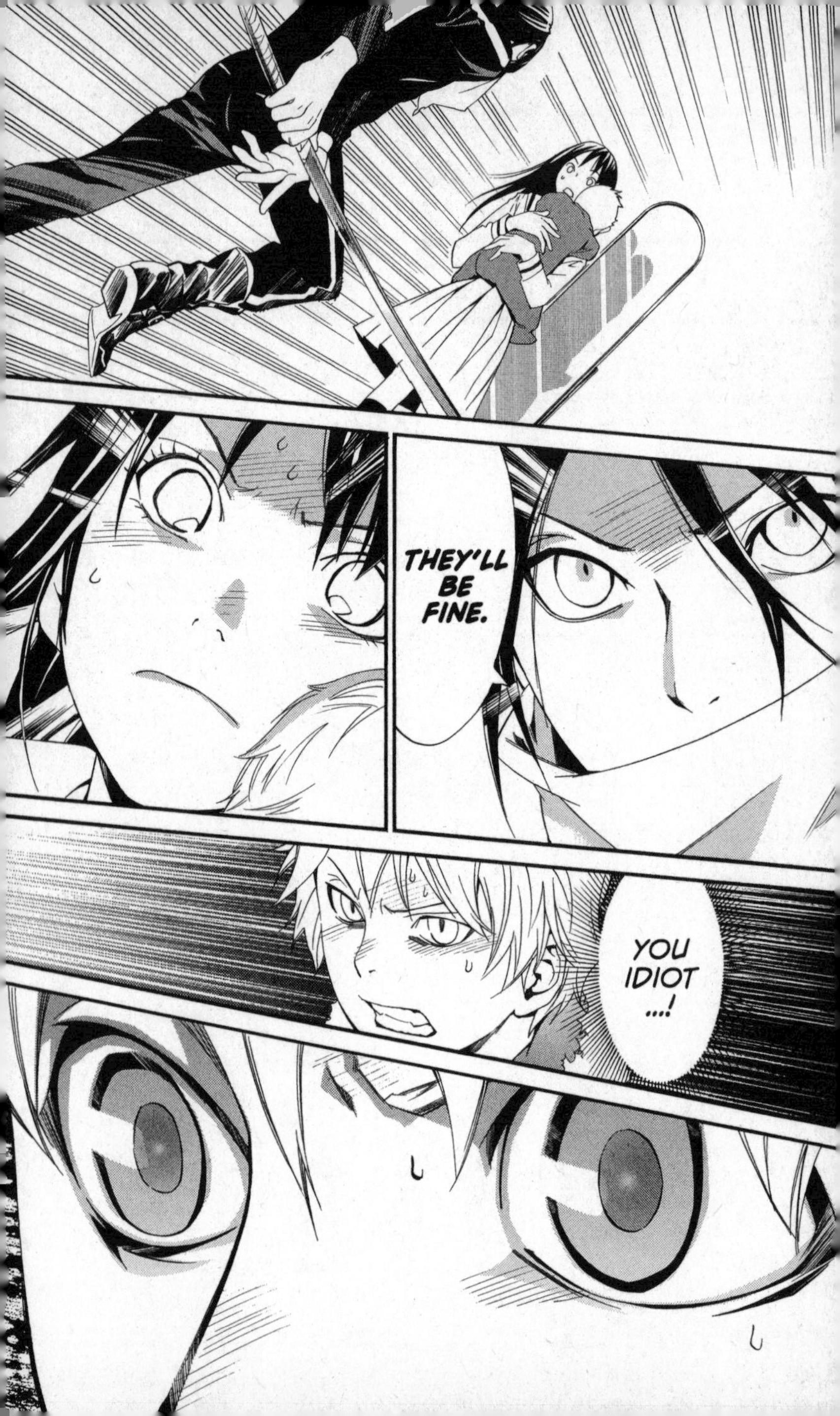
THEY'LL BE FINE.
YOU IDIOT ...!

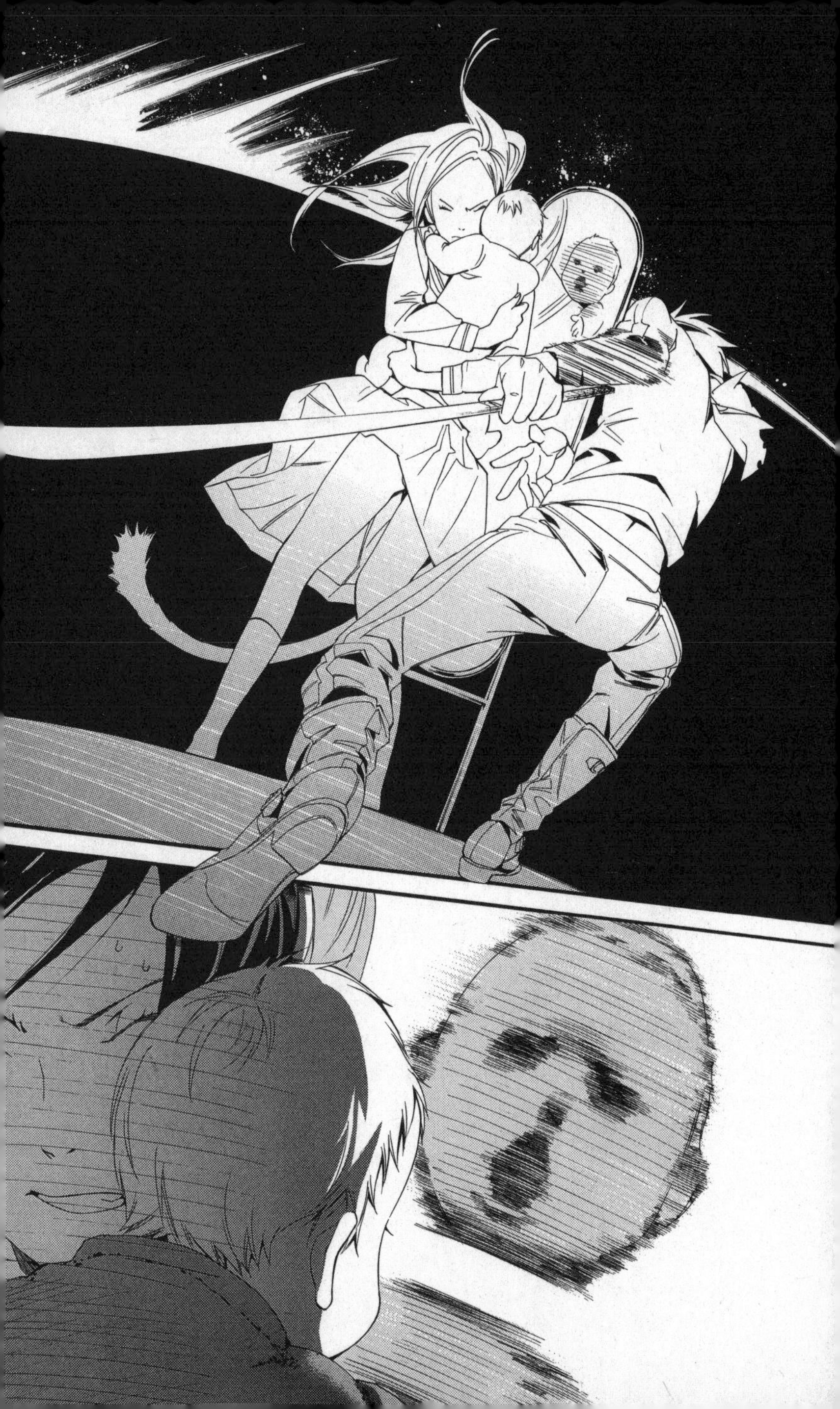

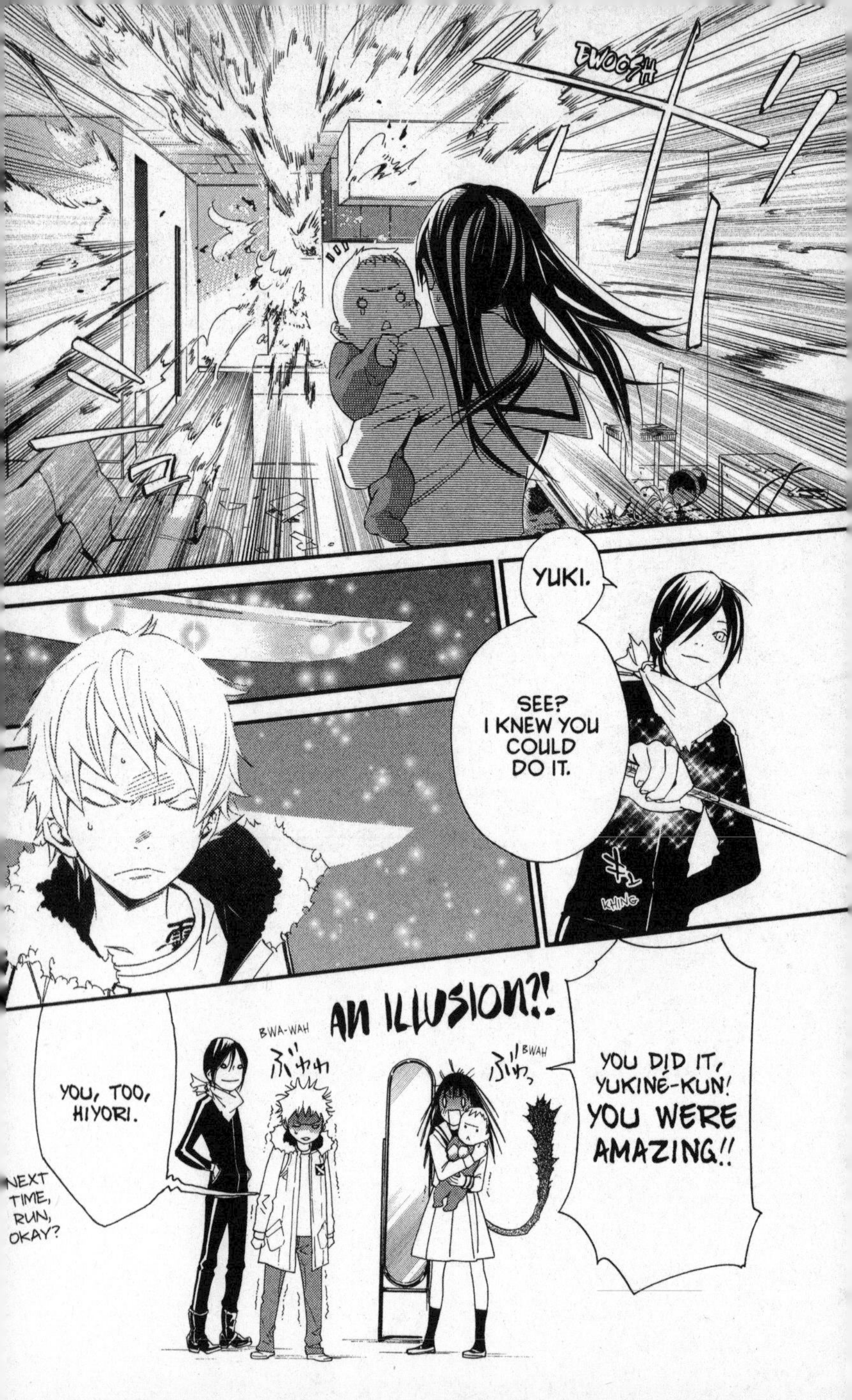
SWOOSH
YUKI.
SEE? I KNEW YOU COULD DO IT.
KHING
YOU DID IT, YUKINE-KUN! YOU WERE AMAZING!!
ぶわっ
BWAH
AN ILLUSION?!
ぶわわ
BWA-WAH
YOU, TOO, HIYORI.
NEXT TIME, RUN, OKAY?

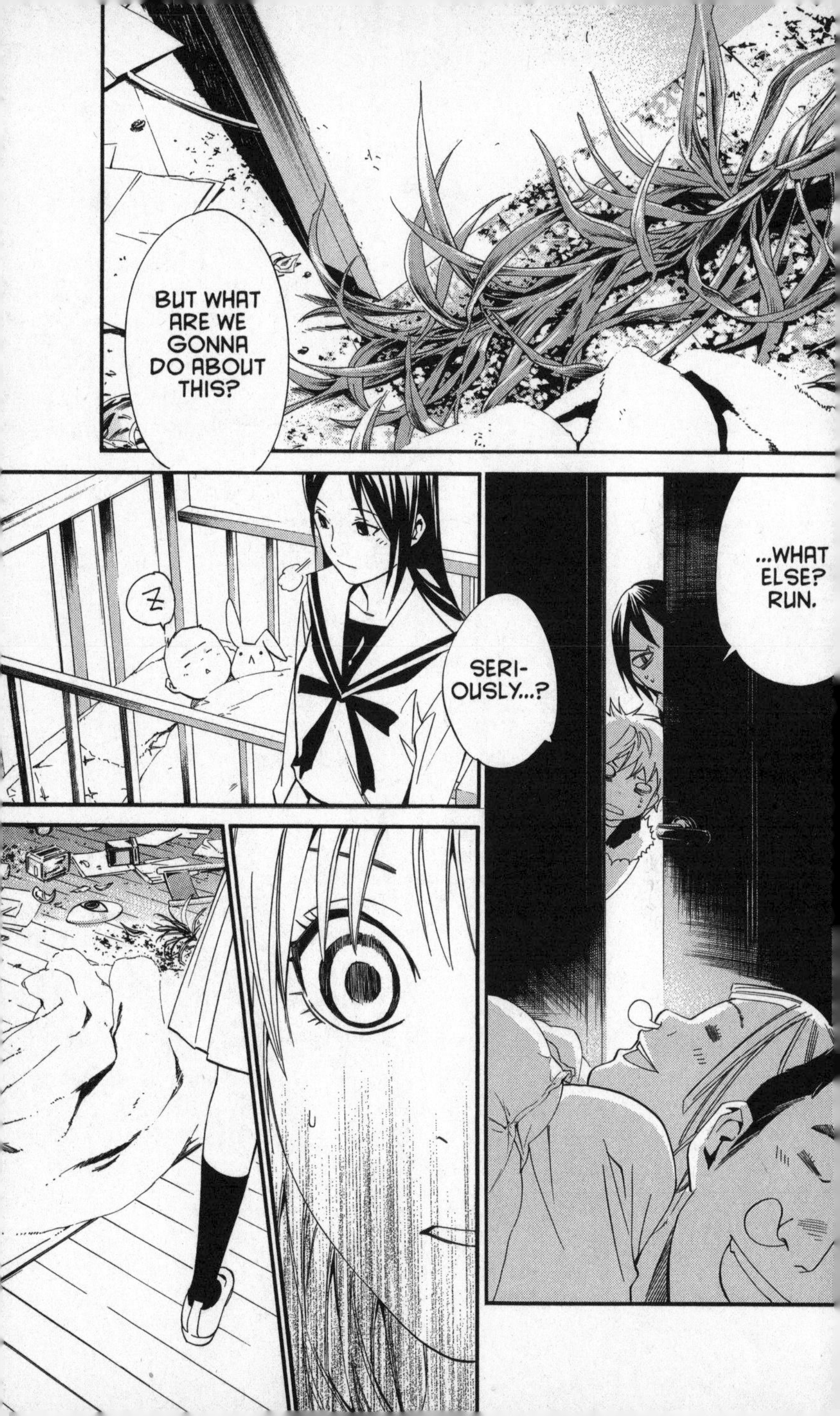
BUT WHAT ARE WE GONNA DO ABOUT THIS?
...WHAT ELSE? RUN.
SERI-OUSLY...?
Z

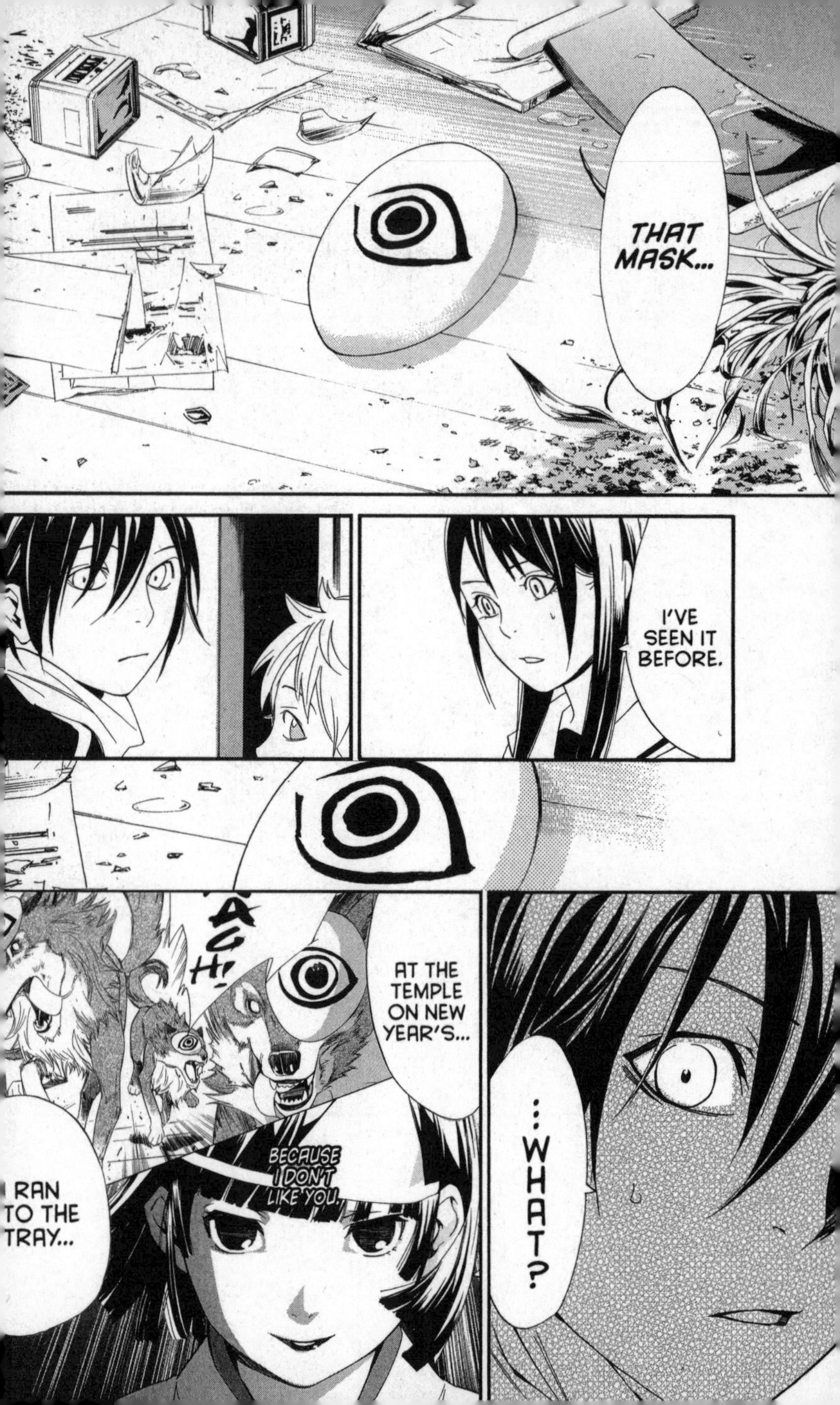
THAT MASK...
I'VE SEEN IT BEFORE.
...WHAT?
AT THE TEMPLE ON NEW YEAR'S...
AGH!
BECAUSE I DON'T LIKE YOU.
I RAN TO THE TRAY...

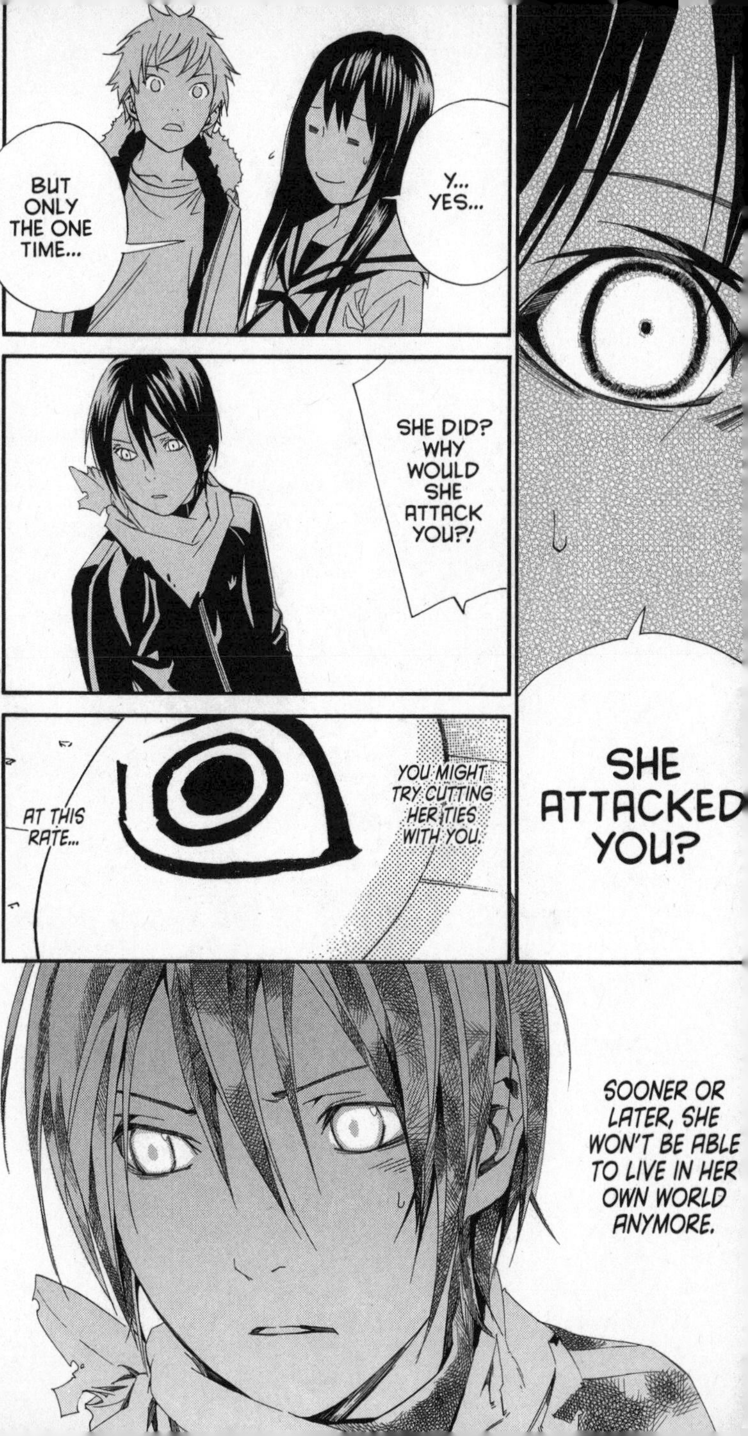

SHE ATTACKED YOU?
Y... YES...
BUT ONLY THE ONE TIME...
SHE DID? WHY WOULD SHE ATTACK YOU?!
YOU MIGHT TRY CUTTING HER TIES WITH YOU.
AT THIS RATE...
SOONER OR LATER, SHE WON'T BE ABLE TO LIVE IN HER OWN WORLD ANYMORE.

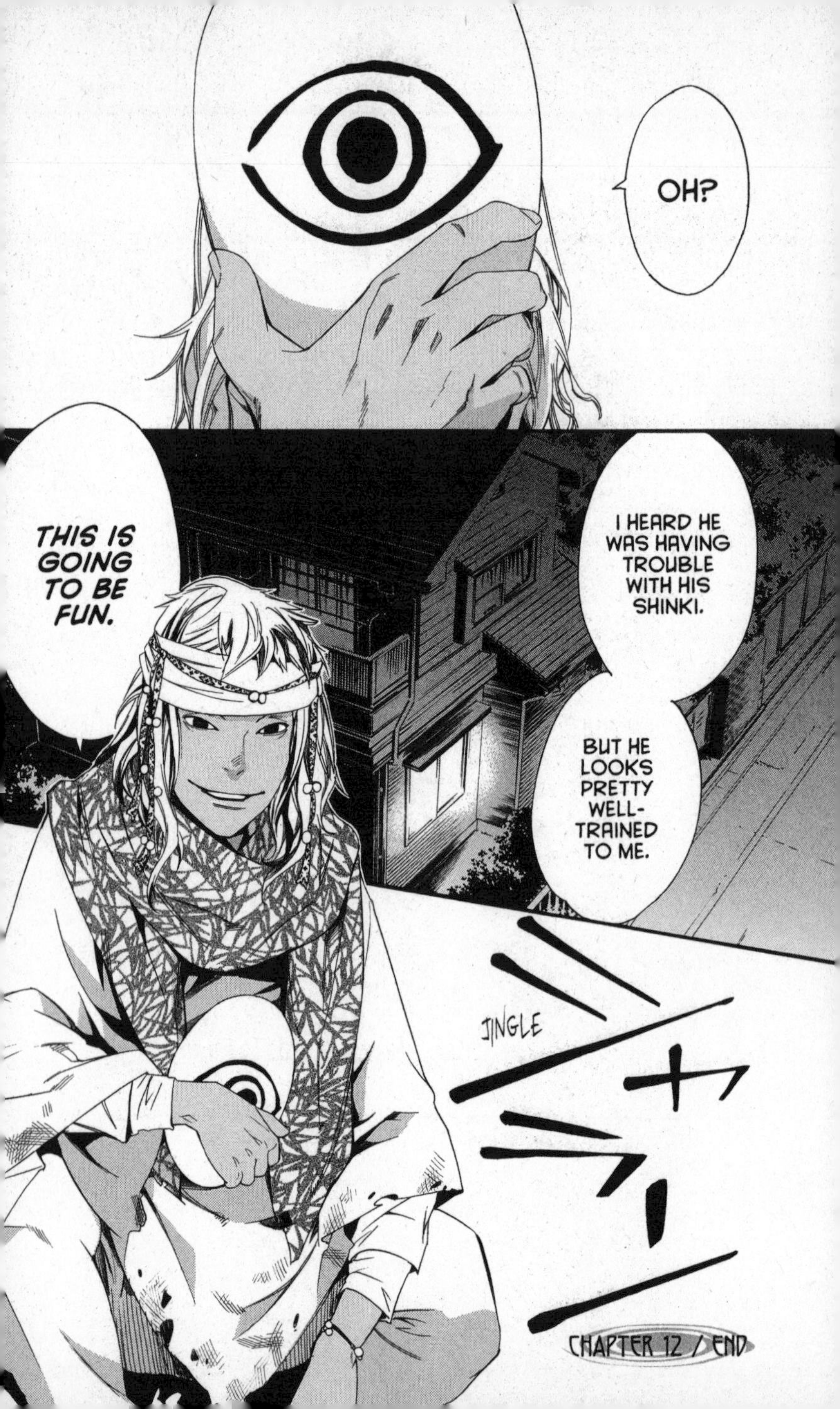
OH?
I HEARD HE WAS HAVING TROUBLE WITH HIS SHINKI.
BUT HE LOOKS PRETTY WELL-TRAINED TO ME.
THIS IS GOING TO BE FUN.
JINGLE
CHAPTER 12 / END

野

邑

神

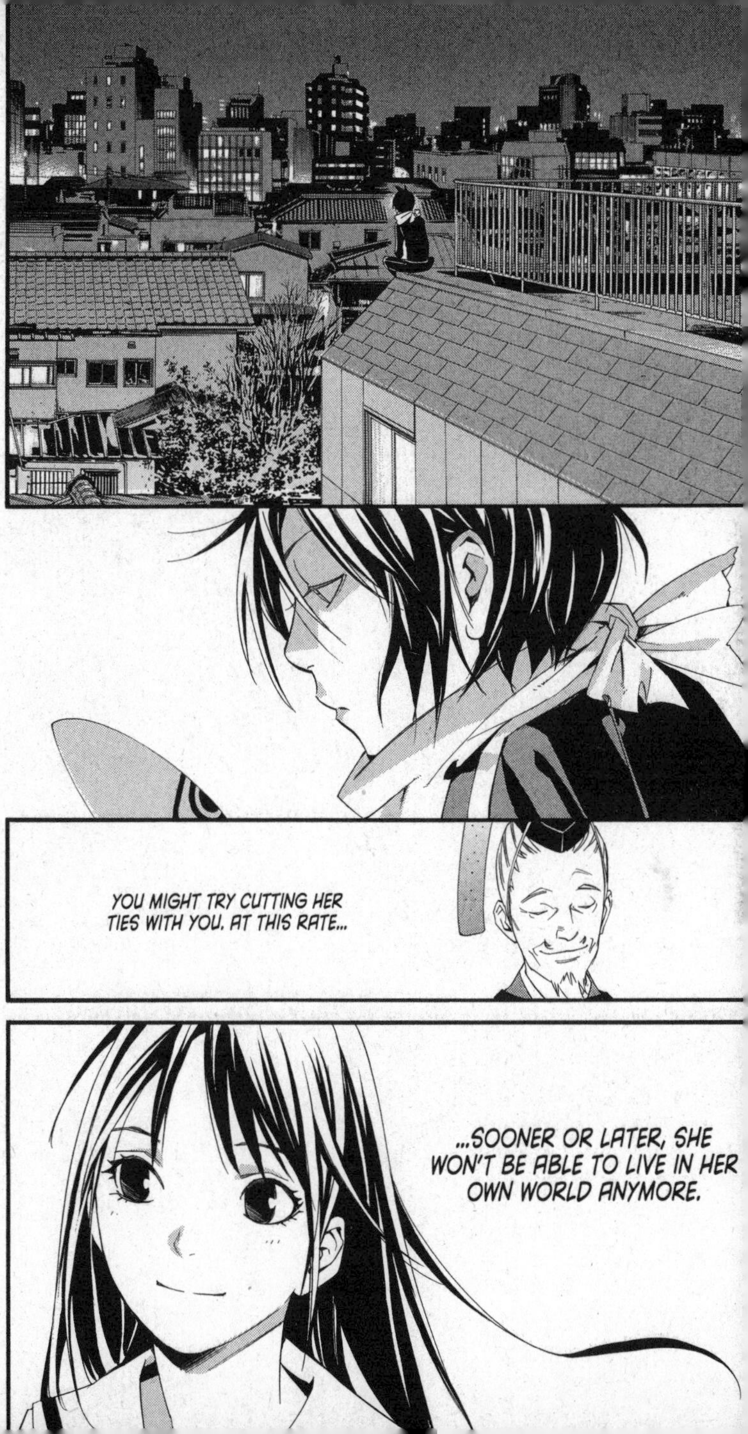
YOU MIGHT TRY CUTTING HER TIES WITH YOU. AT THIS RATE...
...SOONER OR LATER, SHE WON'T BE ABLE TO LIVE IN HER OWN WORLD ANYMORE.

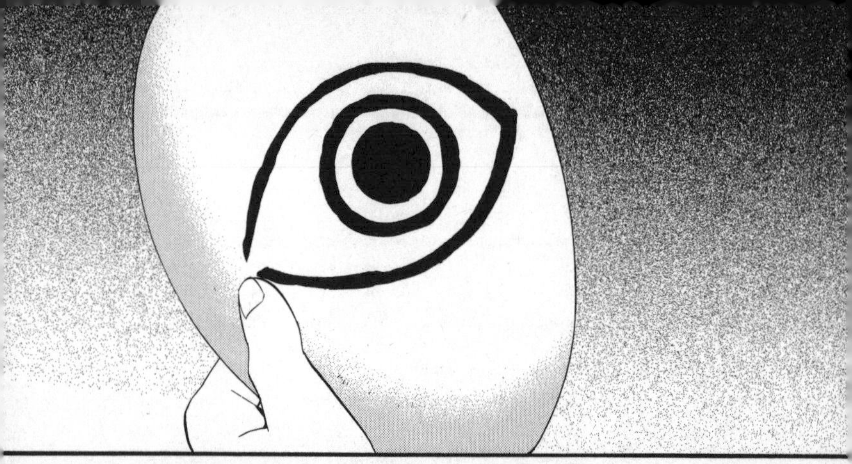

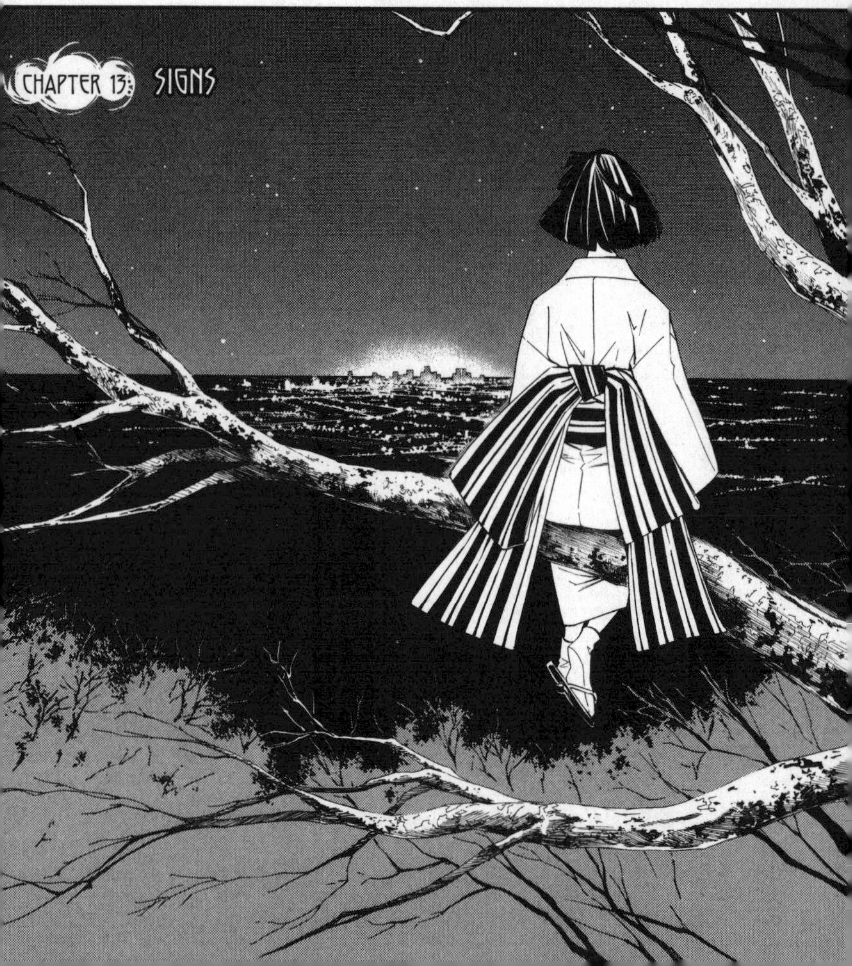
CHAPTER 13: SIGNS

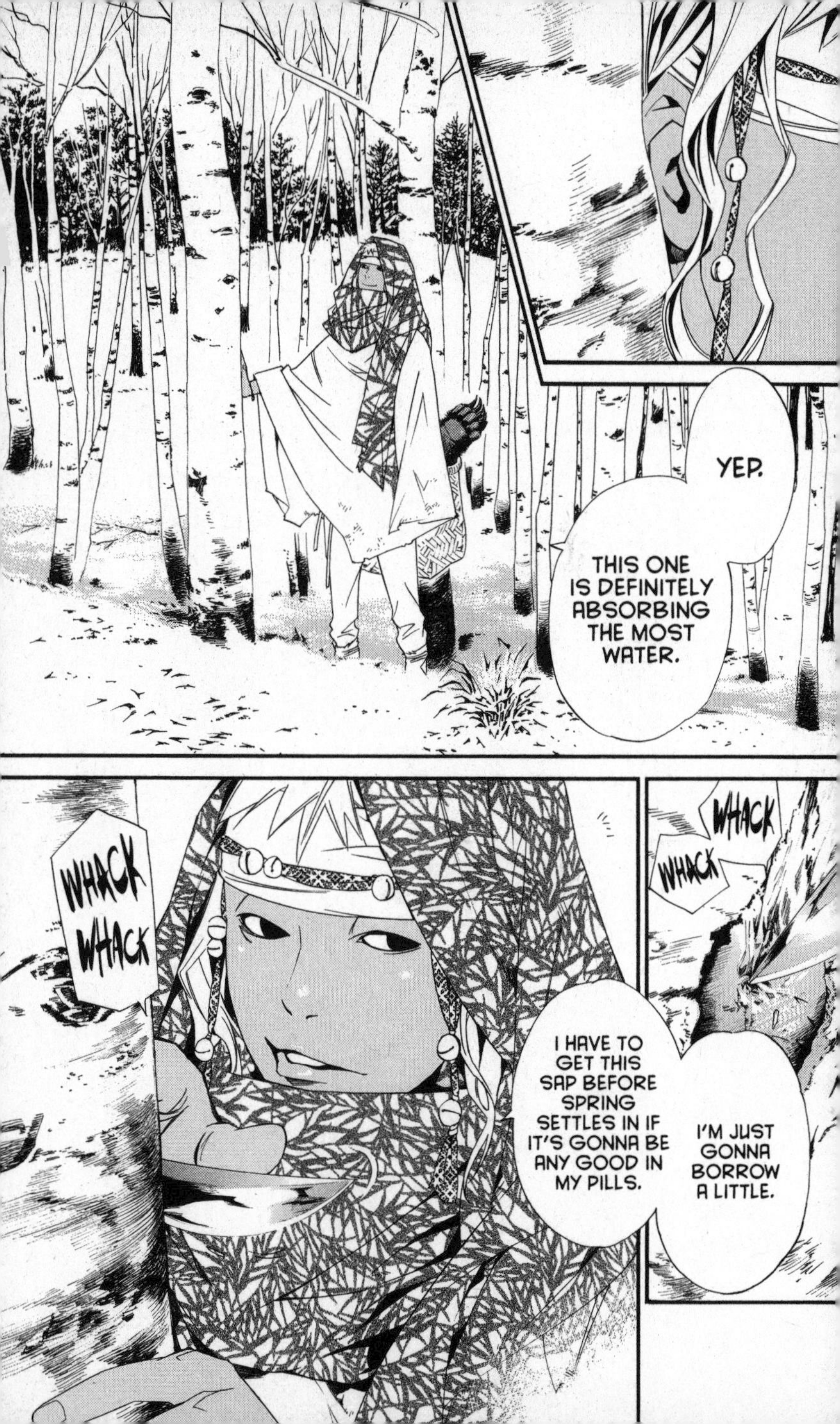
YEP.
THIS ONE IS DEFINITELY ABSORBING THE MOST WATER.
WHACK
WHACK
I'M JUST GONNA BORROW A LITTLE.
WHACK WHACK
I HAVE TO GET THIS SAP BEFORE SPRING SETTLES IN IF IT'S GONNA BE ANY GOOD IN MY PILLS.

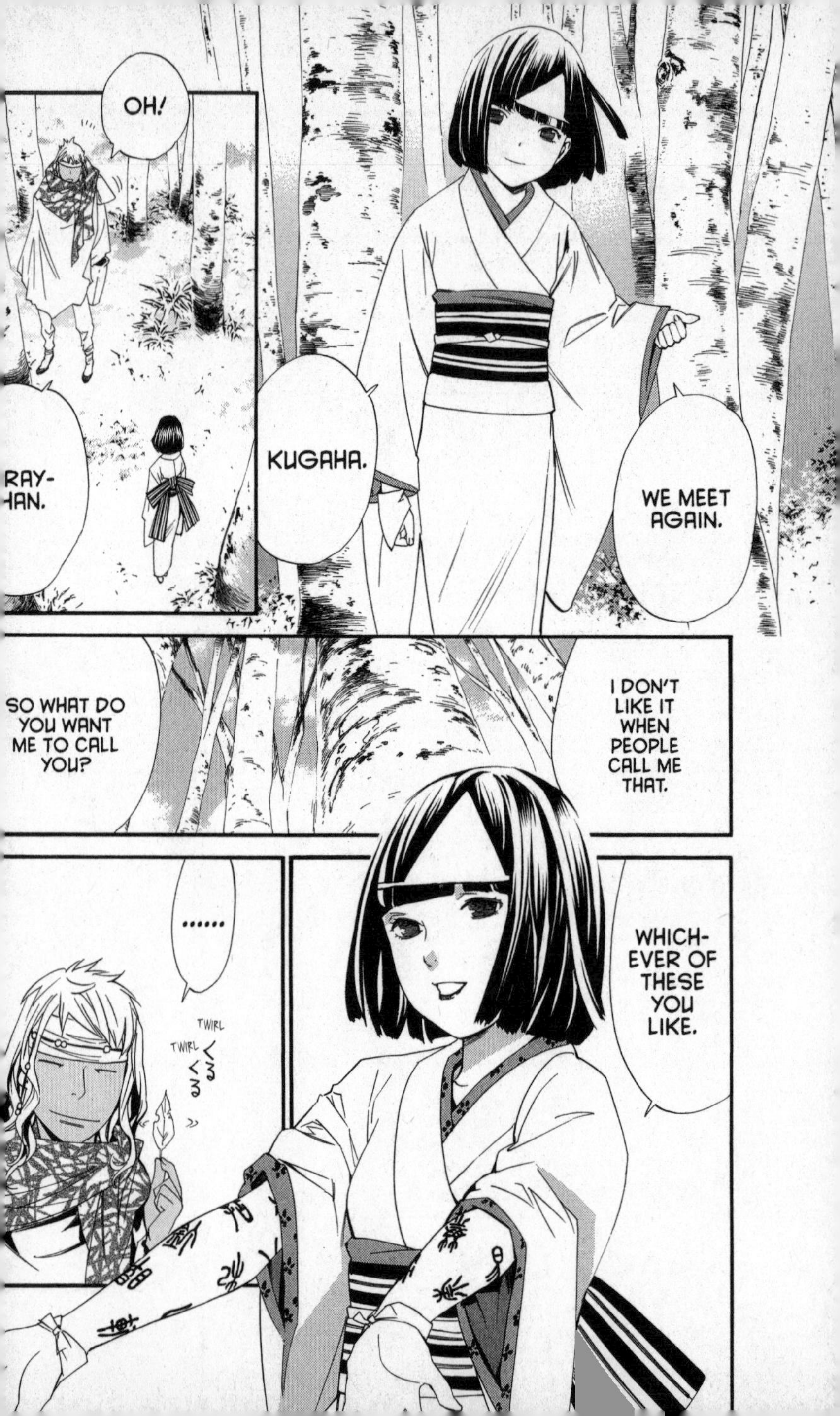
WE MEET AGAIN.
KUGAHA.
OH!
RAY-HAN.
I DON'T LIKE IT WHEN PEOPLE CALL ME THAT.
SO WHAT DO YOU WANT ME TO CALL YOU?
WHICH-EVER OF THESE YOU LIKE.
......
TWIRL くる
TWIRL くる

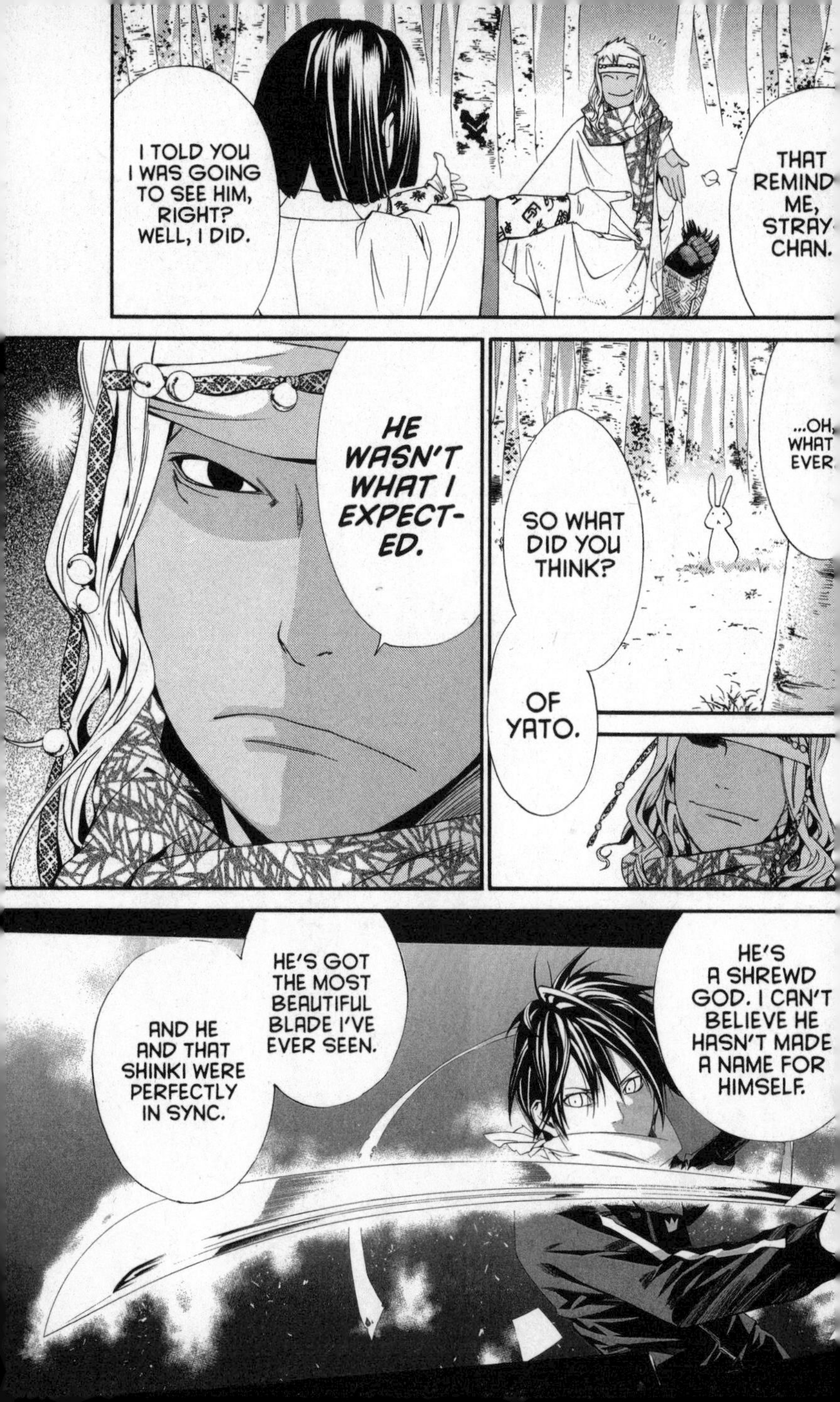

THAT REMIND ME, STRAY CHAN.
I TOLD YOU I WAS GOING TO SEE HIM, RIGHT? WELL, I DID.
...OH, WHAT EVER
SO WHAT DID YOU THINK?
OF YATO.
HE WASN'T WHAT I EXPECTED.
HE'S A SHREWD GOD. I CAN'T BELIEVE HE HASN'T MADE A NAME FOR HIMSELF.
HE'S GOT THE MOST BEAUTIFUL BLADE I'VE EVER SEEN.
AND HE AND THAT SHINKI WERE PERFECTLY IN SYNC.

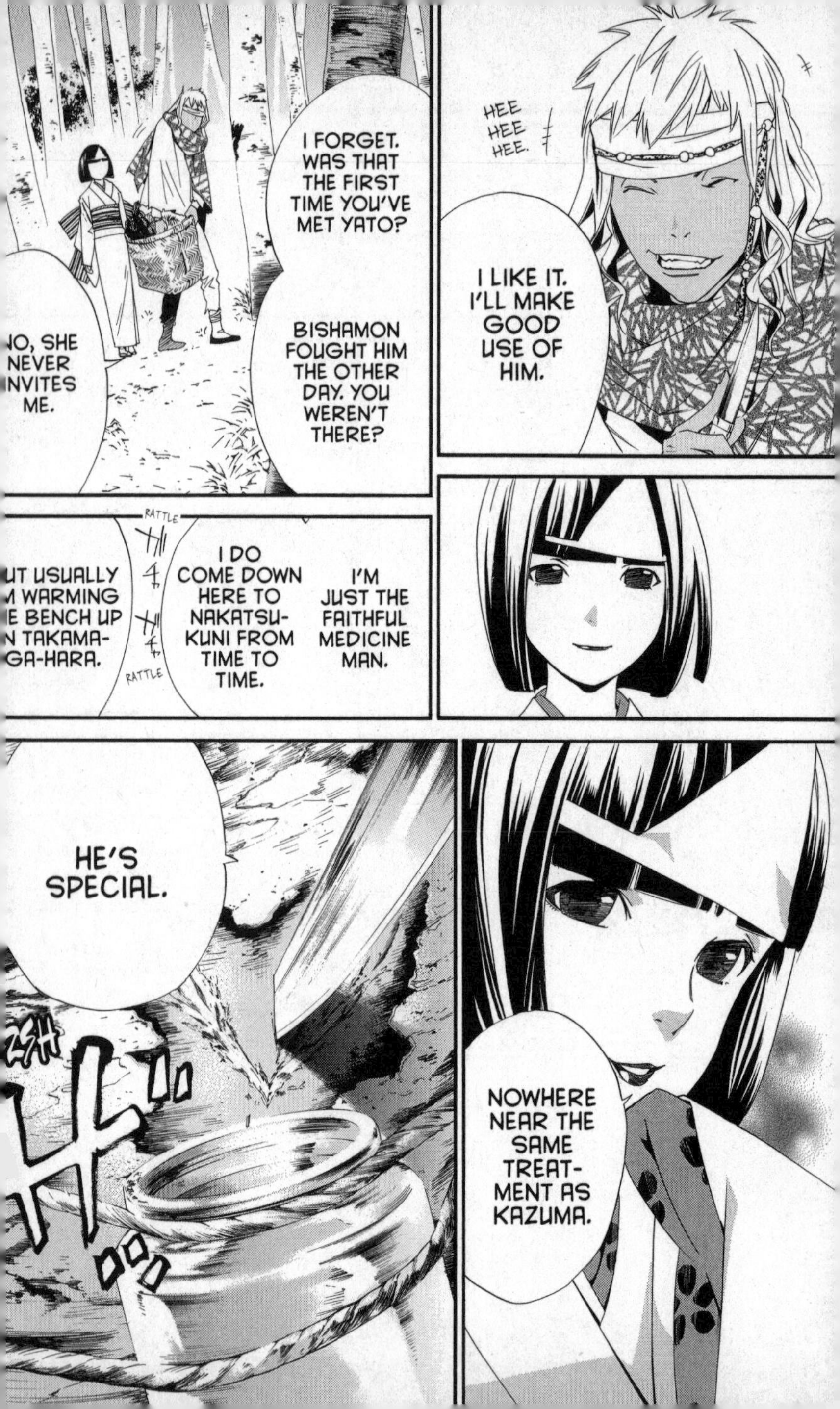
HEE HEE HEE.
I LIKE IT. I'LL MAKE GOOD USE OF HIM.
I FORGET. WAS THAT THE FIRST TIME YOU'VE MET YATO?
BISHAMON FOUGHT HIM THE OTHER DAY. YOU WEREN'T THERE?
O, SHE NEVER NVITES ME.
I'M JUST THE FAITHFUL MEDICINE MAN.
I DO COME DOWN HERE TO NAKATSU-KUNI FROM TIME TO TIME.
RATTLE
UT USUALLY M WARMING E BENCH UP N TAKAMA-GA-HARA.
RATTLE
NOWHERE NEAR THE SAME TREATMENT AS KAZUMA.
HE'S SPECIAL.

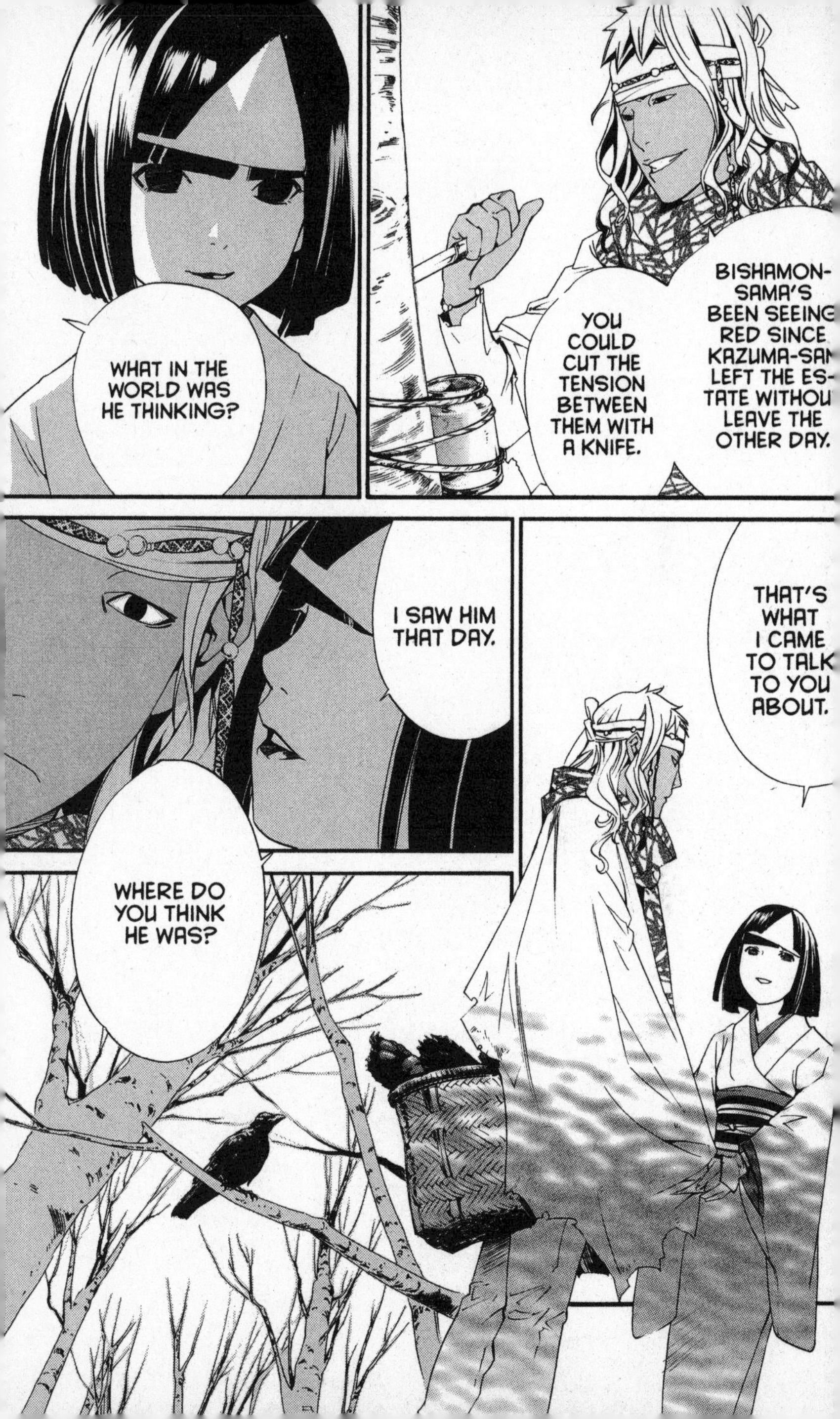
BISHAMON-SAMA'S BEEN SEEING RED SINCE KAZUMA-SAN LEFT THE ES-TATE WITHOU LEAVE THE OTHER DAY.
YOU COULD CUT THE TENSION BETWEEN THEM WITH A KNIFE.
WHAT IN THE WORLD WAS HE THINKING?
THAT'S WHAT I CAME TO TALK TO YOU ABOUT.
I SAW HIM THAT DAY.
WHERE DO YOU THINK HE WAS?

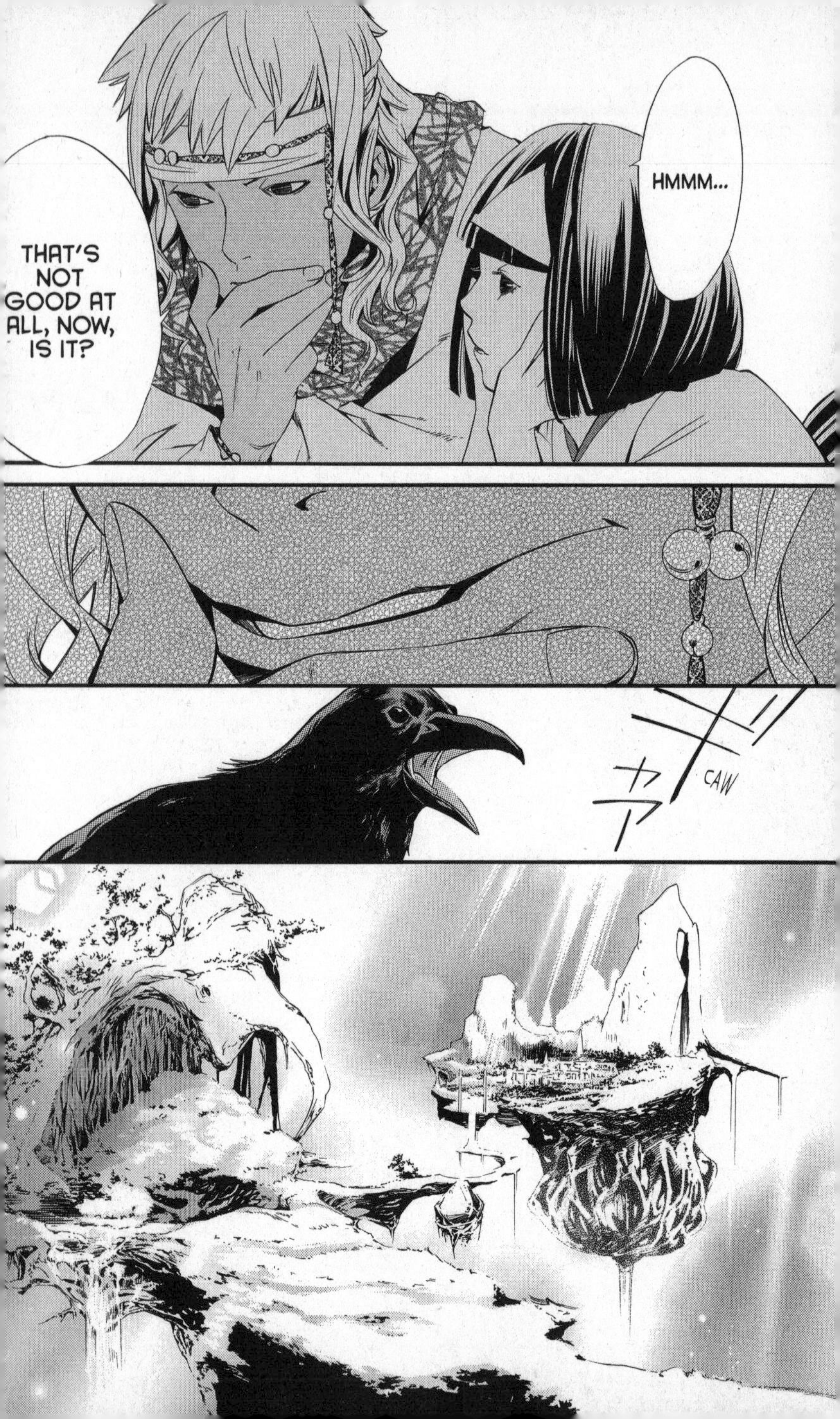
HMMM...
THAT'S NOT GOOD AT ALL, NOW, IS IT?
CAW

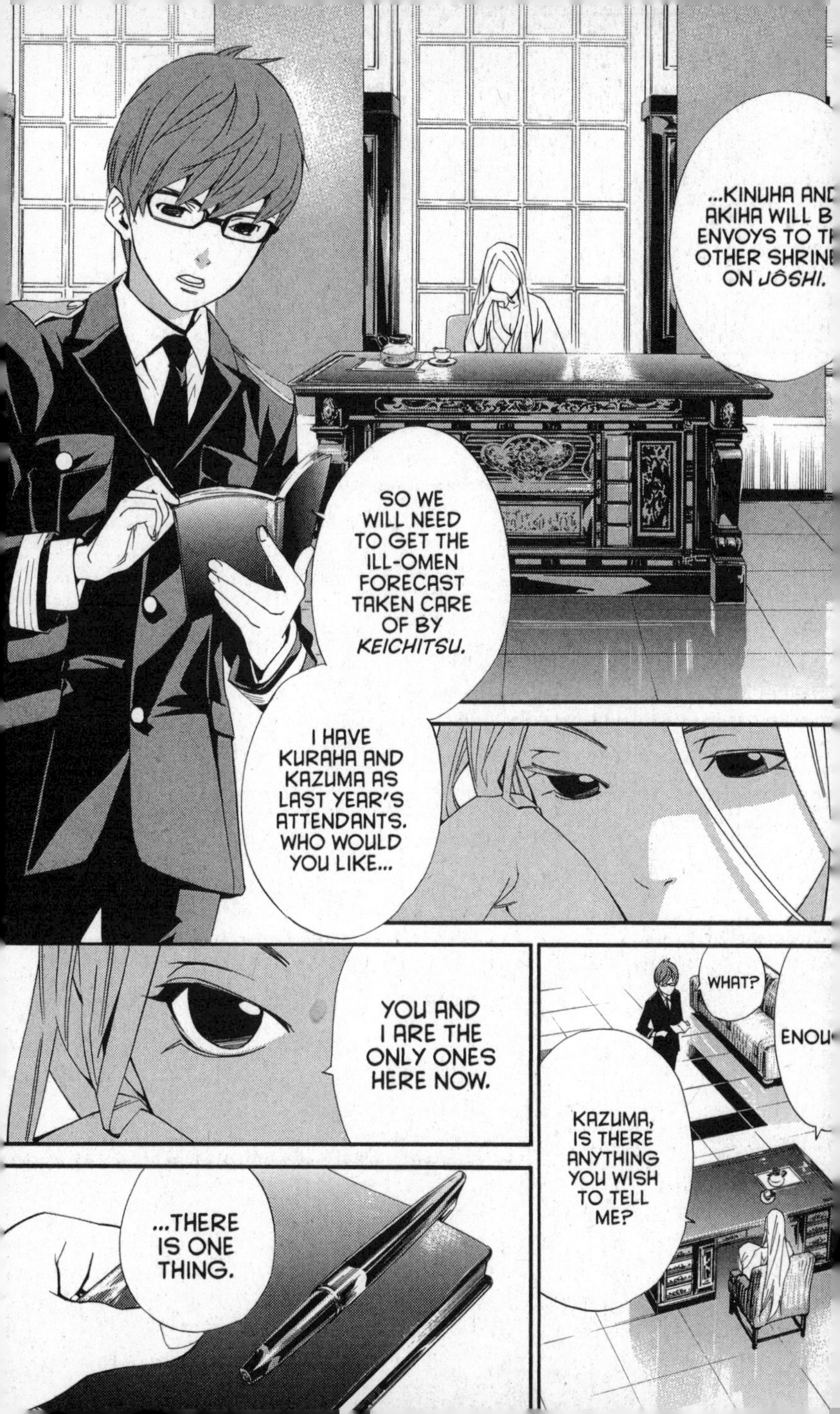
...KINUHA AND AKIHA WILL B ENVOYS TO TH OTHER SHRINE ON *JÔSHI.*
SO WE WILL NEED TO GET THE ILL-OMEN FORECAST TAKEN CARE OF BY *KEICHITSU.*
I HAVE KURAHA AND KAZUMA AS LAST YEAR'S ATTENDANTS. WHO WOULD YOU LIKE...
YOU AND I ARE THE ONLY ONES HERE NOW.
KAZUMA, IS THERE ANYTHING YOU WISH TO TELL ME?
...THERE IS ONE THING.
WHAT?
ENOU

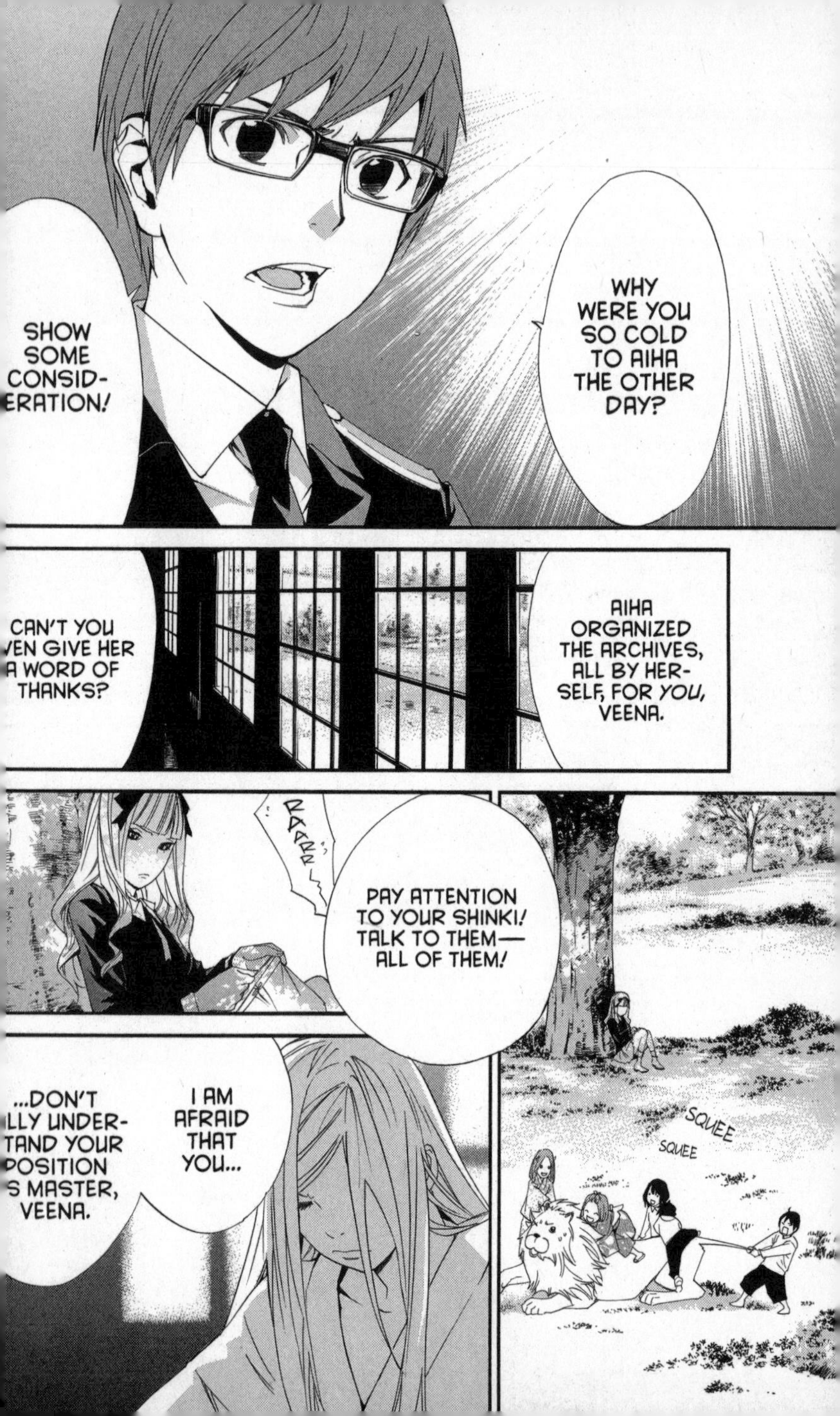
WHY WERE YOU SO COLD TO AIHA THE OTHER DAY?
SHOW SOME CONSID- ERATION!
AIHA ORGANIZED THE ARCHIVES, ALL BY HER- SELF, FOR *YOU*, VEENA.
CAN'T YOU VEN GIVE HER A WORD OF THANKS?
SQUEE
SQUEE
PAY ATTENTION TO YOUR SHINKI! TALK TO THEM— ALL OF THEM!
RAAARR
I AM AFRAID THAT YOU...
...DON'T LLY UNDER- TAND YOUR POSITION S MASTER, VEENA.

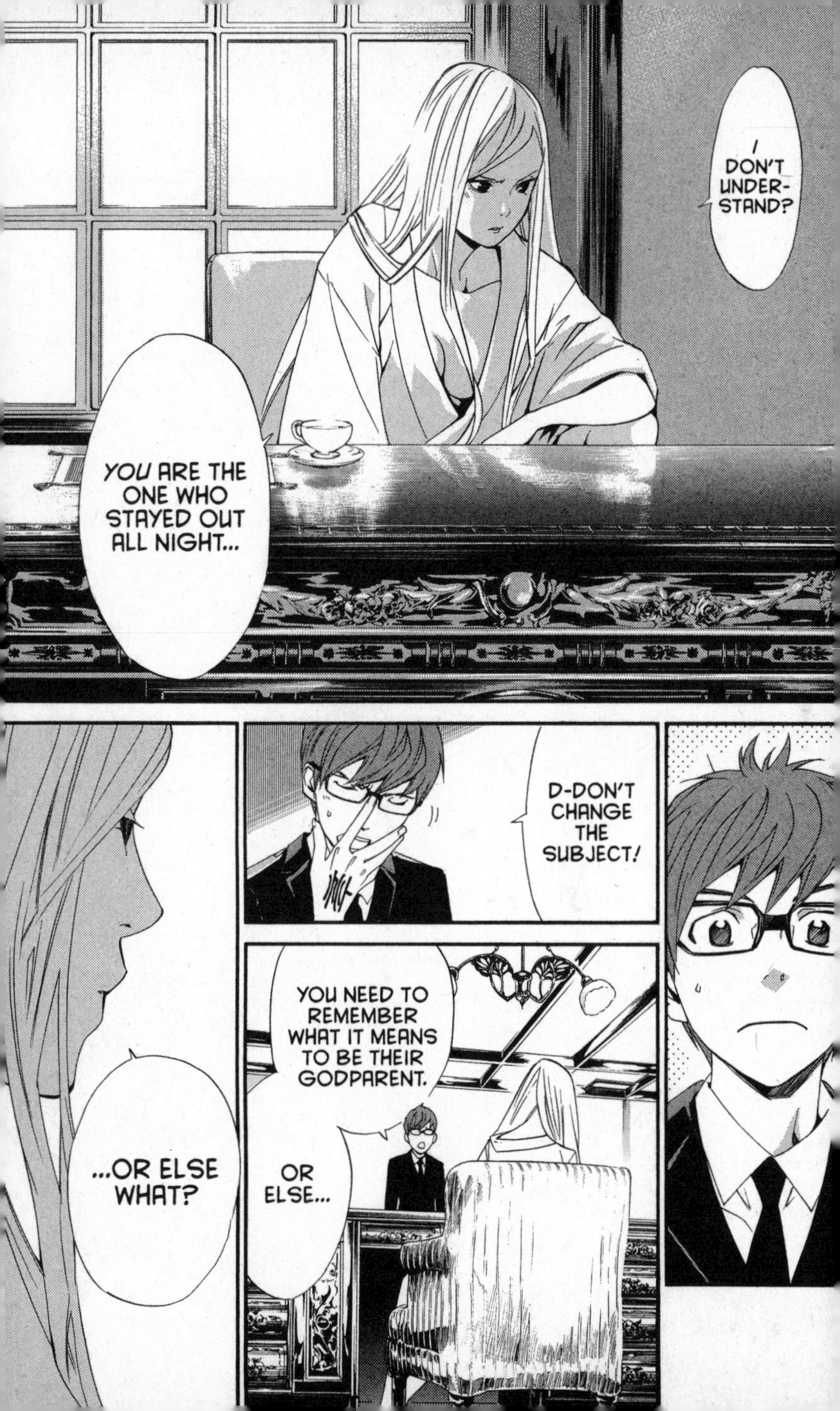
I DON'T UNDERSTAND?
YOU ARE THE ONE WHO STAYED OUT ALL NIGHT...
D-DON'T CHANGE THE SUBJECT!
YOU NEED TO REMEMBER WHAT IT MEANS TO BE THEIR GODPARENT.
OR ELSE...
...OR ELSE WHAT?

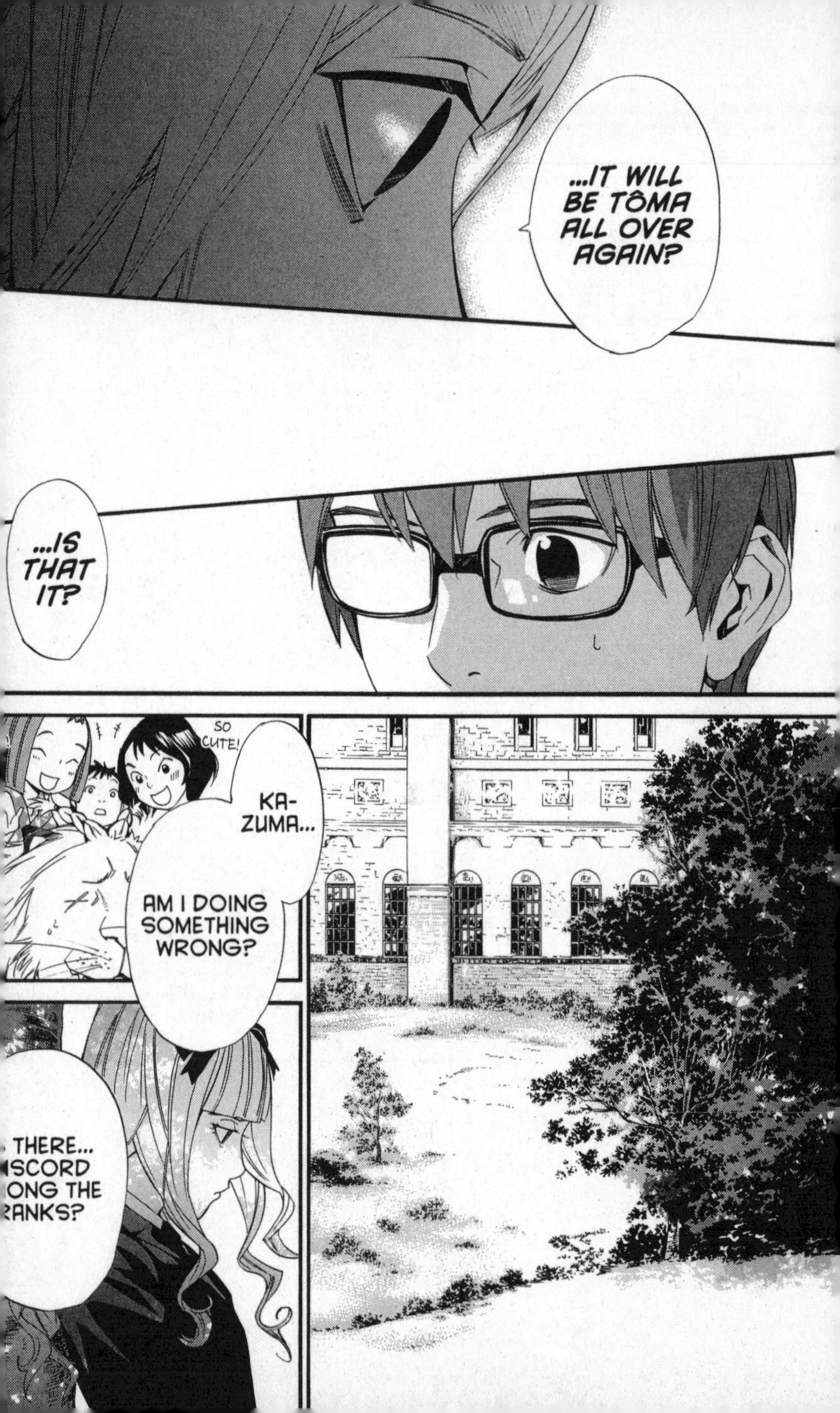
...IT WILL BE TÔMA ALL OVER AGAIN?
...IS THAT IT?
KA-ZUMA...
AM I DOING SOMETHING WRONG?
SO CUTE!
THERE... SCORD ONG THE RANKS?

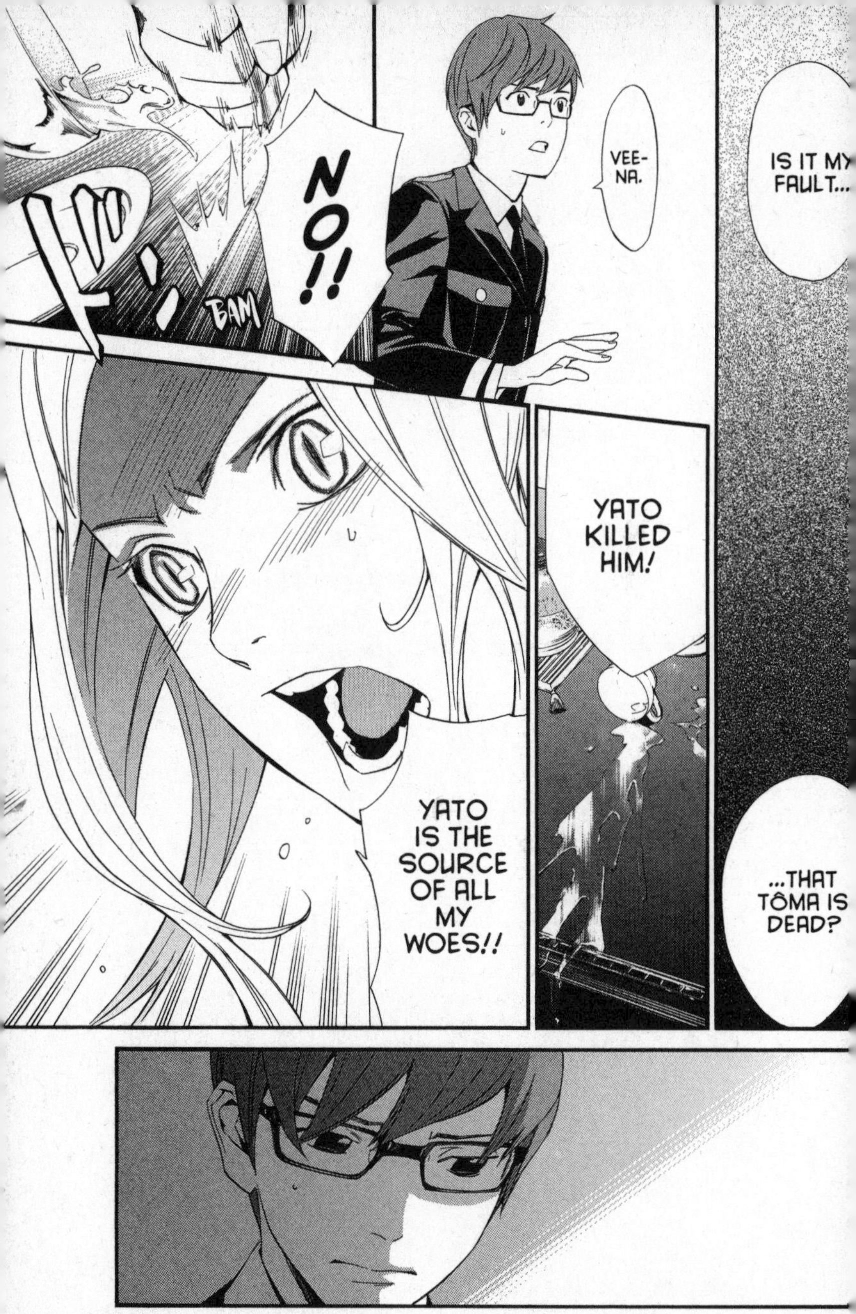
IS IT MY FAULT...
...THAT TÔMA IS DEAD?
VEE-NA.
NO!!
BAM
YATO KILLED HIM!
YATO IS THE SOURCE OF ALL MY WOES!!

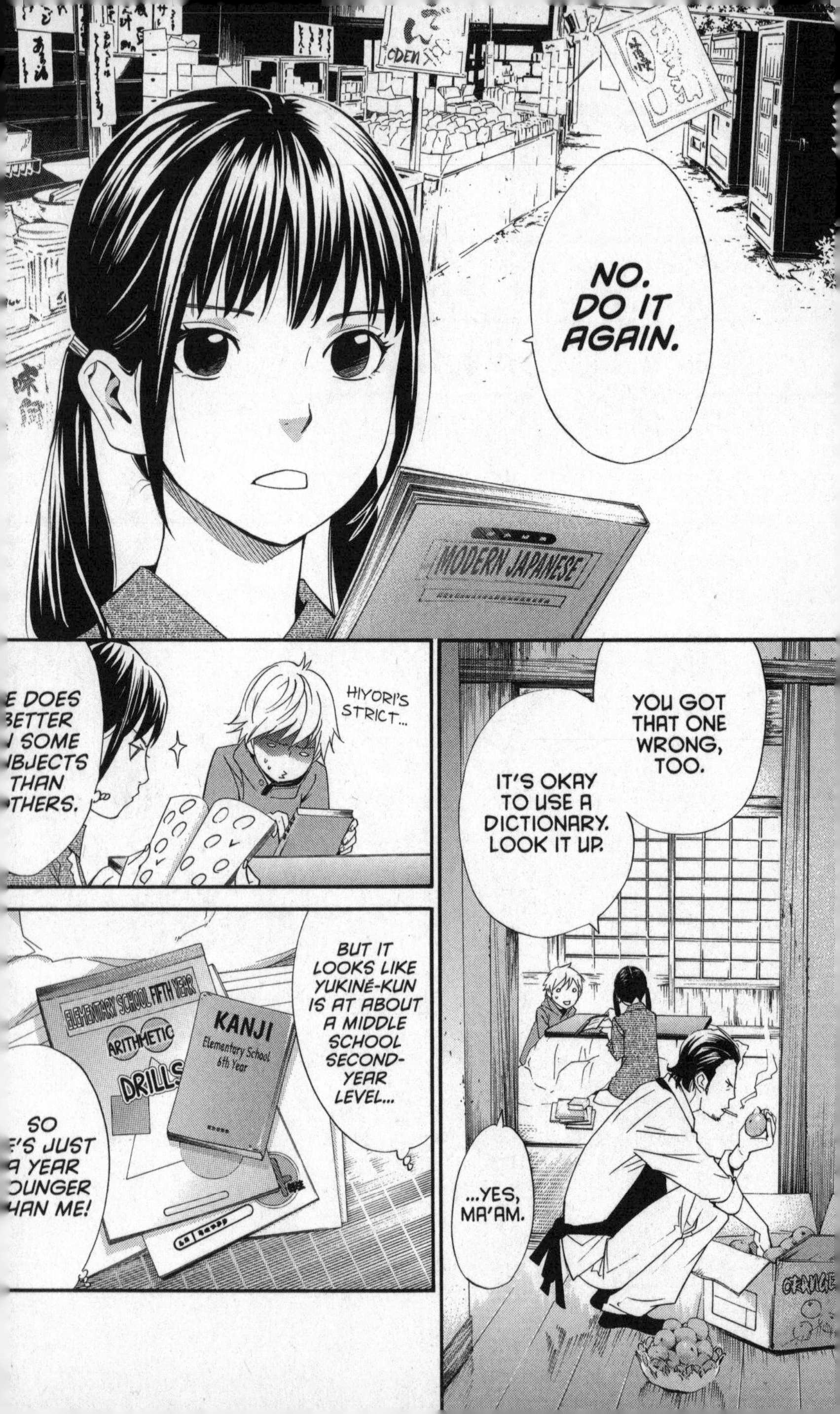
ODEN
NO. DO IT AGAIN.
MODERN JAPANESE
YOU GOT THAT ONE WRONG, TOO.
IT'S OKAY TO USE A DICTIONARY. LOOK IT UP.
...YES, MA'AM.
HIYORI'S STRICT...
E DOES BETTER
I SOME
UBJECTS
THAN
THERS.
BUT IT LOOKS LIKE YUKINÉ-KUN IS AT ABOUT A MIDDLE SCHOOL SECOND-YEAR LEVEL...
ELEMENTARY SCHOOL FIFTH YEAR
ARITHMETIC
DRILLS
KANJI
Elementary School 6th Year
SO
E'S JUST
A YEAR
OUNGER
HAN ME!

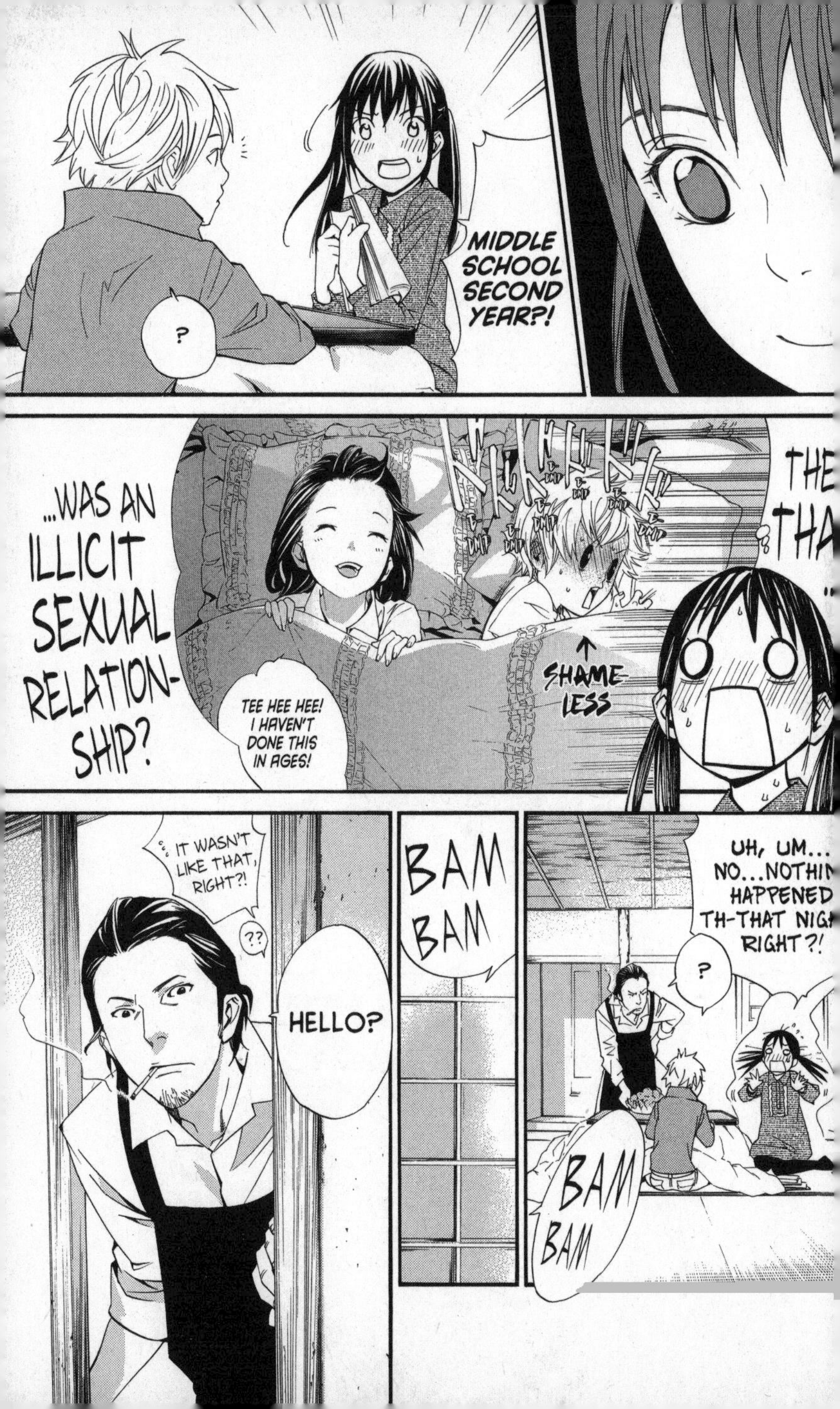
MIDDLE SCHOOL SECOND YEAR?!
?
THE THA
SHAME-LESS
TEE HEE HEE! I HAVEN'T DONE THIS IN AGES!
...WAS AN ILLICIT SEXUAL RELATION-SHIP?
UH, UM... NO...NOTHIN HAPPENED TH-THAT NIG RIGHT?!
?
BAM BAM
BAM BAM
IT WASN'T LIKE THAT, RIGHT?!
??
HELLO?

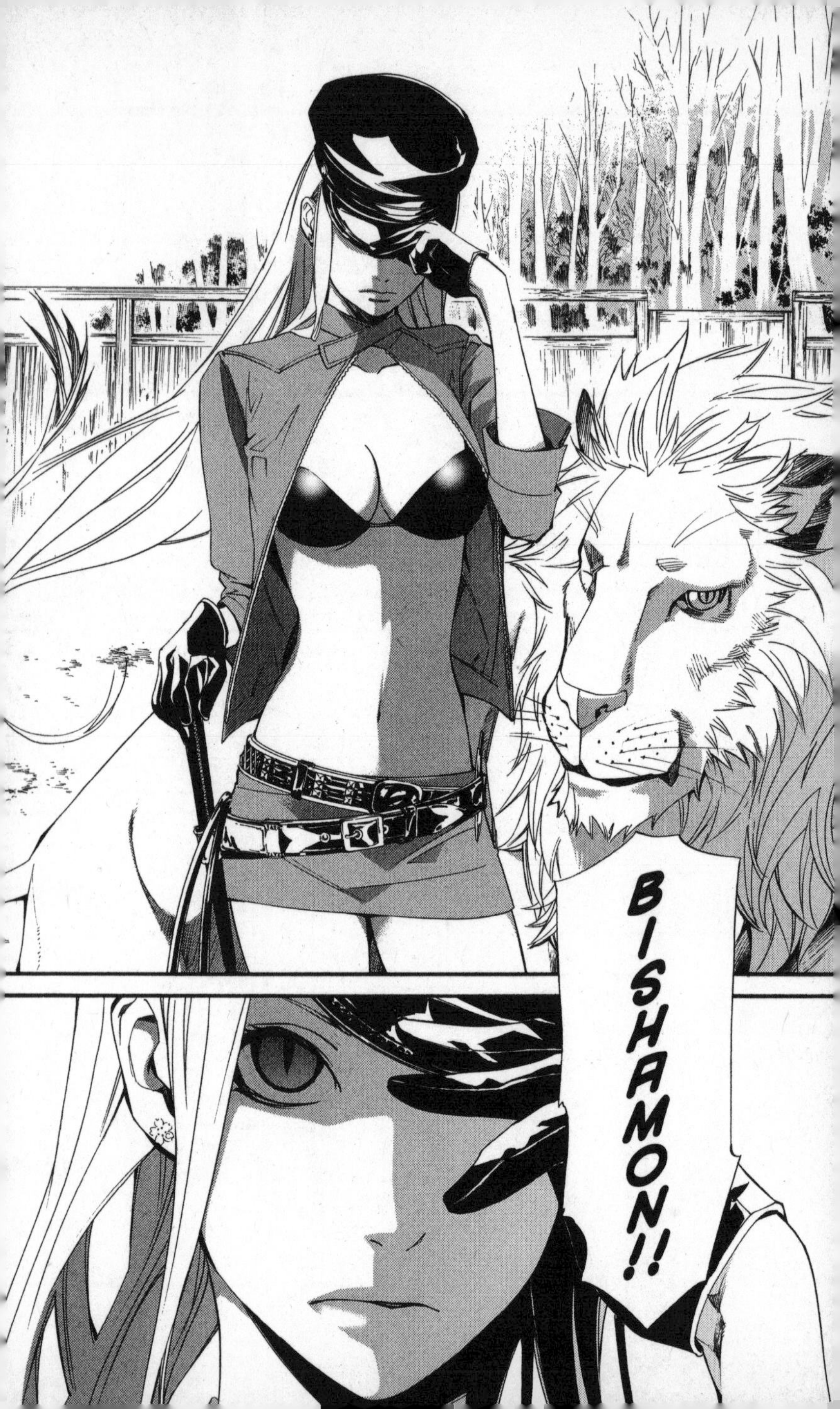
BISHAMON!!

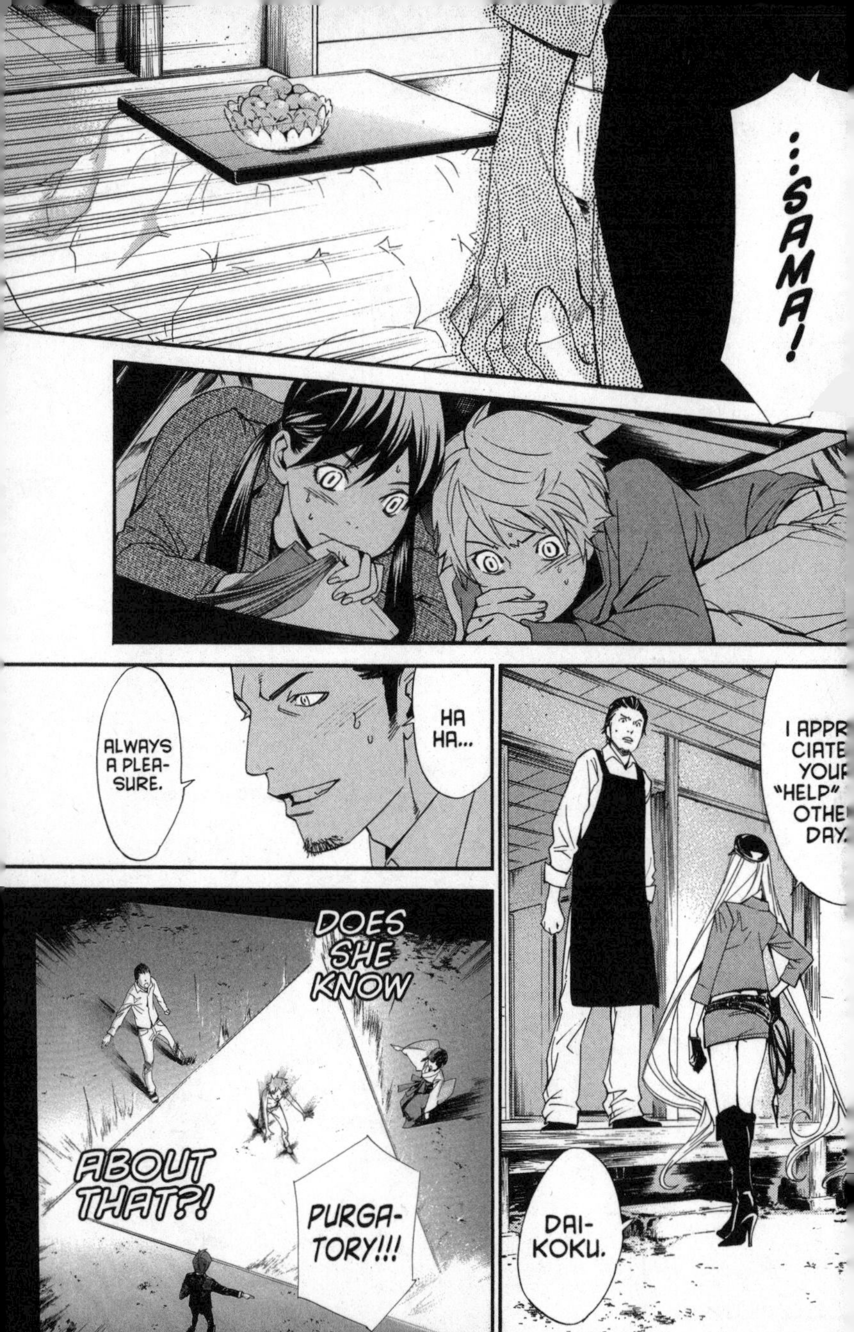
...SAMA!
I APPR CIATE YOUR "HELP" OTHE DAY.
DAI-KOKU.
HA HA...
ALWAYS A PLEA-SURE.
DOES SHE KNOW
ABOUT THAT?!
PURGA-TORY!!!

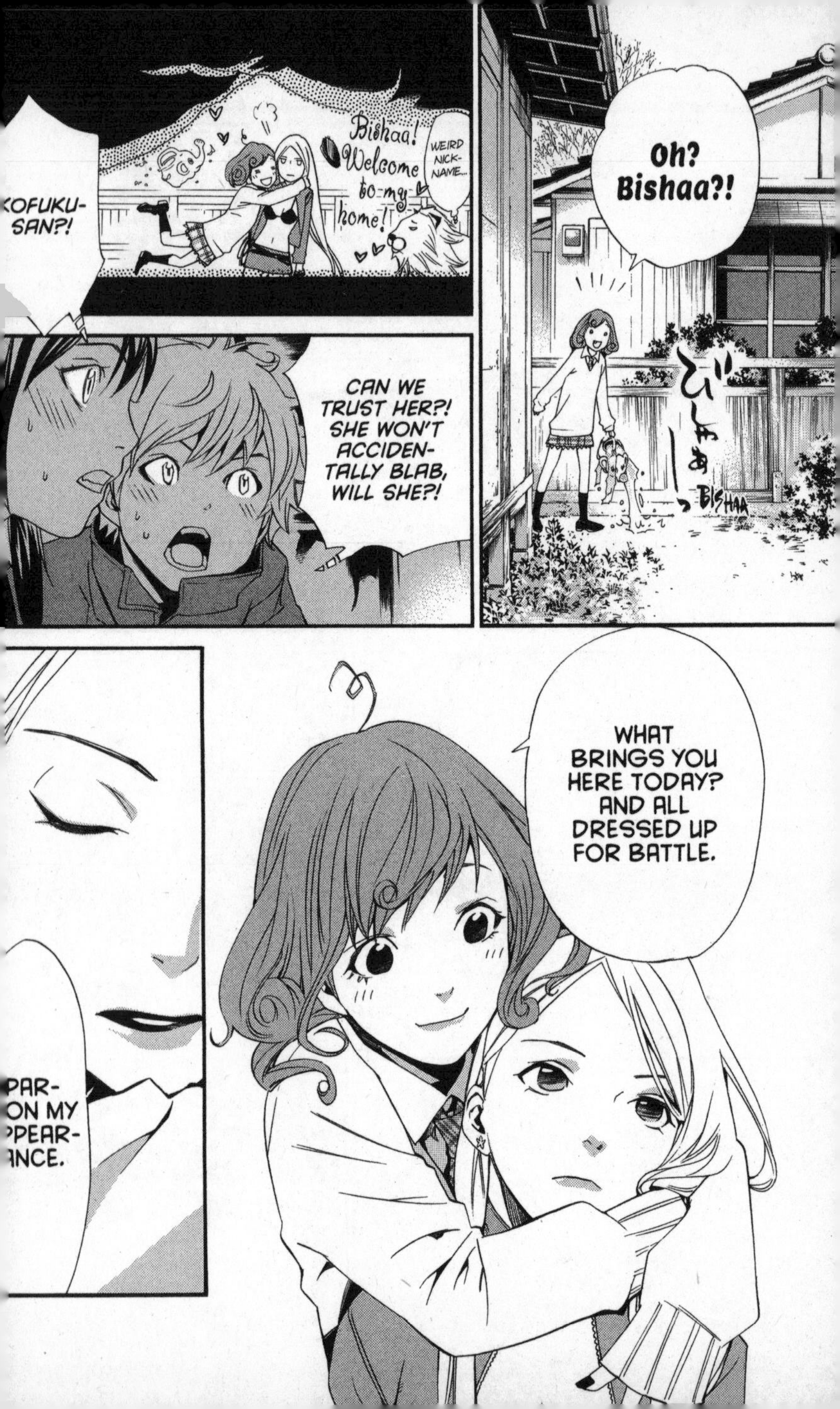
Oh? Bishaa?!
びしゃあ
BISHAA
KOFUKU-SAN?!
Bishaa! Welcome to my home!
WEIRD NICK-NAME...
CAN WE TRUST HER?! SHE WON'T ACCIDEN-TALLY BLAB, WILL SHE?!
WHAT BRINGS YOU HERE TODAY? AND ALL DRESSED UP FOR BATTLE.
PAR- ON MY PPEAR- NCE.

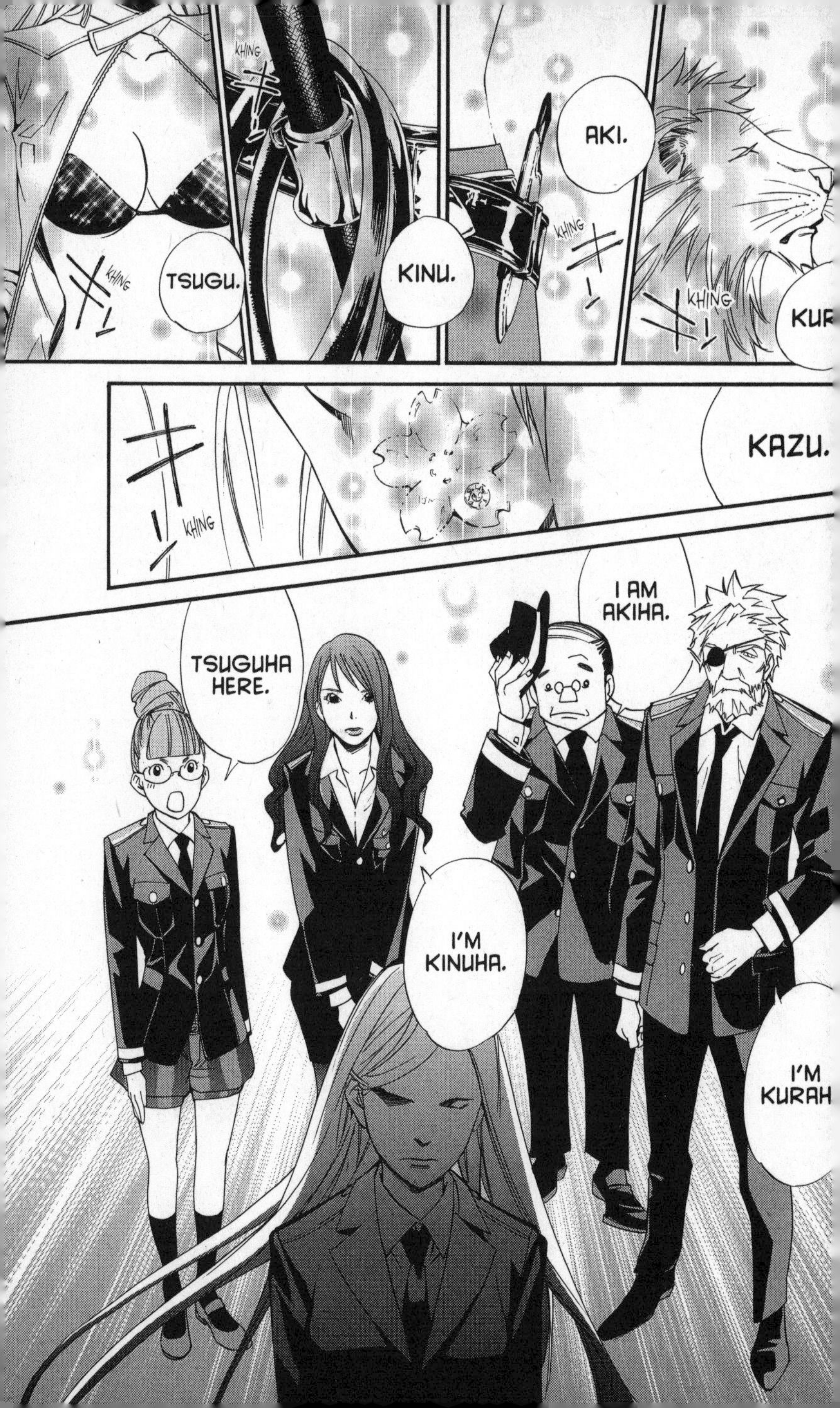
KHING
KUR
AKI.
KHING
KHING
KINU.
TSUGU.
KHING
KAZU.
KHING
I AM AKIHA.
I'M KURAH
I'M KINUHA.
TSUGUHA HERE.

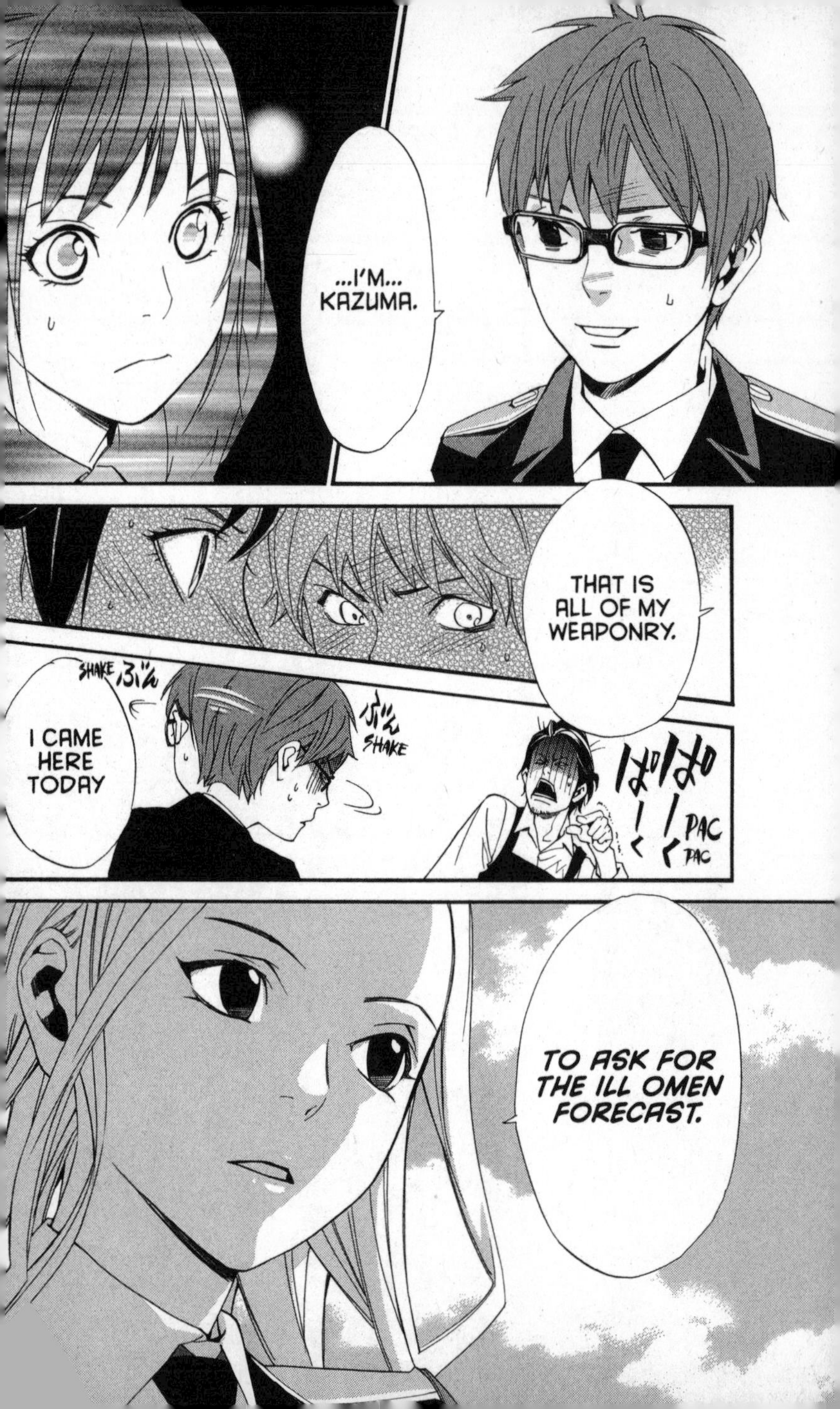
...I'M... KAZUMA.
THAT IS ALL OF MY WEAPONRY.
ぱく ぱく
PAC PAC
ぶん SHAKE
SHAKE ぶん
I CAME HERE TODAY
TO ASK FOR THE ILL OMEN FORECAST.

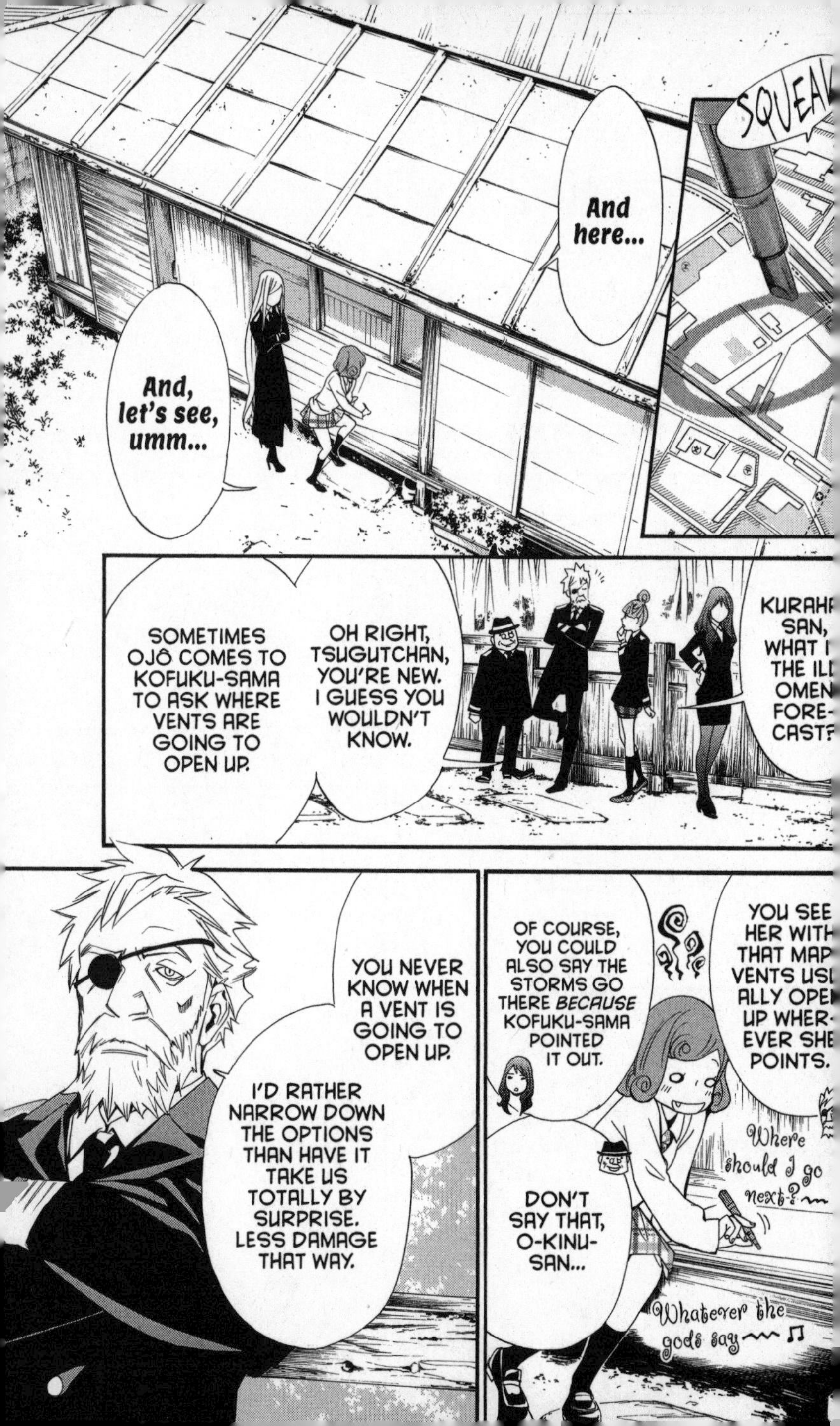
SQUEAK
And here...
And, let's see, umm...
KURAHA SAN, WHAT IS THE ILL OMEN FORE-CAST?
OH RIGHT, TSUGUTCHAN, YOU'RE NEW. I GUESS YOU WOULDN'T KNOW.
SOMETIMES OJÔ COMES TO KOFUKU-SAMA TO ASK WHERE VENTS ARE GOING TO OPEN UP.
YOU SEE HER WITH THAT MAP VENTS USU- ALLY OPEN UP WHER-EVER SHE POINTS.
Where should I go next?~
OF COURSE, YOU COULD ALSO SAY THE STORMS GO THERE *BECAUSE* KOFUKU-SAMA POINTED IT OUT.
DON'T SAY THAT, O-KINU-SAN...
Whatever the gods say~ ♫
YOU NEVER KNOW WHEN A VENT IS GOING TO OPEN UP.
I'D RATHER NARROW DOWN THE OPTIONS THAN HAVE IT TAKE US TOTALLY BY SURPRISE. LESS DAMAGE THAT WAY.

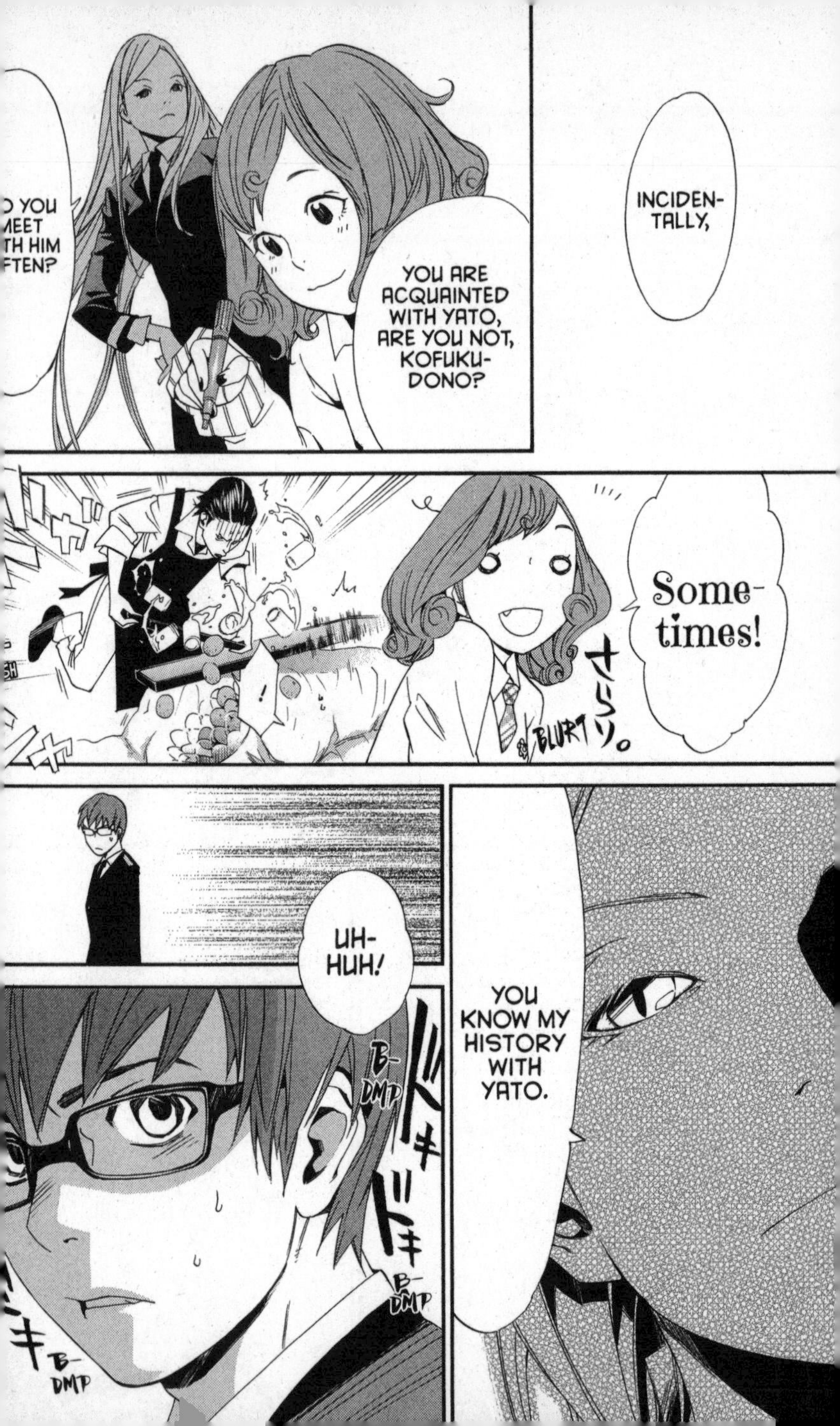
INCIDEN-TALLY,
YOU ARE ACQUAINTED WITH YATO, ARE YOU NOT, KOFUKU-DONO?
D YOU MEET TH HIM FTEN?
Some-times!
BLURT
YOU KNOW MY HISTORY WITH YATO.
UH-HUH!
B-DMP
B-DMP
B-DMP

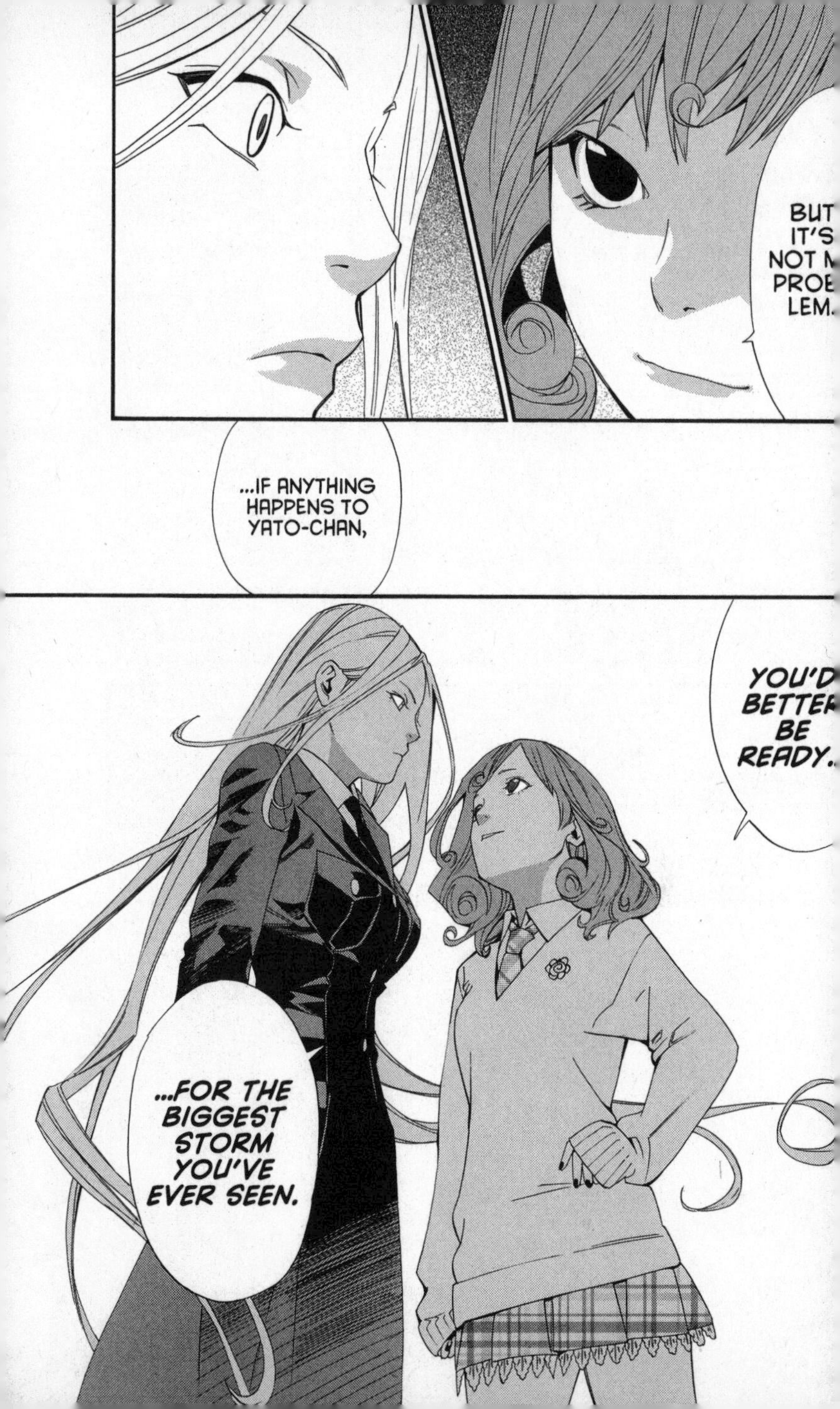
BUT IT'S NOT M PROB LEM.
...IF ANYTHING HAPPENS TO YATO-CHAN,
YOU'D BETTER BE READY..
...FOR THE BIGGEST STORM YOU'VE EVER SEEN.

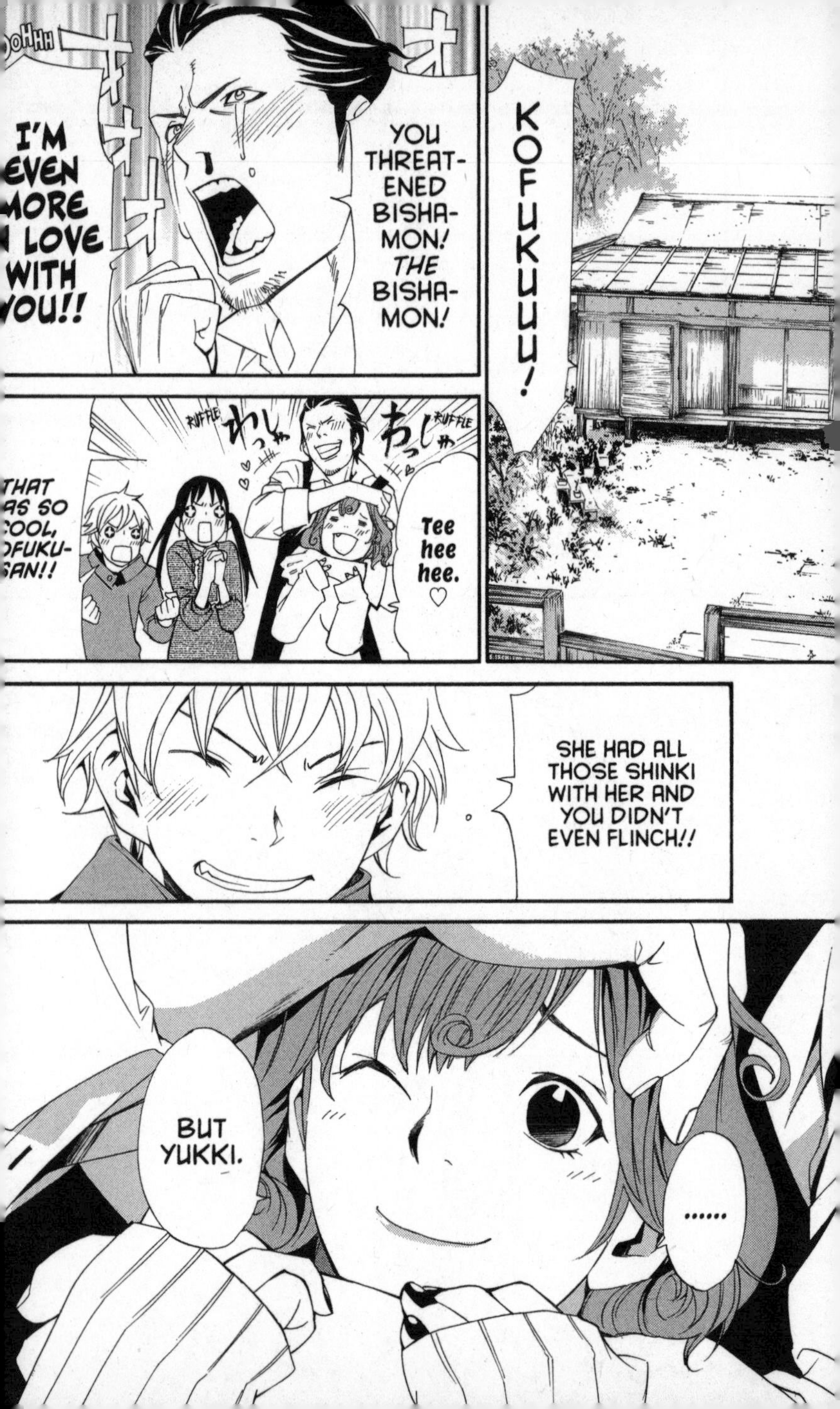
KOFUKUUU!
OOHHH
YOU THREAT-ENED BISHA-MON! THE BISHA-MON!
I'M EVEN ORE I LOVE WITH OU!!
RUFFLE
RUFFLE
Tee hee hee. ♡
THAT AS SO OOL, OFUKU-SAN!!
SHE HAD ALL THOSE SHINKI WITH HER AND YOU DIDN'T EVEN FLINCH!!
......
BUT YUKKI.

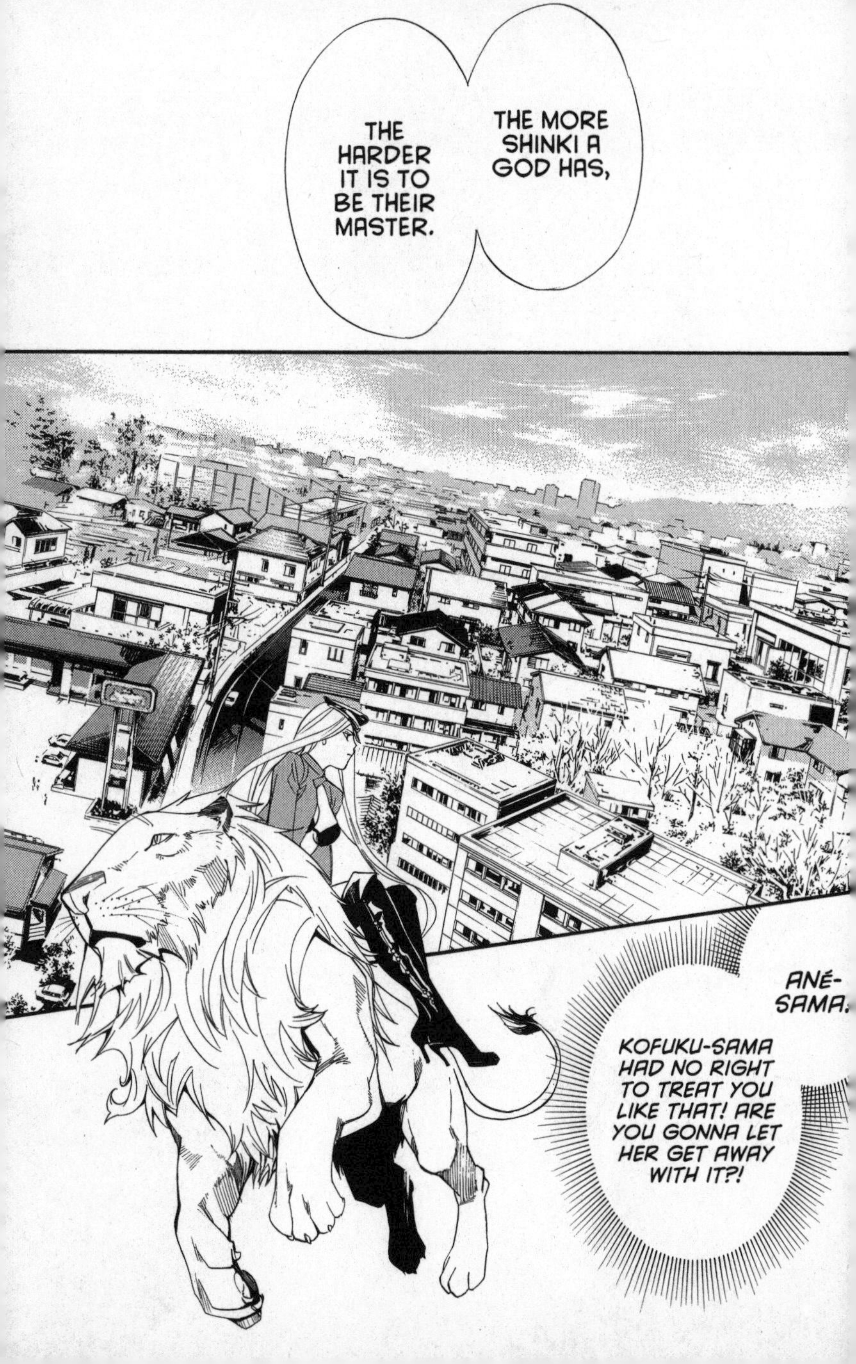
THE MORE SHINKI A GOD HAS,
THE HARDER IT IS TO BE THEIR MASTER.
ANÉ-SAMA.
KOFUKU-SAMA HAD NO RIGHT TO TREAT YOU LIKE THAT! ARE YOU GONNA LET HER GET AWAY WITH IT?!

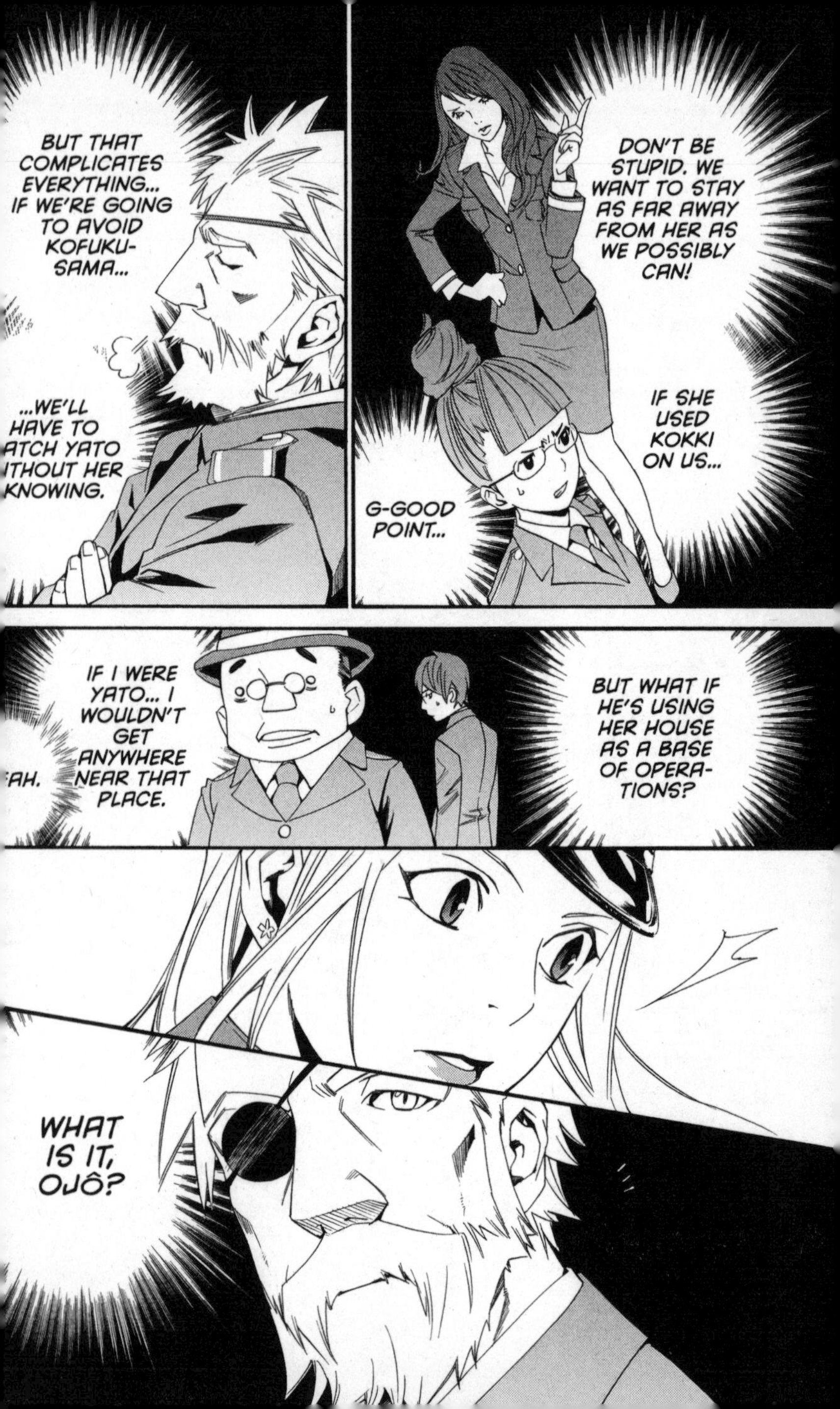

DON'T BE STUPID. WE WANT TO STAY AS FAR AWAY FROM HER AS WE POSSIBLY CAN!
IF SHE USED KOKKI ON US...
G-GOOD POINT...
BUT THAT COMPLICATES EVERYTHING... IF WE'RE GOING TO AVOID KOFUKU-SAMA...
...WE'LL HAVE TO ATCH YATO ITHOUT HER KNOWING.
BUT WHAT IF HE'S USING HER HOUSE AS A BASE OF OPERA-TIONS?
IF I WERE YATO... I WOULDN'T GET ANYWHERE NEAR THAT PLACE.
AH.
WHAT IS IT, OJÔ?

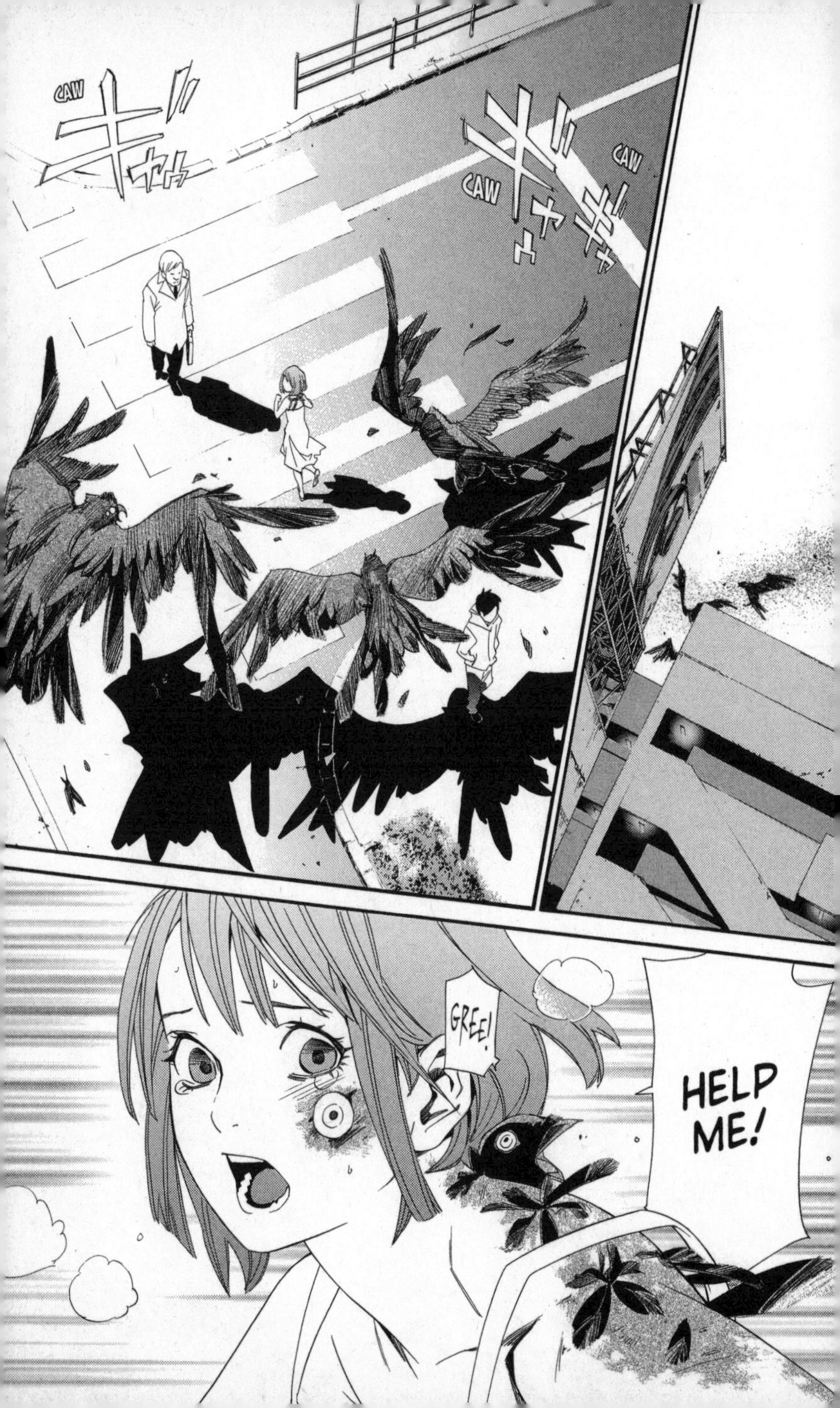
CAW
CAW
CAW
HELP ME!
GREE!

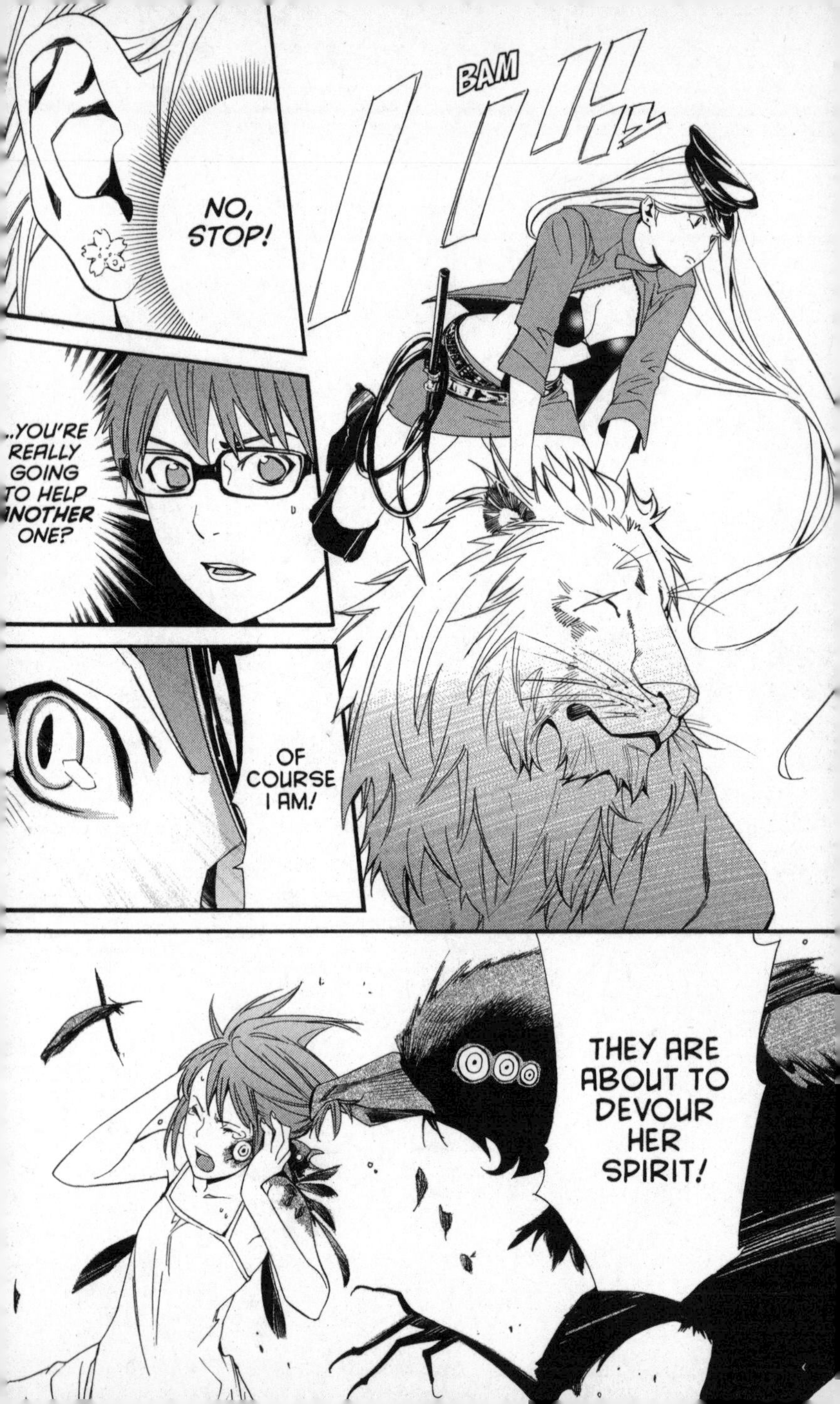
BAM
NO, STOP!
...YOU'RE REALLY GOING TO HELP ANOTHER ONE?
OF COURSE I AM!
THEY ARE ABOUT TO DEVOUR HER SPIRIT!

BUT... YOU ALREADY HAVE MORE THAN ENOUGH SHINKI.
IF YOU ADD TO YOUR ARMAMENTS, YOU'LL BE INCREASING THE STRAIN ON YOUR HEALTH.
YOU KNOW THE WASHINGS AREN'T ENOUG ANYMORE— YOU'RE SOAK-ING IN MEDICIN EVERY DAY!
IT MAY BE BETTER TO LEAVE HER AND SLAY THE...

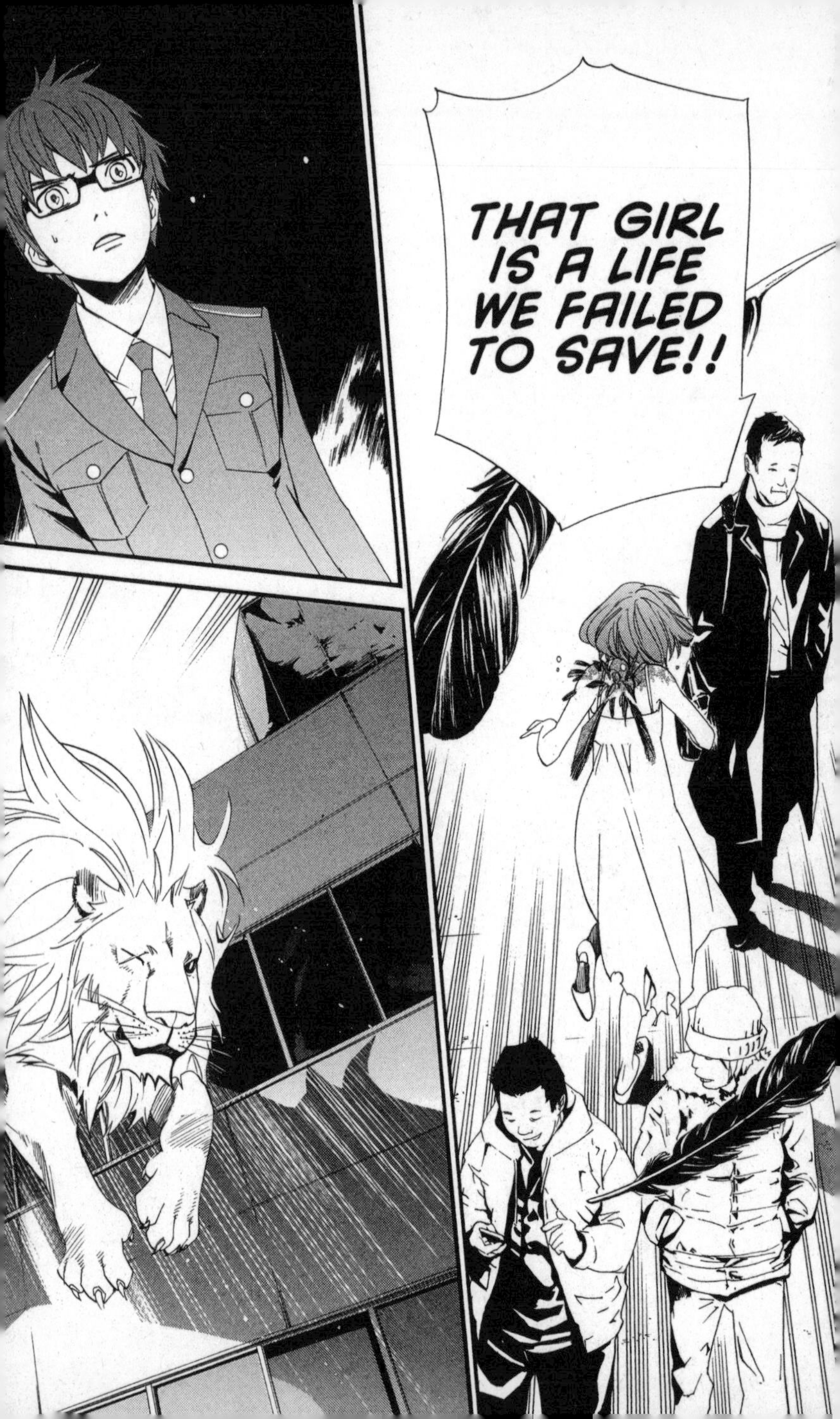
THAT GIRL IS A LIFE WE FAILED TO SAVE!!

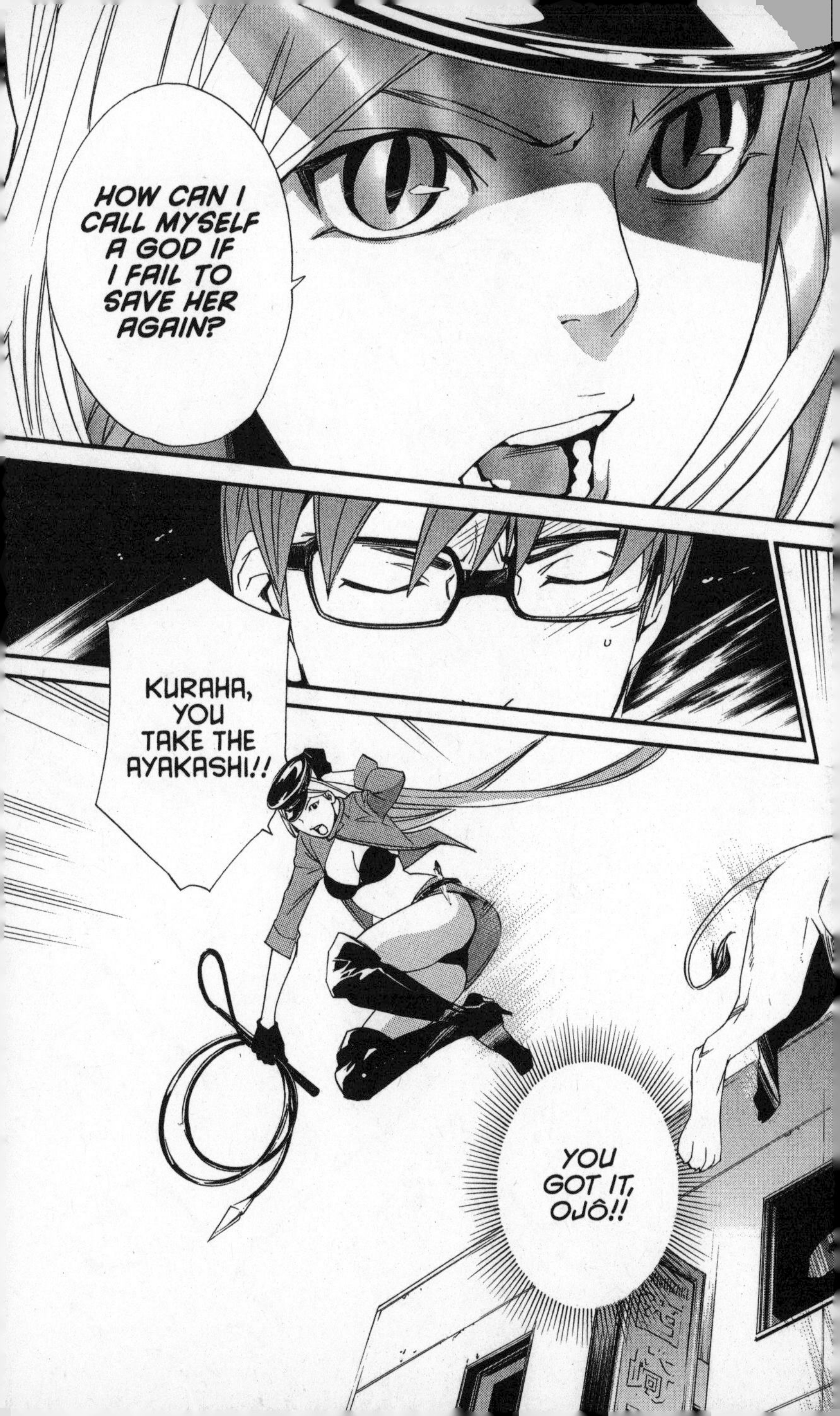
HOW CAN I CALL MYSELF A GOD IF I FAIL TO SAVE HER AGAIN?
KURAHA, YOU TAKE THE AYAKASHI!!
YOU GOT IT, OJÔ!!

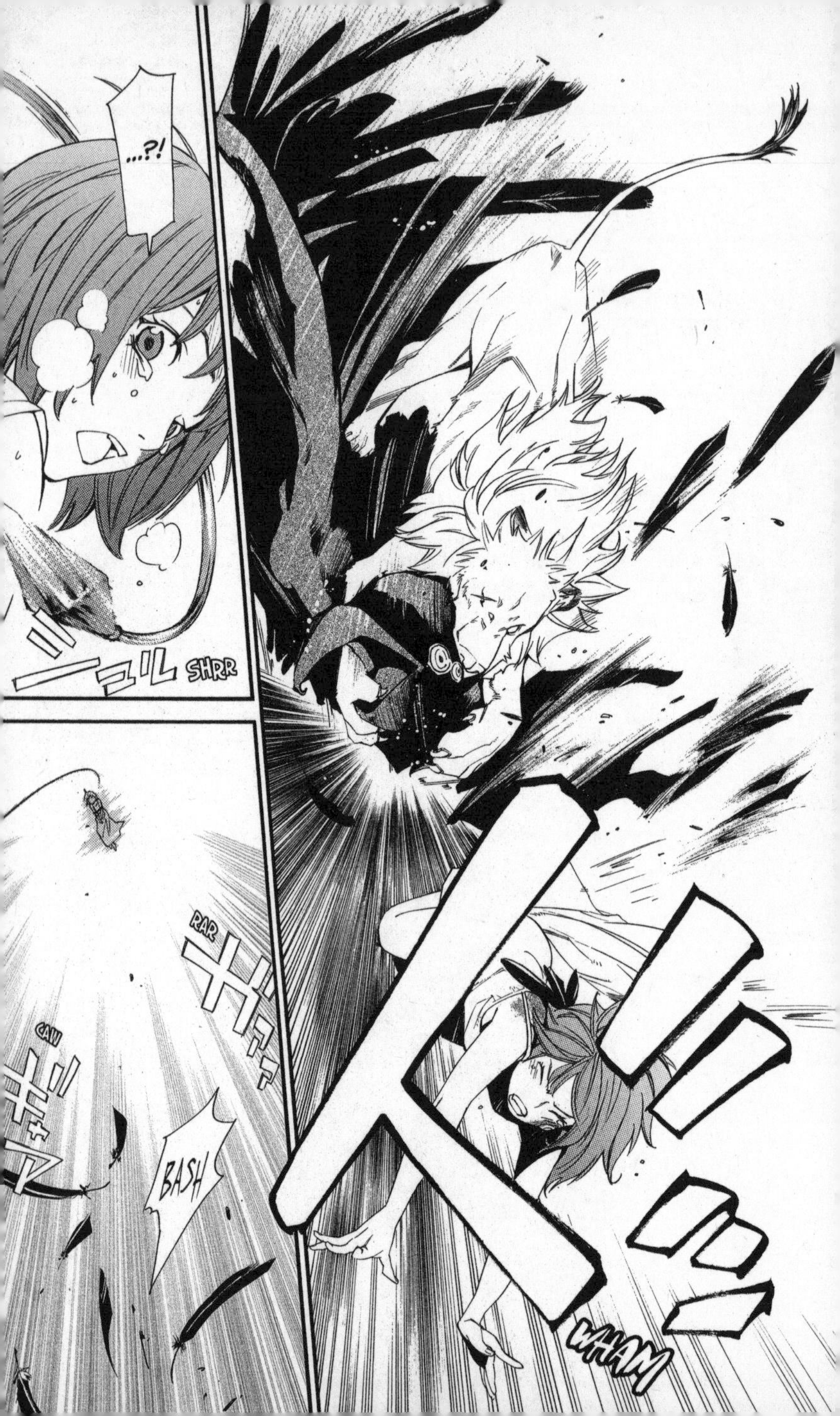
WHAM
...?!
SHRR
RAR
CAW
BASH

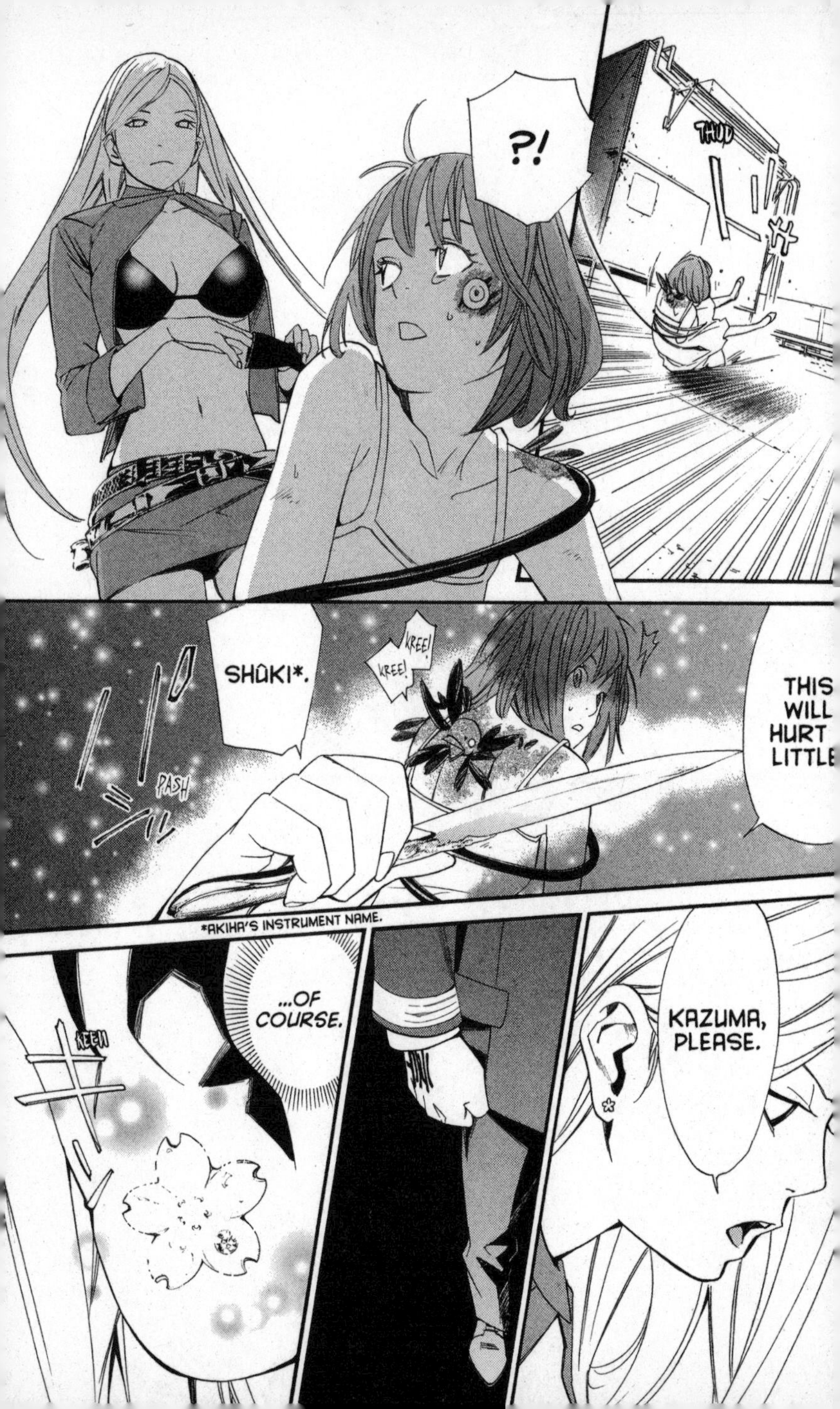
?!
THUD
THIS WILL HURT LITTLE
KREE!
KREE!
SHÛKI*.
PASH
KAZUMA, PLEASE.
...OF COURSE.
KEEN
*AKIHA'S INSTRUMENT NAME.

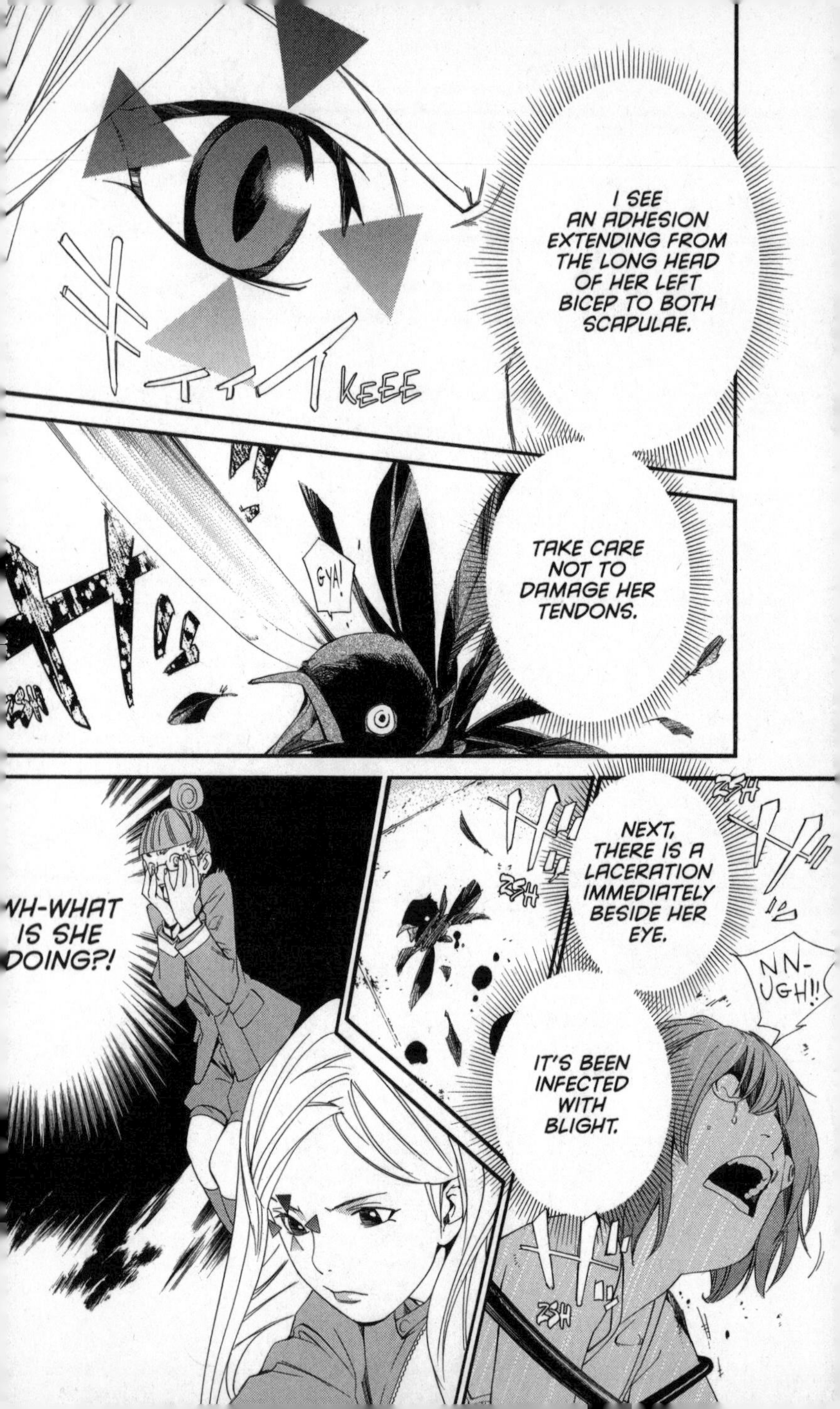
I SEE AN ADHESION EXTENDING FROM THE LONG HEAD OF HER LEFT BICEP TO BOTH SCAPULAE.
KEEE
TAKE CARE NOT TO DAMAGE HER TENDONS.
GYA!
ZSH
ZSH
NEXT, THERE IS A LACERATION IMMEDIATELY BESIDE HER EYE.
NN-UGH!!
ZSH
IT'S BEEN INFECTED WITH BLIGHT.
ZSH
WH-WHAT IS SHE DOING?!

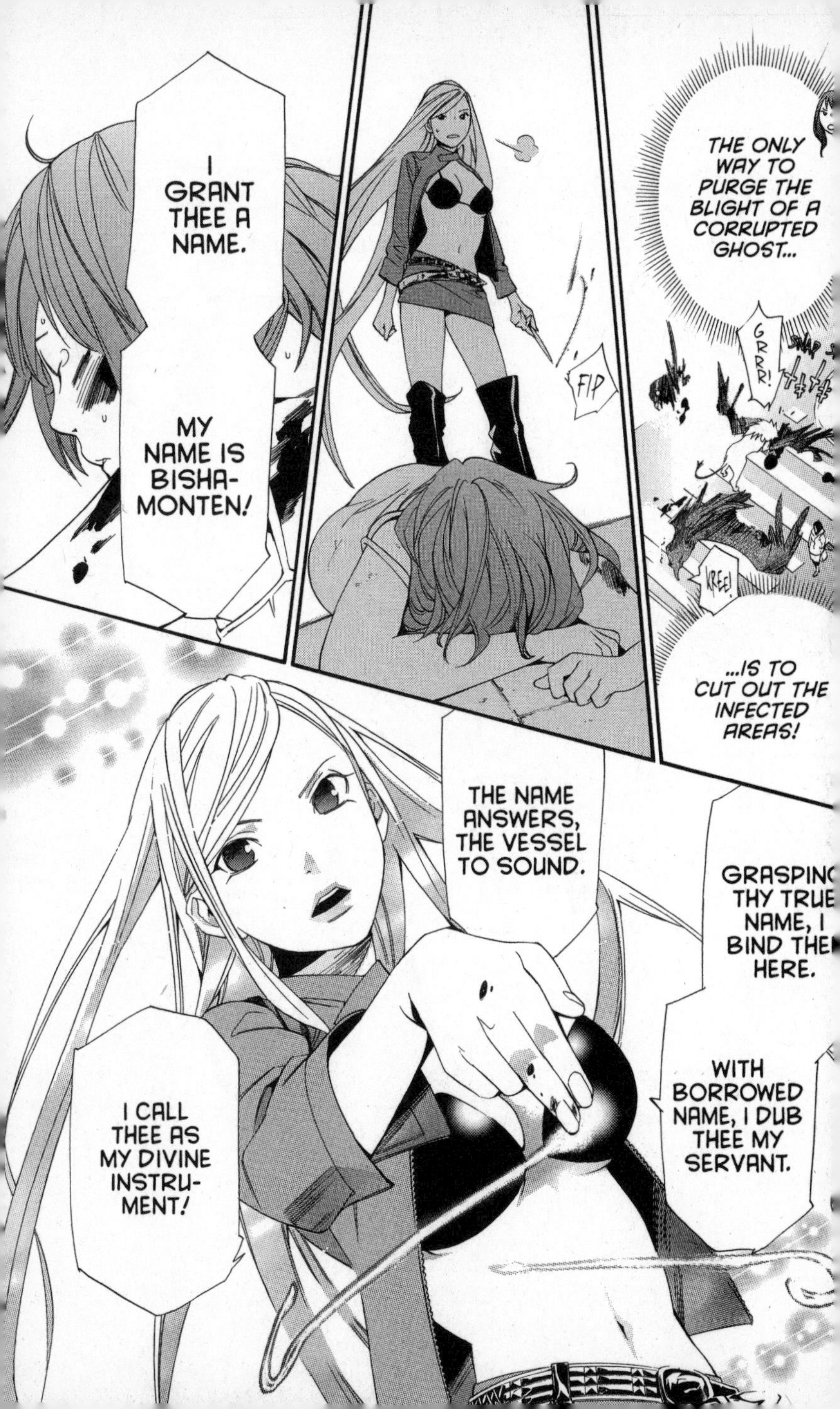
THE ONLY WAY TO PURGE THE BLIGHT OF A CORRUPTED GHOST...
GRRR!
SNAP
KREE!
...IS TO CUT OUT THE INFECTED AREAS!
FIP
I GRANT THEE A NAME.
MY NAME IS BISHAMONTEN!
GRASPING THY TRUE NAME, I BIND THEE HERE.
THE NAME ANSWERS, THE VESSEL TO SOUND.
WITH BORROWED NAME, I DUB THEE MY SERVANT.
I CALL THEE AS MY DIVINE INSTRUMENT!

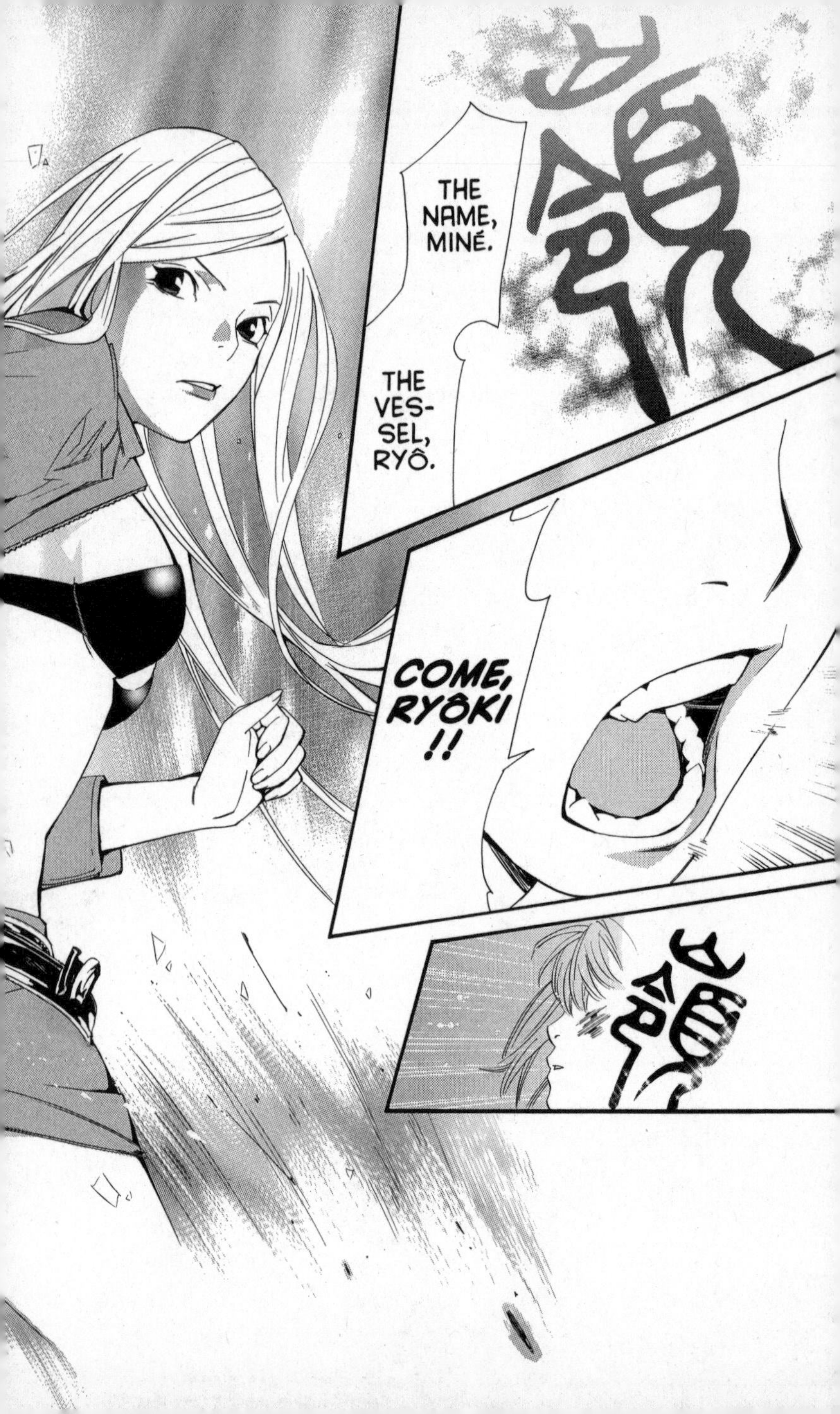
THE NAME, MINÉ.
THE VES-SEL, RYÔ.
COME, RYÔKI !!

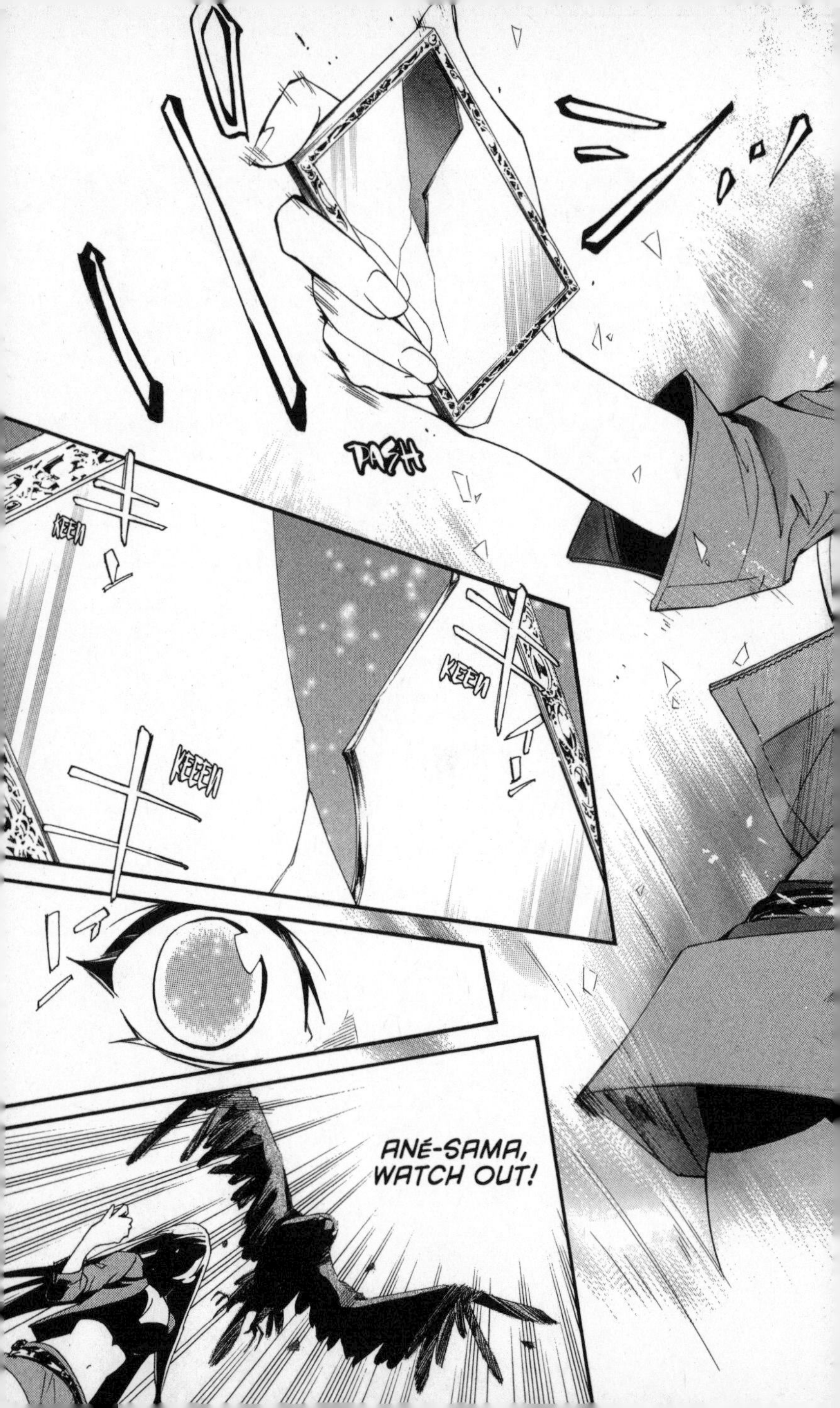
PASH
KEEN
KEEN
KEEEN
ANÉ-SAMA, WATCH OUT!

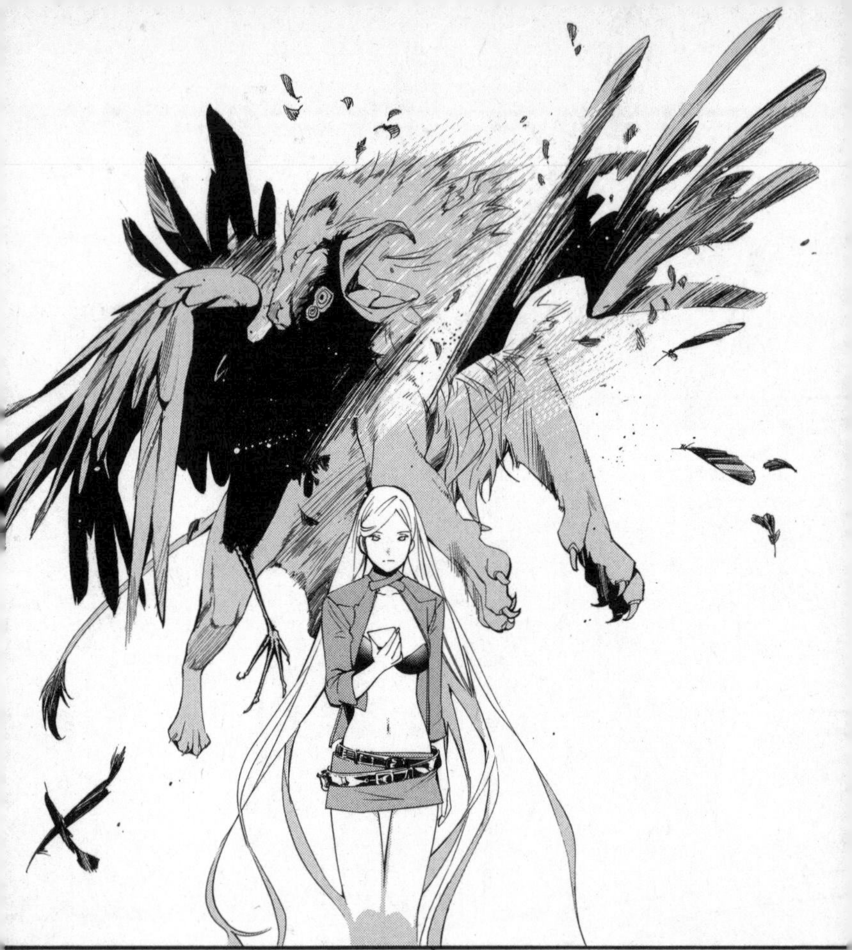

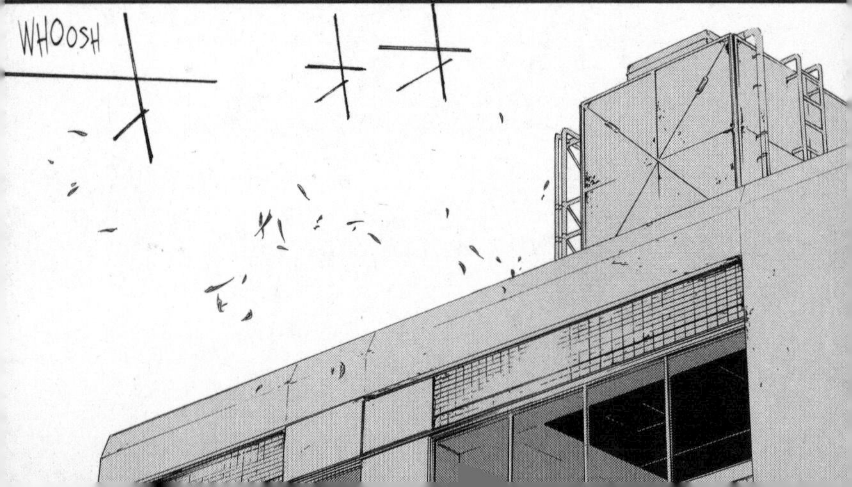
WHOOSH

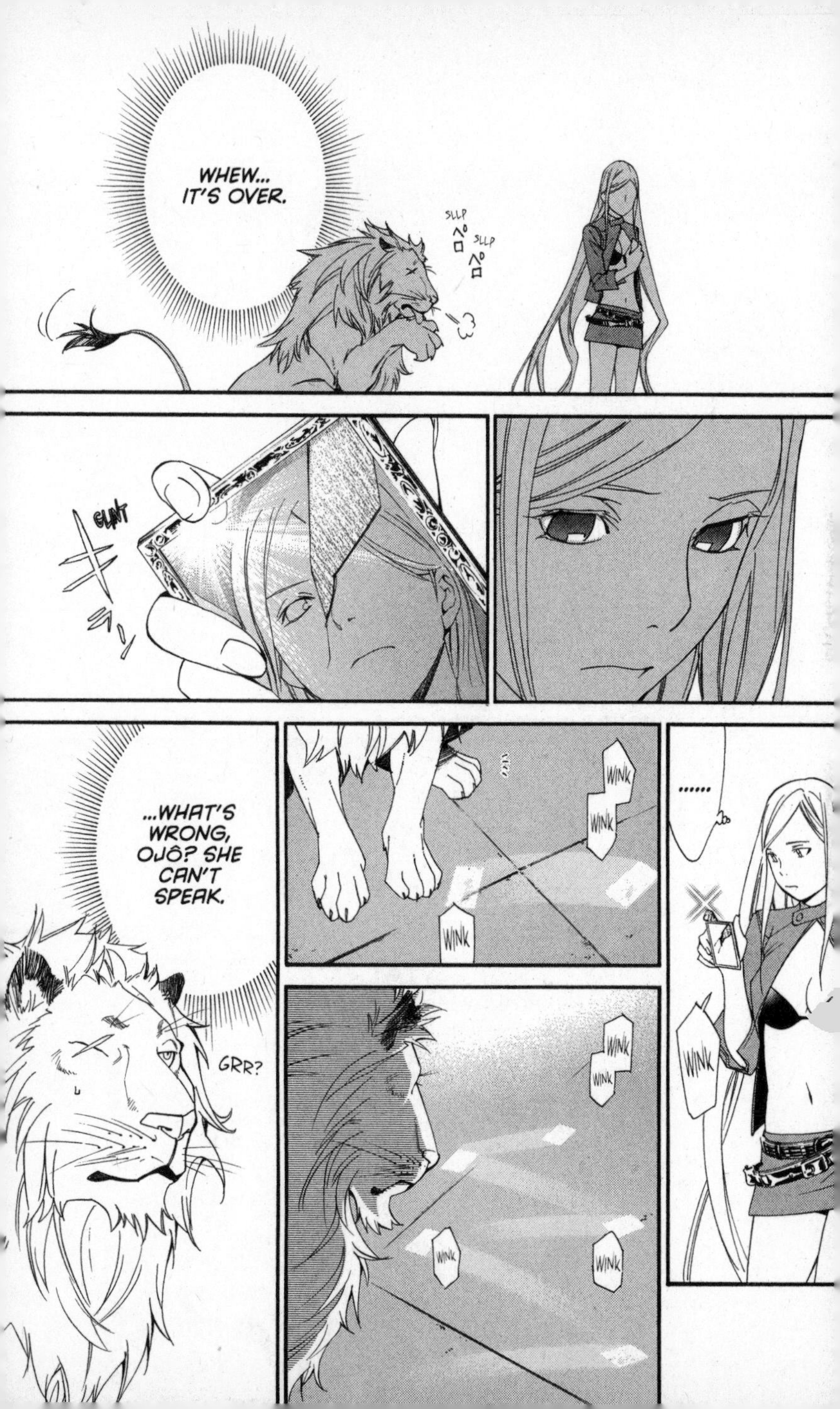
WHEW... IT'S OVER.
SLLP
SLLP
GLINT
......
WINK
WINK
WINK
WINK
WINK
WINK
WINK
WINK
...WHAT'S WRONG, OJÔ? SHE CAN'T SPEAK.
GRR?

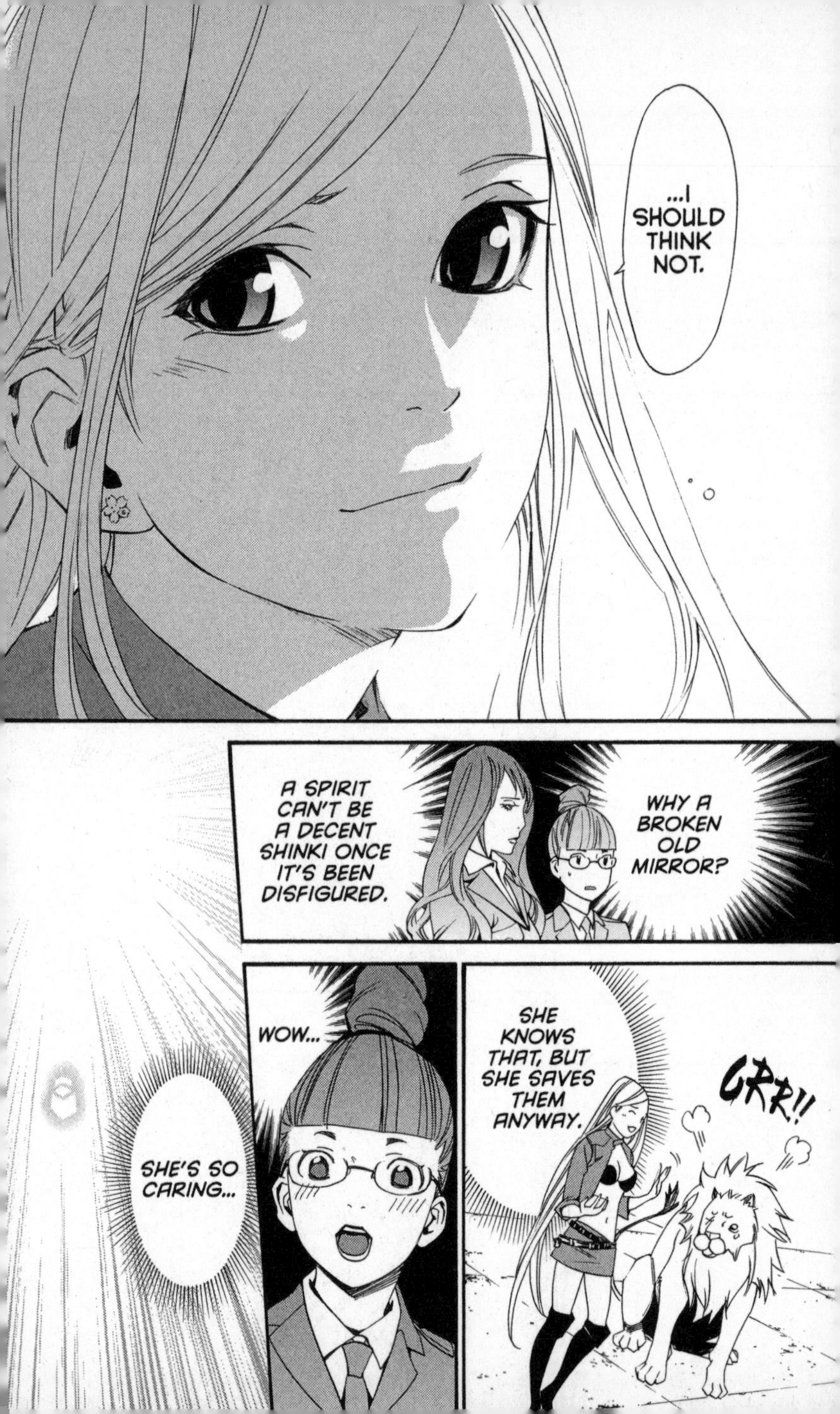
...I SHOULD THINK NOT.
WHY A BROKEN OLD MIRROR?
A SPIRIT CAN'T BE A DECENT SHINKI ONCE IT'S BEEN DISFIGURED.
SHE KNOWS THAT, BUT SHE SAVES THEM ANYWAY.
GRR!!
WOW...
SHE'S SO CARING...

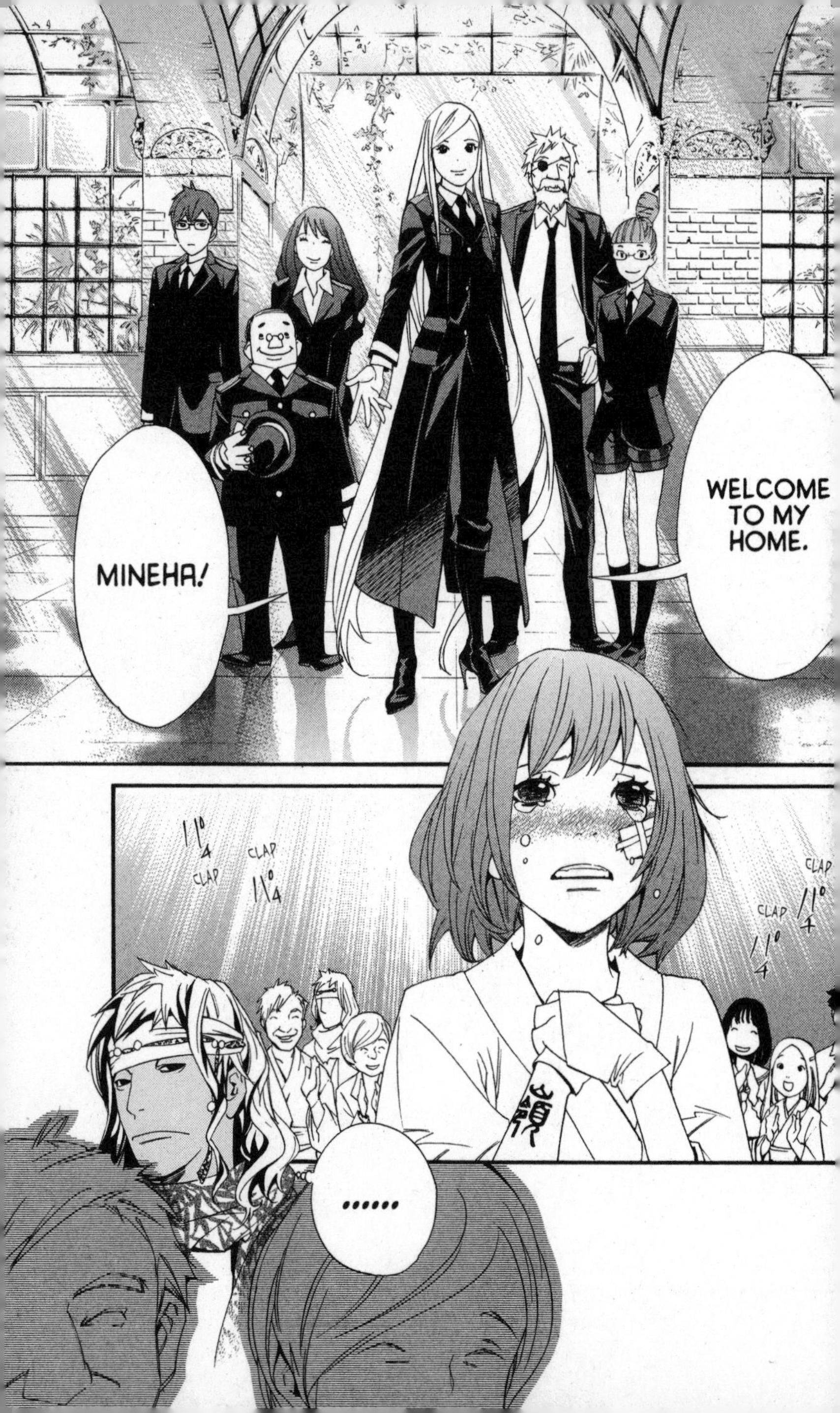
WELCOME TO MY HOME.
MINEHA!
CLAP
CLAP
CLAP
CLAP
......

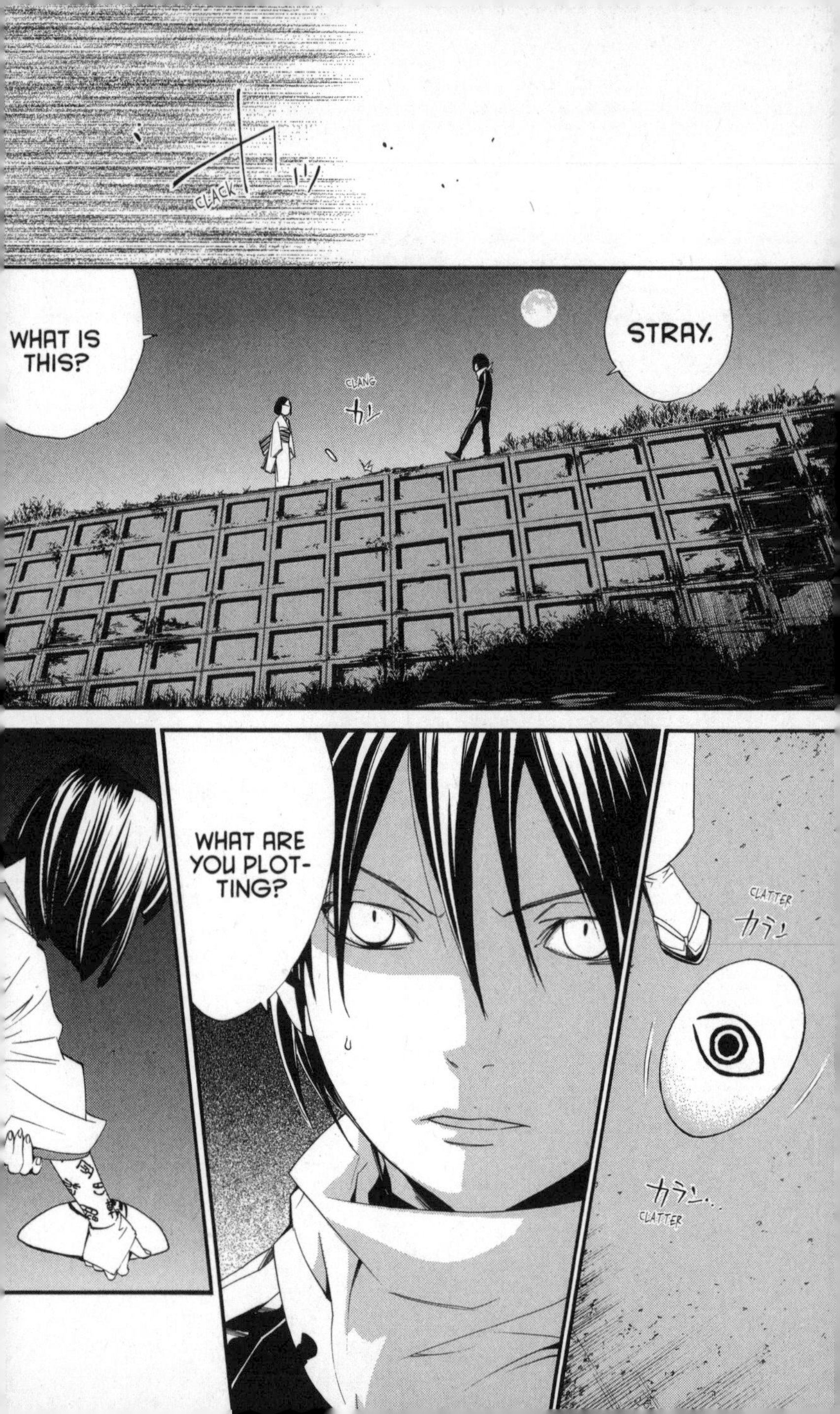

CLACK
STRAY.
WHAT IS THIS?
CLANG
WHAT ARE YOU PLOT-TING?
CLATTER
CLATTER

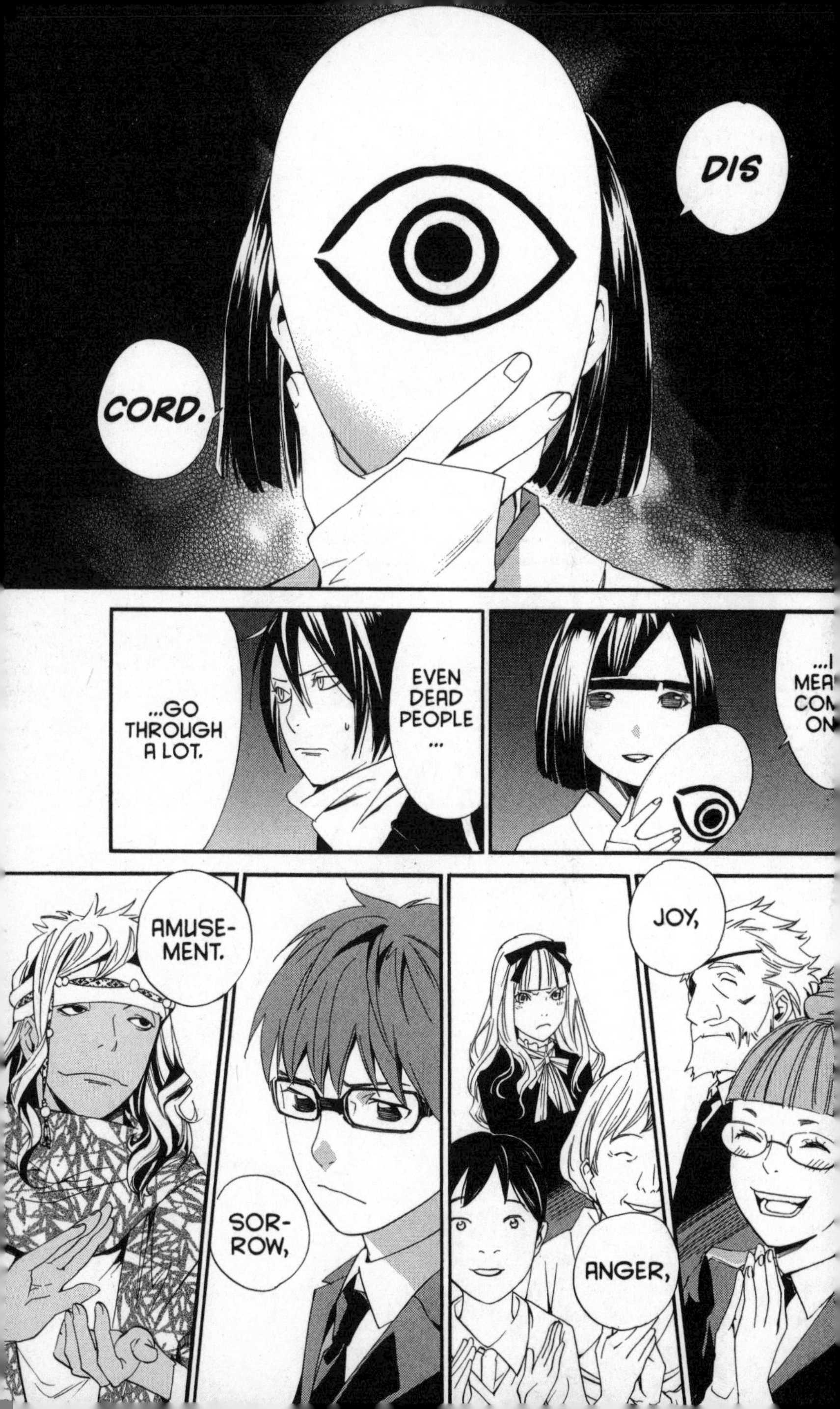
DIS
CORD.
...I MEA COM ON
EVEN DEAD PEOPLE ...
...GO THROUGH A LOT.
JOY,
ANGER,
SORROW,
AMUSEMENT.

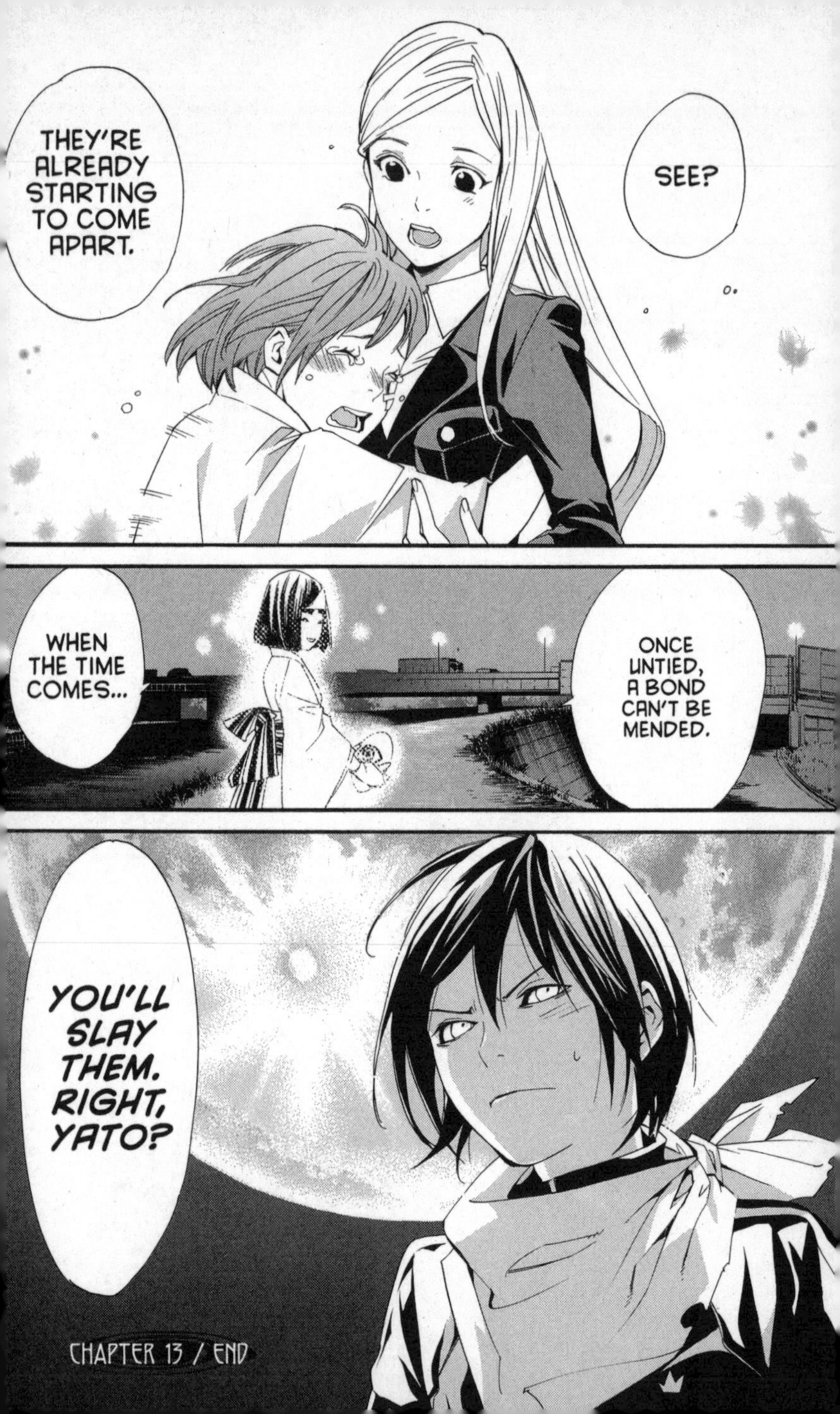
SEE?
THEY'RE ALREADY STARTING TO COME APART.
ONCE UNTIED, A BOND CAN'T BE MENDED.
WHEN THE TIME COMES...
YOU'LL SLAY THEM. RIGHT, YATO?
CHAPTER 13 / END

野

㕙

神

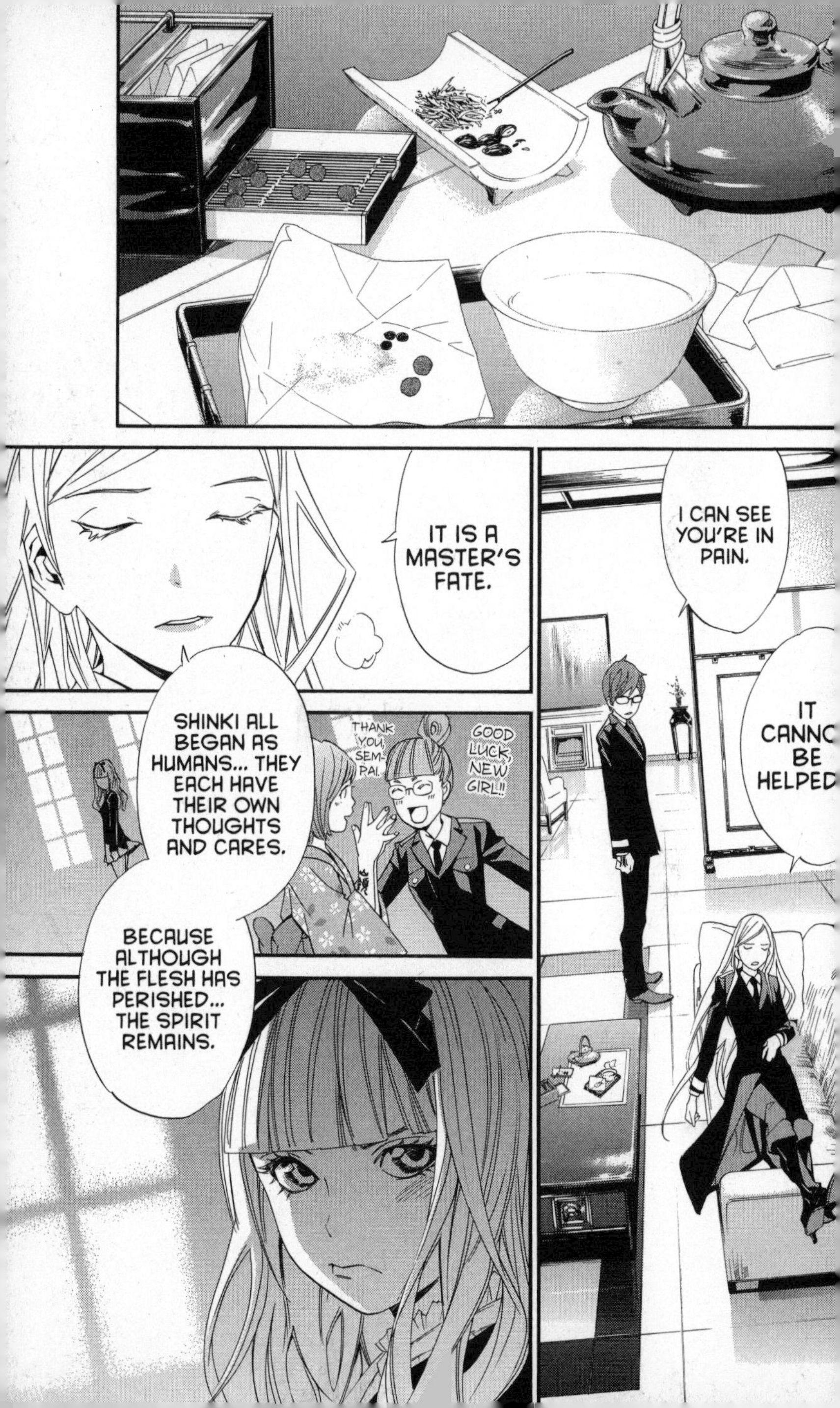
I CAN SEE YOU'RE IN PAIN.
IT CANNO BE HELPED
IT IS A MASTER'S FATE.
SHINKI ALL BEGAN AS HUMANS... THEY EACH HAVE THEIR OWN THOUGHTS AND CARES.
GOOD LUCK, NEW GIRL!!
THANK YOU, SEM-PAI.
BECAUSE ALTHOUGH THE FLESH HAS PERISHED... THE SPIRIT REMAINS.

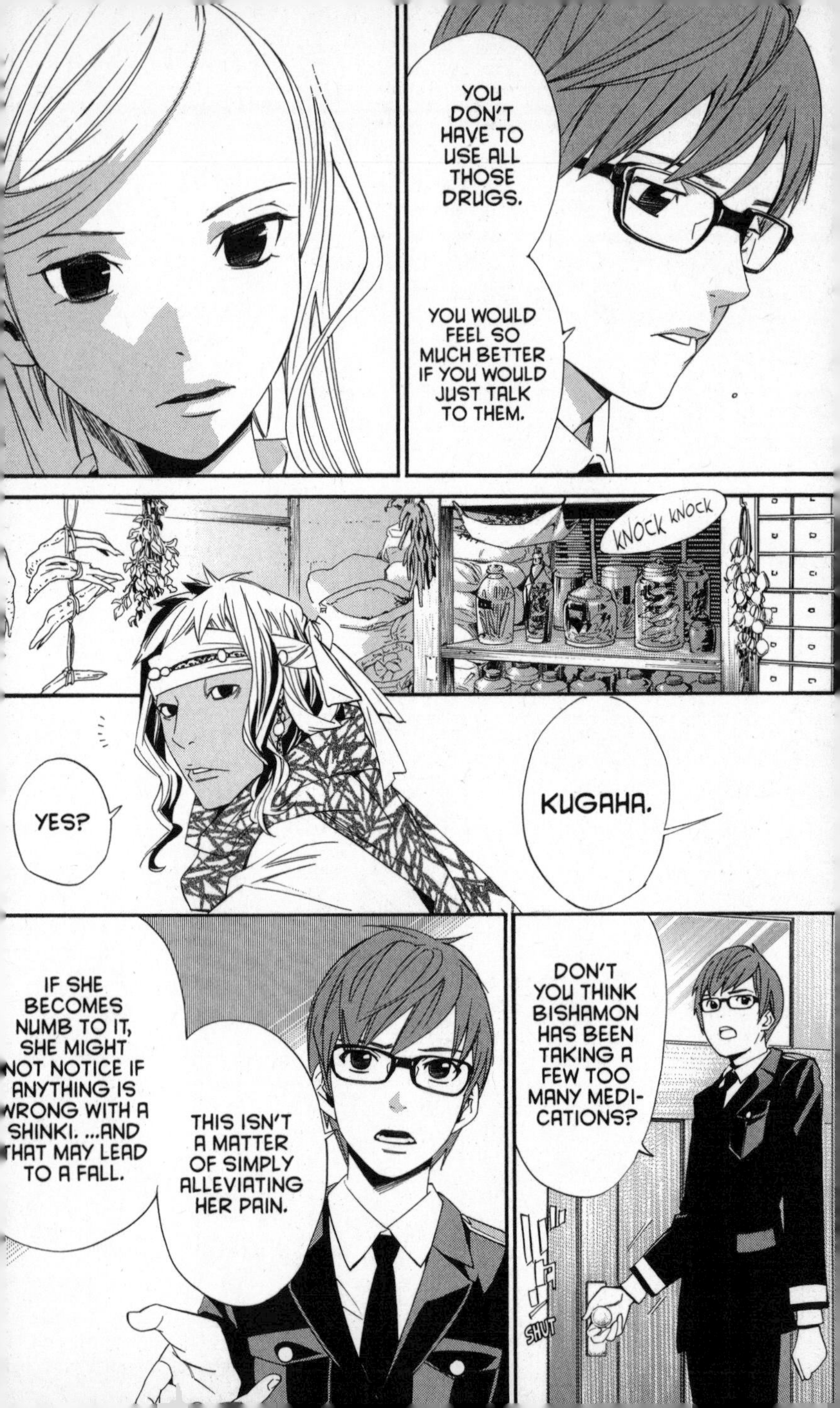
YOU DON'T HAVE TO USE ALL THOSE DRUGS.
YOU WOULD FEEL SO MUCH BETTER IF YOU WOULD JUST TALK TO THEM.
KNOCK KNOCK
KUGAHA.
YES?
DON'T YOU THINK BISHAMON HAS BEEN TAKING A FEW TOO MANY MEDI-CATIONS?
SHUT
THIS ISN'T A MATTER OF SIMPLY ALLEVIATING HER PAIN.
IF SHE BECOMES NUMB TO IT, SHE MIGHT NOT NOTICE IF ANYTHING IS WRONG WITH A SHINKI. ...AND THAT MAY LEAD TO A FALL.

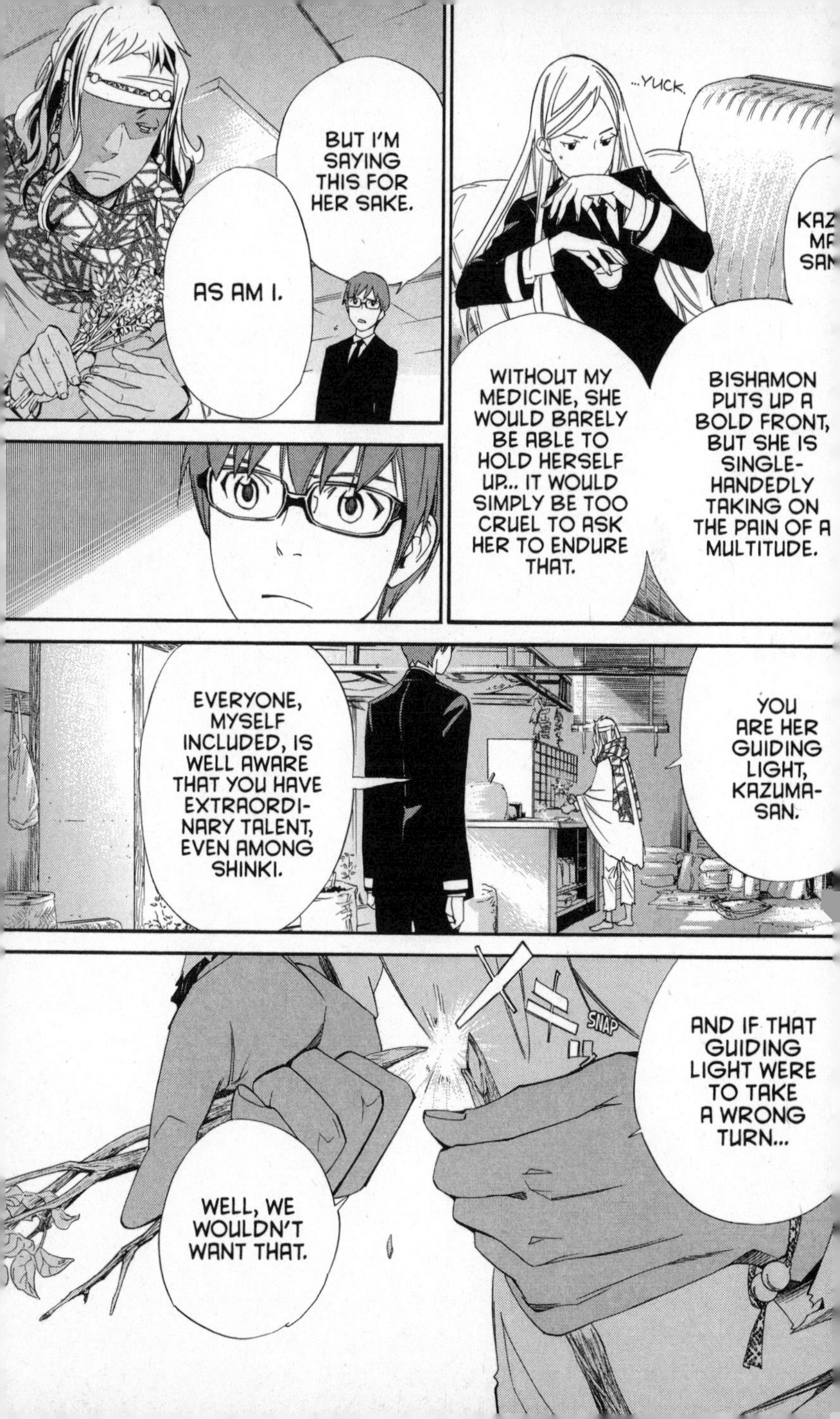
...YUCK.
BISHAMON PUTS UP A BOLD FRONT, BUT SHE IS SINGLE-HANDEDLY TAKING ON THE PAIN OF A MULTITUDE.
WITHOUT MY MEDICINE, SHE WOULD BARELY BE ABLE TO HOLD HERSELF UP... IT WOULD SIMPLY BE TOO CRUEL TO ASK HER TO ENDURE THAT.
BUT I'M SAYING THIS FOR HER SAKE.
AS AM I.
YOU ARE HER GUIDING LIGHT, KAZUMA-SAN.
EVERYONE, MYSELF INCLUDED, IS WELL AWARE THAT YOU HAVE EXTRAORDINARY TALENT, EVEN AMONG SHINKI.
AND IF THAT GUIDING LIGHT WERE TO TAKE A WRONG TURN...
SNAP
WELL, WE WOULDN'T WANT THAT.

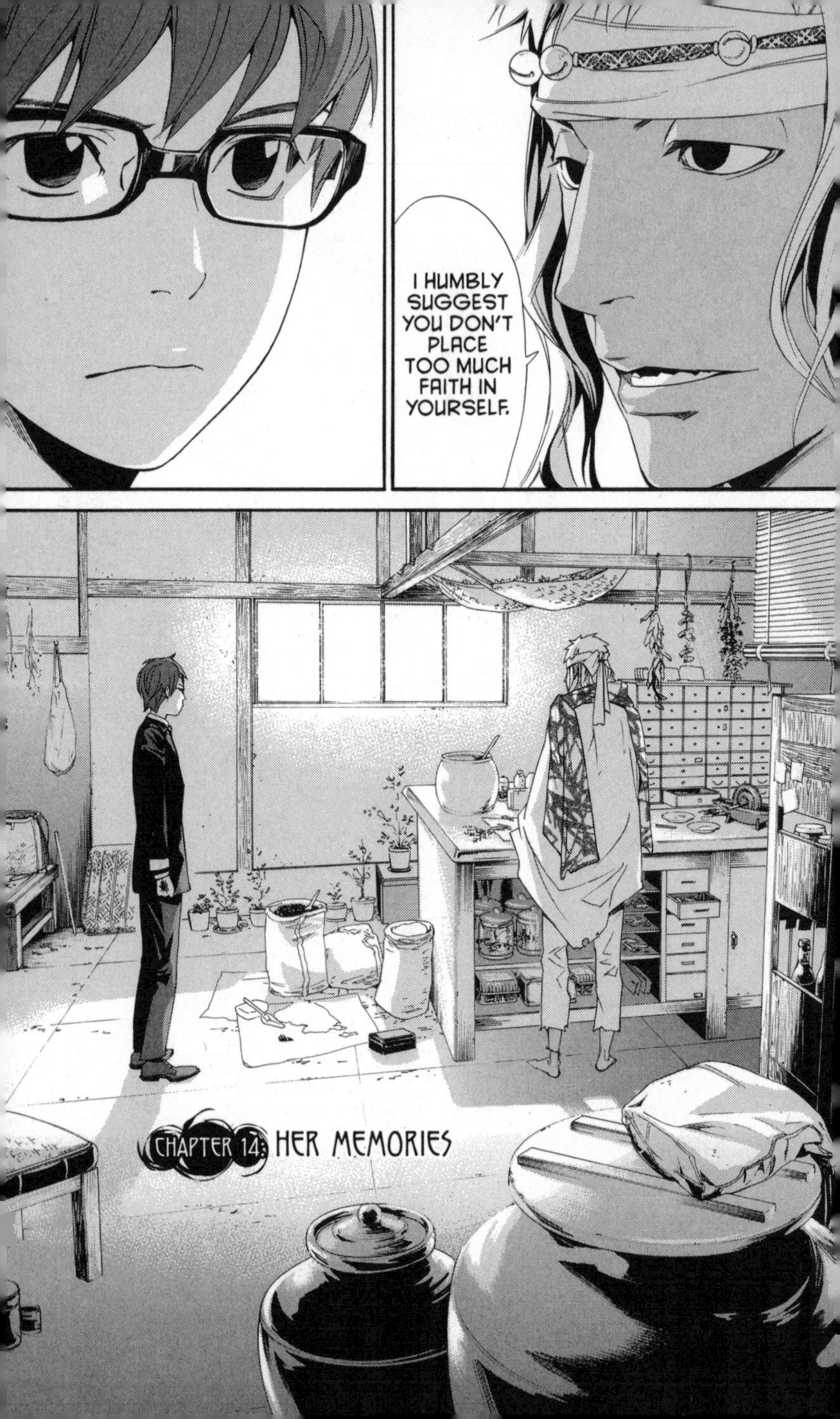
I HUMBLY SUGGEST YOU DON'T PLACE TOO MUCH FAITH IN YOURSELF.
CHAPTER 14: HER MEMORIES

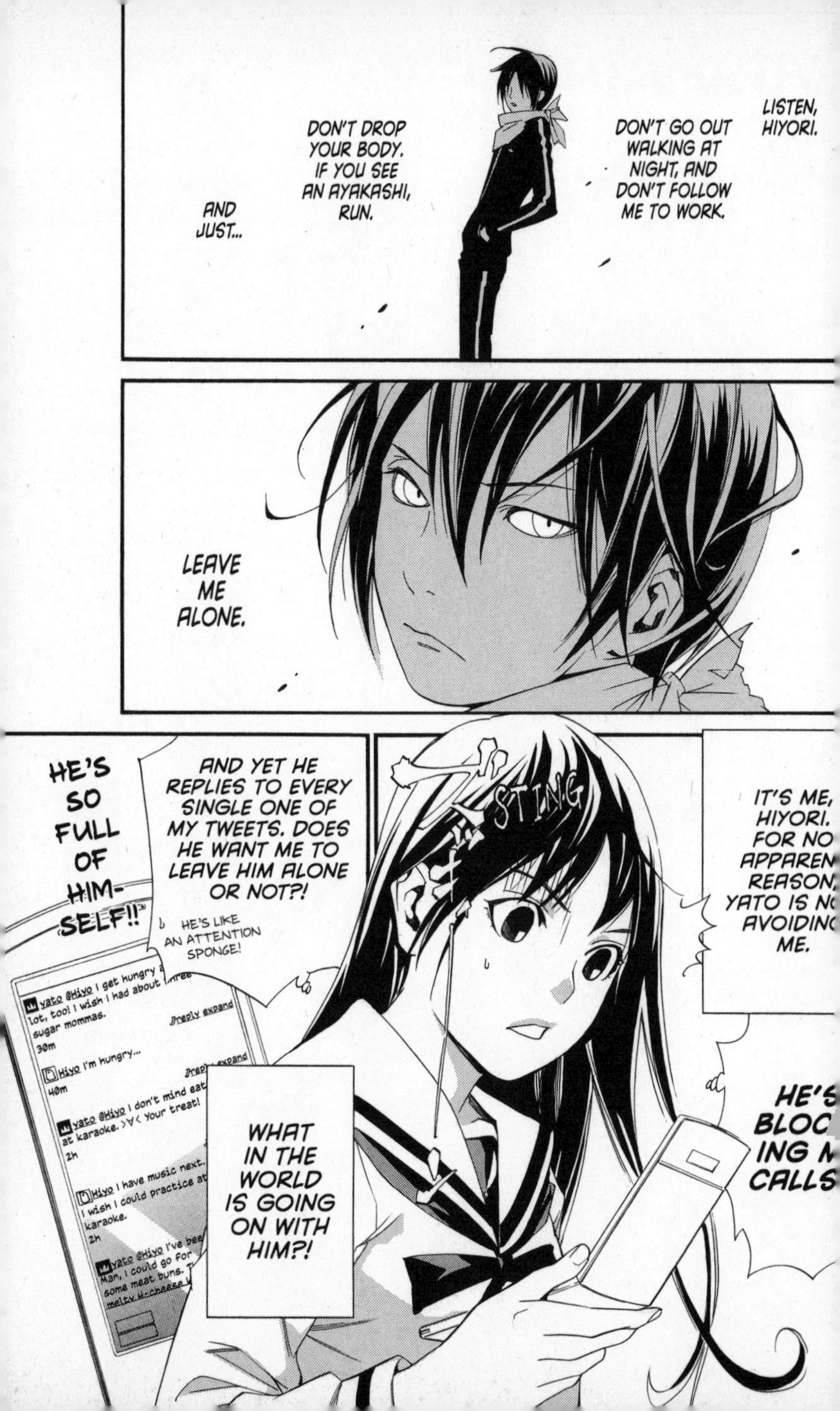

LISTEN, HIYORI.
DON'T GO OUT WALKING AT NIGHT, AND DON'T FOLLOW ME TO WORK.
DON'T DROP YOUR BODY. IF YOU SEE AN AYAKASHI, RUN.
AND JUST...
LEAVE ME ALONE.
IT'S ME, HIYORI. FOR NO APPAREN REASON, YATO IS N AVOIDIN ME.
HE'S BLOC ING M CALLS
STING
WHAT IN THE WORLD IS GOING ON WITH HIM?!
AND YET HE REPLIES TO EVERY SINGLE ONE OF MY TWEETS. DOES HE WANT ME TO LEAVE HIM ALONE OR NOT?!
HE'S LIKE AN ATTENTION SPONGE!
HE'S SO FULL OF HIM-SELF!!
yato @Hiyo I get hungry a
lot, too! I wish I had about three
sugar mommas.
30m
Hiyo I'm hungry...
40m
yato @Hiyo I don't mind eat
at karaoke. >∀< Your treat!
2h
Hiyo I have music next.
I wish I could practice at
karaoke.
2h
yato @Hiyo I've bee
Man, I could go for
some meat buns.

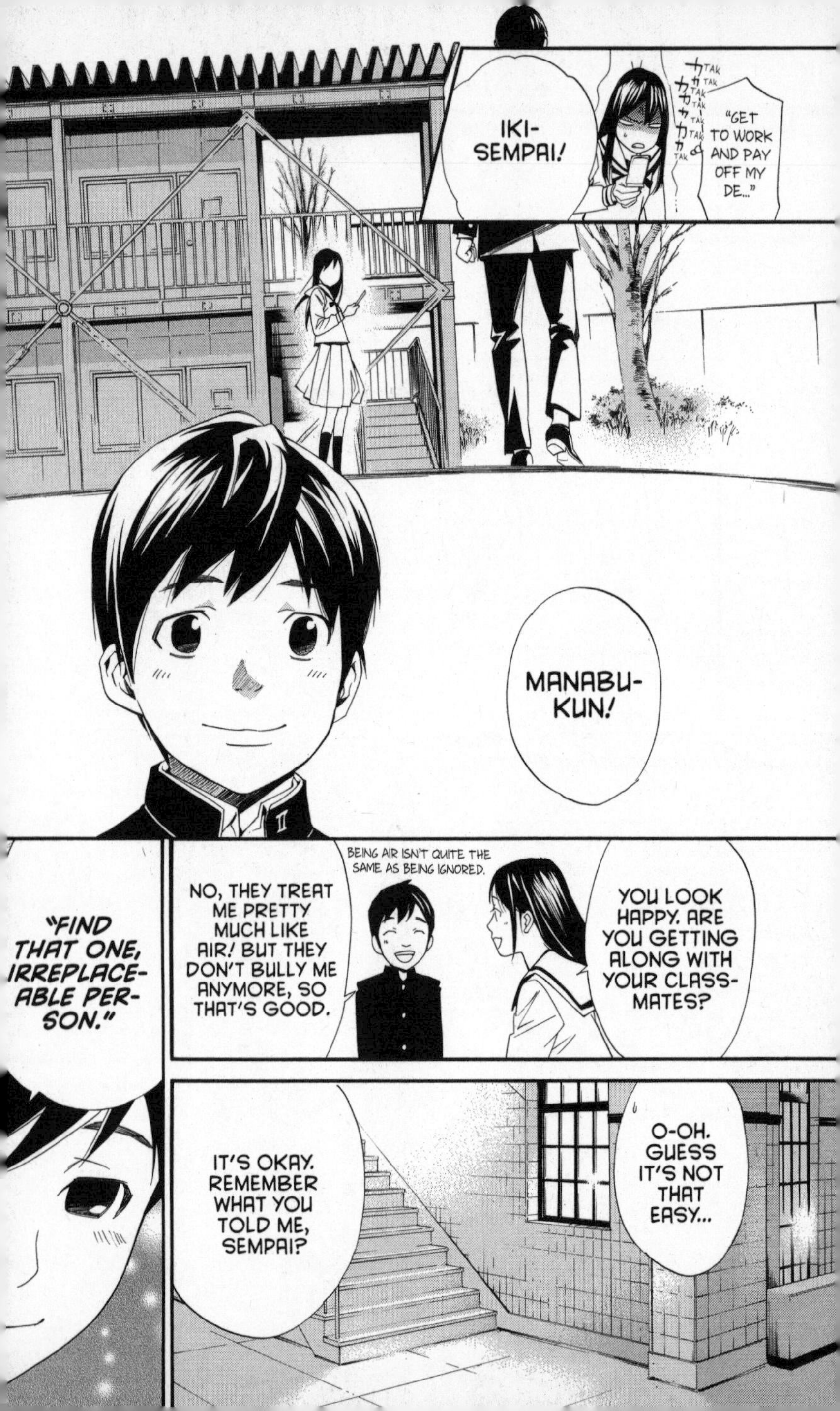

"GET TO WORK AND PAY OFF MY DE..."
TAK TAK TAK TAK TAK TAK TAK
IKI-SEMPAI!
MANABU-KUN!
YOU LOOK HAPPY. ARE YOU GETTING ALONG WITH YOUR CLASSMATES?
BEING AIR ISN'T QUITE THE SAME AS BEING IGNORED.
NO, THEY TREAT ME PRETTY MUCH LIKE AIR! BUT THEY DON'T BULLY ME ANYMORE, SO THAT'S GOOD.
O-OH. GUESS IT'S NOT THAT EASY...
IT'S OKAY. REMEMBER WHAT YOU TOLD ME, SEMPAI?
"FIND THAT ONE, IRREPLACEABLE PERSON."

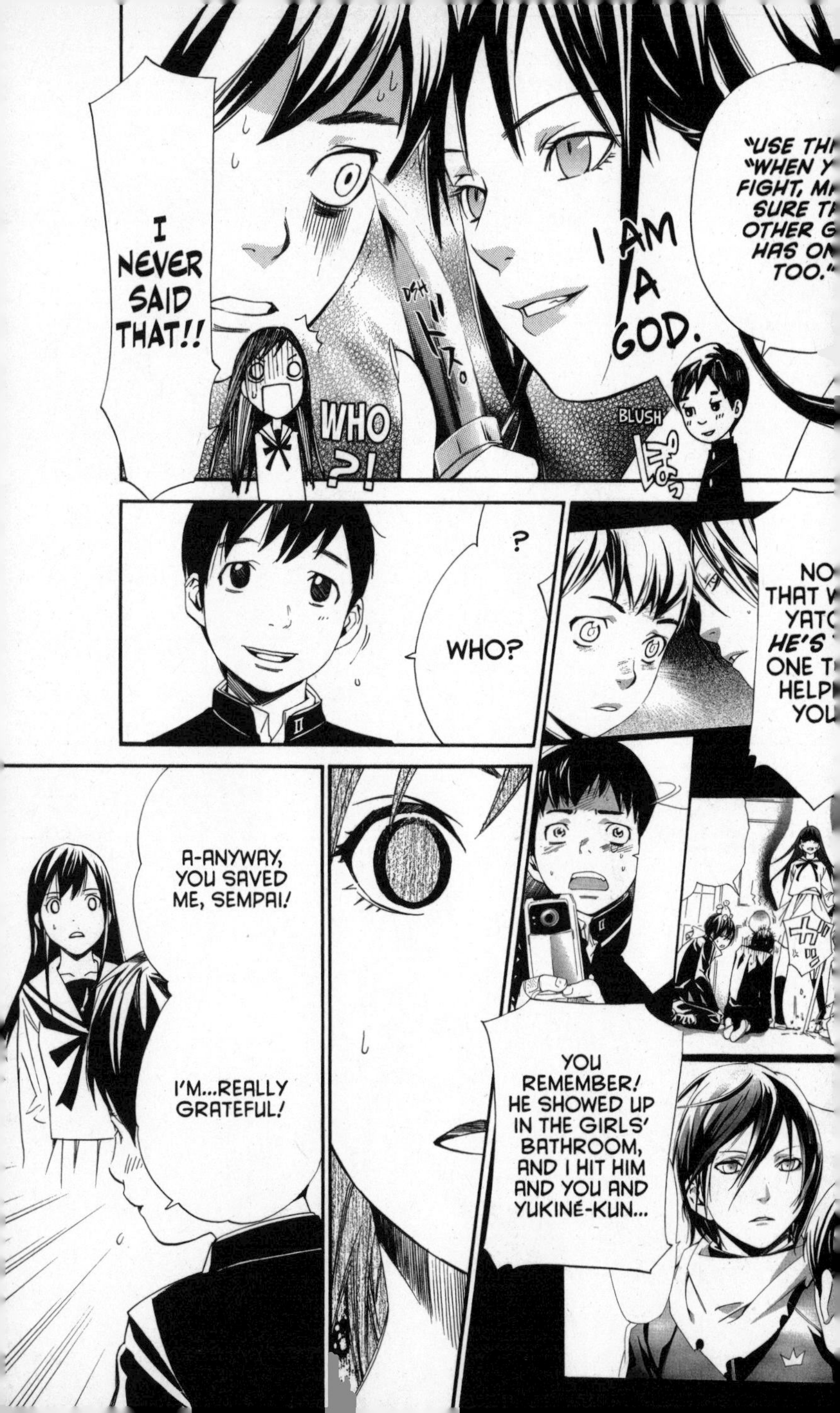
"USE THI
"WHEN Y
FIGHT, MA
SURE TH
OTHER G
HAS ON
TOO."
I AM A GOD.
BLUSH
DSH
WHO ?!
I NEVER SAID THAT!!
NO
THAT W
YATO
HE'S
ONE T
HELP
YOU
?
WHO?
YOU REMEMBER! HE SHOWED UP IN THE GIRLS' BATHROOM, AND I HIT HIM AND YOU AND YUKINÉ-KUN...
A-ANYWAY, YOU SAVED ME, SEMPAI!
I'M...REALLY GRATEFUL!

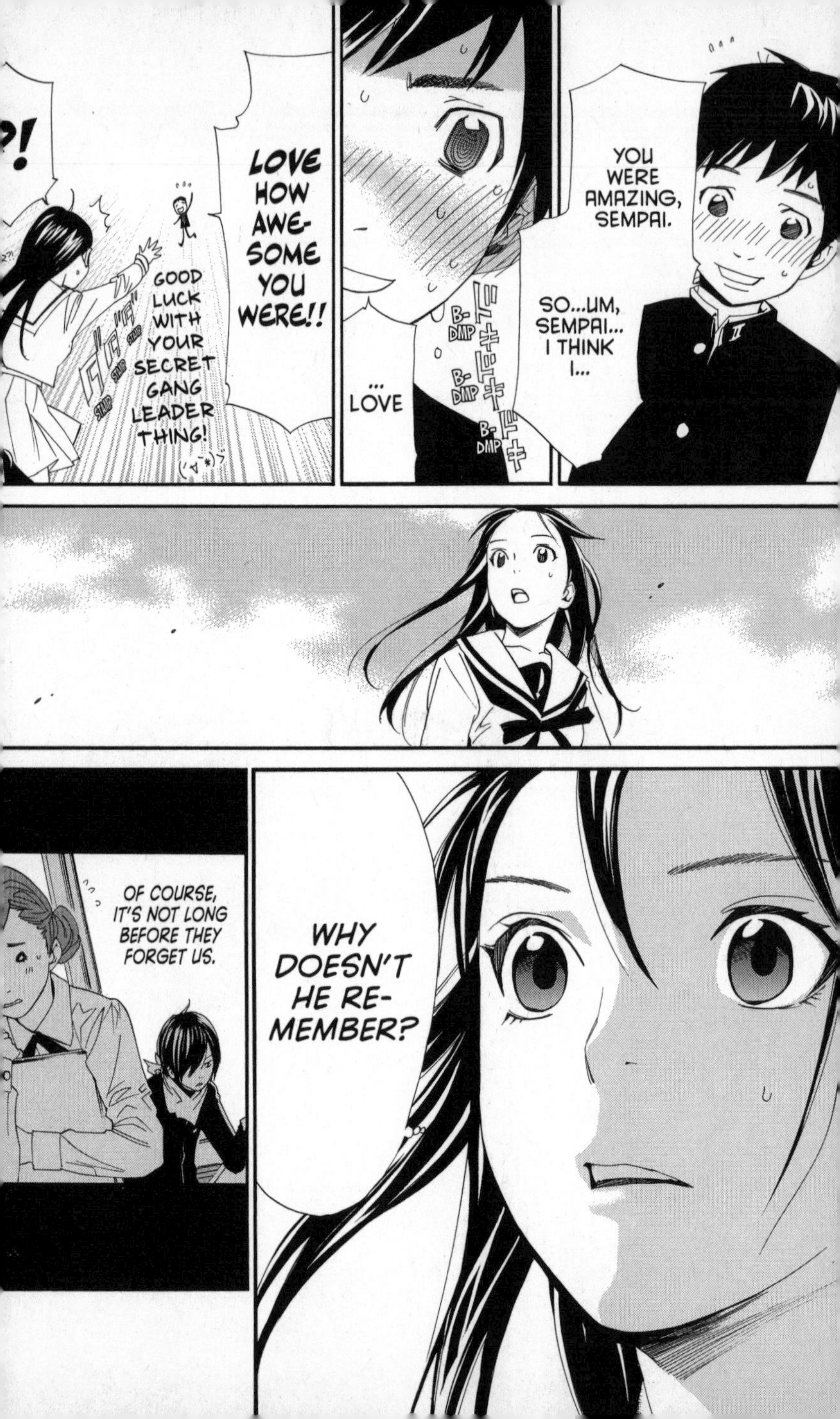
YOU WERE AMAZING, SEMPAI.
SO...UM, SEMPAI... I THINK I...
...LOVE
B-DMP
B-DMP
B-DMP
LOVE HOW AWE-SOME YOU WERE!!
GOOD LUCK WITH YOUR SECRET GANG LEADER THING!
STAMP
STAMP
STAMP
?!
WHY DOESN'T HE RE-MEMBER?
OF COURSE, IT'S NOT LONG BEFORE THEY FORGET US.

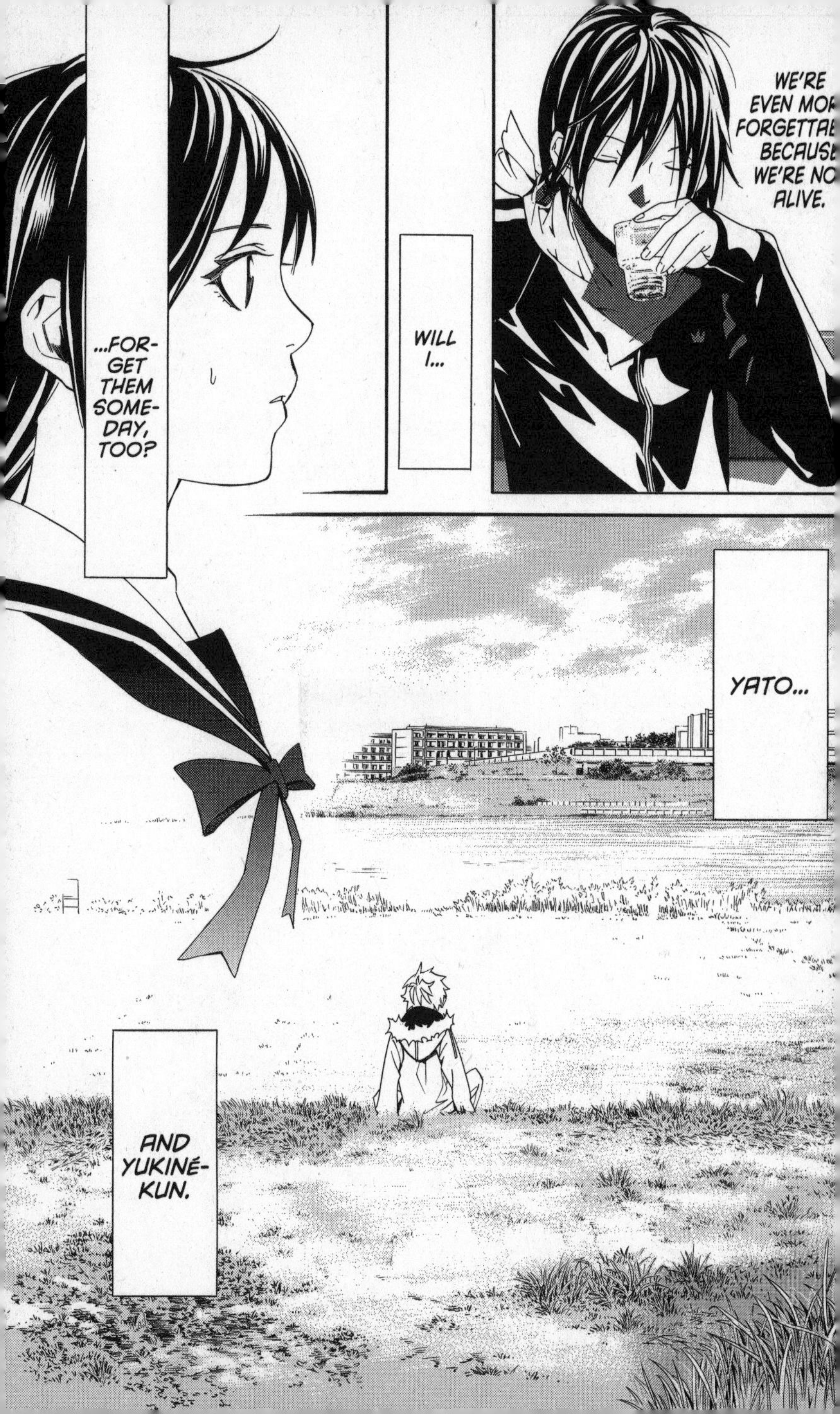
WE'RE EVEN MOR FORGETTAB BECAUSE WE'RE NO ALIVE.
WILL I...
...FOR-GET THEM SOME-DAY, TOO?
YATO...
AND YUKINÉ-KUN.

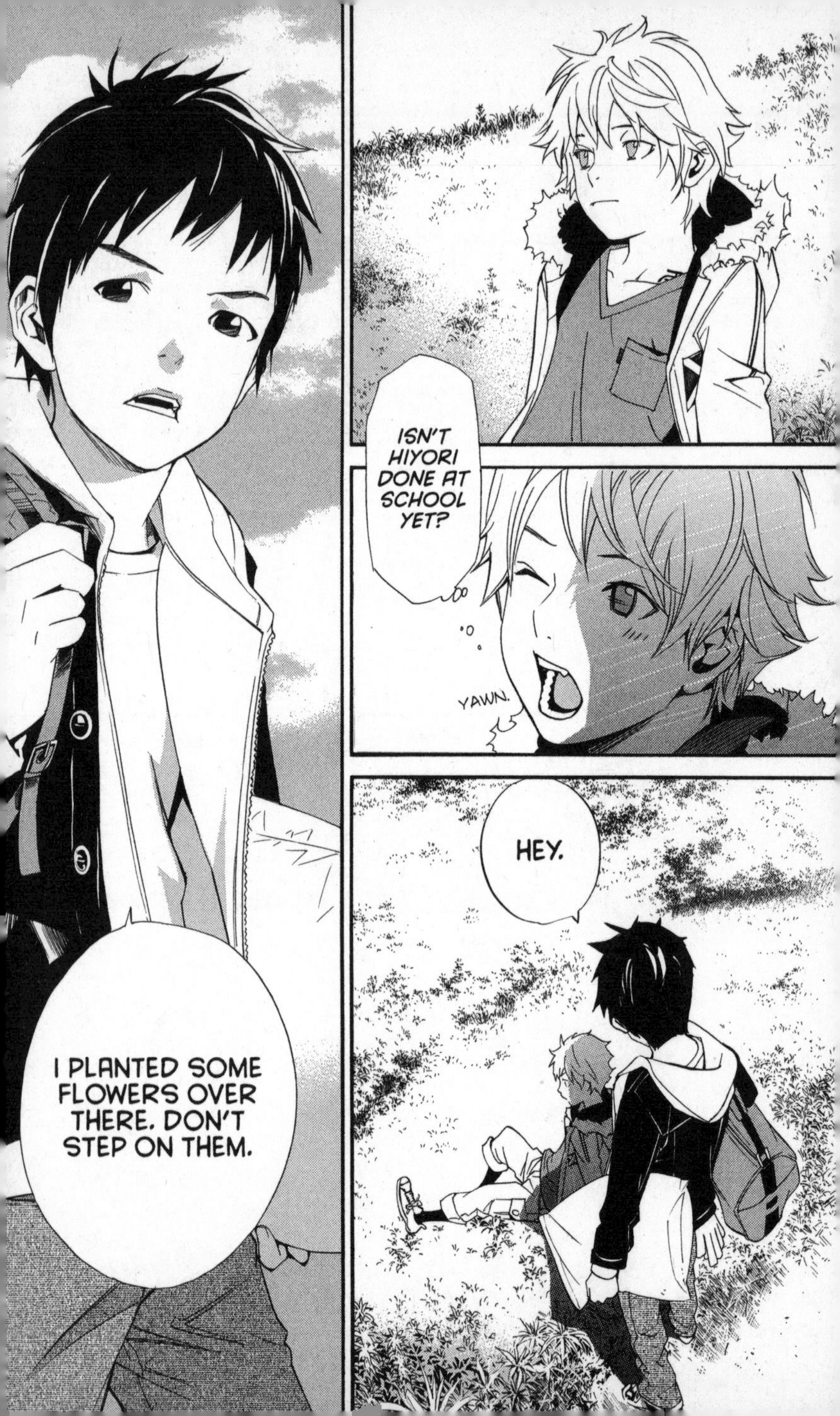
ISN'T HIYORI DONE AT SCHOOL YET?
YAWN.
HEY.
I PLANTED SOME FLOWERS OVER THERE. DON'T STEP ON THEM.

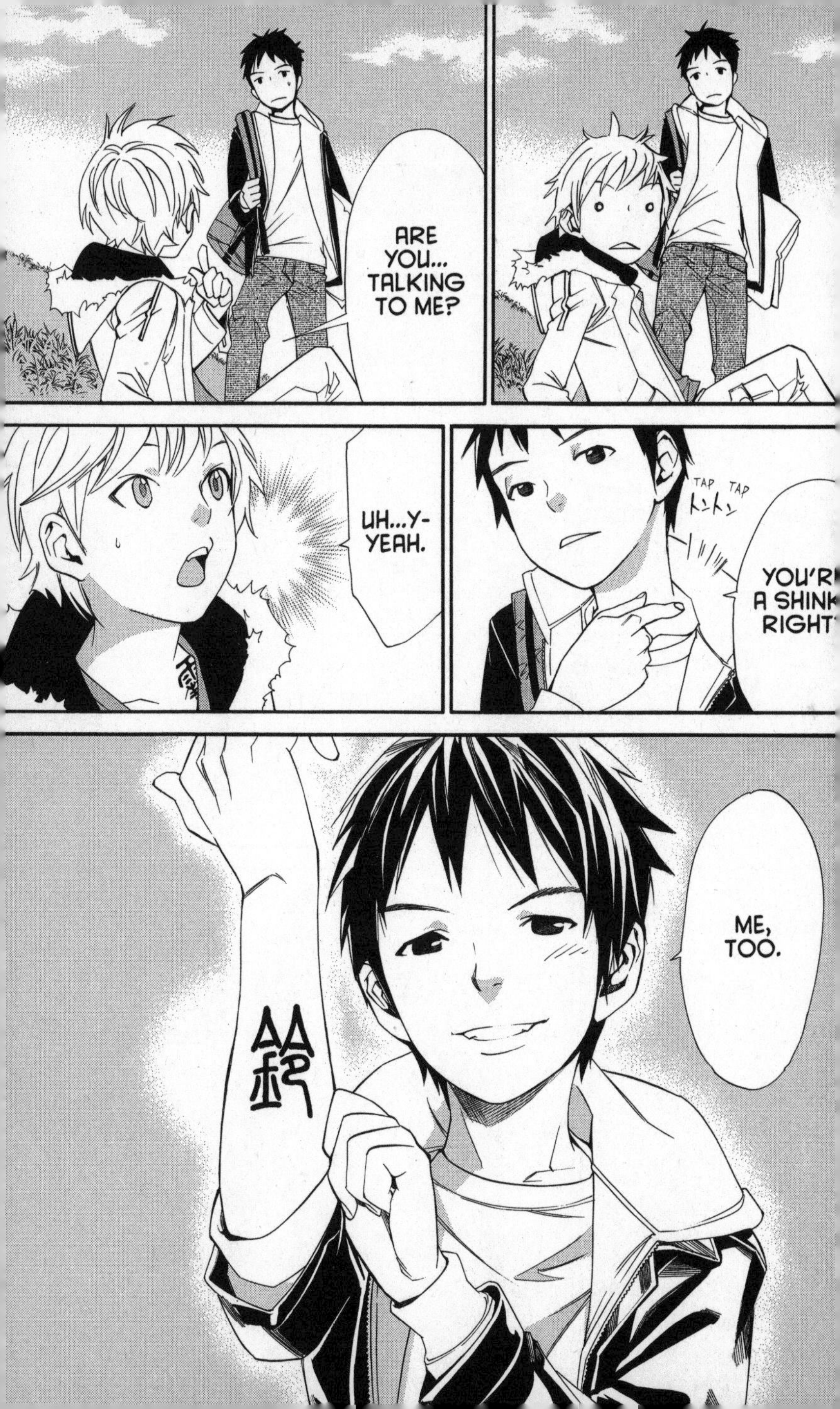
ARE YOU... TALKING TO ME?
TAP TAP
トントン
YOU'R
A SHINK
RIGHT
UH...Y-YEAH.
ME, TOO.

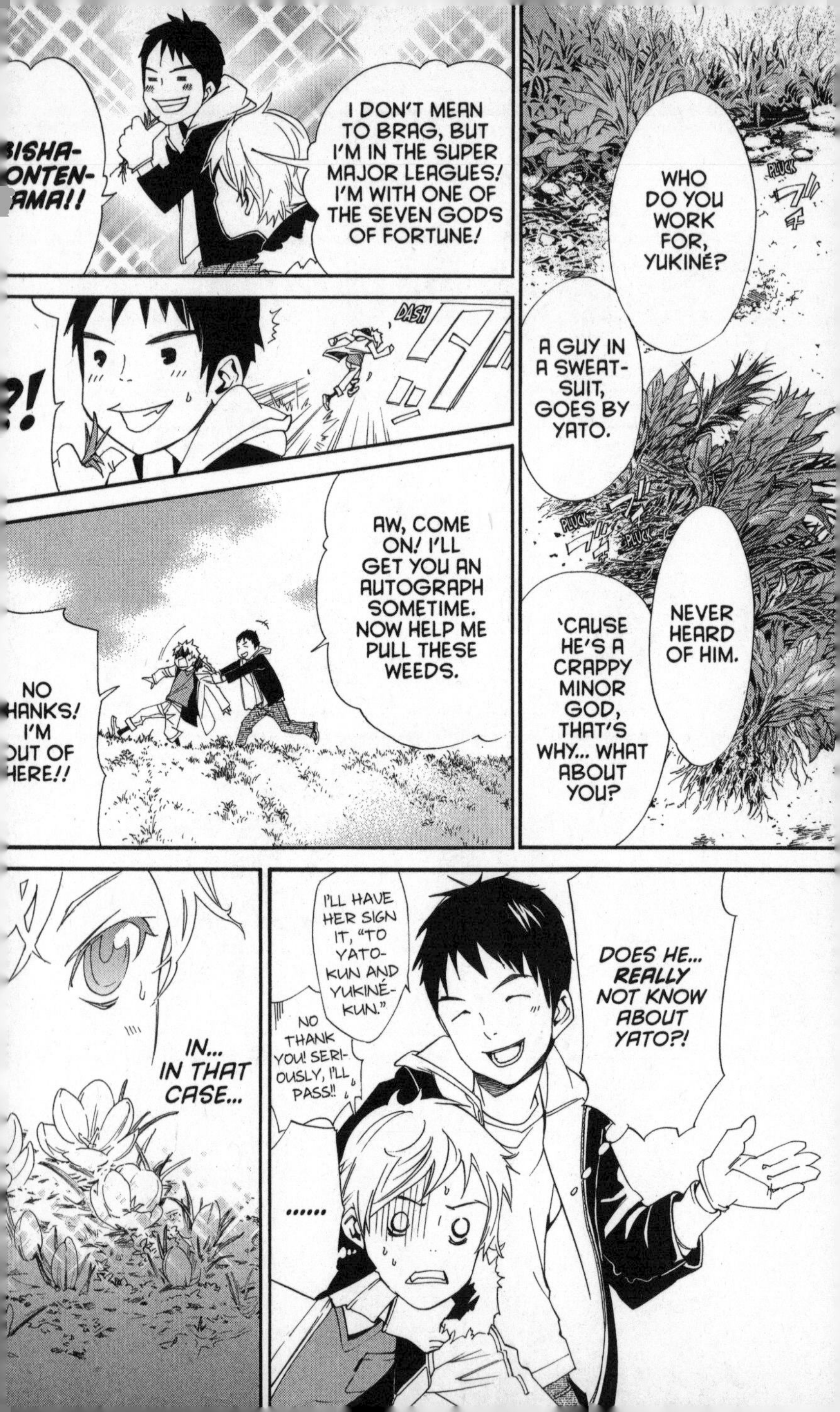
WHO DO YOU WORK FOR, YUKINÉ?
PLUCK
A GUY IN A SWEAT-SUIT, GOES BY YATO.
PLUCK
PLUCK
NEVER HEARD OF HIM.
'CAUSE HE'S A CRAPPY MINOR GOD, THAT'S WHY... WHAT ABOUT YOU?
I DON'T MEAN TO BRAG, BUT I'M IN THE SUPER MAJOR LEAGUES! I'M WITH ONE OF THE SEVEN GODS OF FORTUNE!
BISHA-ONTEN-AMA!!
DASH
?!
AW, COME ON! I'LL GET YOU AN AUTOGRAPH SOMETIME. NOW HELP ME PULL THESE WEEDS.
NO HANKS! I'M OUT OF HERE!!
DOES HE... REALLY NOT KNOW ABOUT YATO?!
I'LL HAVE HER SIGN IT, "TO YATO-KUN AND YUKINÉ-KUN."
NO THANK YOU! SERI-OUSLY, I'LL PASS!!
......
IN... IN THAT CASE...

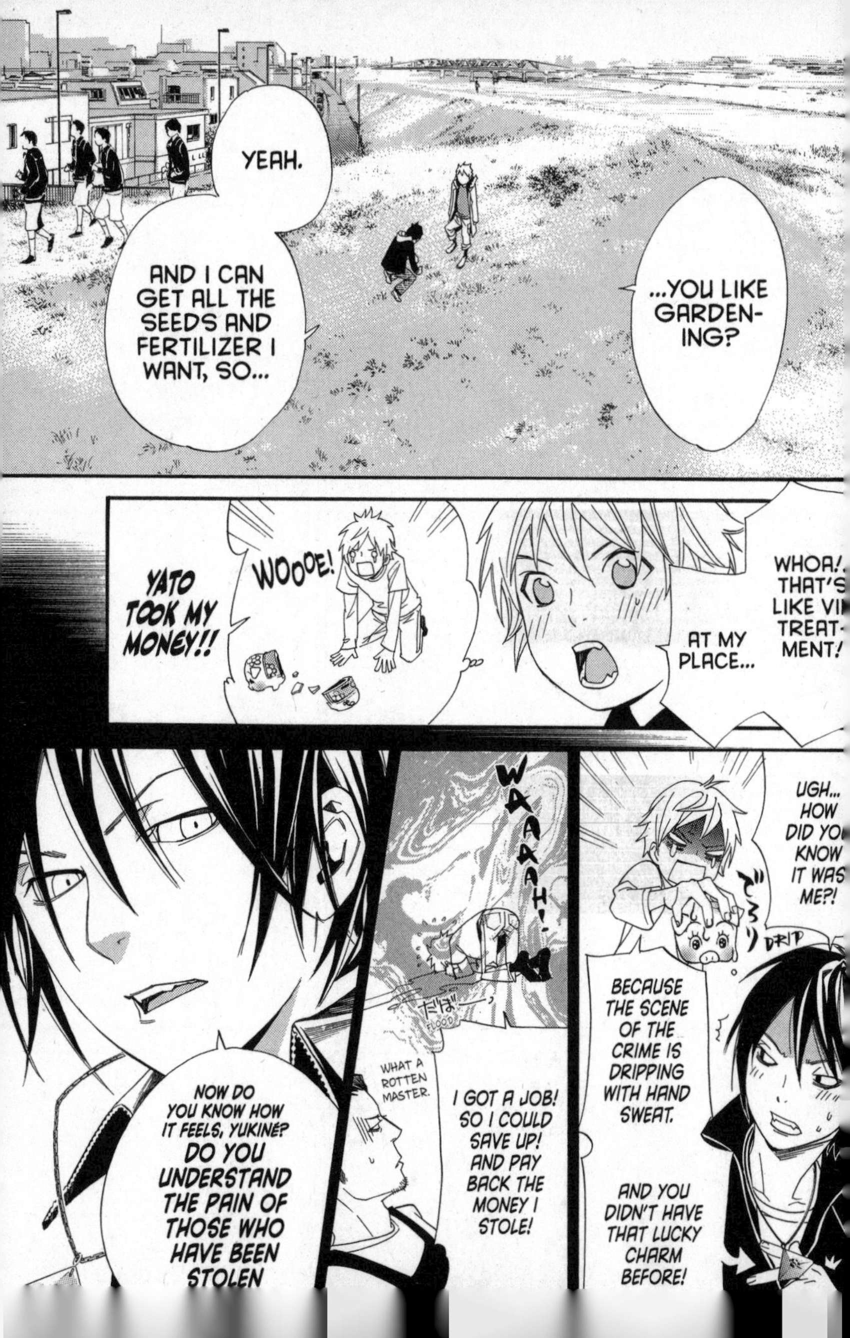
...YOU LIKE GARDEN-ING?
YEAH.
AND I CAN GET ALL THE SEEDS AND FERTILIZER I WANT, SO...
WHOA!. THAT'S LIKE VI TREAT-MENT!
AT MY PLACE...
WOOOE!
YATO TOOK MY MONEY!!
UGH... HOW DID YO KNOW IT WAS ME?!
DRIP
BECAUSE THE SCENE OF THE CRIME IS DRIPPING WITH HAND SWEAT.
AND YOU DIDN'T HAVE THAT LUCKY CHARM BEFORE!
WAAAAH!
FLOOD
I GOT A JOB! SO I COULD SAVE UP! AND PAY BACK THE MONEY I STOLE!
WHAT A ROTTEN MASTER.
NOW DO YOU KNOW HOW IT FEELS, YUKINE? DO YOU UNDERSTAND THE PAIN OF THOSE WHO HAVE BEEN STOLEN

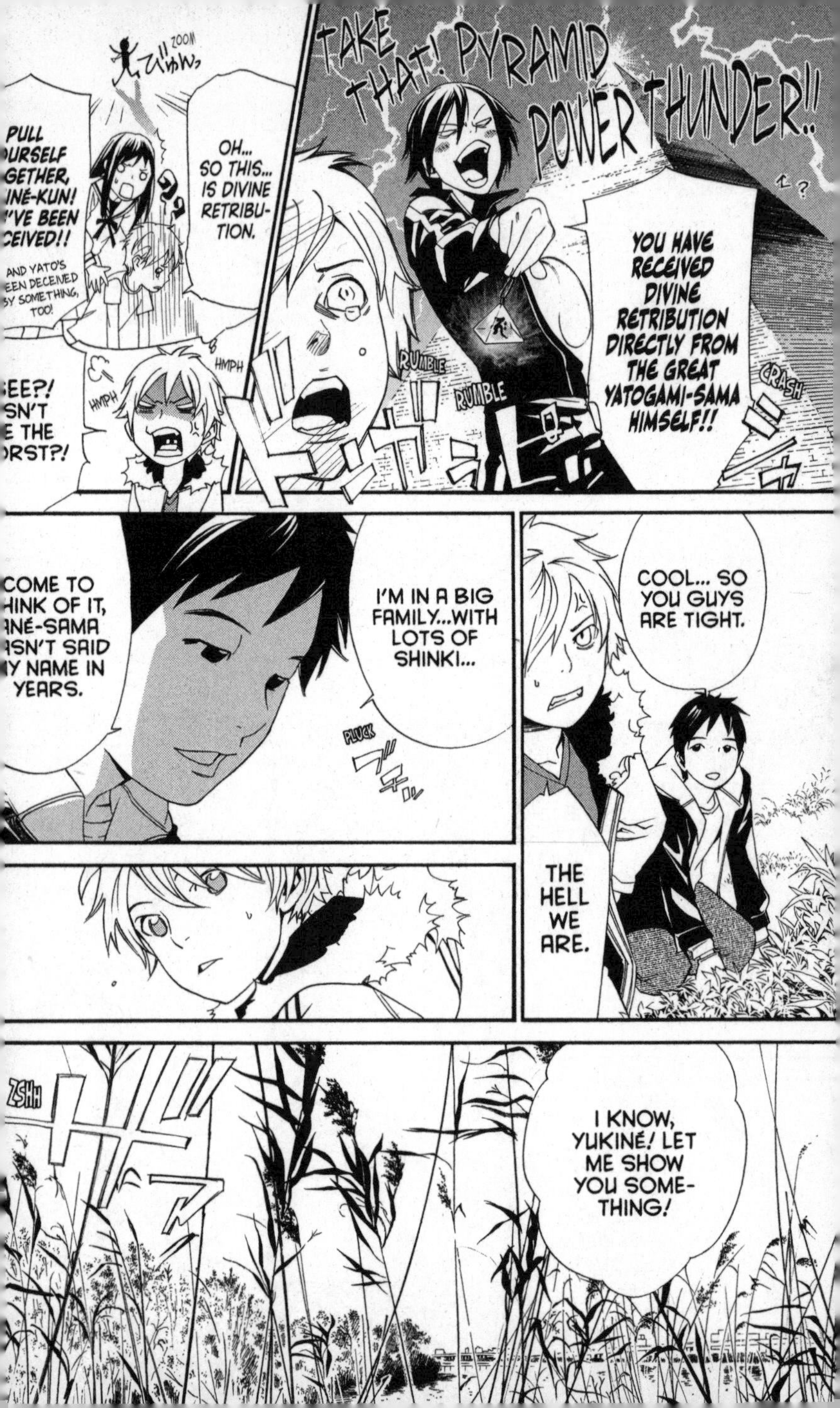

TAKE THAT! PYRAMID POWER THUNDER!!
YOU HAVE RECEIVED DIVINE RETRIBUTION DIRECTLY FROM THE GREAT YATOGAMI-SAMA HIMSELF!!
RUMBLE
RUMBLE
CRASH
OH... SO THIS... IS DIVINE RETRIBUTION.
ZOOM
PULL OURSELF GETHER, INÉ-KUN! 'VE BEEN CEIVED!!
AND YATO'S EEN DECEIVED BY SOMETHING, TOO!
HMPH
HMPH
EE?! SN'T E THE ORST?!
COOL... SO YOU GUYS ARE TIGHT.
THE HELL WE ARE.
I'M IN A BIG FAMILY...WITH LOTS OF SHINKI...
COME TO HINK OF IT, NÉ-SAMA ASN'T SAID Y NAME IN YEARS.
PLUCK
ZSHH
I KNOW, YUKINÉ! LET ME SHOW YOU SOMETHING!

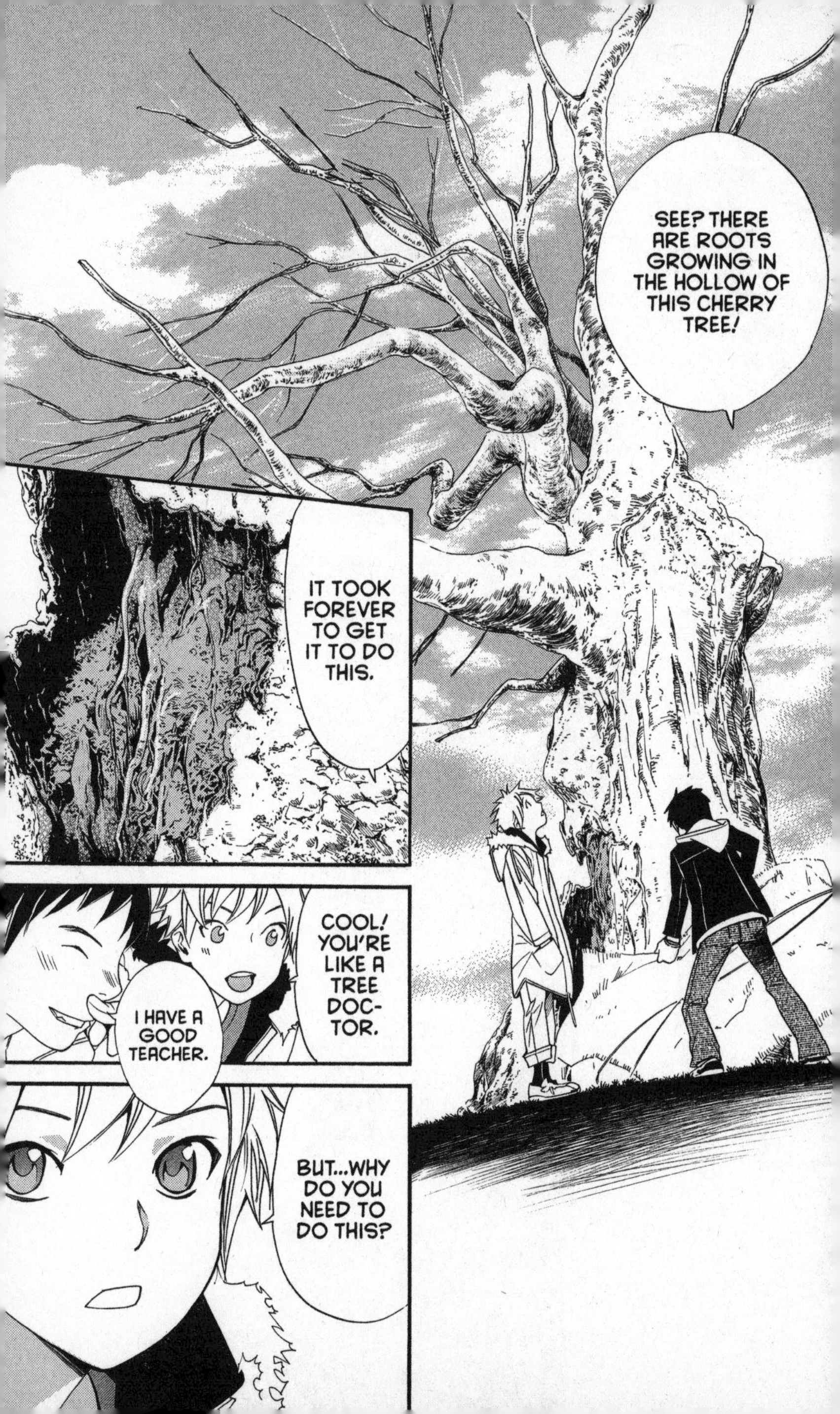
SEE? THERE ARE ROOTS GROWING IN THE HOLLOW OF THIS CHERRY TREE!
IT TOOK FOREVER TO GET IT TO DO THIS.
COOL! YOU'RE LIKE A TREE DOC-TOR.
I HAVE A GOOD TEACHER.
BUT...WHY DO YOU NEED TO DO THIS?

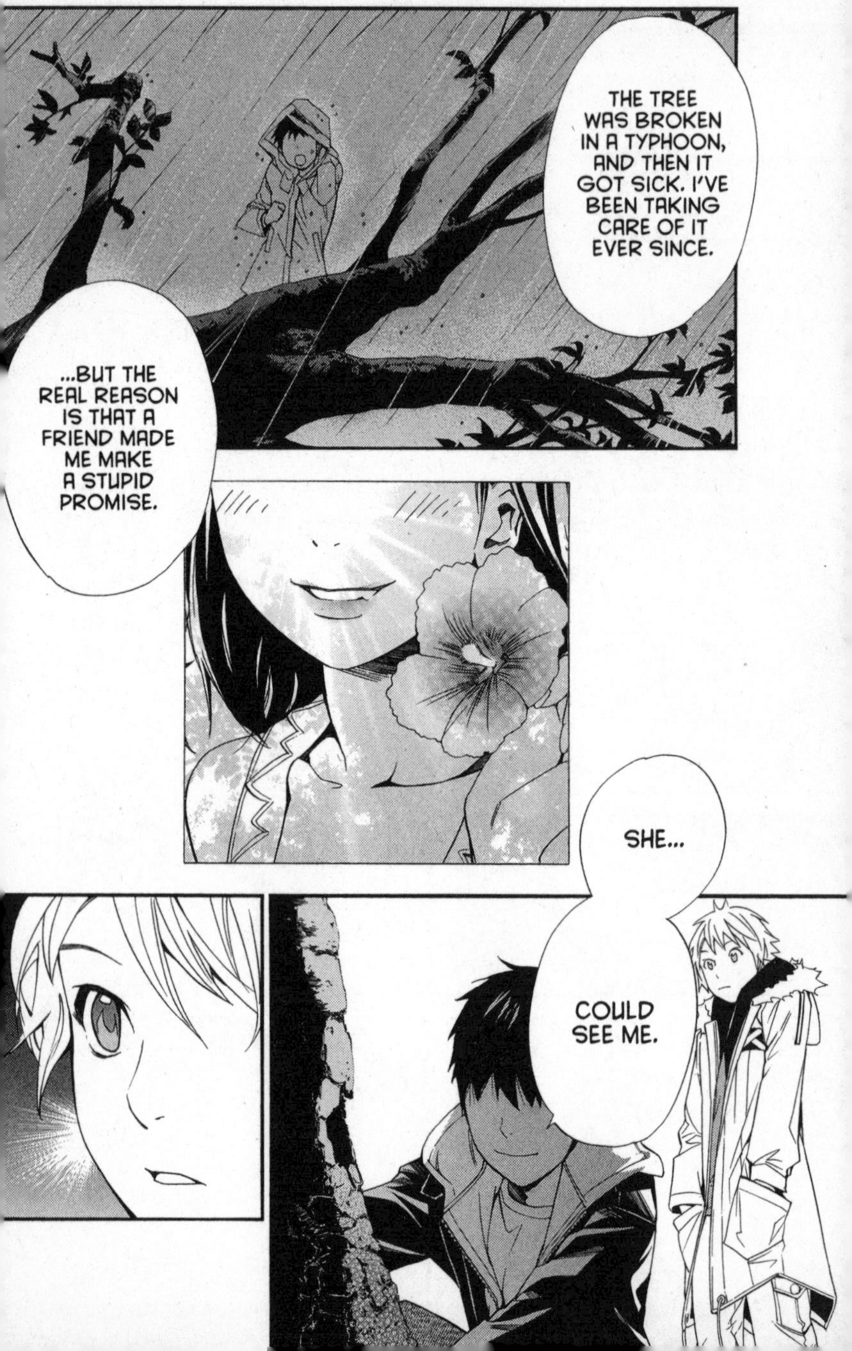
THE TREE WAS BROKEN IN A TYPHOON, AND THEN IT GOT SICK. I'VE BEEN TAKING CARE OF IT EVER SINCE.
...BUT THE REAL REASON IS THAT A FRIEND MADE ME MAKE A STUPID PROMISE.
SHE...
COULD SEE ME.

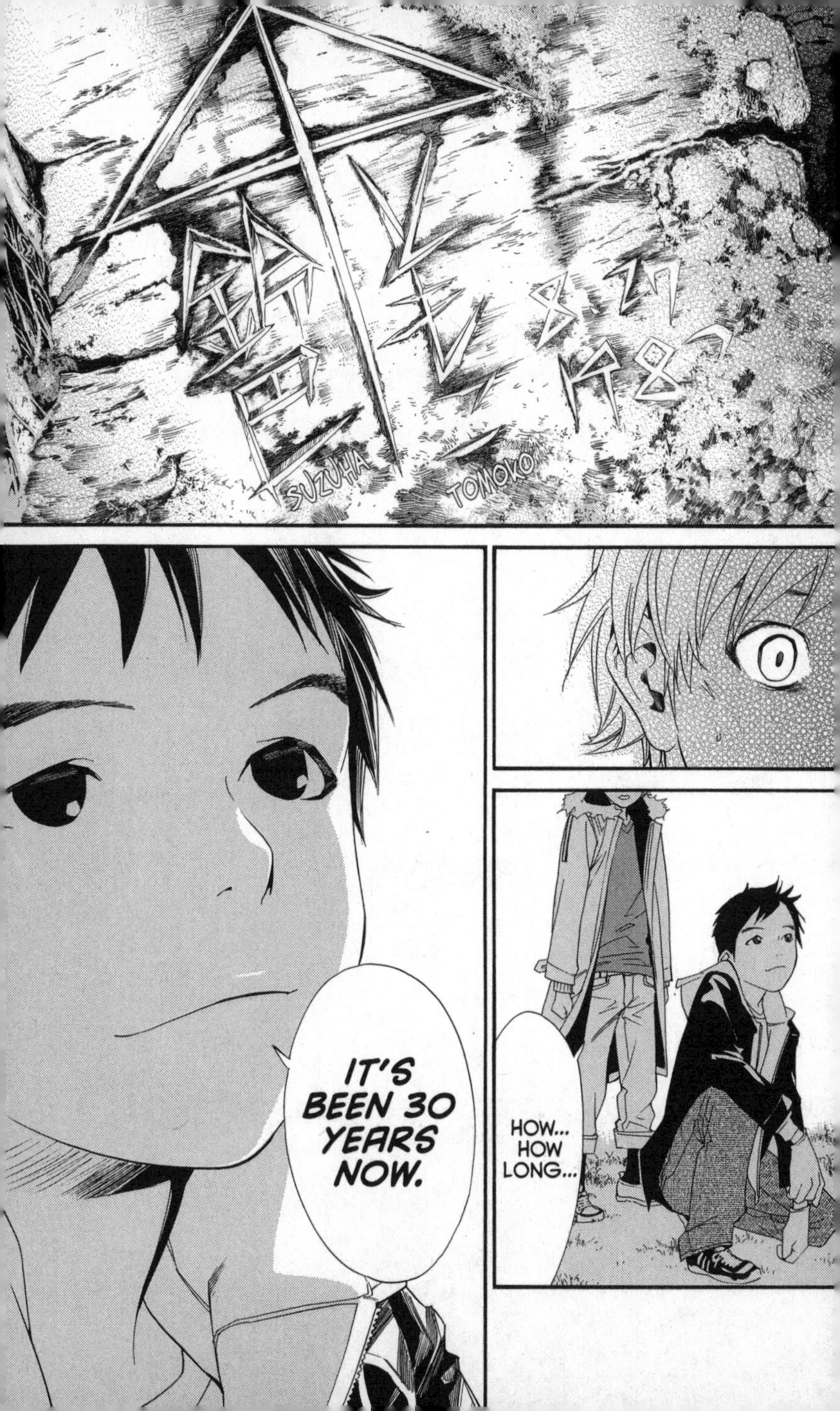
SUZUHA
TOMOKO
HOW... HOW LONG...
IT'S BEEN 30 YEARS NOW.

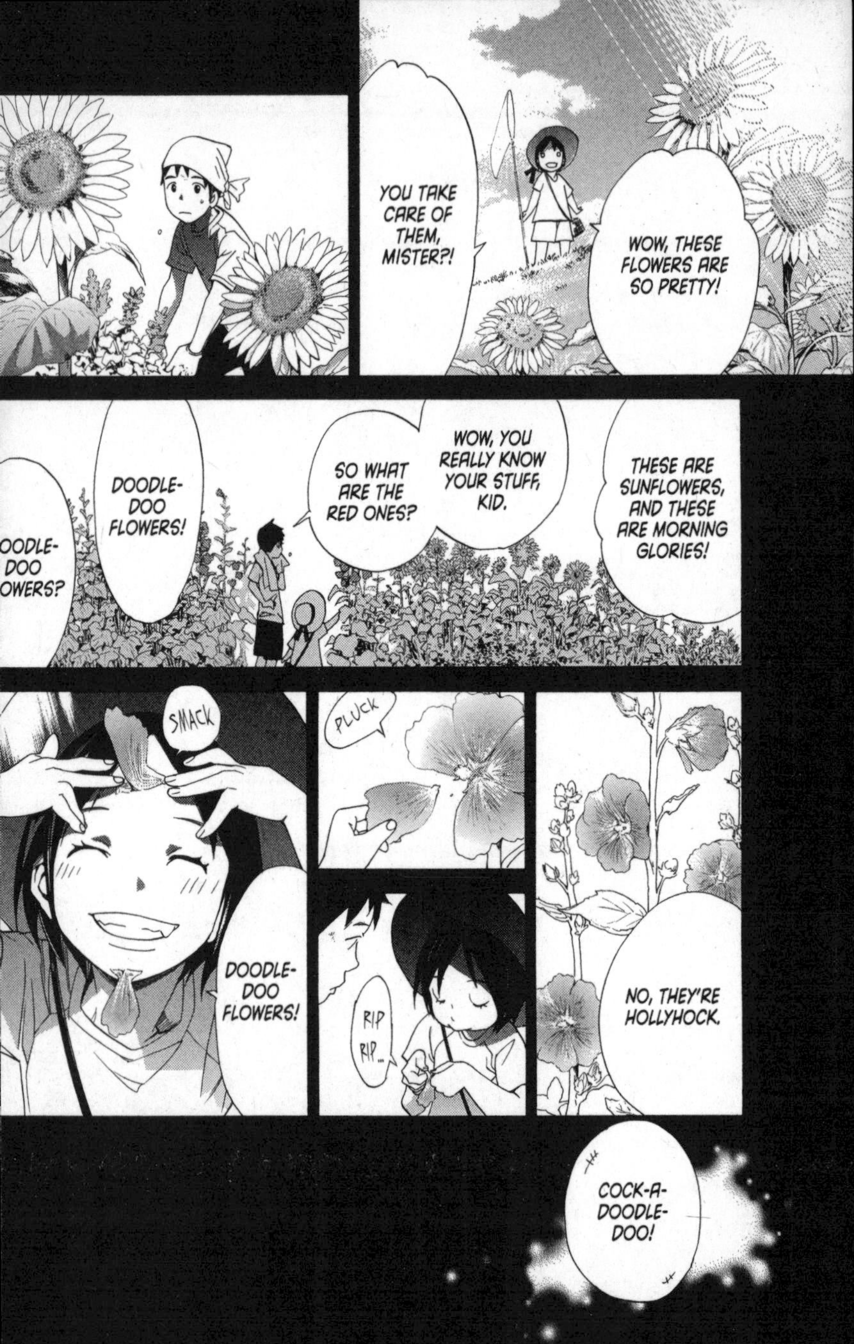
WOW, THESE FLOWERS ARE SO PRETTY!
YOU TAKE CARE OF THEM, MISTER?!
THESE ARE SUNFLOWERS, AND THESE ARE MORNING GLORIES!
WOW, YOU REALLY KNOW YOUR STUFF, KID.
SO WHAT ARE THE RED ONES?
DOODLE-DOO FLOWERS!
OODLE-DOO OWERS?
NO, THEY'RE HOLLYHOCK.
PLUCK
RIP RIP...
SMACK
DOODLE-DOO FLOWERS!
COCK-A-DOODLE-DOO!

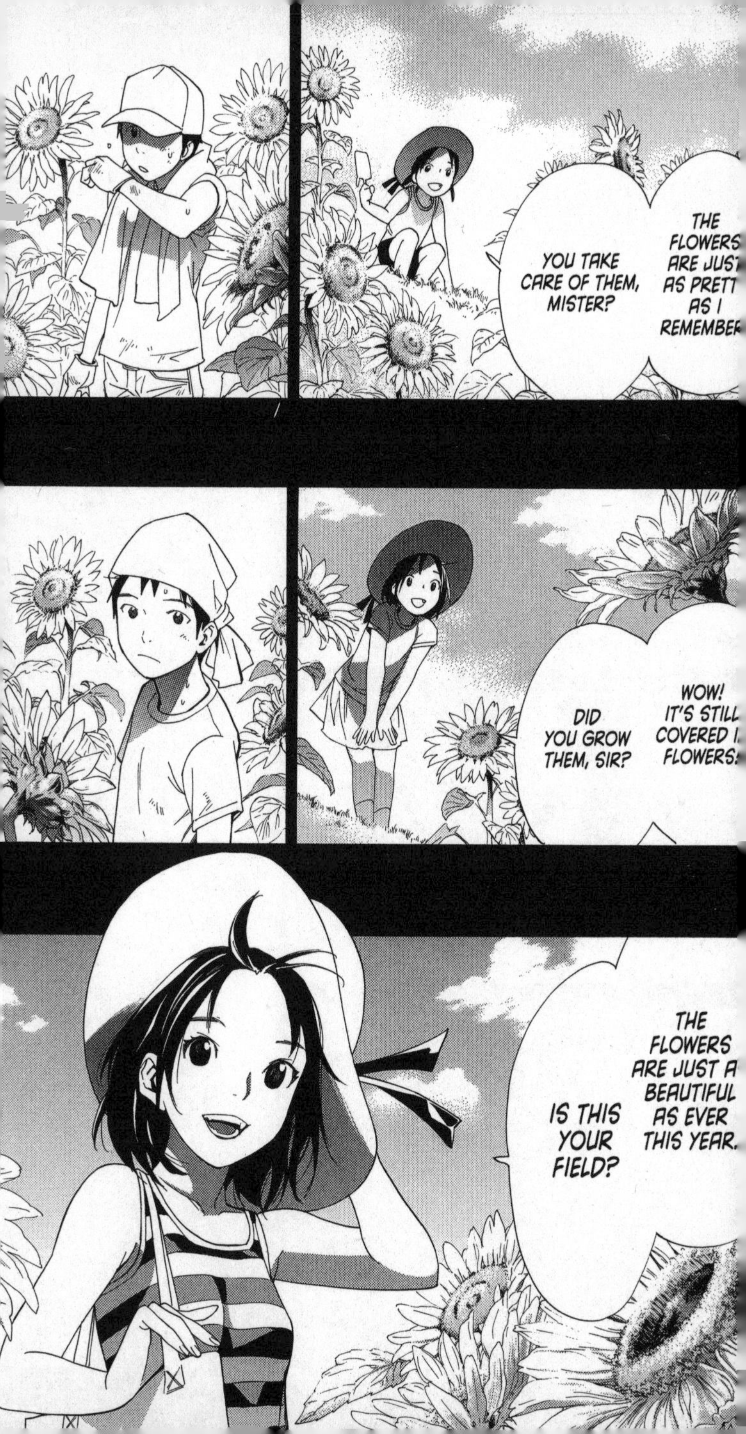
THE FLOWERS ARE JUST AS PRETT AS I REMEMBER
YOU TAKE CARE OF THEM, MISTER?
WOW! IT'S STILL COVERED I FLOWERS!
DID YOU GROW THEM, SIR?
THE FLOWERS ARE JUST A BEAUTIFUL AS EVER THIS YEAR.
IS THIS YOUR FIELD?

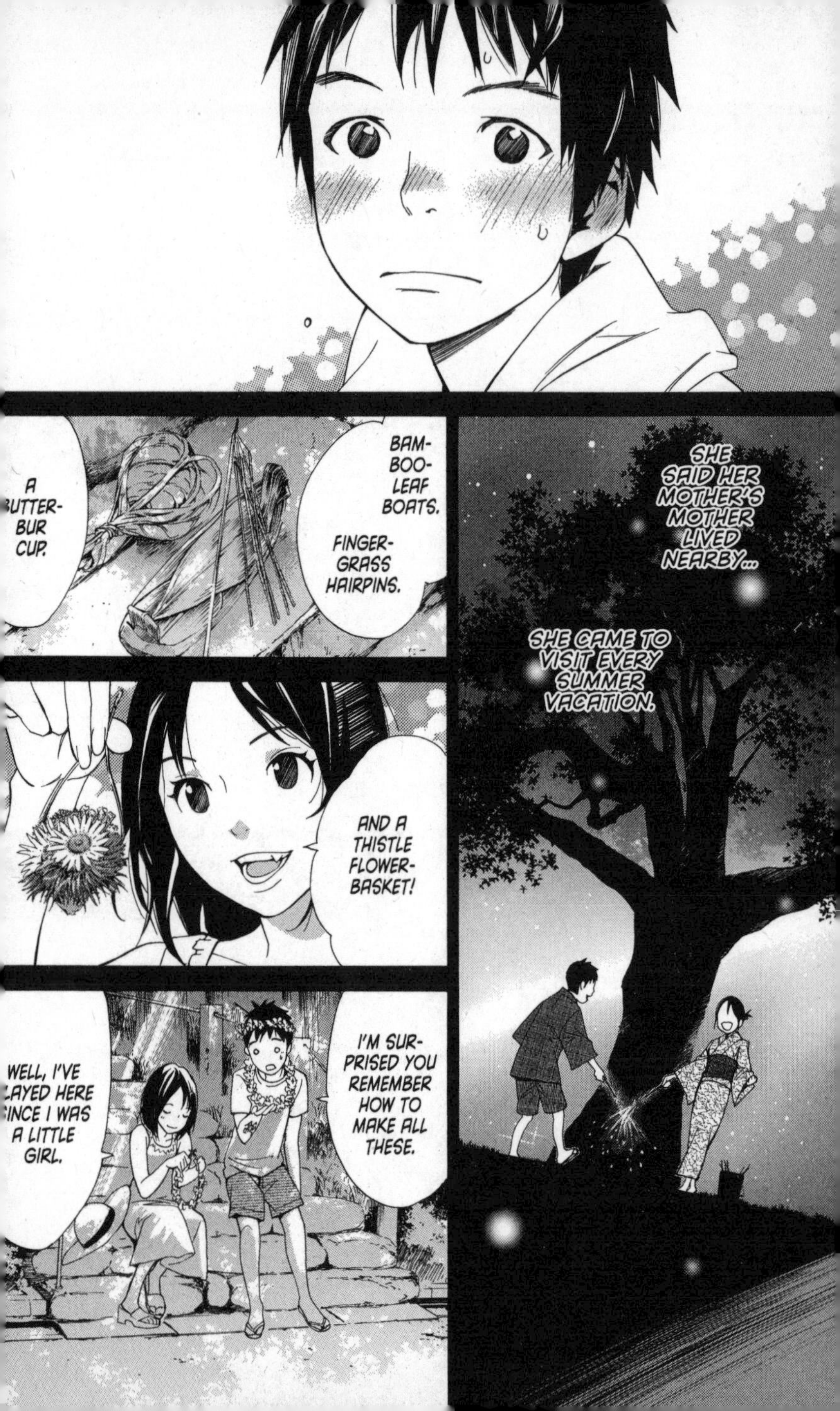
SHE SAID HER MOTHER'S MOTHER LIVED NEARBY...
SHE CAME TO VISIT EVERY SUMMER VACATION.
BAMBOO-LEAF BOATS.
FINGER-GRASS HAIRPINS.
A BUTTER-BUR CUP.
AND A THISTLE FLOWER-BASKET!
I'M SURPRISED YOU REMEMBER HOW TO MAKE ALL THESE.
WELL, I'VE LAYED HERE SINCE I WAS A LITTLE GIRL.

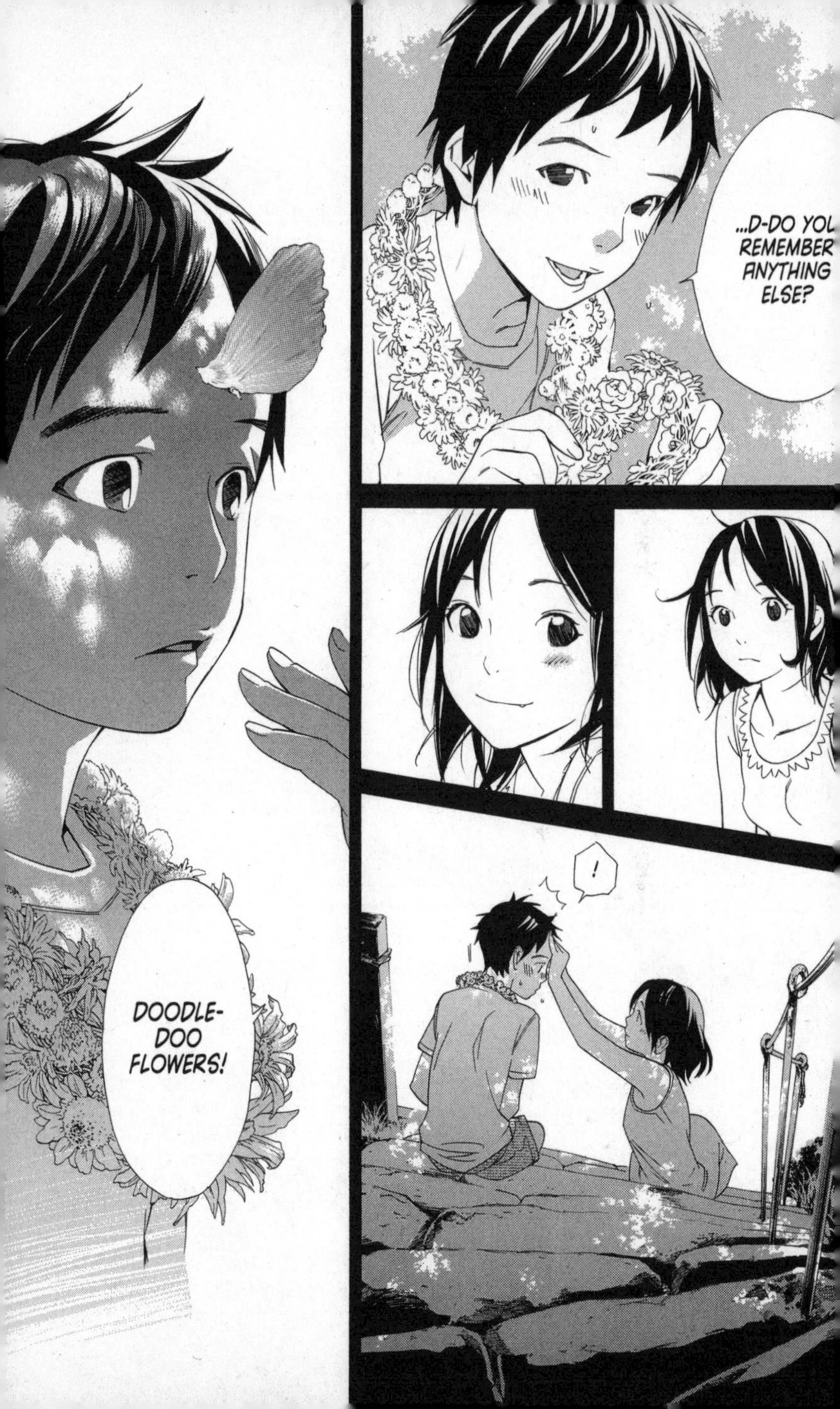
...D-DO YOU REMEMBER ANYTHING ELSE?
!
DOODLE-DOO FLOWERS!

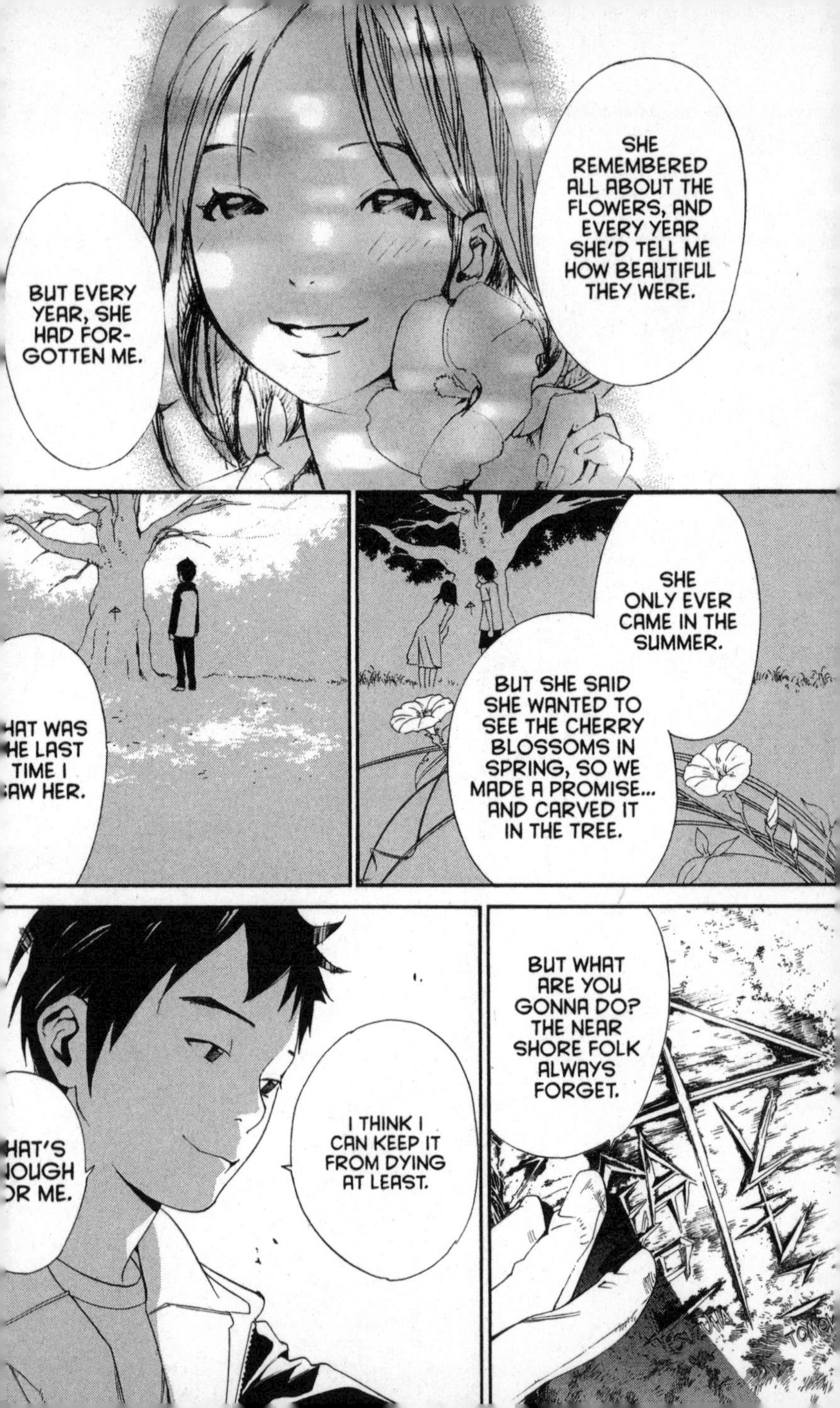
SHE REMEMBERED ALL ABOUT THE FLOWERS, AND EVERY YEAR SHE'D TELL ME HOW BEAUTIFUL THEY WERE.
BUT EVERY YEAR, SHE HAD FOR-GOTTEN ME.
SHE ONLY EVER CAME IN THE SUMMER.
BUT SHE SAID SHE WANTED TO SEE THE CHERRY BLOSSOMS IN SPRING, SO WE MADE A PROMISE... AND CARVED IT IN THE TREE.
HAT WAS HE LAST TIME I AW HER.
BUT WHAT ARE YOU GONNA DO? THE NEAR SHORE FOLK ALWAYS FORGET.
I THINK I CAN KEEP IT FROM DYING AT LEAST.
HAT'S NOUGH OR ME.

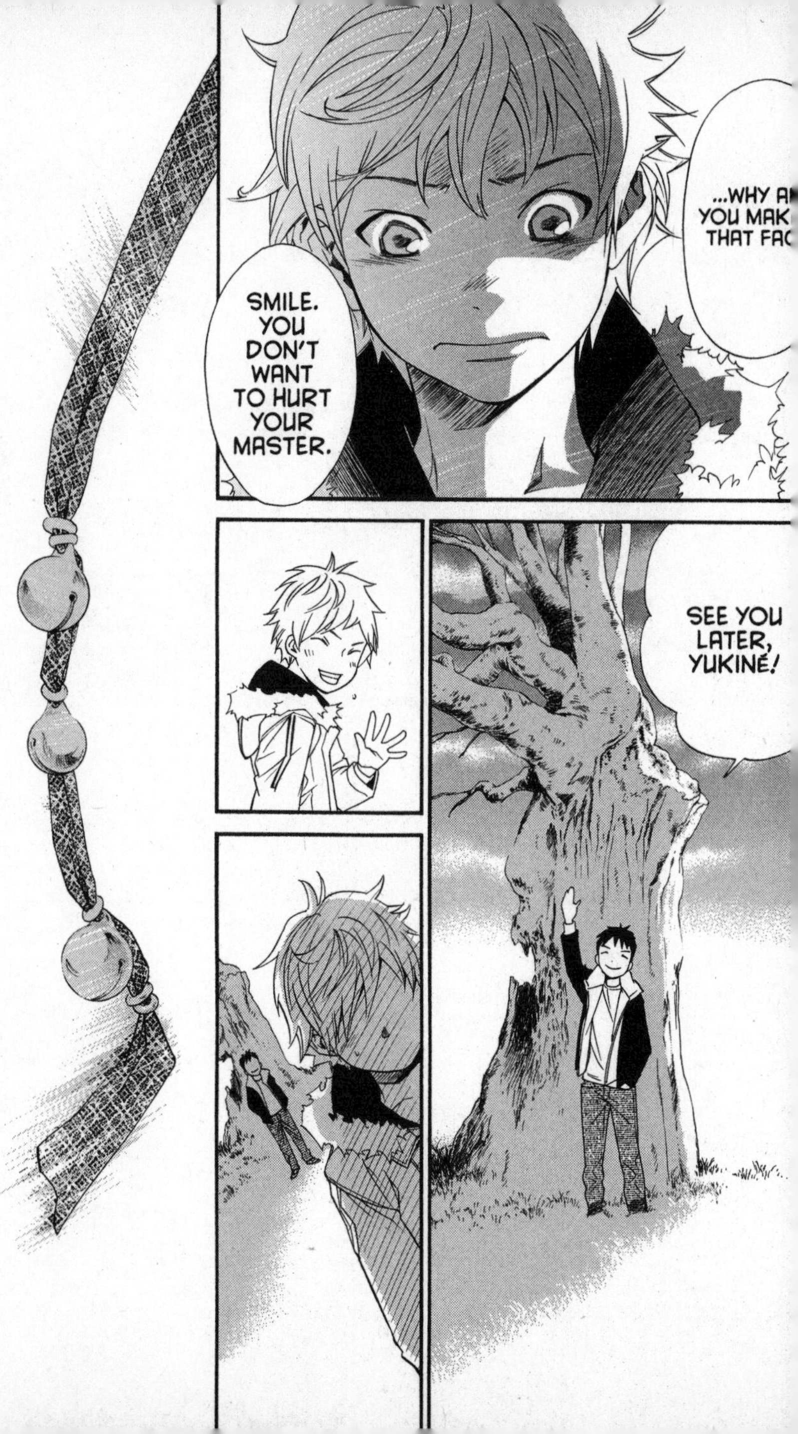
...WHY A YOU MAK THAT FAC
SMILE. YOU DON'T WANT TO HURT YOUR MASTER.
SEE YOU LATER, YUKINÉ!

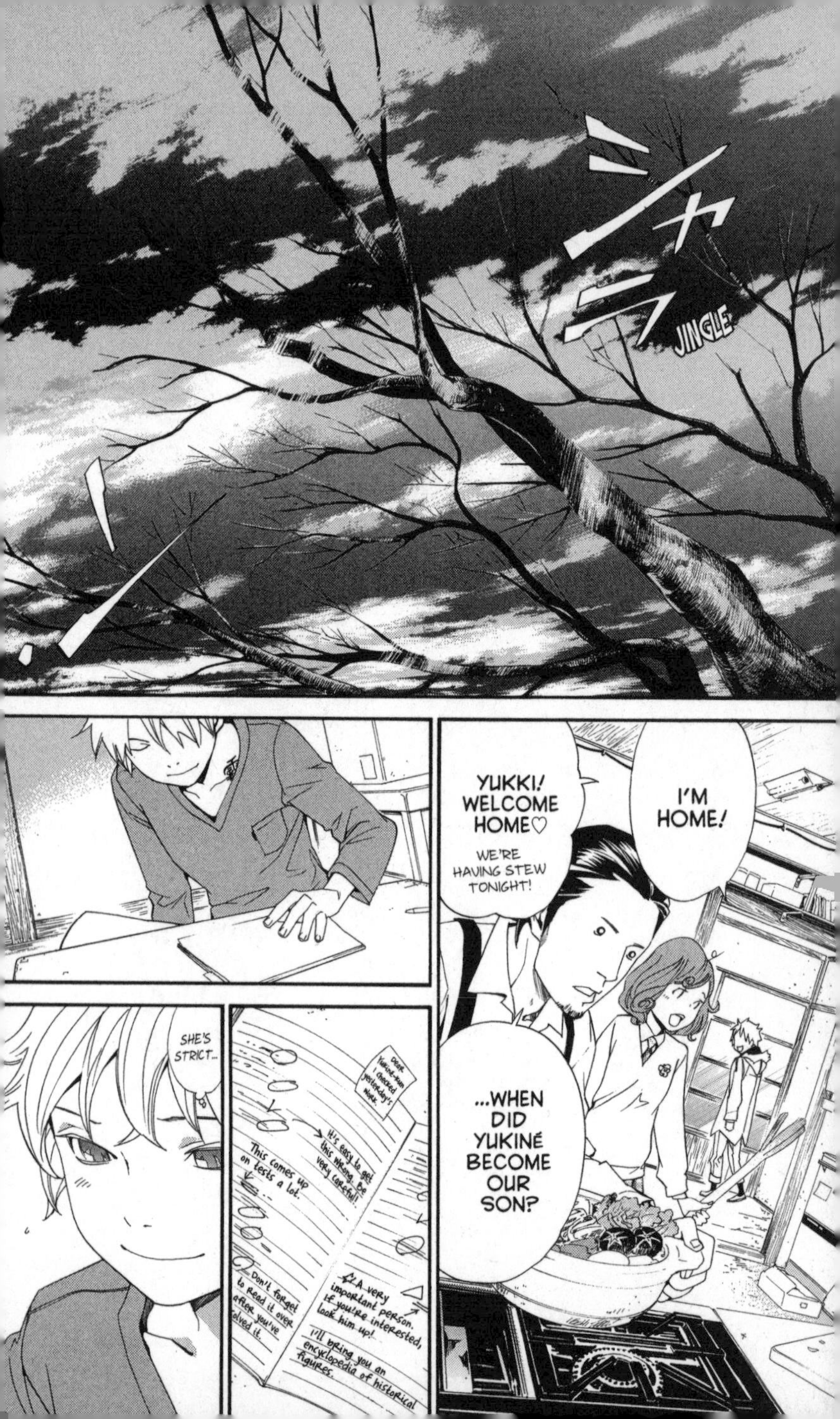
シャラ
JINGLE
I'M HOME!
YUKKI! WELCOME HOME♡
WE'RE HAVING STEW TONIGHT!
...WHEN DID YUKINÉ BECOME OUR SON?
Dear Yukine-kun I checked yesterday's work.
It's easy to get this wrong. Be very careful!
This comes up on tests a lot.
A very important person. If you're interested, look him up!
I'll bring you an encyclopedia of historical figures.
Don't forget to read it over after you've solved it.
SHE'S STRICT...

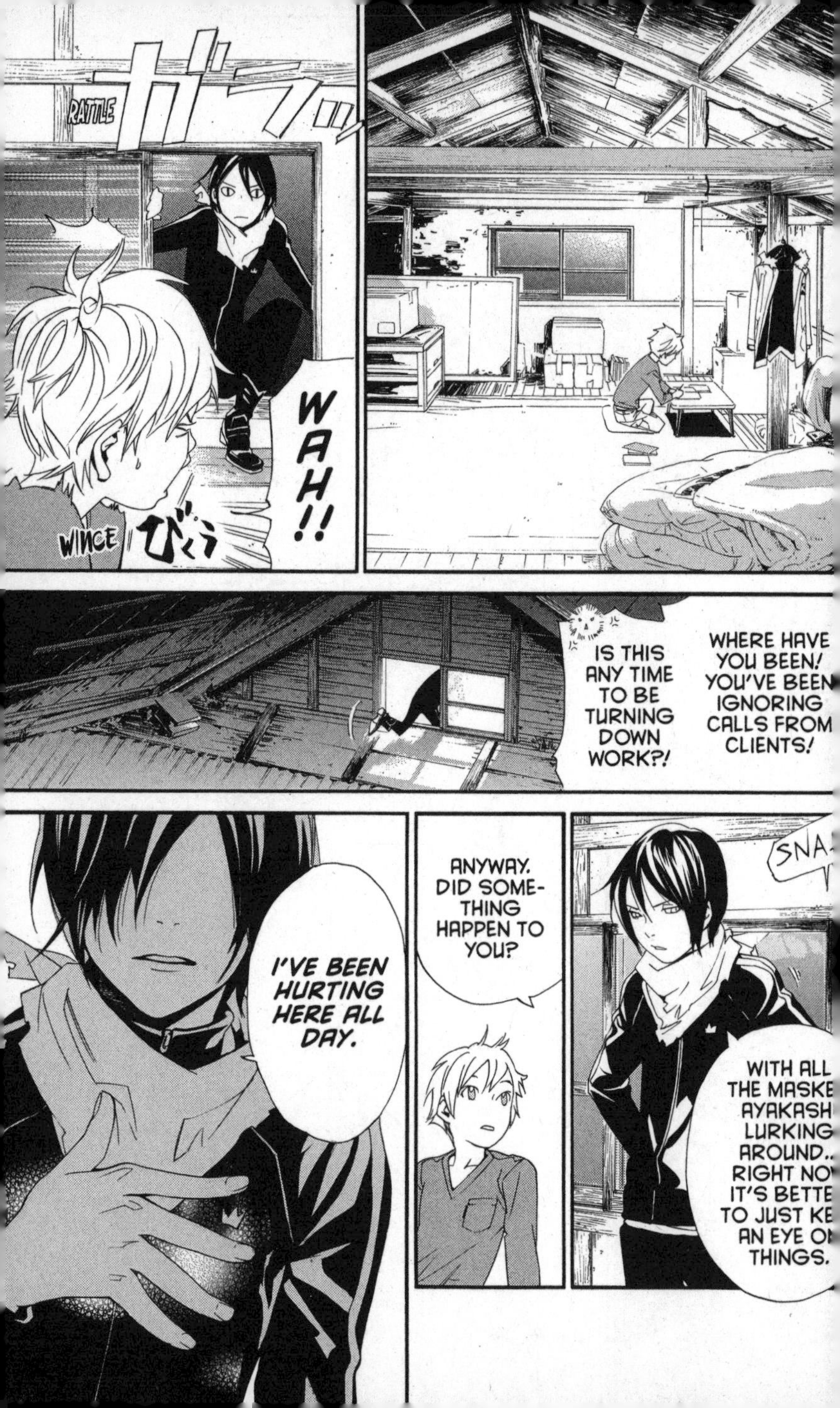

RATTLE
ガラッ
WAH!!
WINCE
びくっ
WHERE HAVE YOU BEEN! YOU'VE BEEN IGNORING CALLS FROM CLIENTS!
IS THIS ANY TIME TO BE TURNING DOWN WORK?!
SNA-
WITH ALL THE MASKE AYAKASH LURKING AROUND.. RIGHT NO IT'S BETTE TO JUST KE AN EYE ON THINGS.
ANYWAY. DID SOME-THING HAPPEN TO YOU?
I'VE BEEN HURTING HERE ALL DAY.

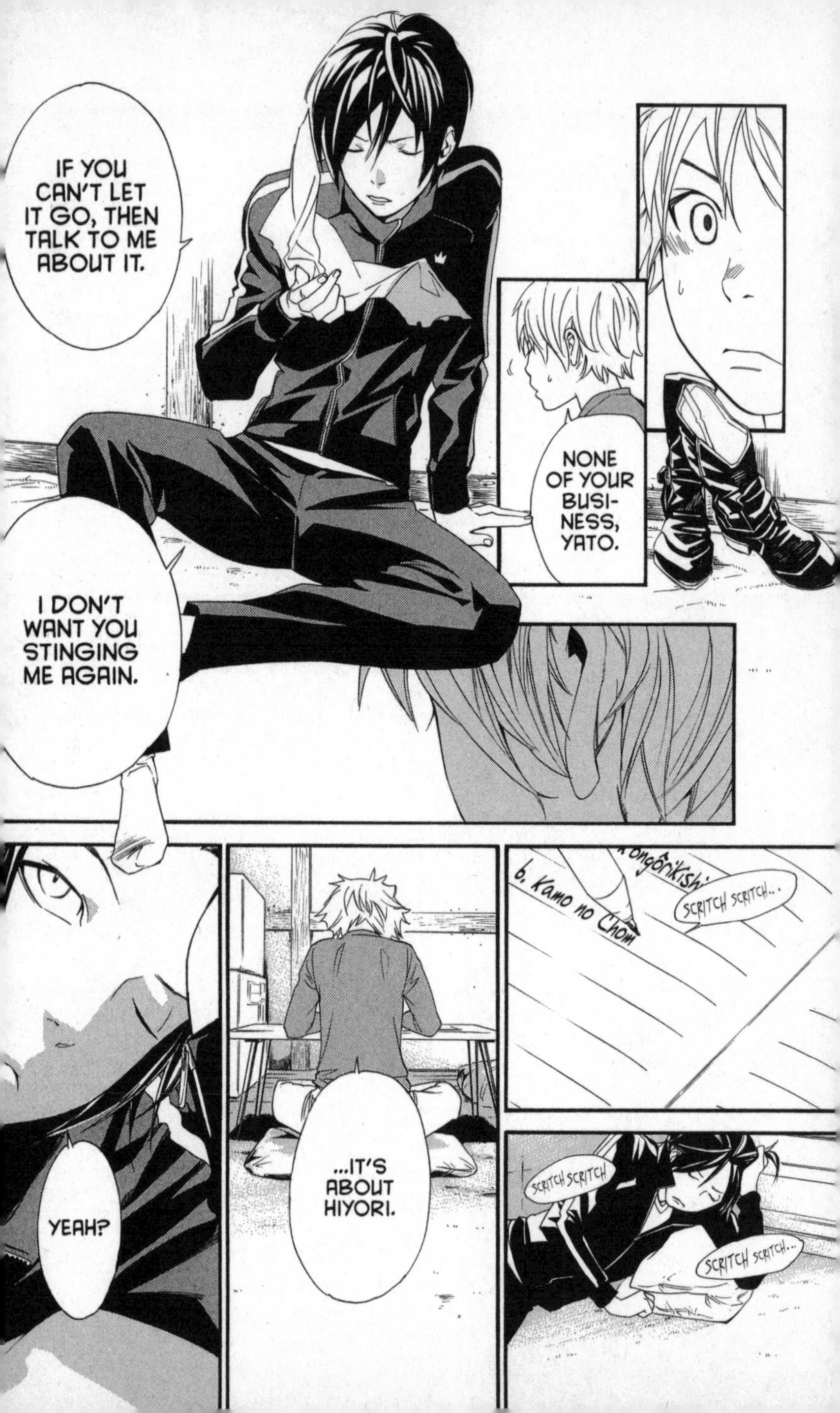
NONE OF YOUR BUSINESS, YATO.
IF YOU CAN'T LET IT GO, THEN TALK TO ME ABOUT IT.
I DON'T WANT YOU STINGING ME AGAIN.
6. Kamo no Chom
SCRITCH SCRITCH...
SCRITCH SCRITCH
SCRITCH SCRITCH...
...IT'S ABOUT HIYORI.
YEAH?

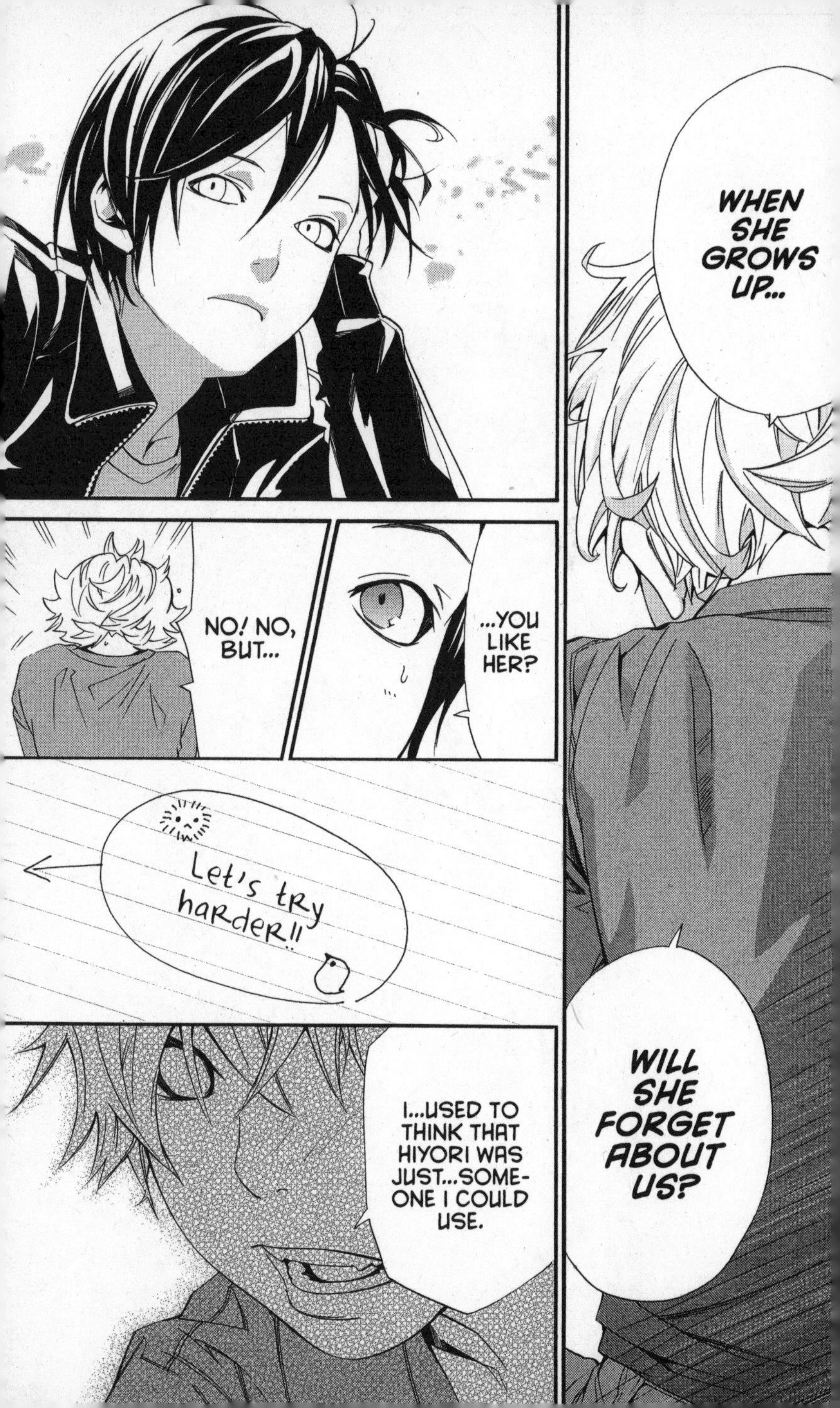
WHEN SHE GROWS UP...
WILL SHE FORGET ABOUT US?
...YOU LIKE HER?
NO! NO, BUT...
Let's try harder!!
I...USED TO THINK THAT HIYORI WAS JUST...SOME-ONE I COULD USE.

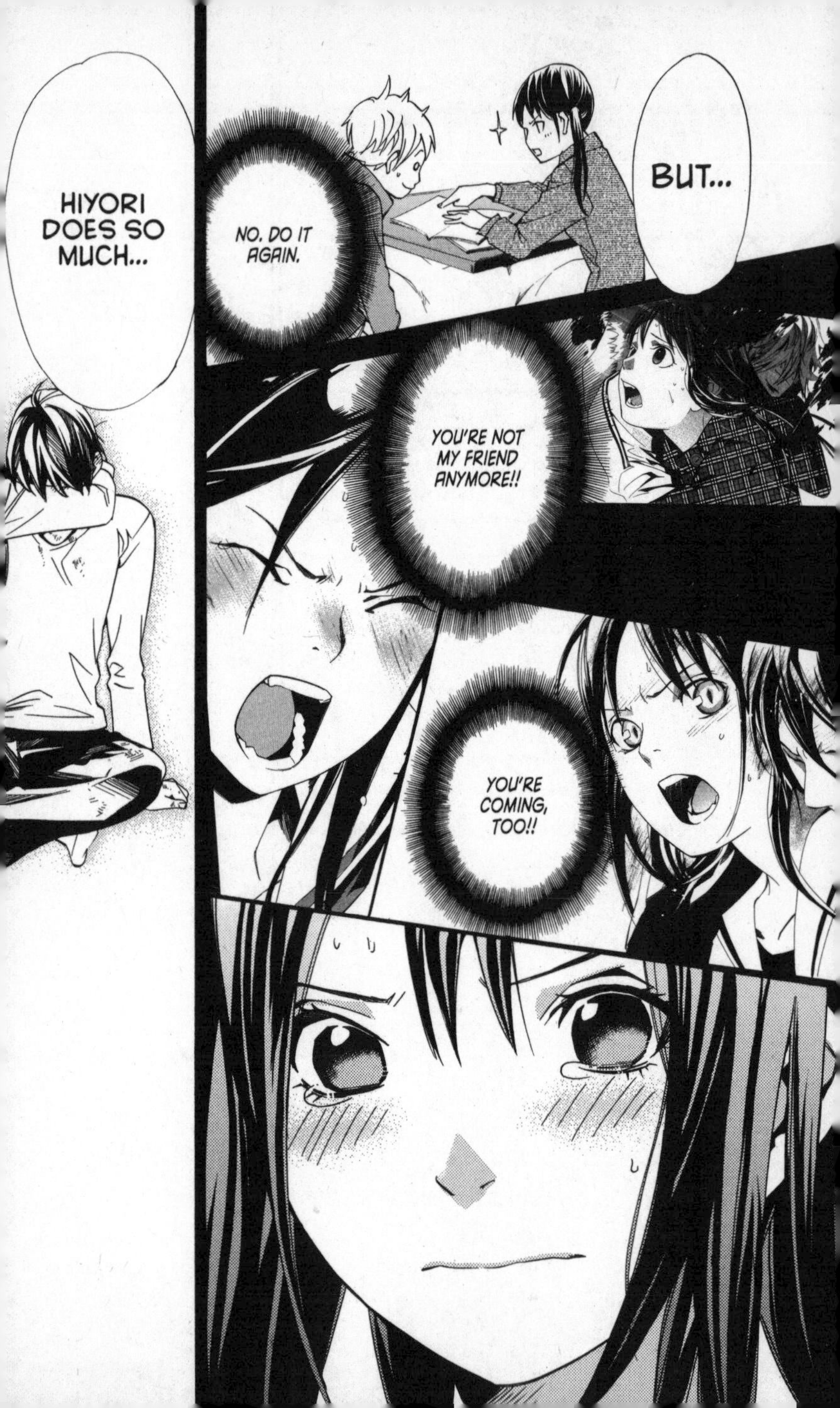
BUT...
NO. DO IT AGAIN.
YOU'RE NOT MY FRIEND ANYMORE!!
YOU'RE COMING, TOO!!
HIYORI DOES SO MUCH...

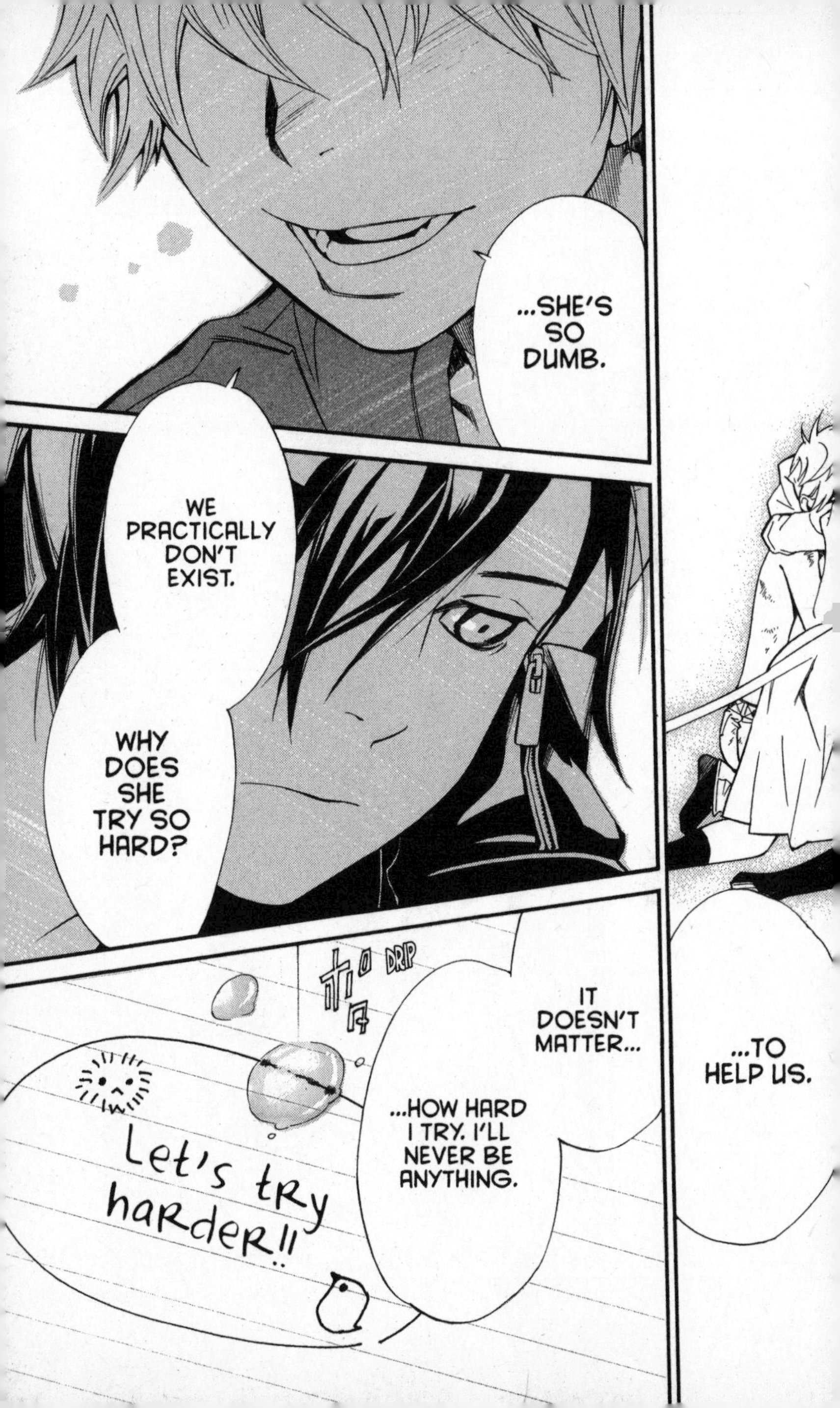
...SHE'S SO DUMB.
WE PRACTICALLY DON'T EXIST.
WHY DOES SHE TRY SO HARD?
...TO HELP US.
DRIP
IT DOESN'T MATTER...
...HOW HARD I TRY. I'LL NEVER BE ANYTHING.
Let's try harder!!

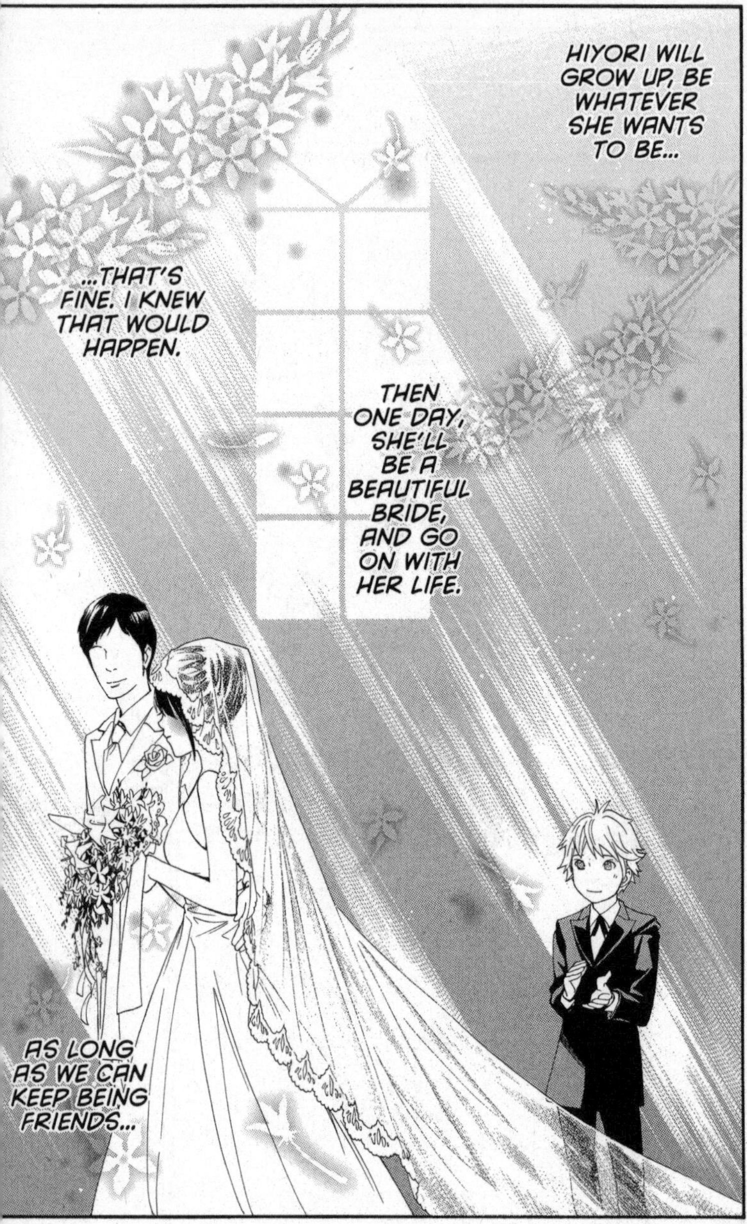
HIYORI WILL GROW UP, BE WHATEVER SHE WANTS TO BE...
THEN ONE DAY, SHE'LL BE A BEAUTIFUL BRIDE, AND GO ON WITH HER LIFE.
...THAT'S FINE. I KNEW THAT WOULD HAPPEN.
AS LONG AS WE CAN KEEP BEING FRIENDS...

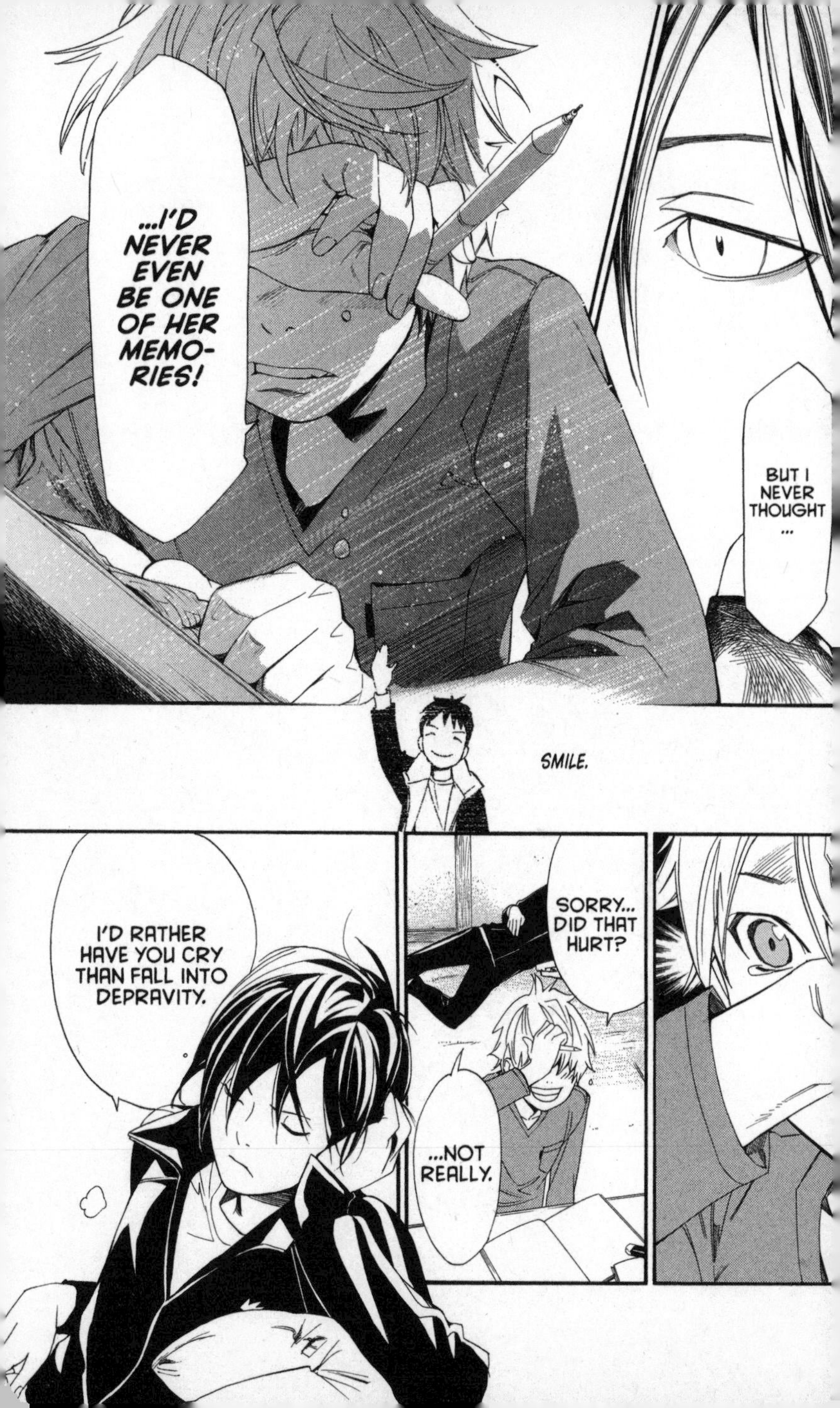
BUT I NEVER THOUGHT...
...I'D NEVER EVEN BE ONE OF HER MEMORIES!
SMILE.
SORRY... DID THAT HURT?
...NOT REALLY.
I'D RATHER HAVE YOU CRY THAN FALL INTO DEPRAVITY.

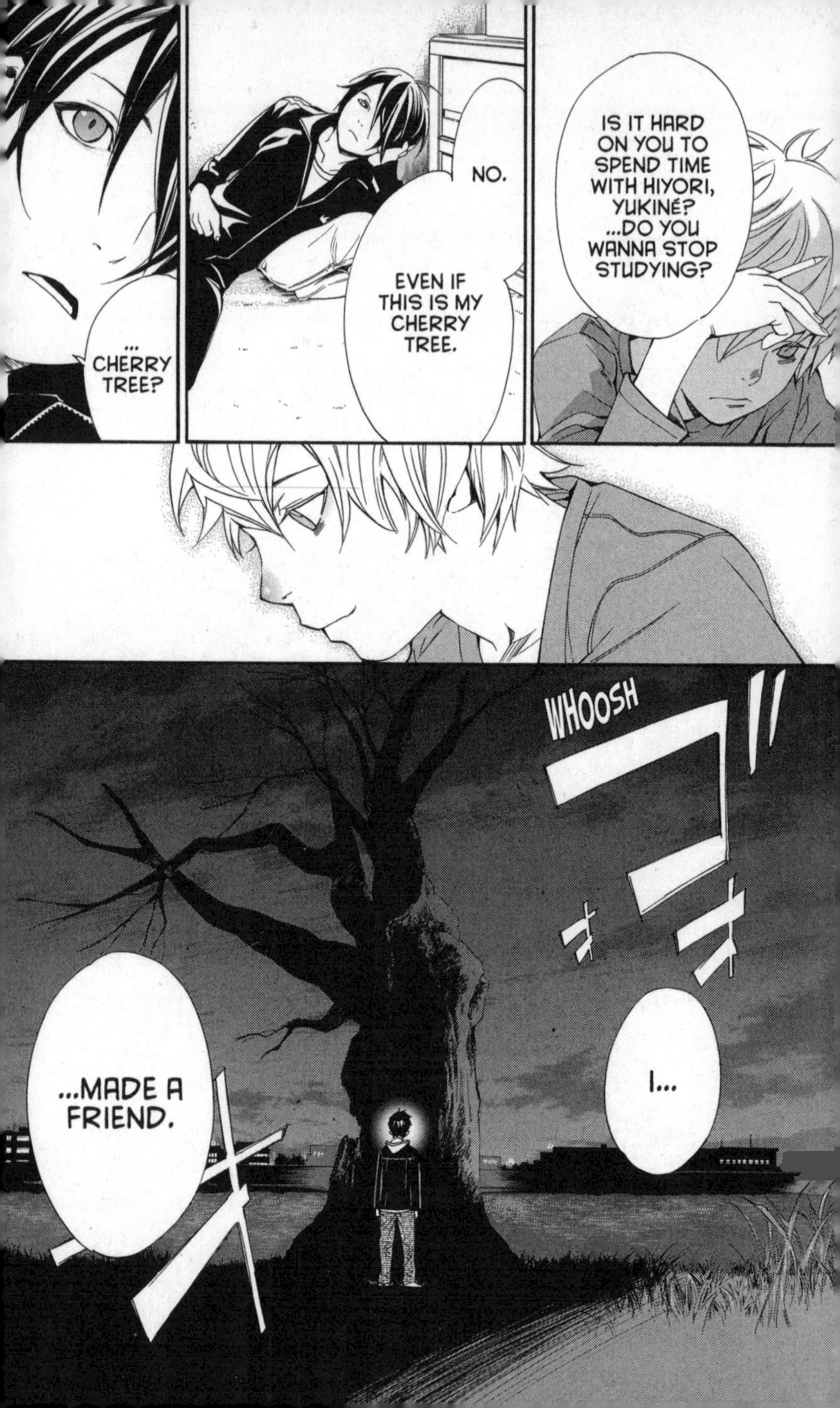
IS IT HARD ON YOU TO SPEND TIME WITH HIYORI, YUKINÉ? ...DO YOU WANNA STOP STUDYING?
NO.
EVEN IF THIS IS MY CHERRY TREE.
...CHERRY TREE?
WHOOSH
I...
...MADE A FRIEND.

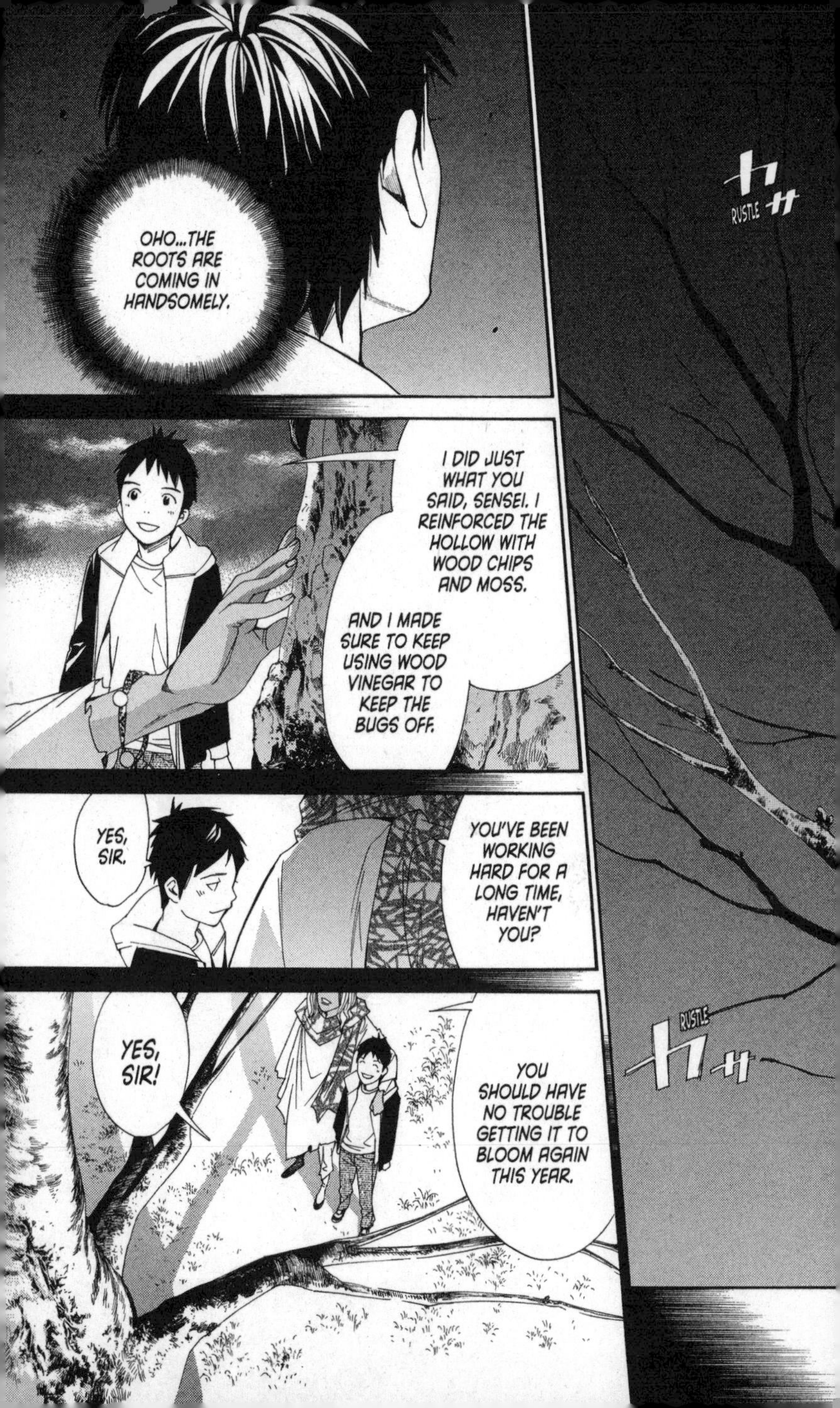
RUSTLE
RUSTLE
OHO...THE ROOTS ARE COMING IN HANDSOMELY.
I DID JUST WHAT YOU SAID, SENSEI. I REINFORCED THE HOLLOW WITH WOOD CHIPS AND MOSS.
AND I MADE SURE TO KEEP USING WOOD VINEGAR TO KEEP THE BUGS OFF.
YOU'VE BEEN WORKING HARD FOR A LONG TIME, HAVEN'T YOU?
YES, SIR.
YOU SHOULD HAVE NO TROUBLE GETTING IT TO BLOOM AGAIN THIS YEAR.
YES, SIR!

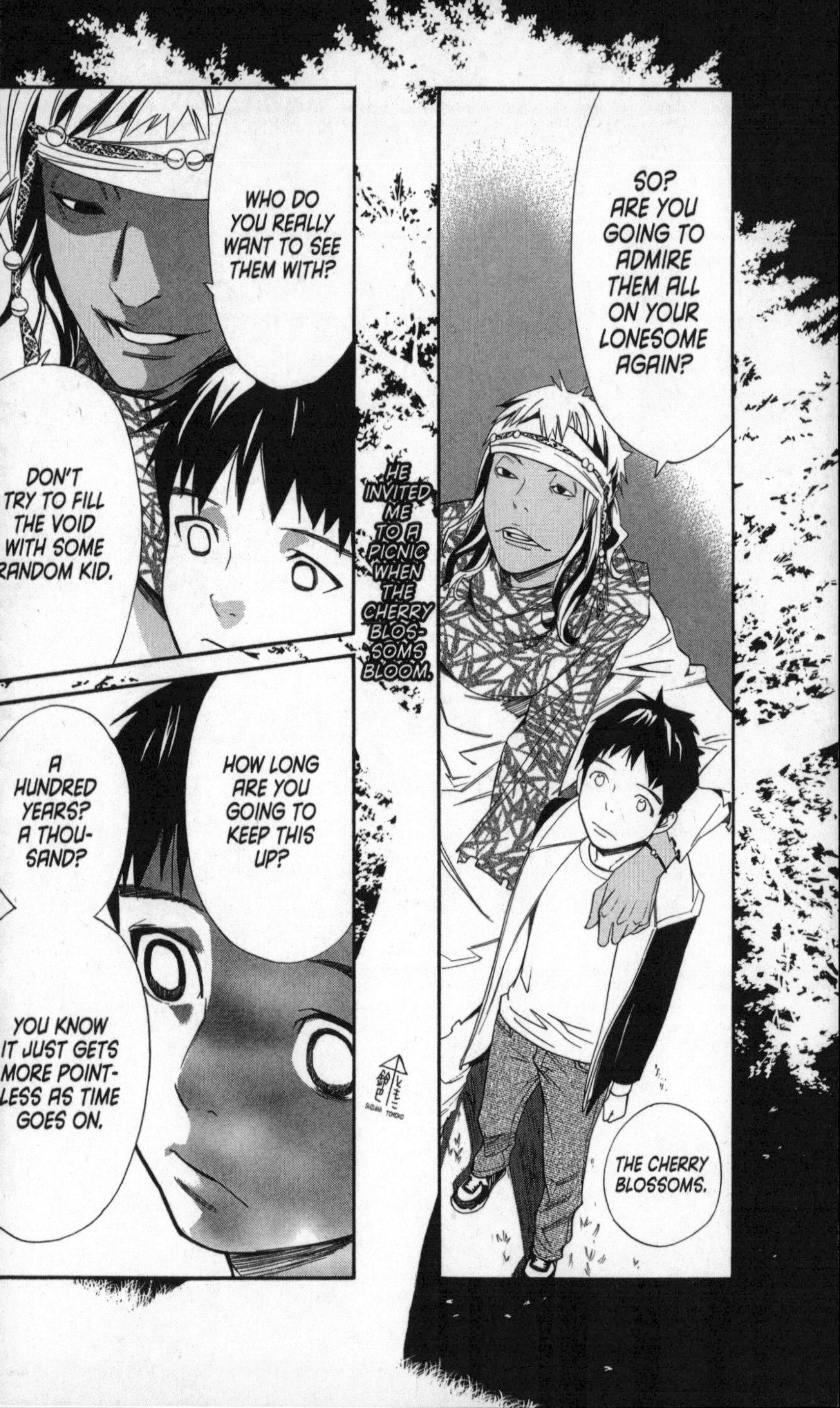
SO? ARE YOU GOING TO ADMIRE THEM ALL ON YOUR LONESOME AGAIN?
THE CHERRY BLOSSOMS.
HE INVITED ME TO A PICNIC WHEN THE CHERRY BLOSSOMS BLOOM.
WHO DO YOU REALLY WANT TO SEE THEM WITH?
DON'T TRY TO FILL THE VOID WITH SOME RANDOM KID.
HOW LONG ARE YOU GOING TO KEEP THIS UP?
A HUNDRED YEARS? A THOUSAND?
YOU KNOW IT JUST GETS MORE POINT-LESS AS TIME GOES ON.

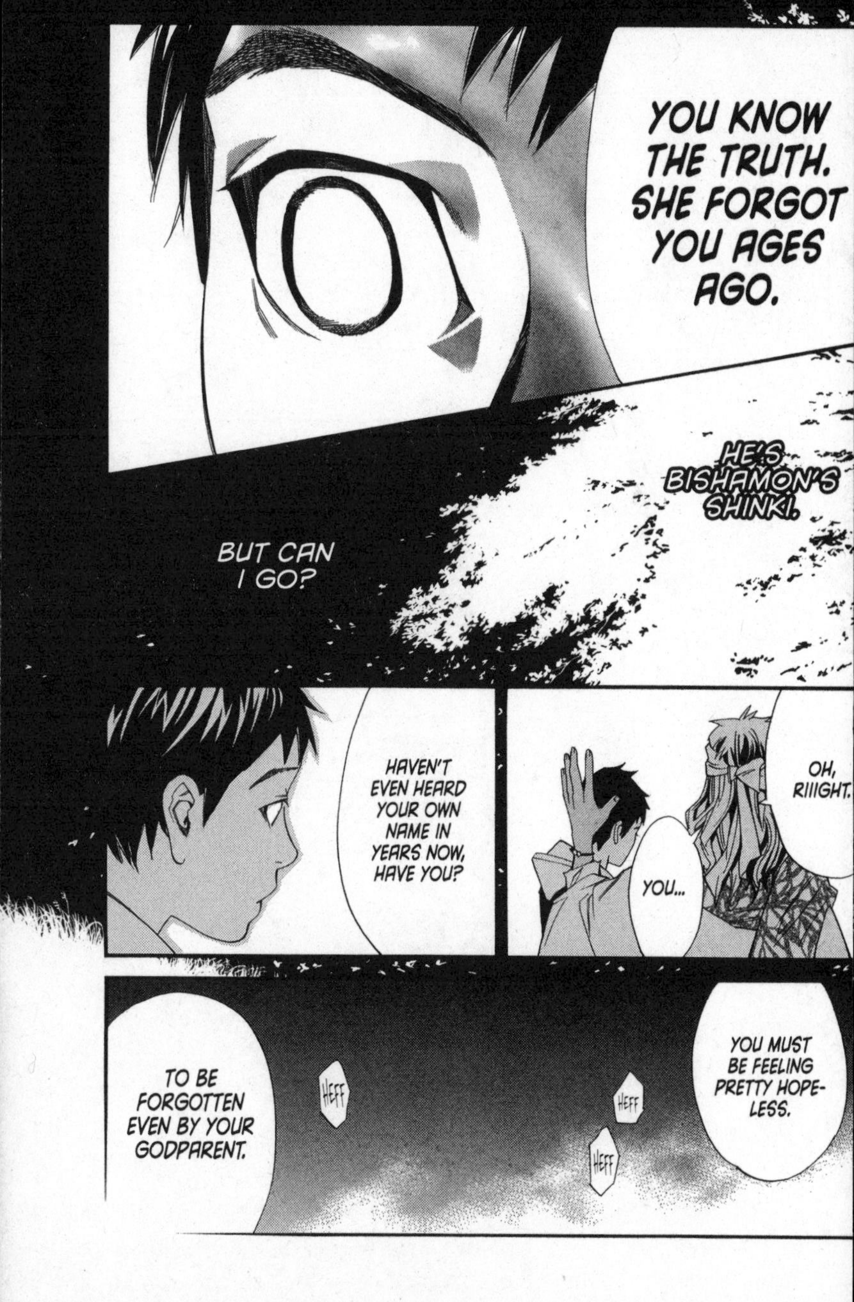
YOU KNOW THE TRUTH. SHE FORGOT YOU AGES AGO.
HE'S BISHAMON'S SHINKI.
BUT CAN I GO?
OH, RIIIGHT.
YOU...
HAVEN'T EVEN HEARD YOUR OWN NAME IN YEARS NOW, HAVE YOU?
YOU MUST BE FEELING PRETTY HOPE-LESS.
HEFF
HEFF
HEFF
TO BE FORGOTTEN EVEN BY YOUR GODPARENT.

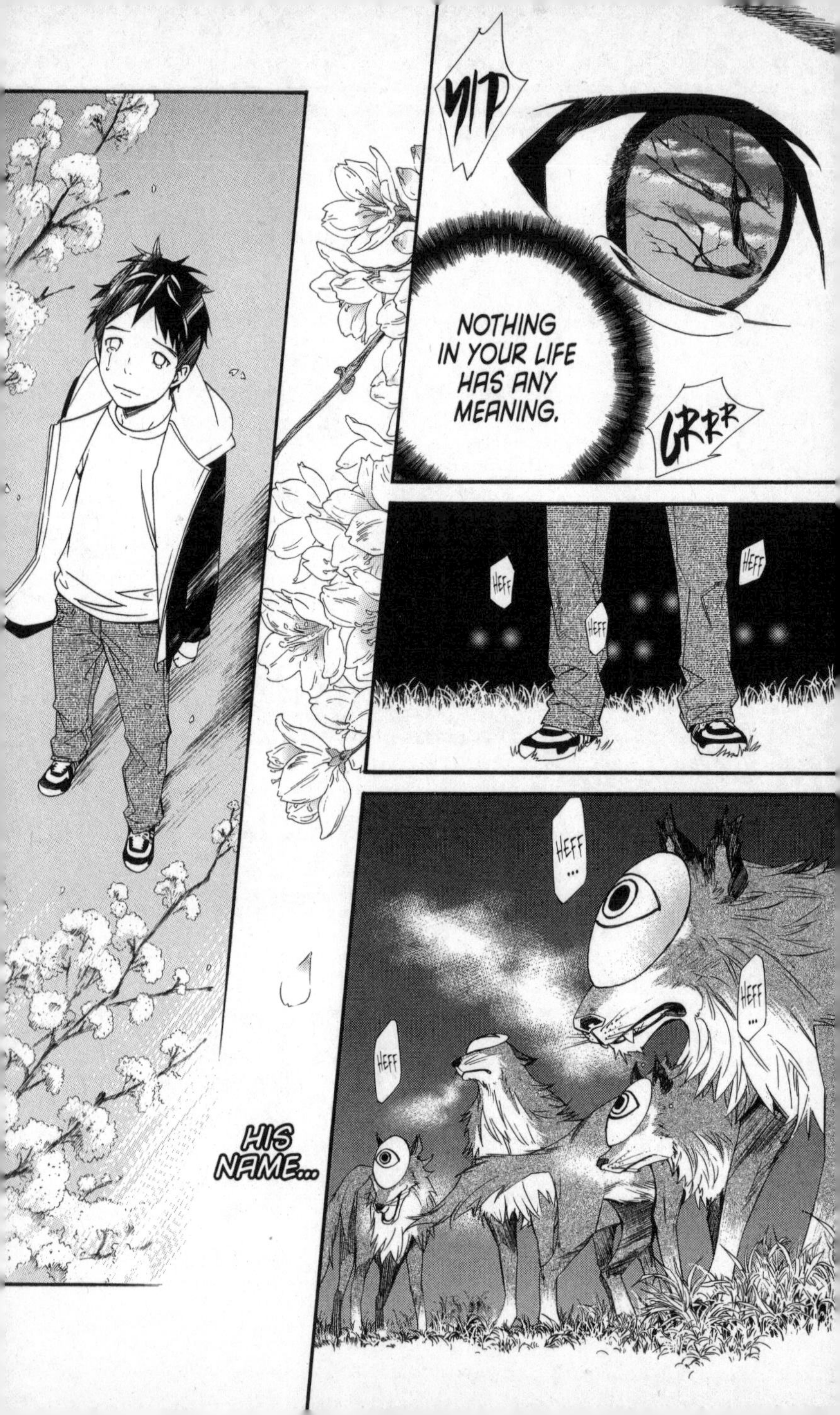
YIP
NOTHING IN YOUR LIFE HAS ANY MEANING.
GRRR
HEFF
HEFF
HEFF
HEFF...
HEFF...
HEFF
HIS NAME...

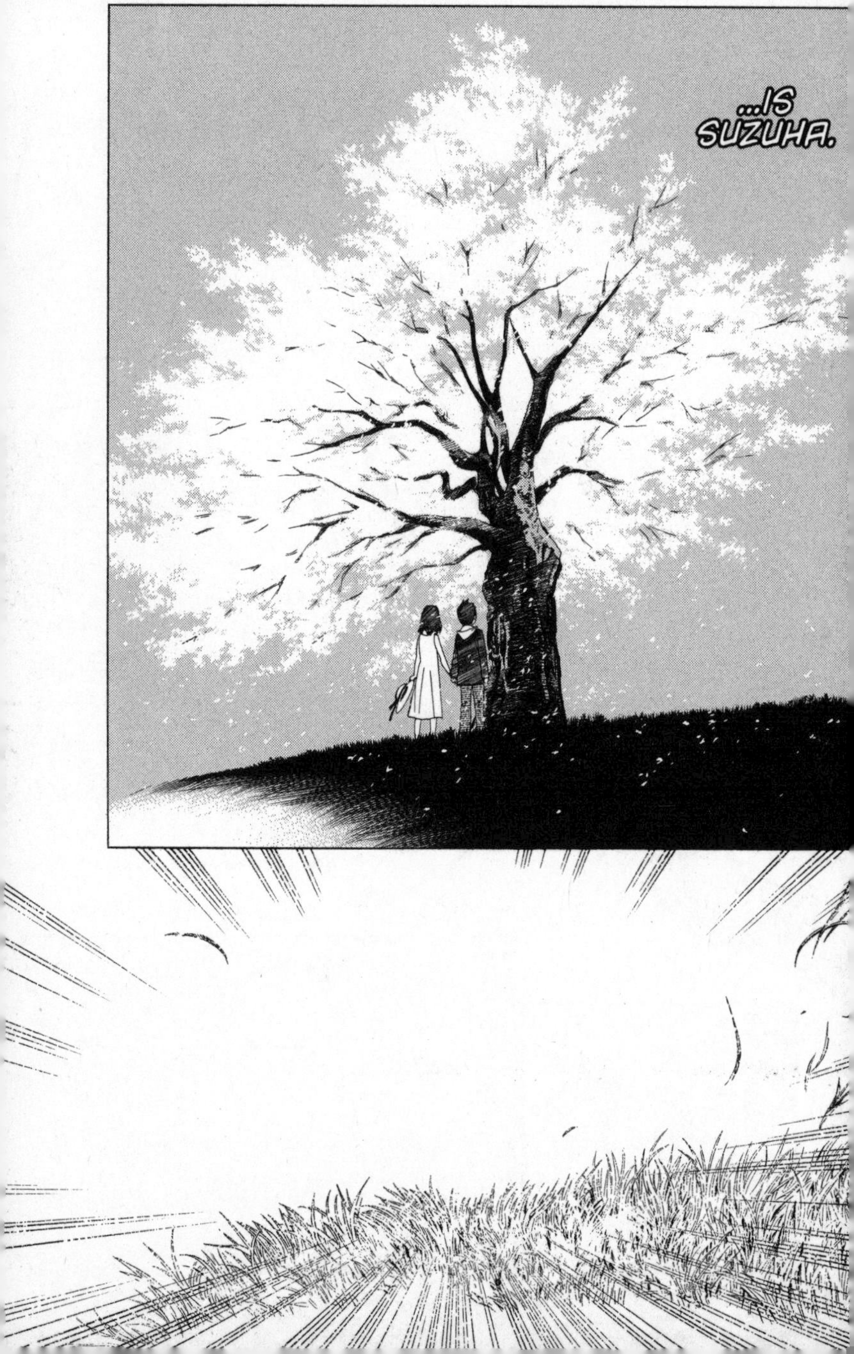
...IS SUZUHA.

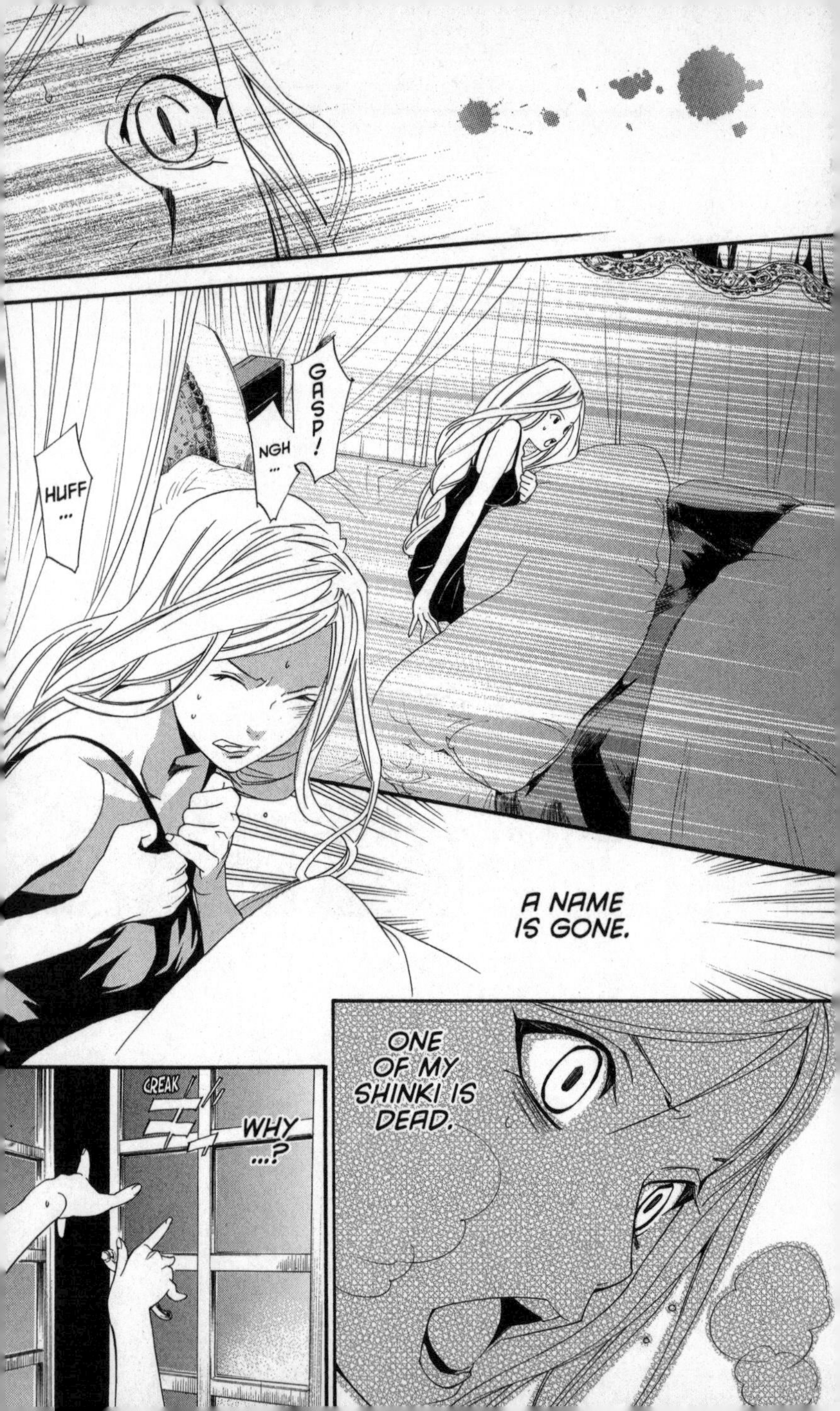
GASP!
NGH...
HUFF...
A NAME IS GONE.
ONE OF MY SHINKI IS DEAD.
CREAK
WHY...?

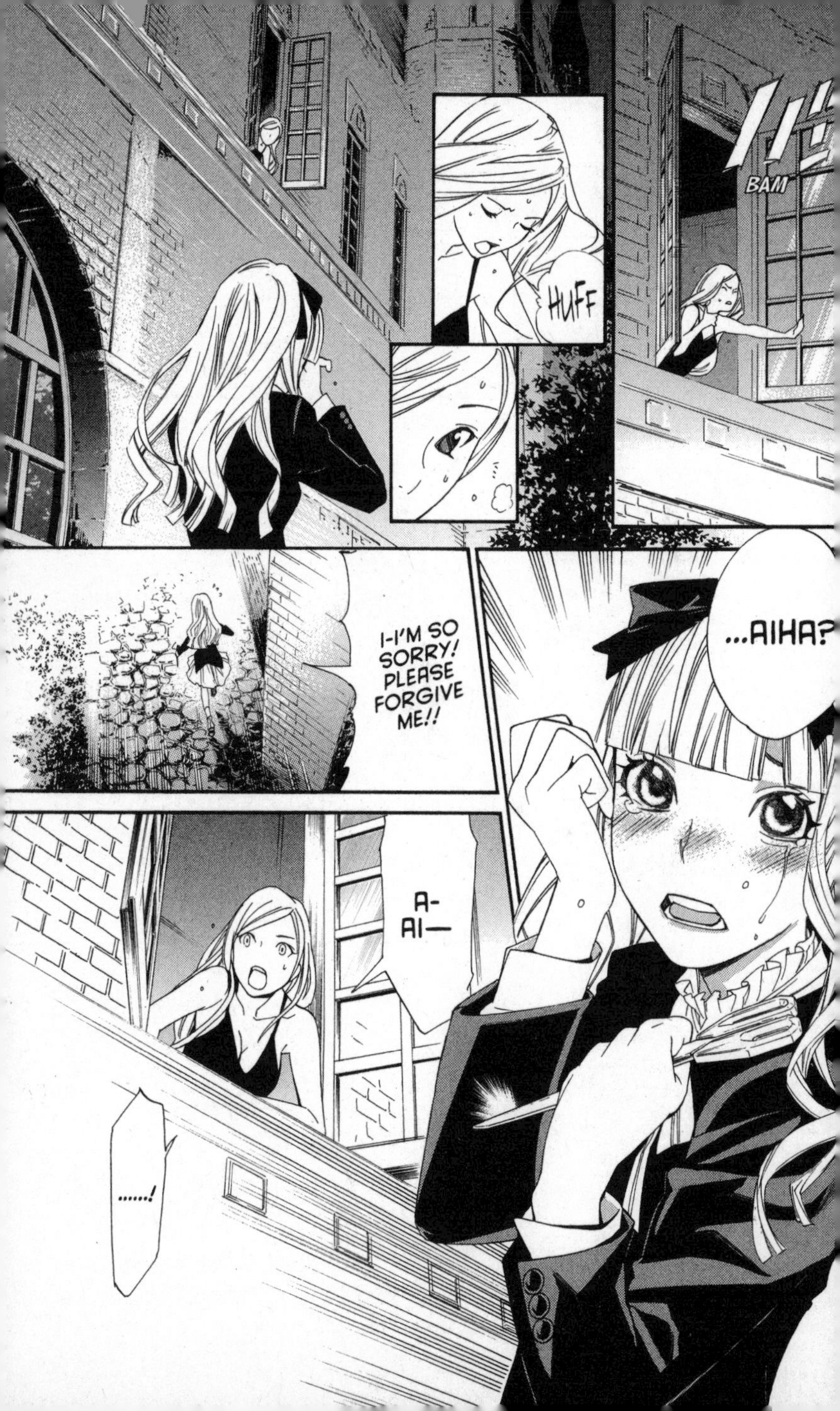
BAM
HUFF
...AIHA?
I-I'M SO SORRY! PLEASE FORGIVE ME!!
A- AI—
......!

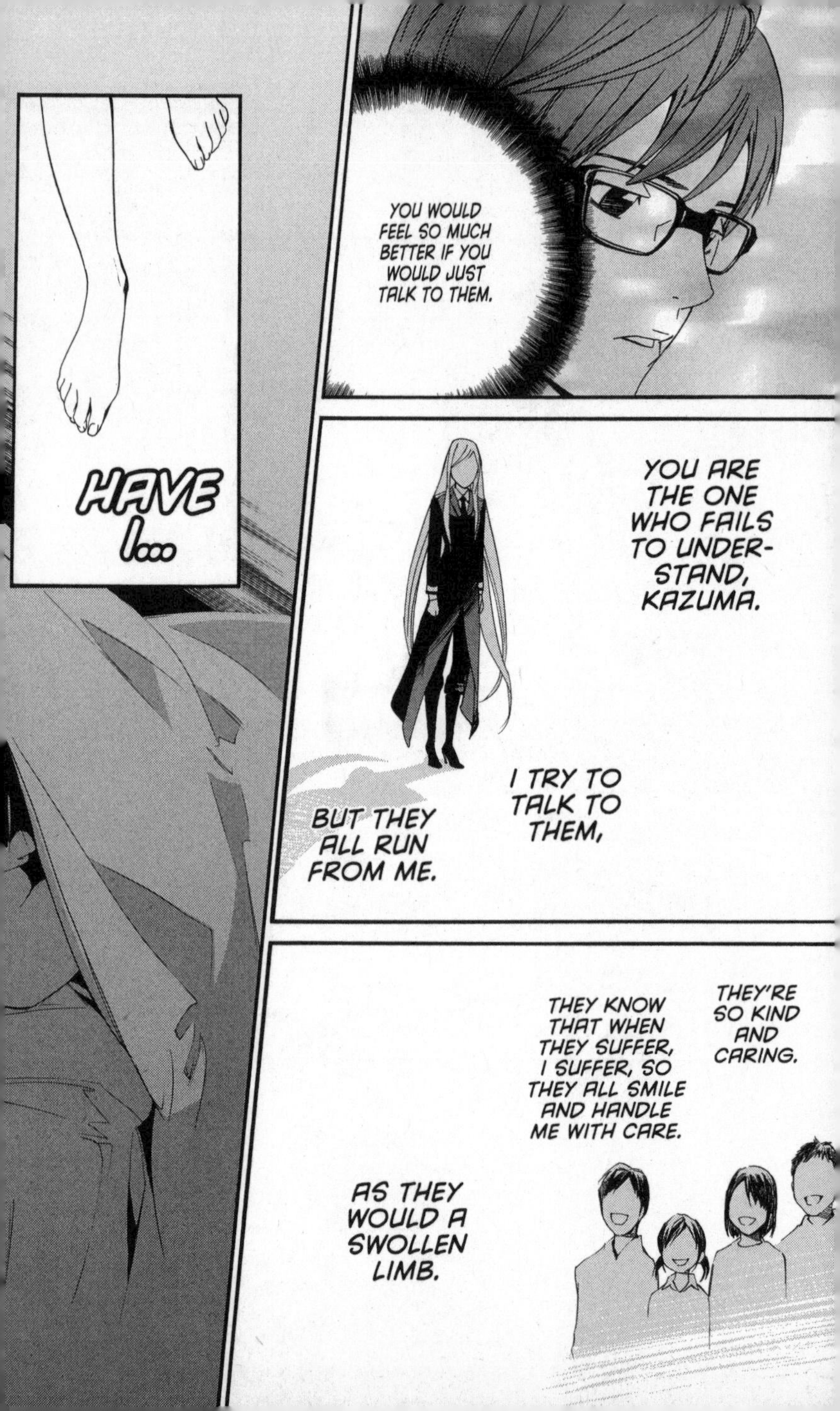
YOU WOULD FEEL SO MUCH BETTER IF YOU WOULD JUST TALK TO THEM.
HAVE I...
YOU ARE THE ONE WHO FAILS TO UNDER-STAND, KAZUMA.
I TRY TO TALK TO THEM,
BUT THEY ALL RUN FROM ME.
THEY'RE SO KIND AND CARING.
THEY KNOW THAT WHEN THEY SUFFER, I SUFFER, SO THEY ALL SMILE AND HANDLE ME WITH CARE.
AS THEY WOULD A SWOLLEN LIMB.

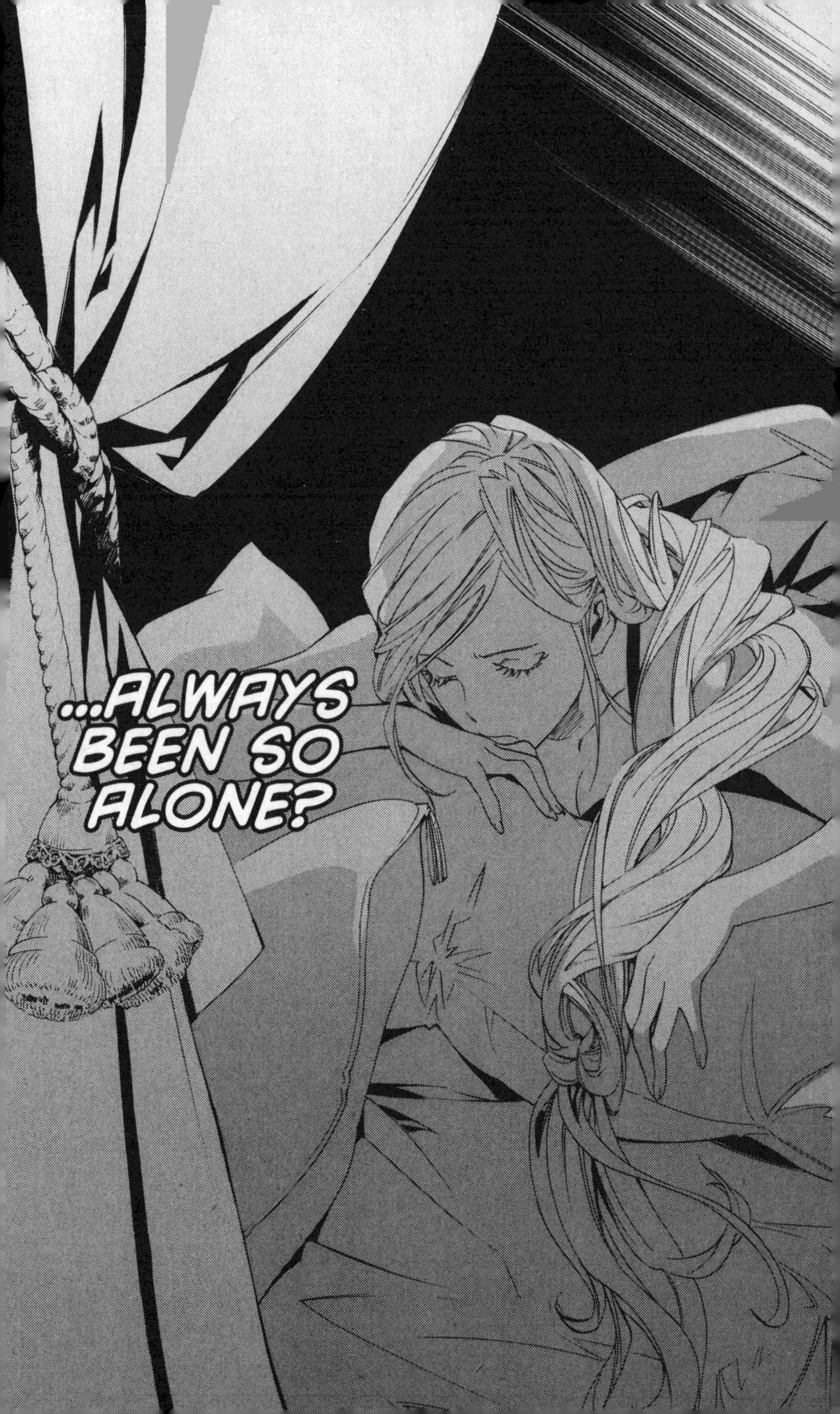
...ALWAYS BEEN SO ALONE?

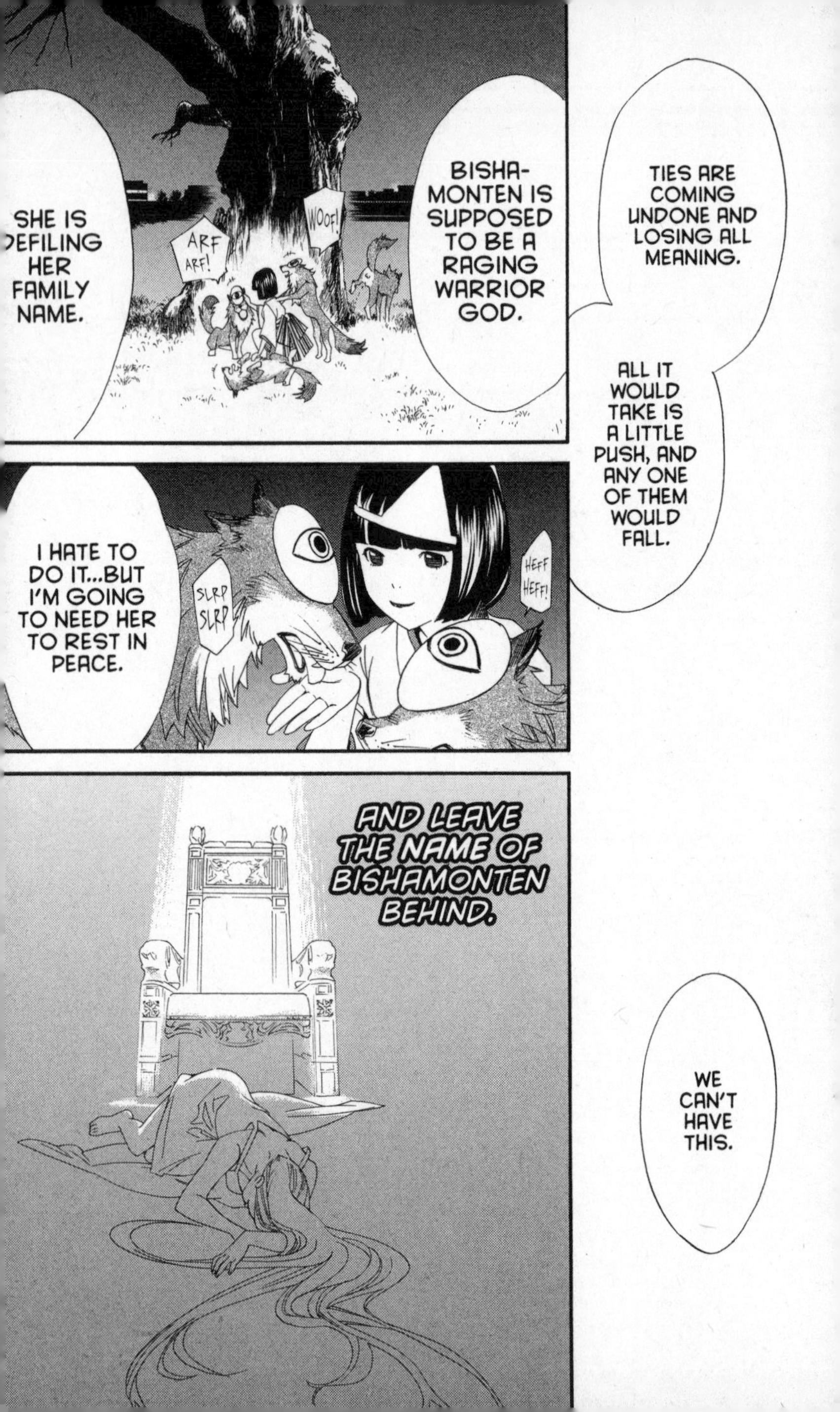
TIES ARE COMING UNDONE AND LOSING ALL MEANING.
BISHAMONTEN IS SUPPOSED TO BE A RAGING WARRIOR GOD.
WOOF!
ARF ARF!
SHE IS DEFILING HER FAMILY NAME.
ALL IT WOULD TAKE IS A LITTLE PUSH, AND ANY ONE OF THEM WOULD FALL.
HEFF HEFF!
SLRP SLRP
I HATE TO DO IT...BUT I'M GOING TO NEED HER TO REST IN PEACE.
AND LEAVE THE NAME OF BISHAMONTEN BEHIND.
WE CAN'T HAVE THIS.

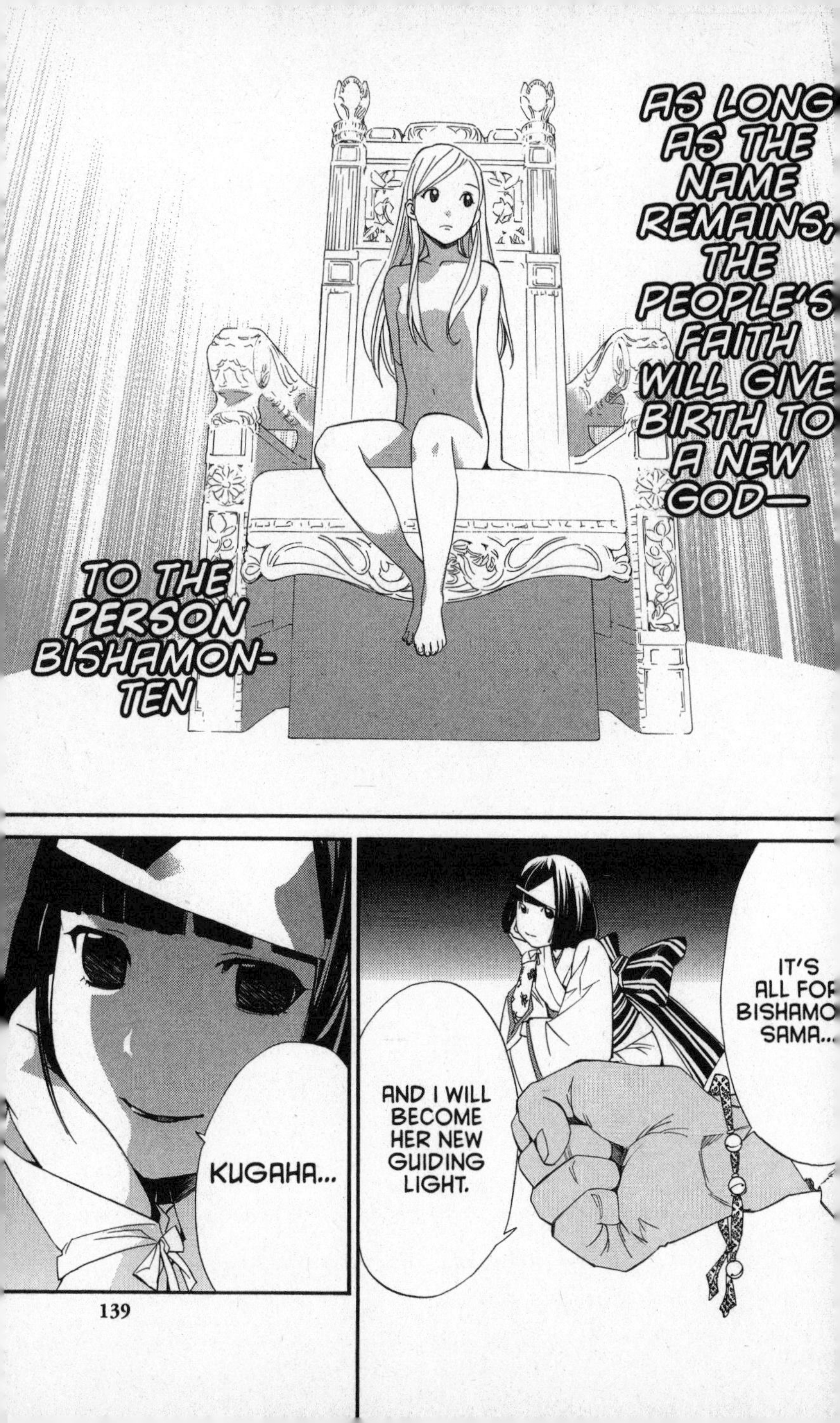
AS LONG AS THE NAME REMAINS, THE PEOPLE'S FAITH WILL GIVE BIRTH TO A NEW GOD—
TO THE PERSON BISHAMON-TEN
IT'S ALL FOR BISHAMO SAMA...
AND I WILL BECOME HER NEW GUIDING LIGHT.
KUGAHA...

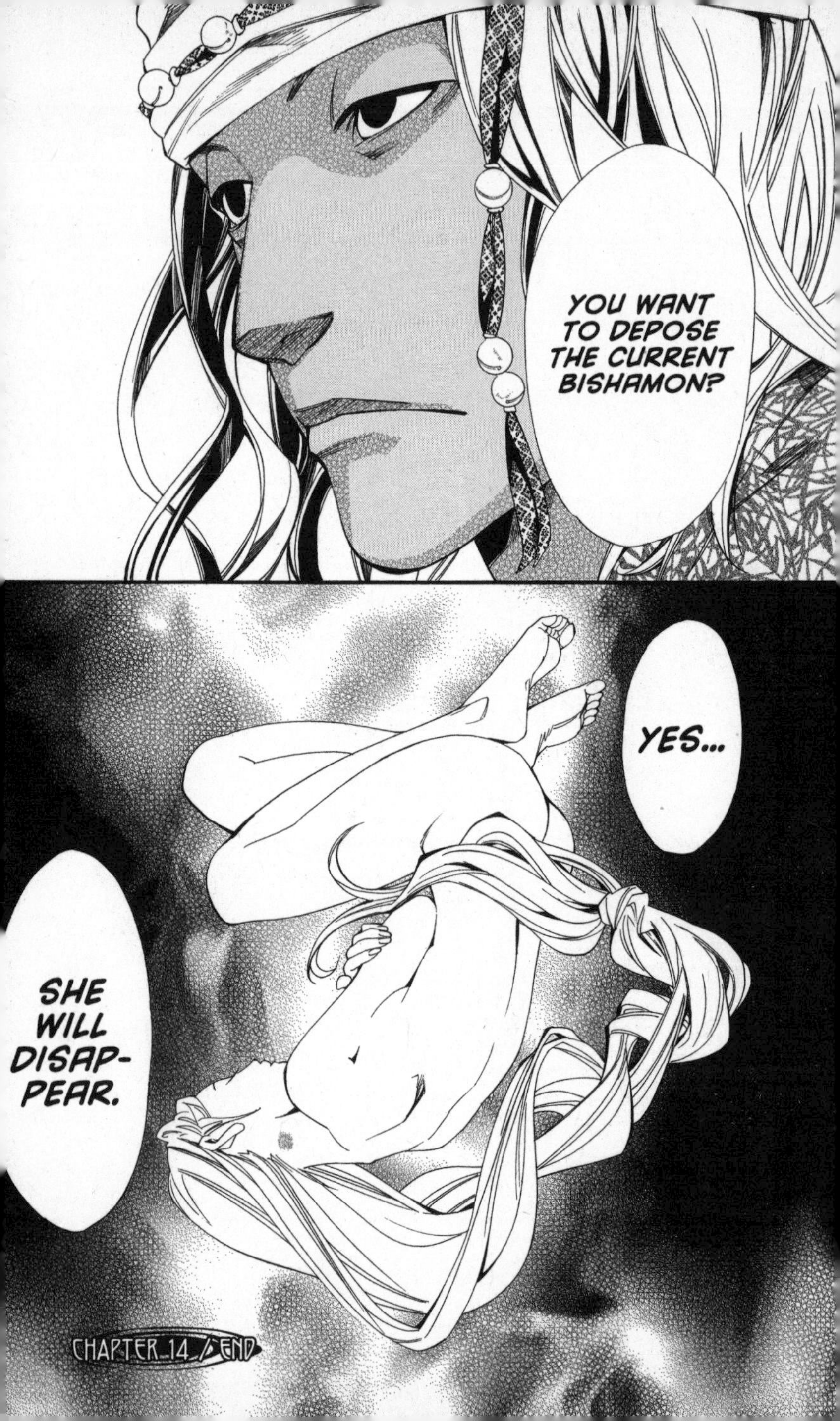
YOU WANT TO DEPOSE THE CURRENT BISHAMON?
YES...
SHE WILL DISAP-PEAR.
CHAPTER 14 / END

野

曳

神

壐

首

帥

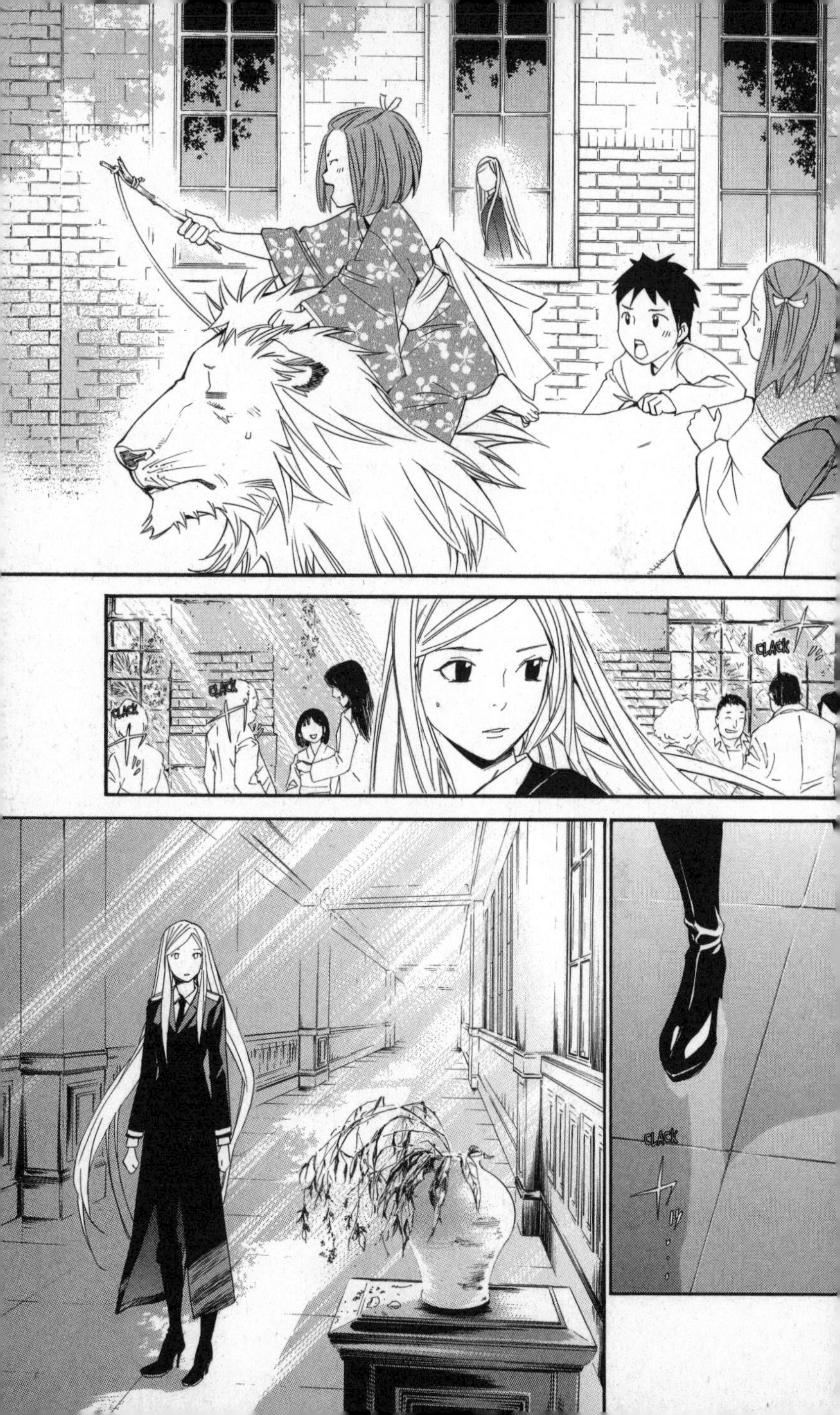
CLACK
CLACK
CLACK
CLACK

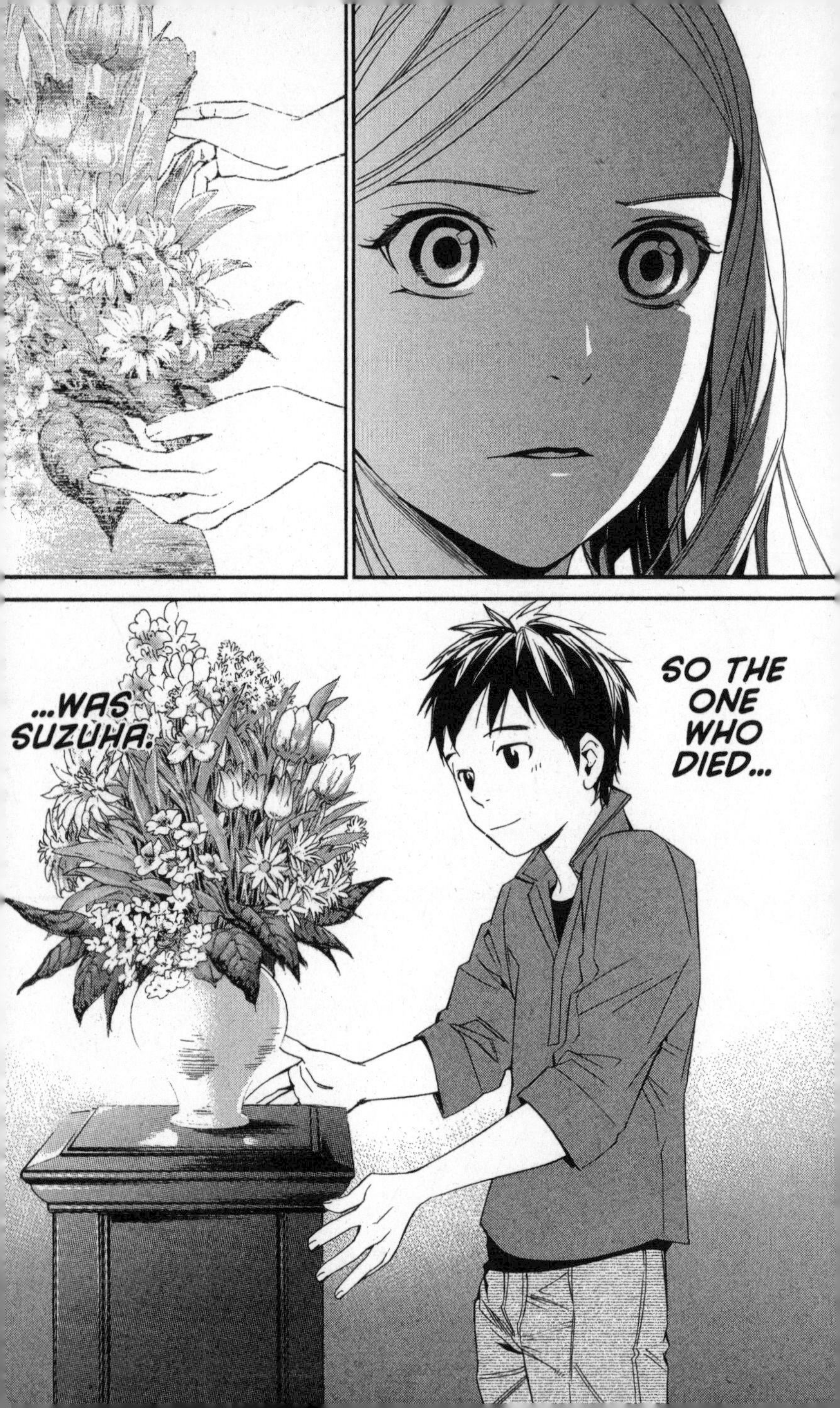
SO THE ONE WHO DIED...
...WAS SUZUHA.

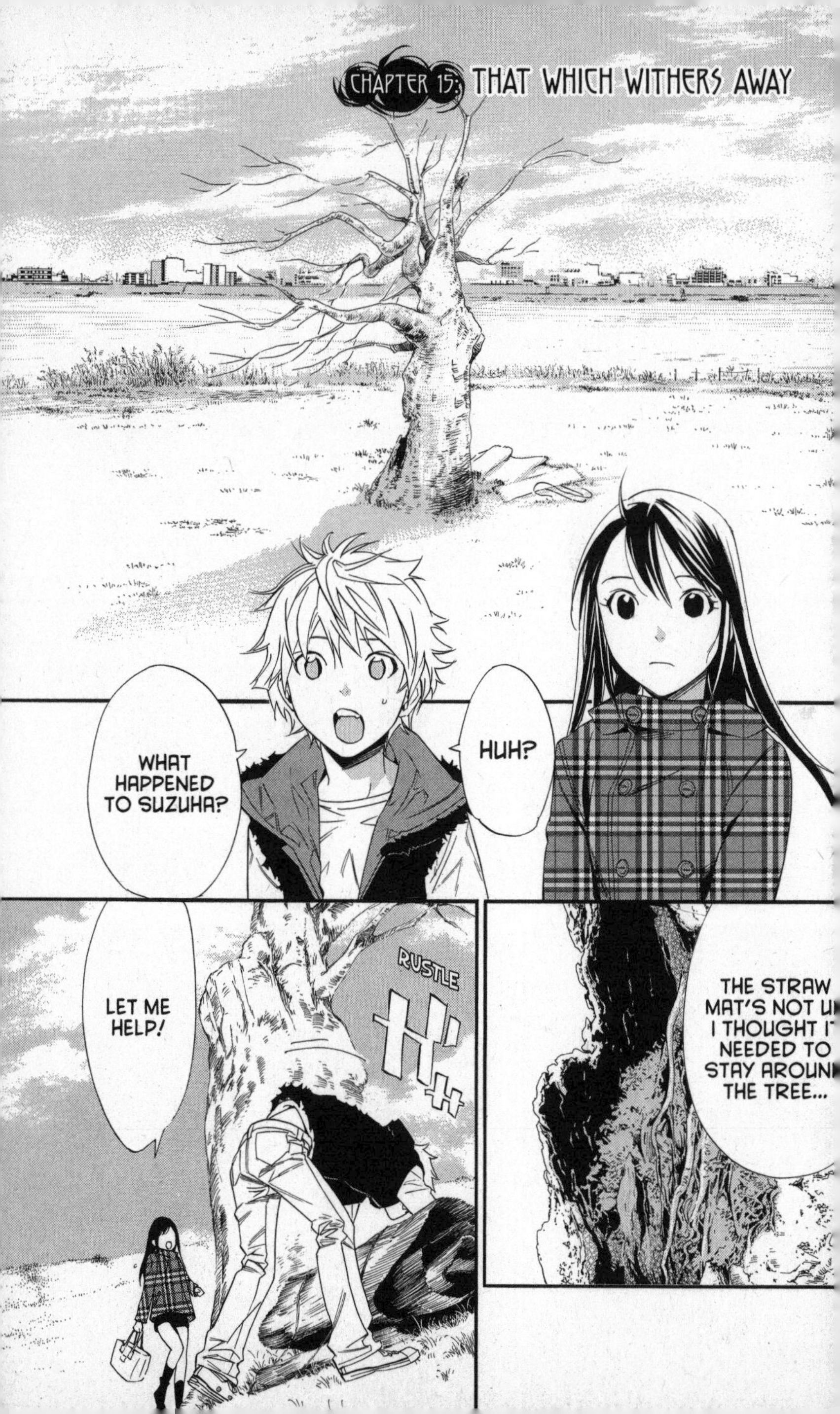
CHAPTER 15: THAT WHICH WITHERS AWAY
HUH?
WHAT HAPPENED TO SUZUHA?
THE STRAW MAT'S NOT U I THOUGHT I NEEDED TO STAY AROUN THE TREE...
RUSTLE
LET ME HELP!

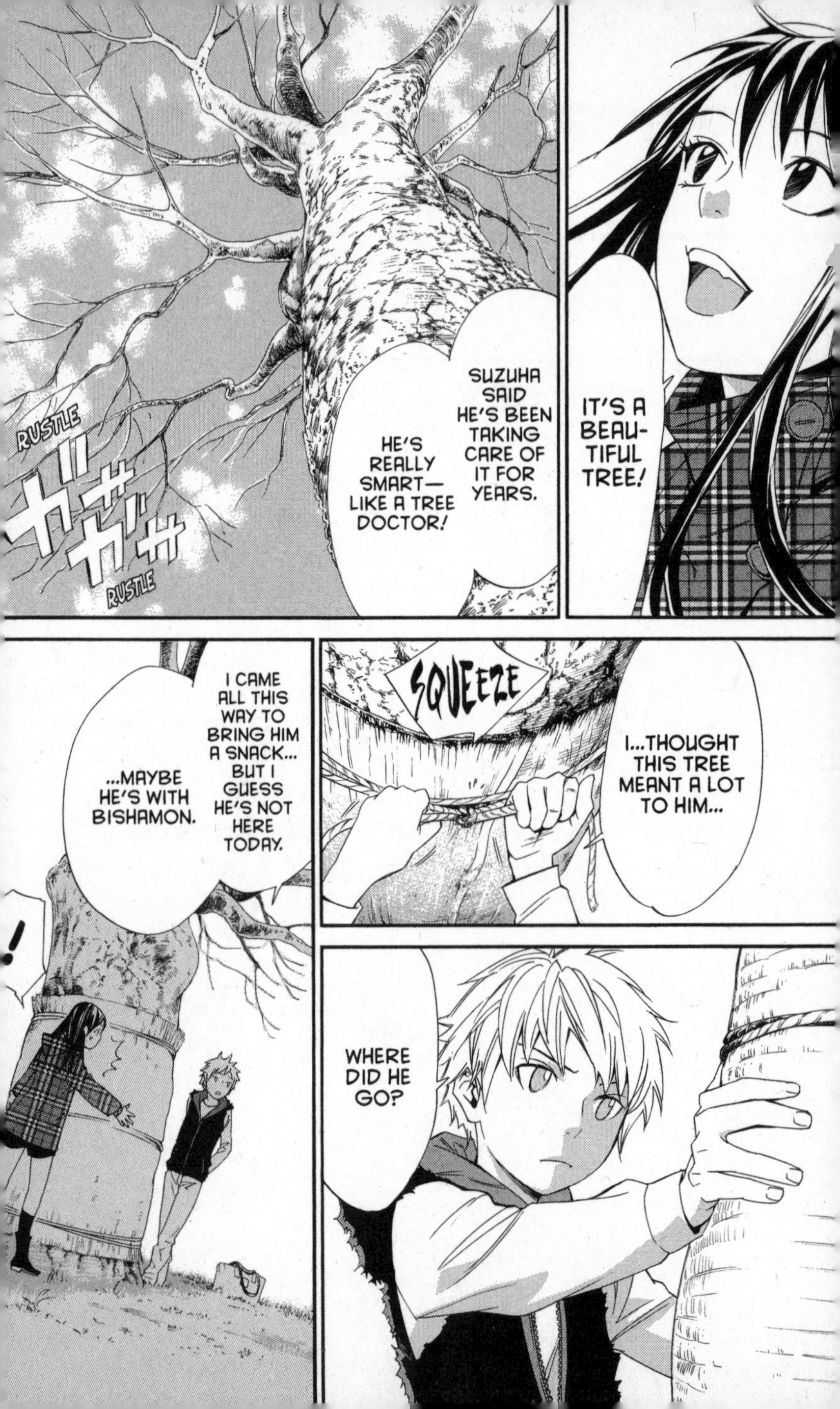
IT'S A BEAU-TIFUL TREE!
SUZUHA SAID HE'S BEEN TAKING CARE OF IT FOR YEARS.
HE'S REALLY SMART—LIKE A TREE DOCTOR!
RUSTLE
ガサガサ
RUSTLE
SQUEEZE
I...THOUGHT THIS TREE MEANT A LOT TO HIM...
WHERE DID HE GO?
I CAME ALL THIS WAY TO BRING HIM A SNACK... BUT I GUESS HE'S NOT HERE TODAY.
...MAYBE HE'S WITH BISHAMON.
!

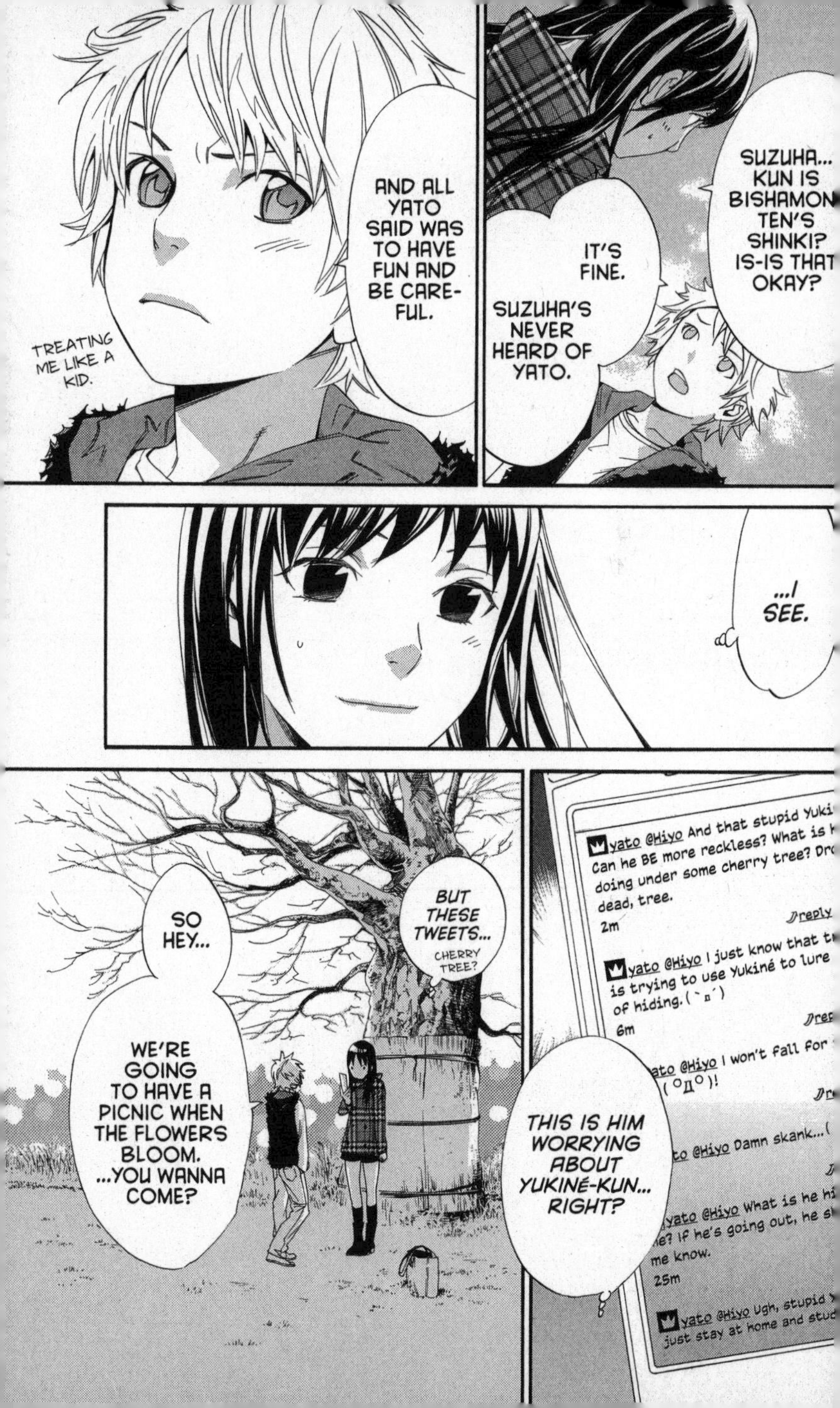
SUZUHA... KUN IS BISHAMON TEN'S SHINKI? IS-IS THAT OKAY?
IT'S FINE.
SUZUHA'S NEVER HEARD OF YATO.
AND ALL YATO SAID WAS TO HAVE FUN AND BE CARE-FUL.
TREATING ME LIKE A KID.
...I SEE.
yato @Hiyo And that stupid Yuki
Can he BE more reckless? What is
doing under some cherry tree? Dr
dead, tree.
2m
reply
yato @Hiyo I just know that t
is trying to use Yukiné to lure
of hiding. (`д´)
6m
rep
ato @Hiyo I won't fall for
(ºДº)!
to @Hiyo Damn skank...
yato @Hiyo What is he h
e? If he's going out, he s
me know.
25m
yato @Hiyo Ugh, stupid
just stay at home and stu
THIS IS HIM WORRYING ABOUT YUKINÉ-KUN... RIGHT?
BUT THESE TWEETS...
CHERRY TREE?
SO HEY...
WE'RE GOING TO HAVE A PICNIC WHEN THE FLOWERS BLOOM. ...YOU WANNA COME?

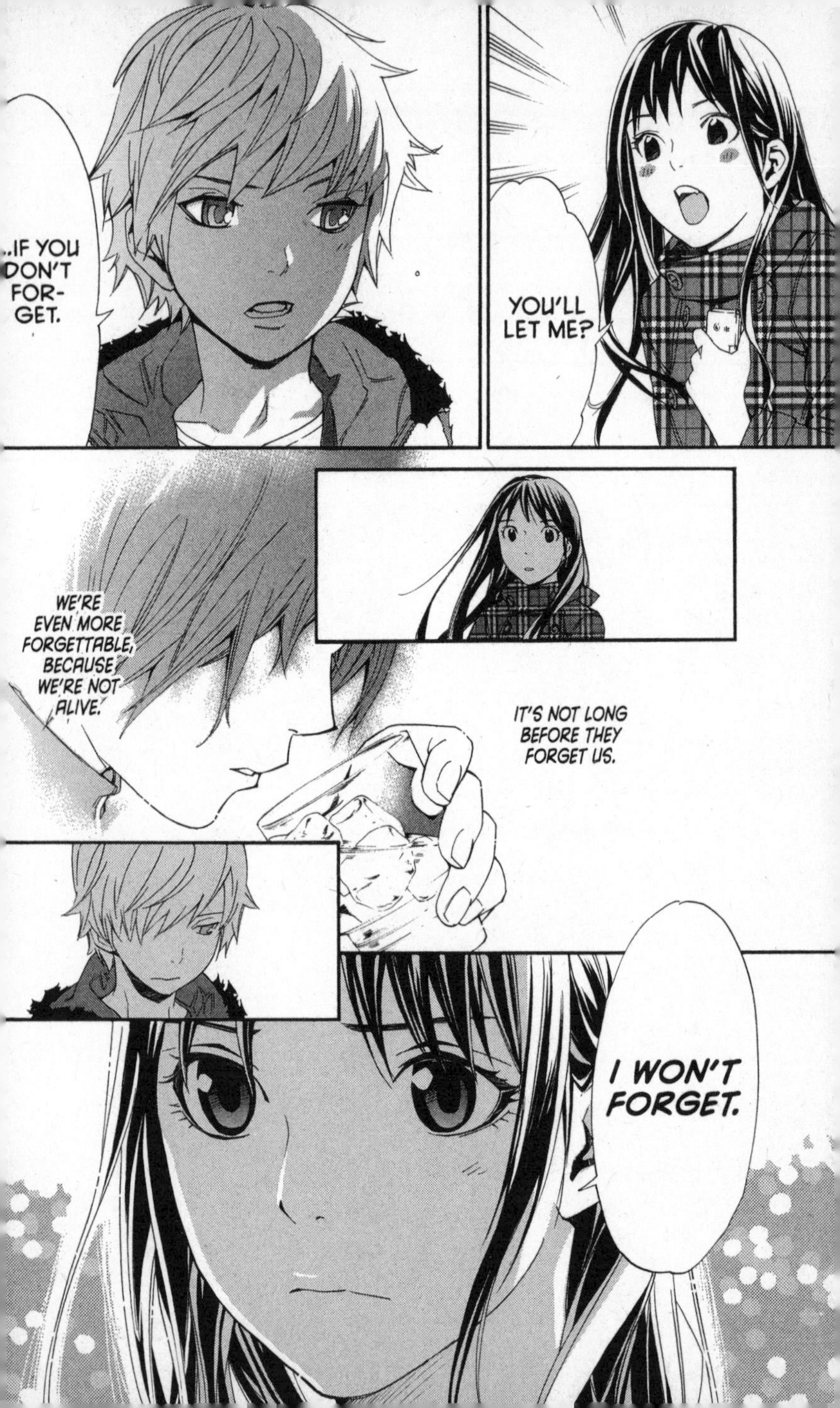
YOU'LL LET ME?
..IF YOU DON'T FORGET.
IT'S NOT LONG BEFORE THEY FORGET US.
WE'RE EVEN MORE FORGETTABLE, BECAUSE WE'RE NOT ALIVE.
I WON'T FORGET.

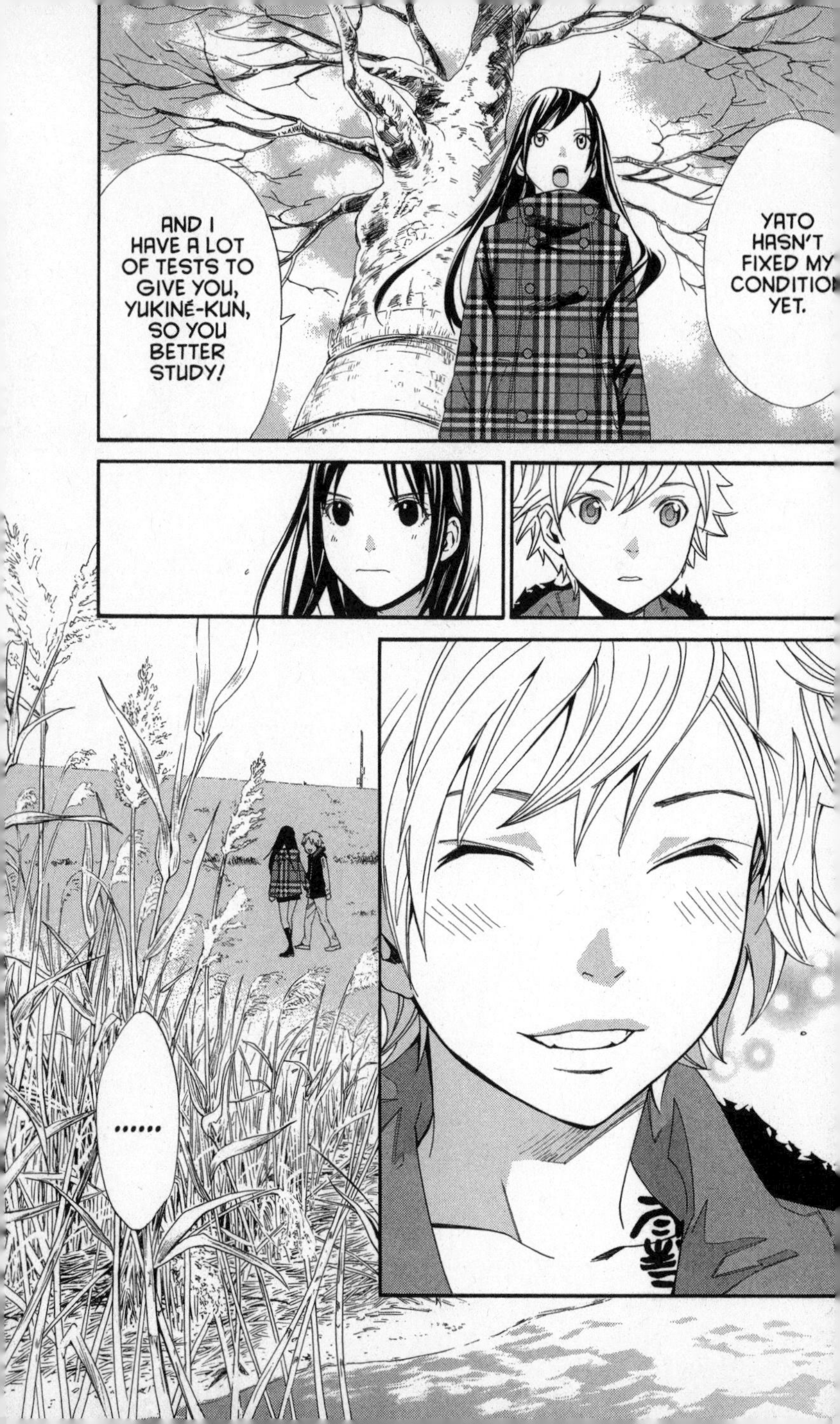
YATO HASN'T FIXED MY CONDITIO YET.
AND I HAVE A LOT OF TESTS TO GIVE YOU, YUKINÉ-KUN, SO YOU BETTER STUDY!
......

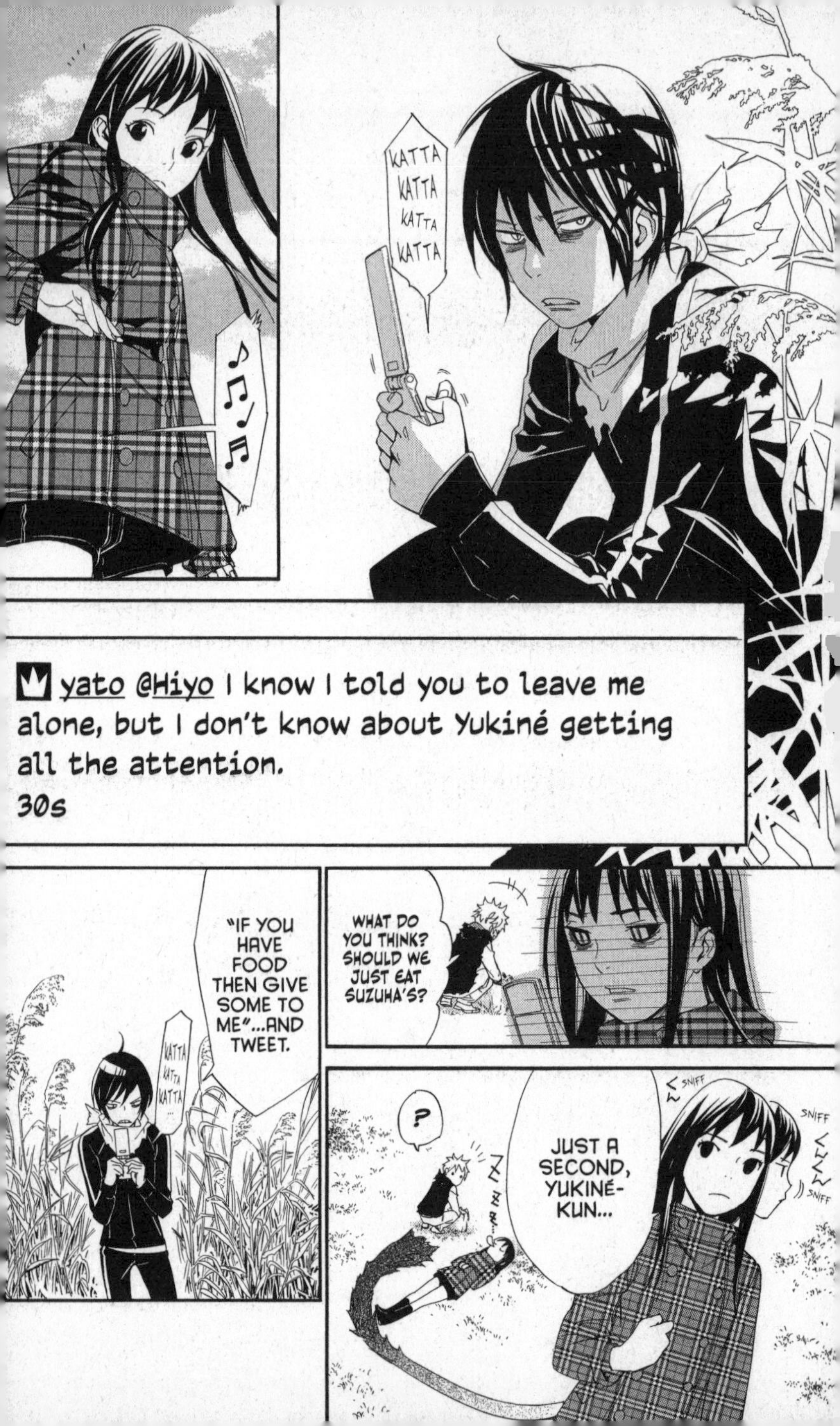
KATTA KATTA KATTA KATTA
♪ ♫ ♩ ♬
yato @Hiyo I know I told you to leave me alone, but I don't know about Yukiné getting all the attention.
30s
WHAT DO YOU THINK? SHOULD WE JUST EAT SUZUHA'S?
SNIFF
SNIFF
SNIFF
JUST A SECOND, YUKINÉ-KUN...
?
"IF YOU HAVE FOOD THEN GIVE SOME TO ME"...AND TWEET.
KATTA KATTA KATTA

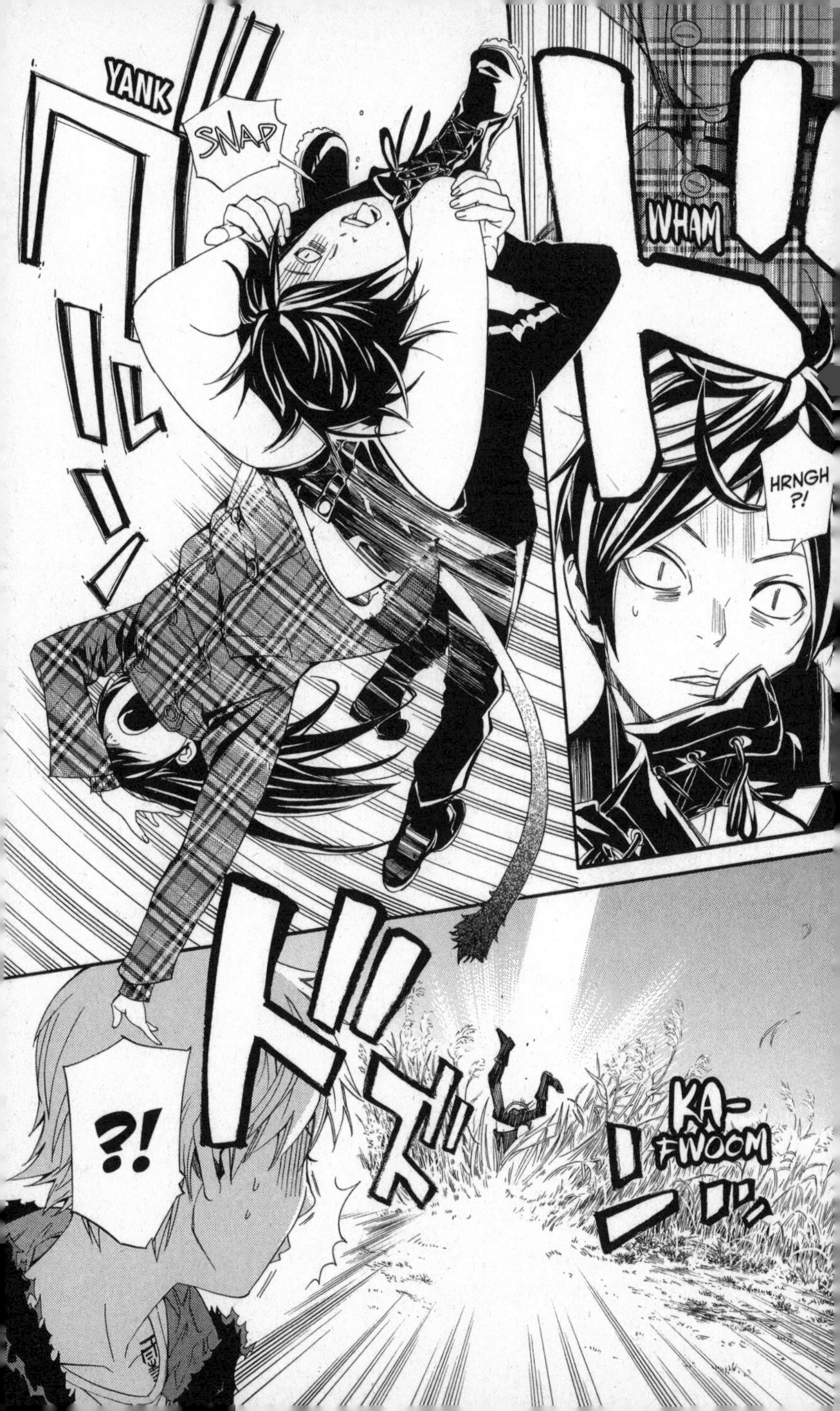
WHAM
HRNGH ?!
SNAP
YANK
KA-FWOOM
?!

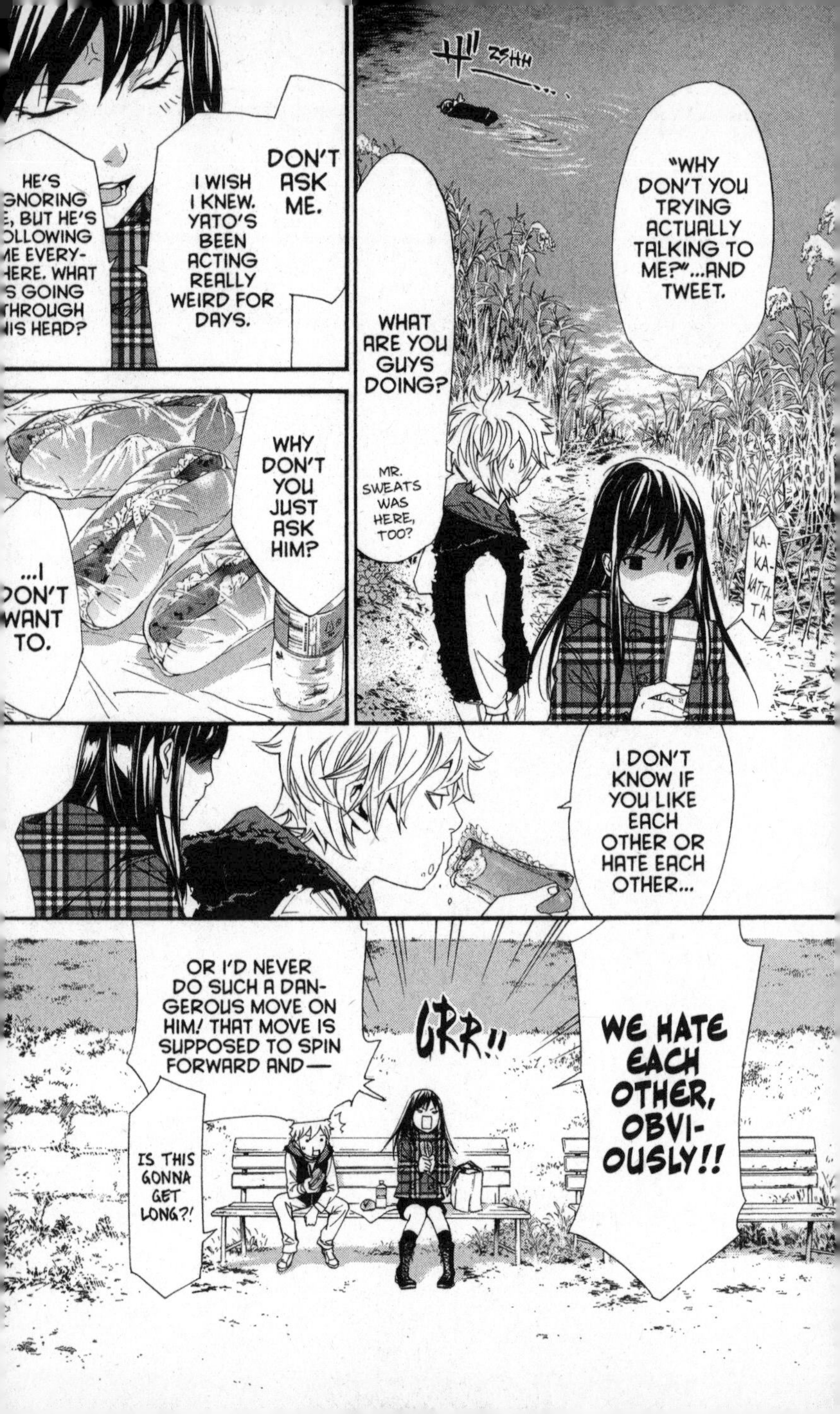
ZSHH
"WHY DON'T YOU TRYING ACTUALLY TALKING TO ME?"...AND TWEET.
WHAT ARE YOU GUYS DOING?
MR. SWEATS WAS HERE, TOO?
KA-KA-KATTA-TA
DON'T ASK ME.
I WISH I KNEW. YATO'S BEEN ACTING REALLY WEIRD FOR DAYS.
HE'S GNORING E, BUT HE'S OLLOWING ME EVERY-HERE. WHAT S GOING THROUGH IS HEAD?
WHY DON'T YOU JUST ASK HIM?
...I DON'T WANT TO.
I DON'T KNOW IF YOU LIKE EACH OTHER OR HATE EACH OTHER...
WE HATE EACH OTHER, OBVIOUSLY!!
GRR!!
OR I'D NEVER DO SUCH A DANGEROUS MOVE ON HIM! THAT MOVE IS SUPPOSED TO SPIN FORWARD AND—
IS THIS GONNA GET LONG?!

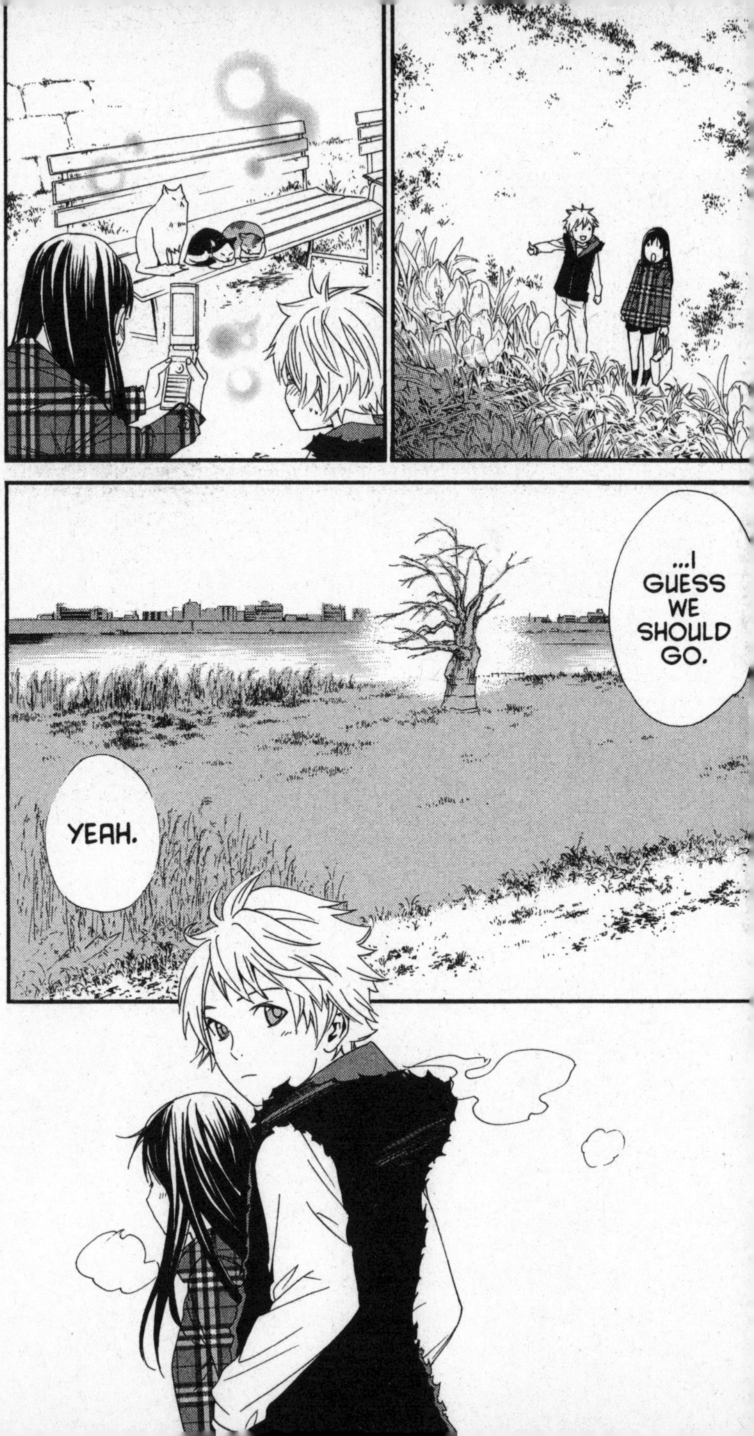
...I GUESS WE SHOULD GO.
YEAH.

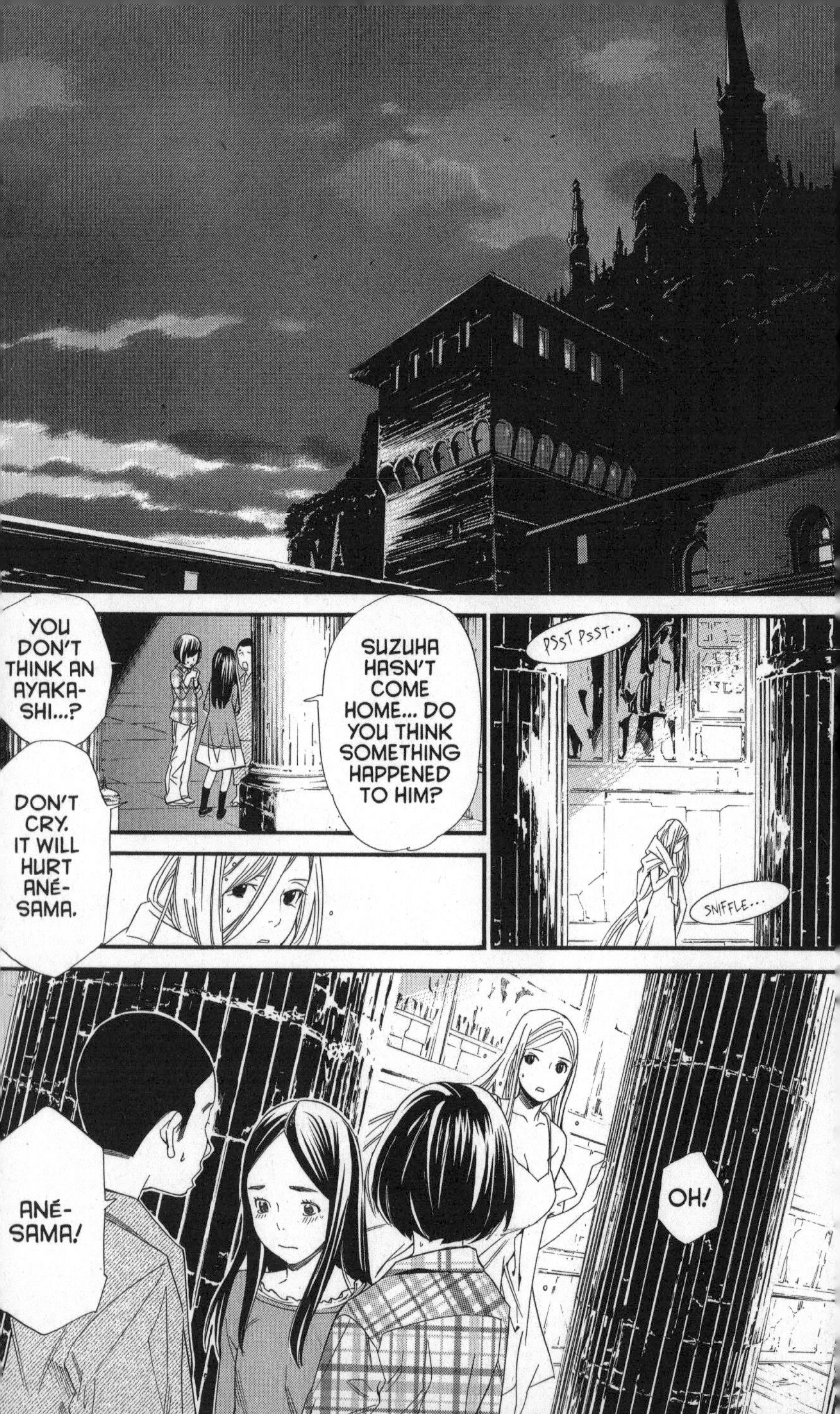
PSST PSST...
SNIFFLE...
SUZUHA HASN'T COME HOME... DO YOU THINK SOMETHING HAPPENED TO HIM?
YOU DON'T THINK AN AYAKA-SHI...?
DON'T CRY. IT WILL HURT ANÉ-SAMA.
OH!
ANÉ-SAMA!

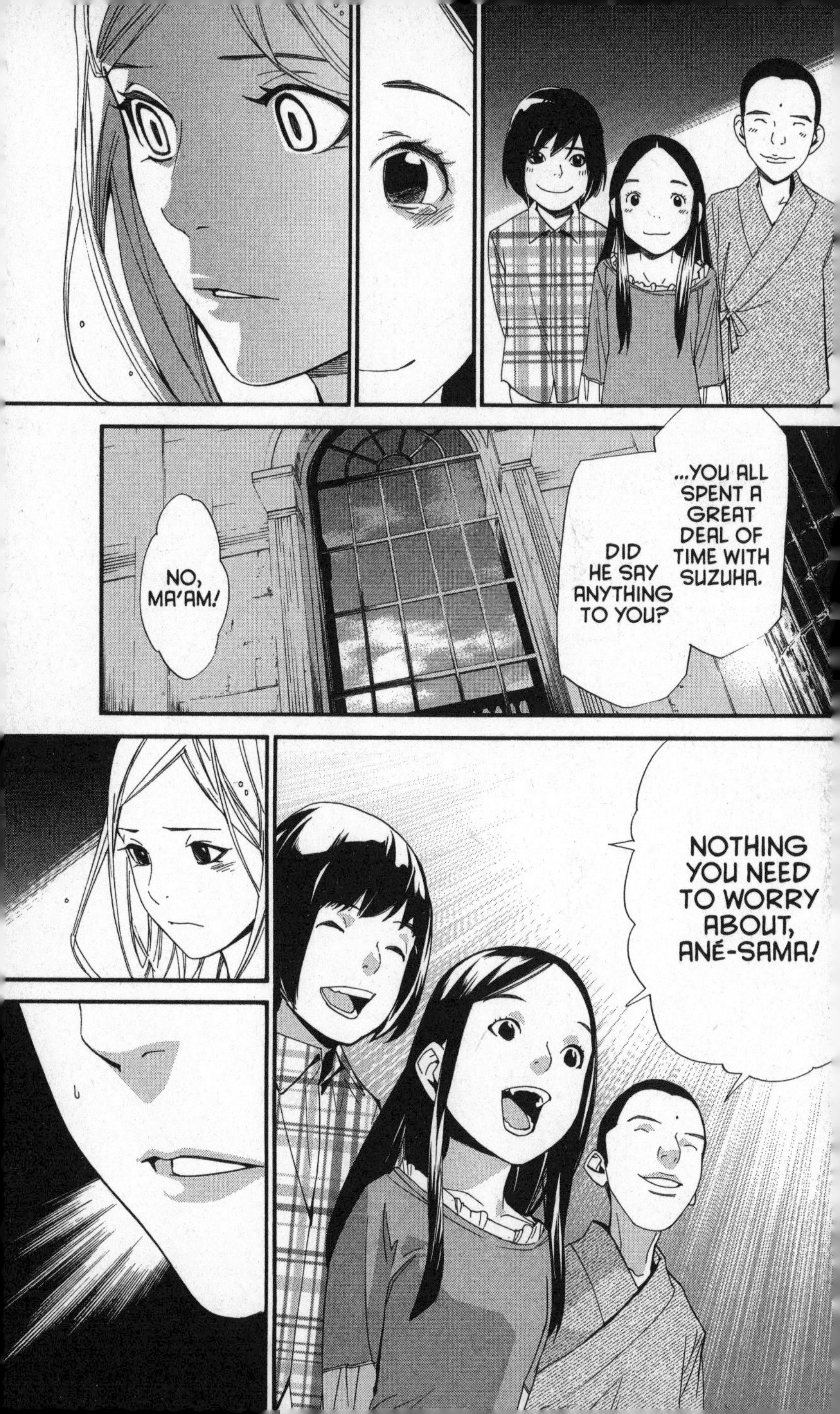
...YOU ALL SPENT A GREAT DEAL OF TIME WITH SUZUHA.
DID HE SAY ANYTHING TO YOU?
NO, MA'AM!
NOTHING YOU NEED TO WORRY ABOUT, ANÉ-SAMA!

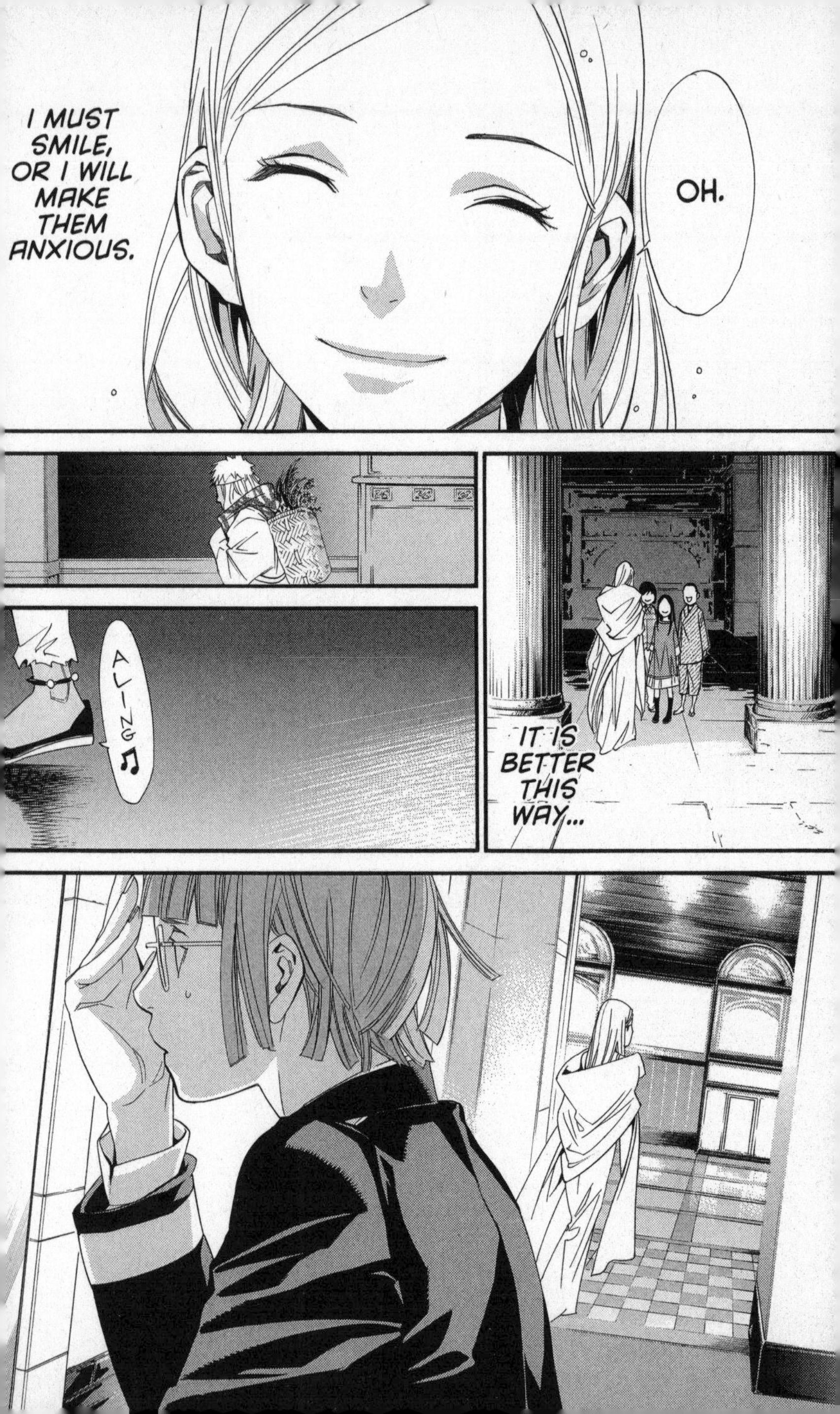
OH.
I MUST SMILE, OR I WILL MAKE THEM ANXIOUS.
IT IS BETTER THIS WAY...
ALING♫

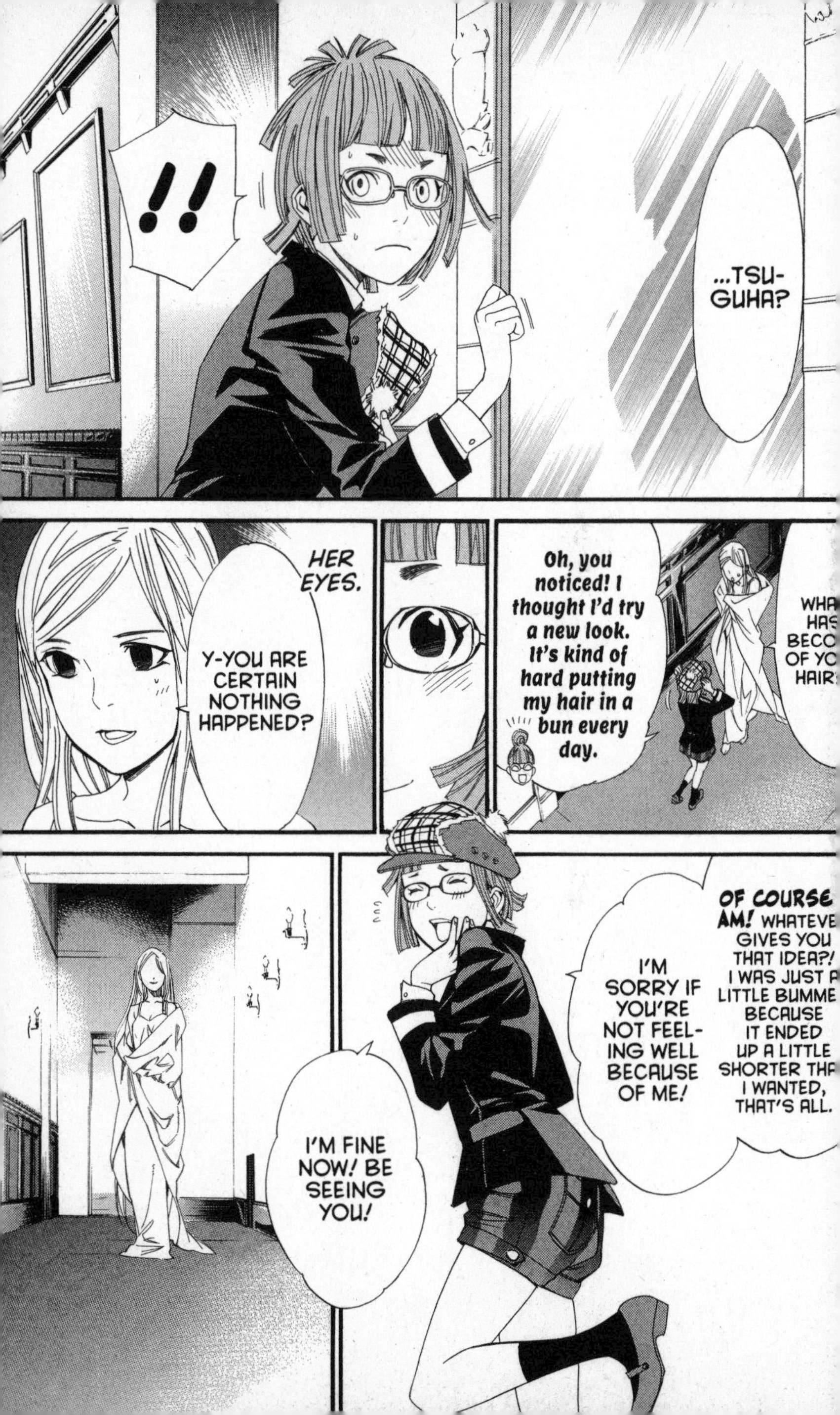
...TSU-GUHA?
!!
WHA HAS BECO OF YO HAIR
Oh, you noticed! I thought I'd try a new look. It's kind of hard putting my hair in a bun every day.
HER EYES.
Y-YOU ARE CERTAIN NOTHING HAPPENED?
OF COURSE AM! WHATEVE GIVES YOU THAT IDEA?! I WAS JUST A LITTLE BUMME BECAUSE IT ENDED UP A LITTLE SHORTER THA I WANTED, THAT'S ALL.
I'M SORRY IF YOU'RE NOT FEEL-ING WELL BECAUSE OF ME!
I'M FINE NOW! BE SEEING YOU!

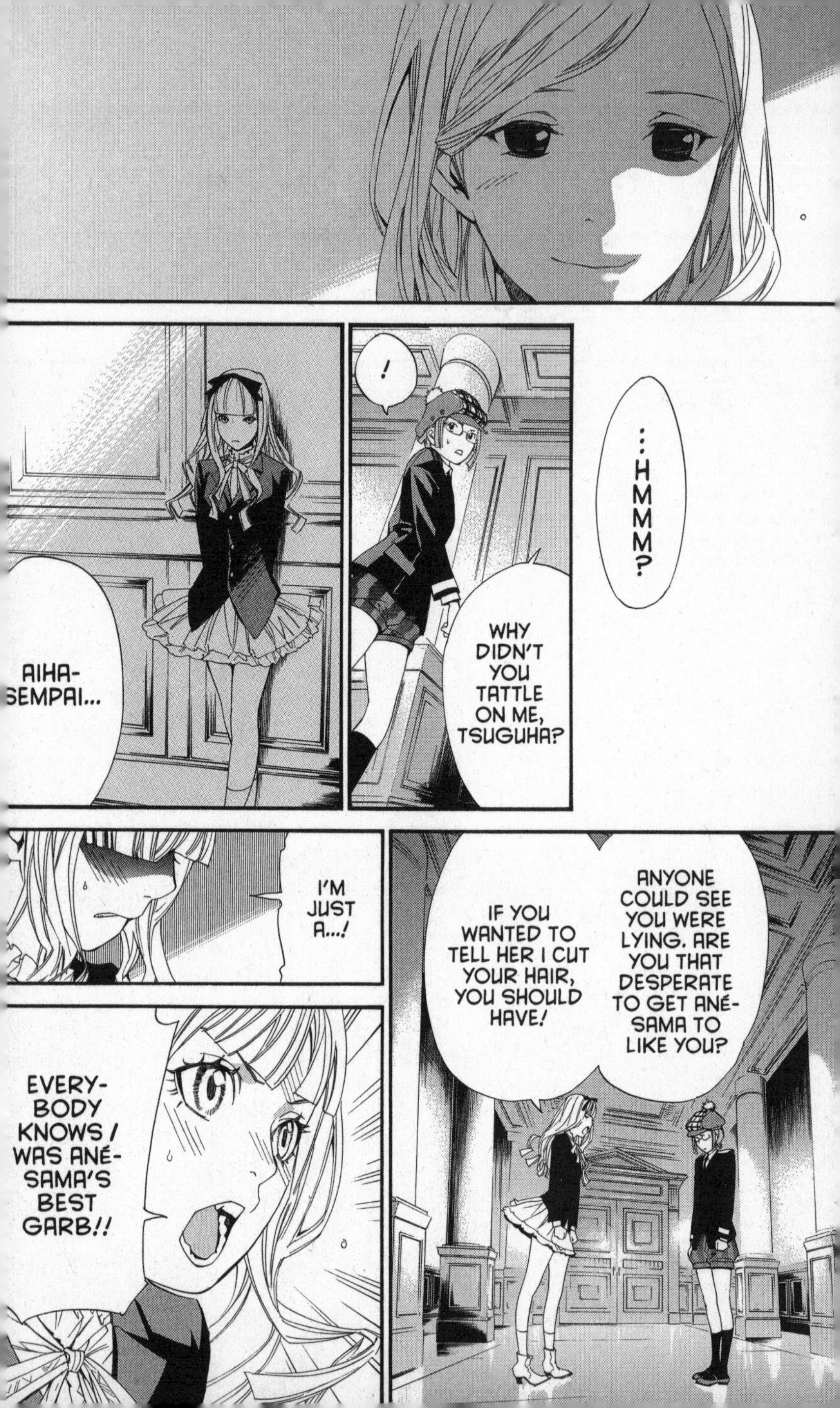
...HMMM?
!
WHY DIDN'T YOU TATTLE ON ME, TSUGUHA?
AIHA-SEMPAI...
ANYONE COULD SEE YOU WERE LYING. ARE YOU THAT DESPERATE TO GET ANÉ-SAMA TO LIKE YOU?
IF YOU WANTED TO TELL HER I CUT YOUR HAIR, YOU SHOULD HAVE!
I'M JUST A...!
EVERYBODY KNOWS I WAS ANÉ-SAMA'S BEST GARB!!

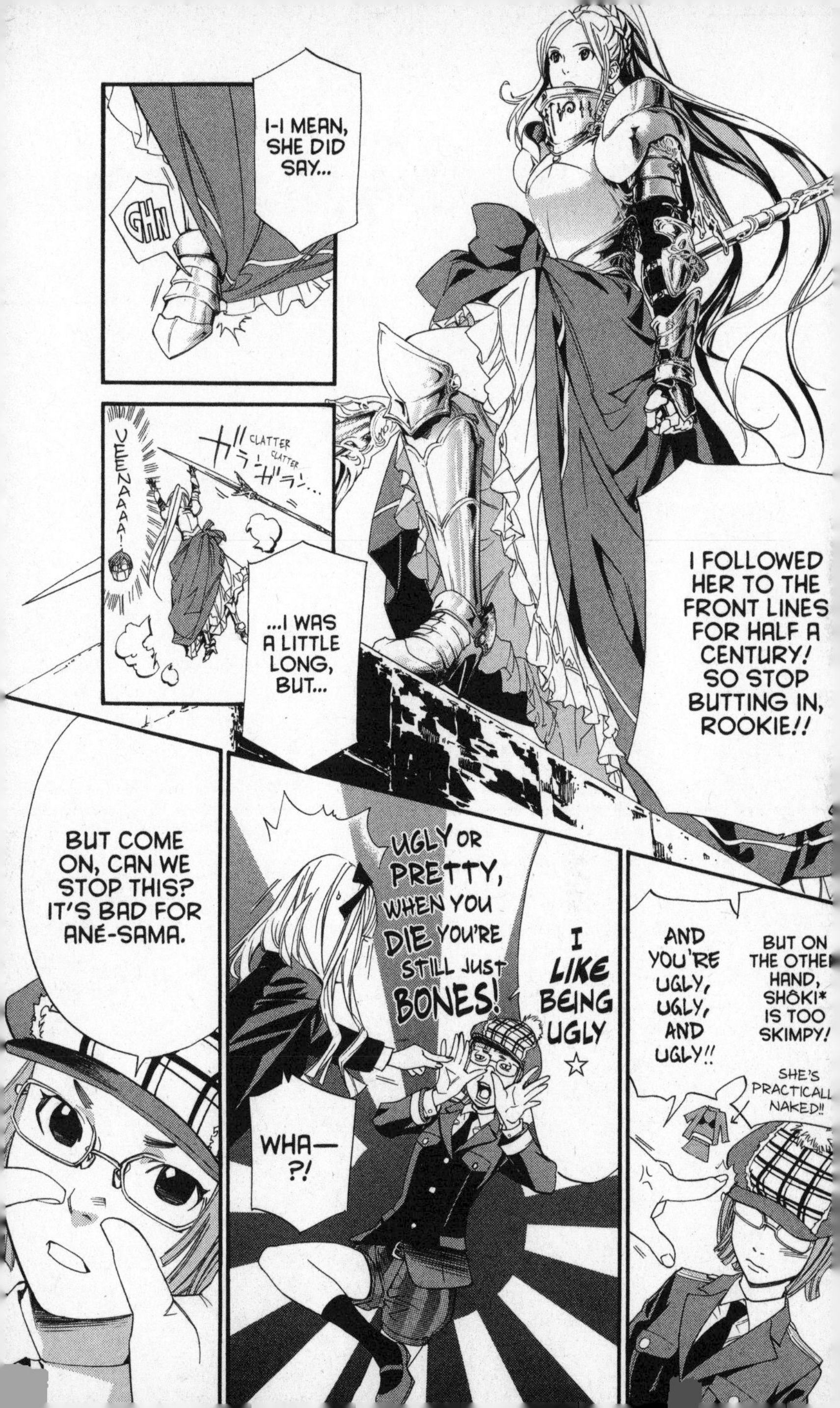
I FOLLOWED HER TO THE FRONT LINES FOR HALF A CENTURY! SO STOP BUTTING IN, ROOKIE!!
I-I MEAN, SHE DID SAY...
GHN
VEENAAAA!
CLATTER CLATTER
...I WAS A LITTLE LONG, BUT...
BUT ON THE OTHE HAND, SHÔKI* IS TOO SKIMPY!
SHE'S PRACTICALL NAKED!!
AND YOU'RE UGLY, UGLY, AND UGLY!!
I LIKE BEING UGLY ☆
UGLY OR PRETTY, WHEN YOU DIE YOU'RE STILL JUST BONES!
WHA—?!
BUT COME ON, CAN WE STOP THIS? IT'S BAD FOR ANÉ-SAMA.

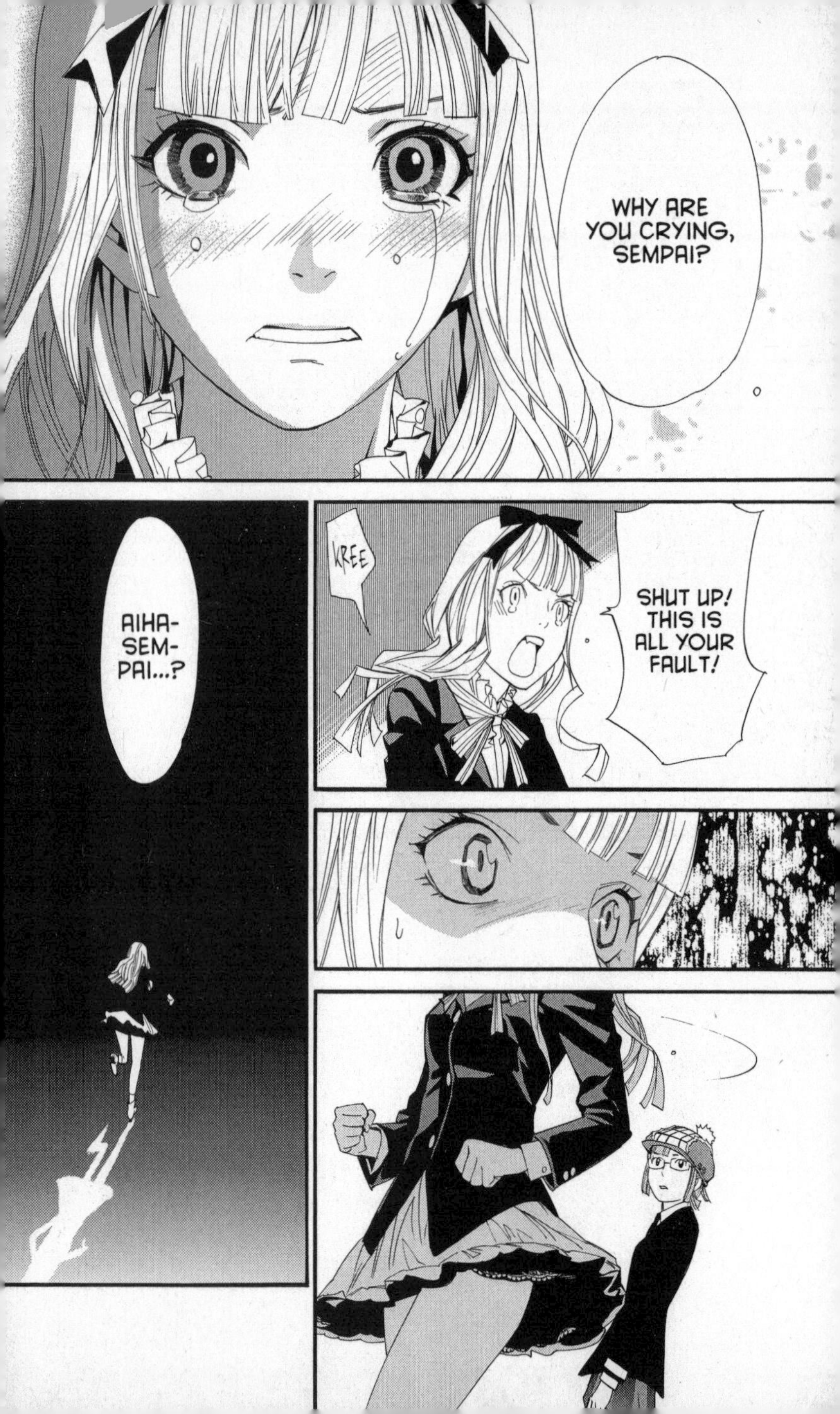
WHY ARE YOU CRYING, SEMPAI?
SHUT UP! THIS IS ALL YOUR FAULT!
KREE
AIHA-SEMPAI...?

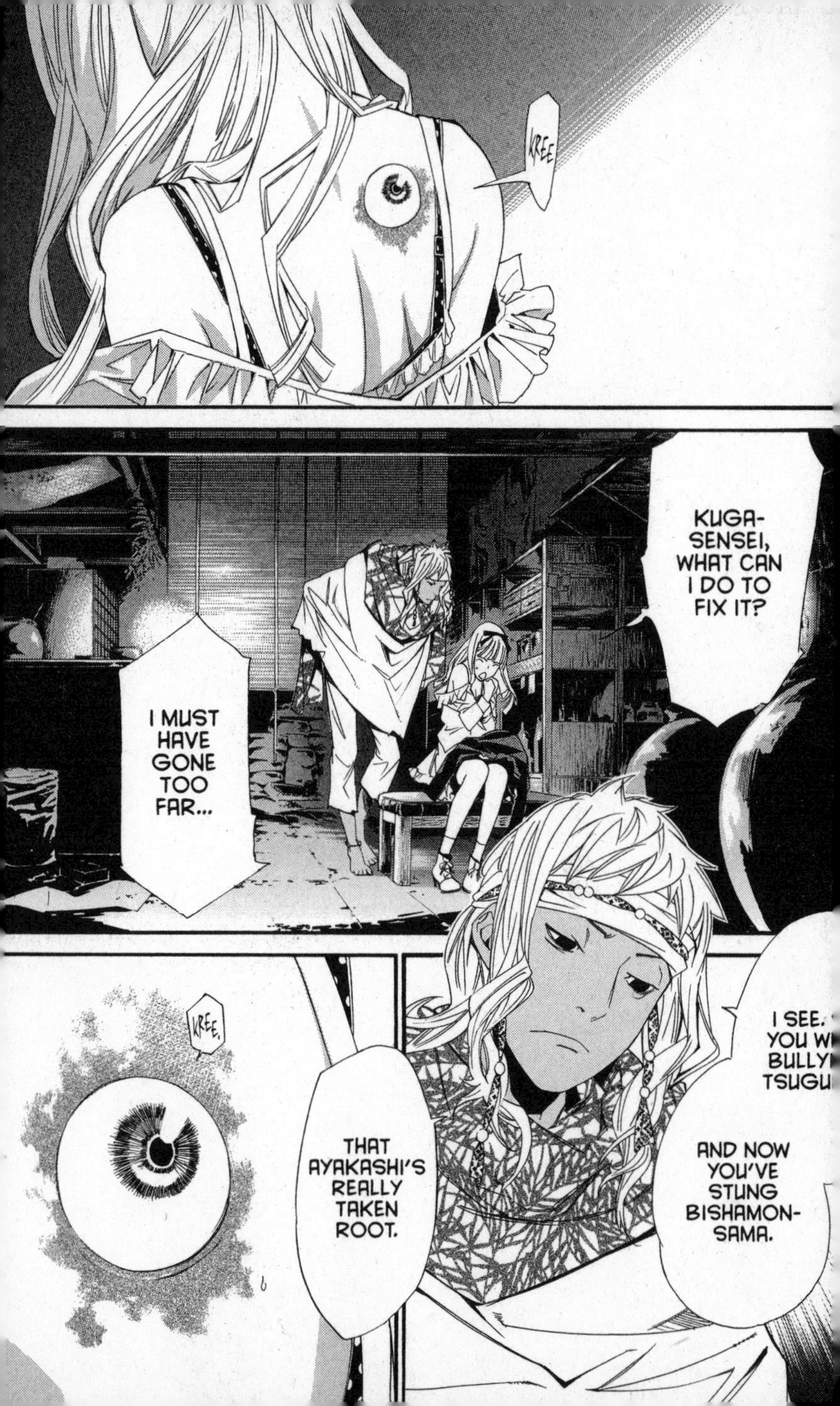
KREE
KUGA-SENSEI, WHAT CAN I DO TO FIX IT?
I MUST HAVE GONE TOO FAR...
I SEE. YOU WI BULLY TSUGU
AND NOW YOU'VE STUNG BISHAMON-SAMA.
THAT AYAKASHI'S REALLY TAKEN ROOT.
KREE.

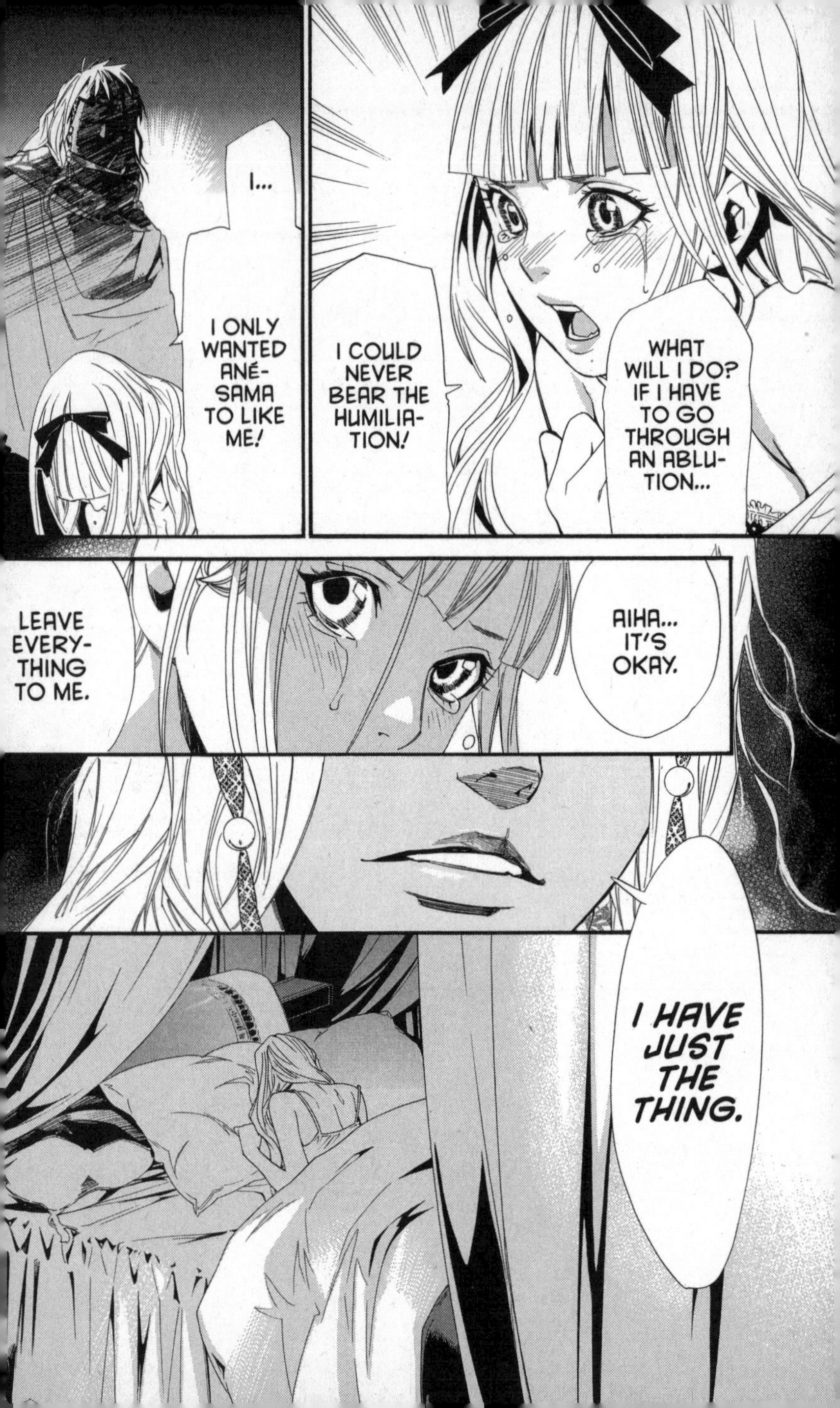
WHAT WILL I DO? IF I HAVE TO GO THROUGH AN ABLUTION...
I COULD NEVER BEAR THE HUMILIATION!
I...
I ONLY WANTED ANÉ-SAMA TO LIKE ME!
AIHA... IT'S OKAY.
LEAVE EVERYTHING TO ME.
I HAVE JUST THE THING.

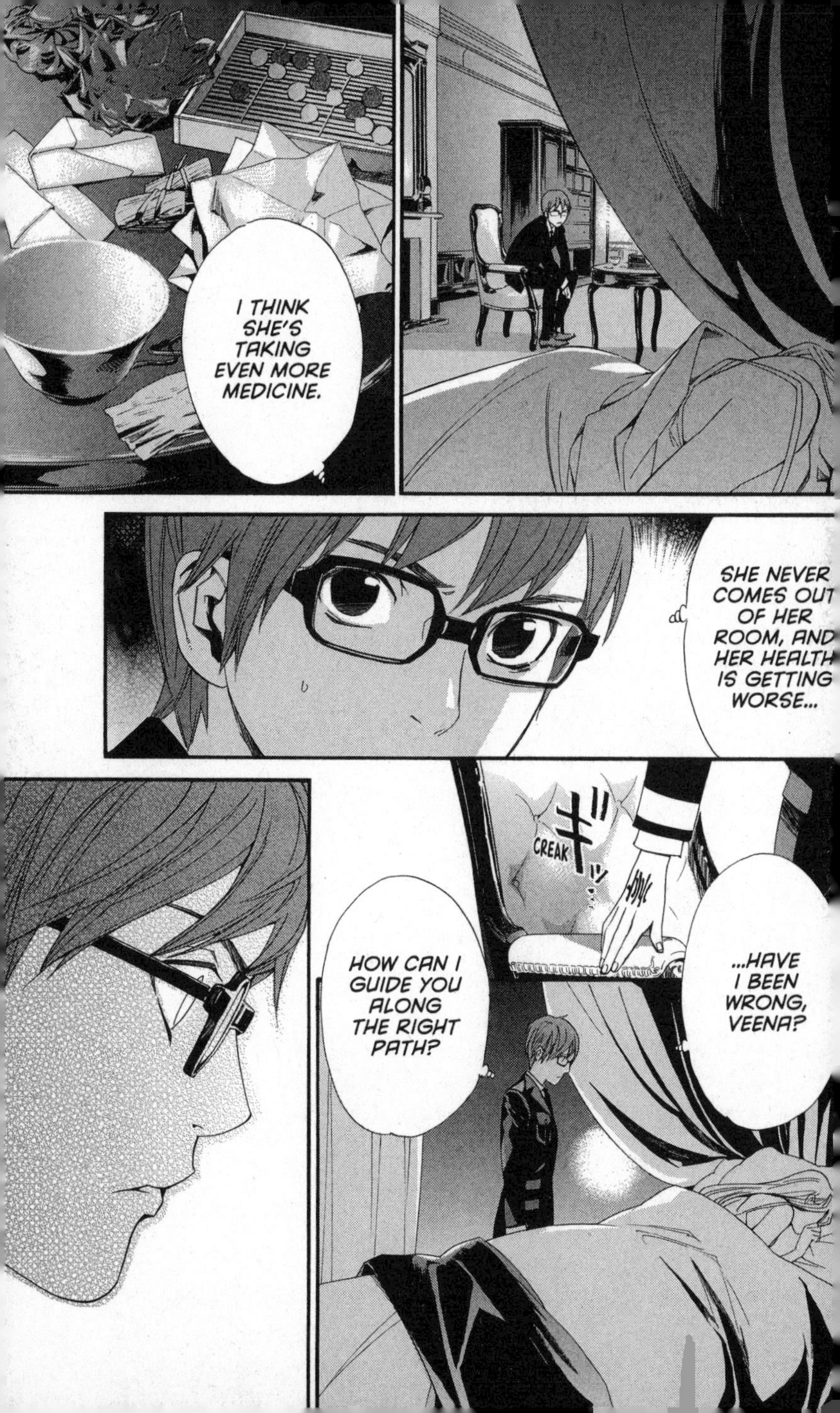
I THINK SHE'S TAKING EVEN MORE MEDICINE.
SHE NEVER COMES OUT OF HER ROOM, AND HER HEALTH IS GETTING WORSE...
CREAK
...HAVE I BEEN WRONG, VEENA?
HOW CAN I GUIDE YOU ALONG THE RIGHT PATH?

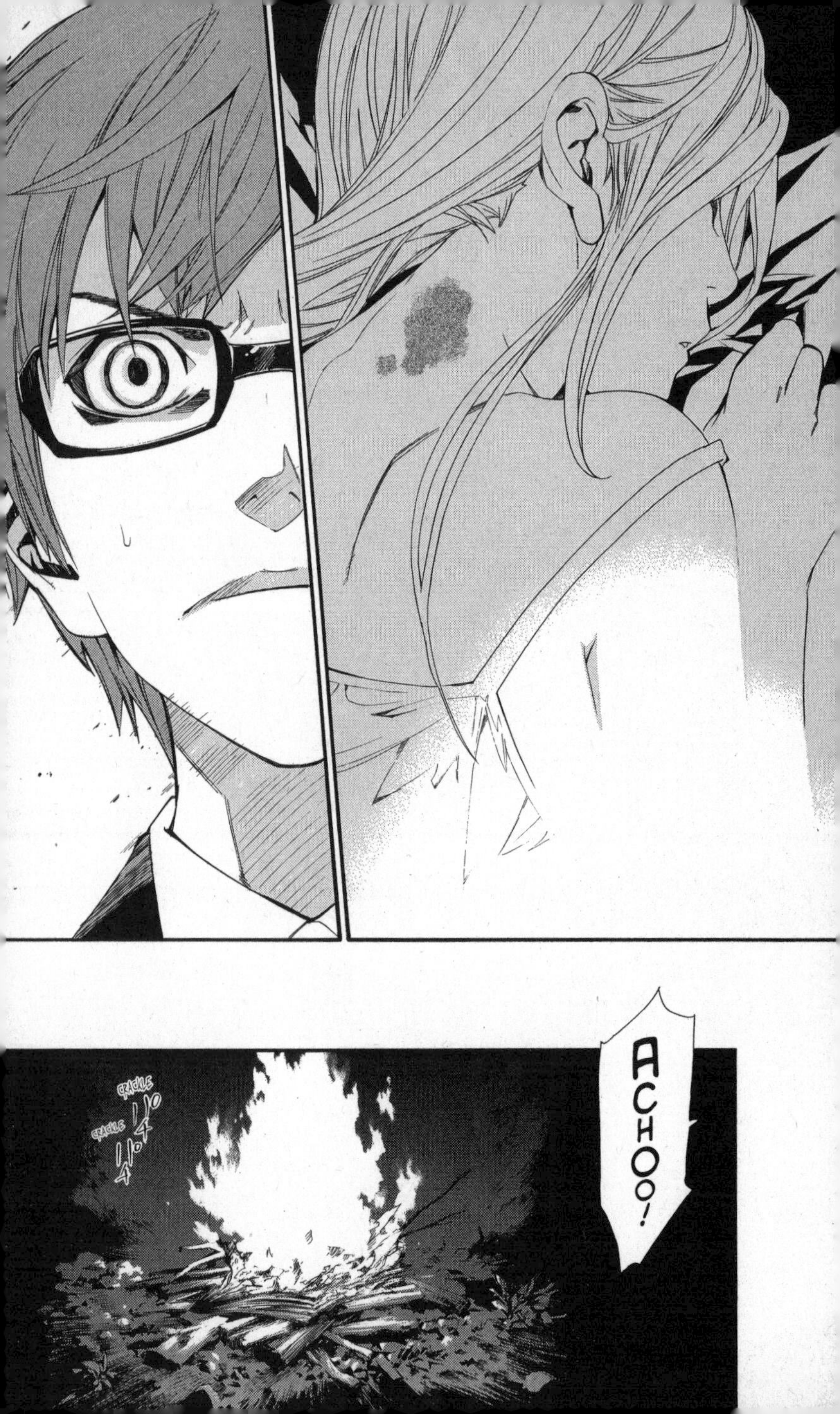
ACHOO!
CRACKLE
CRACKLE

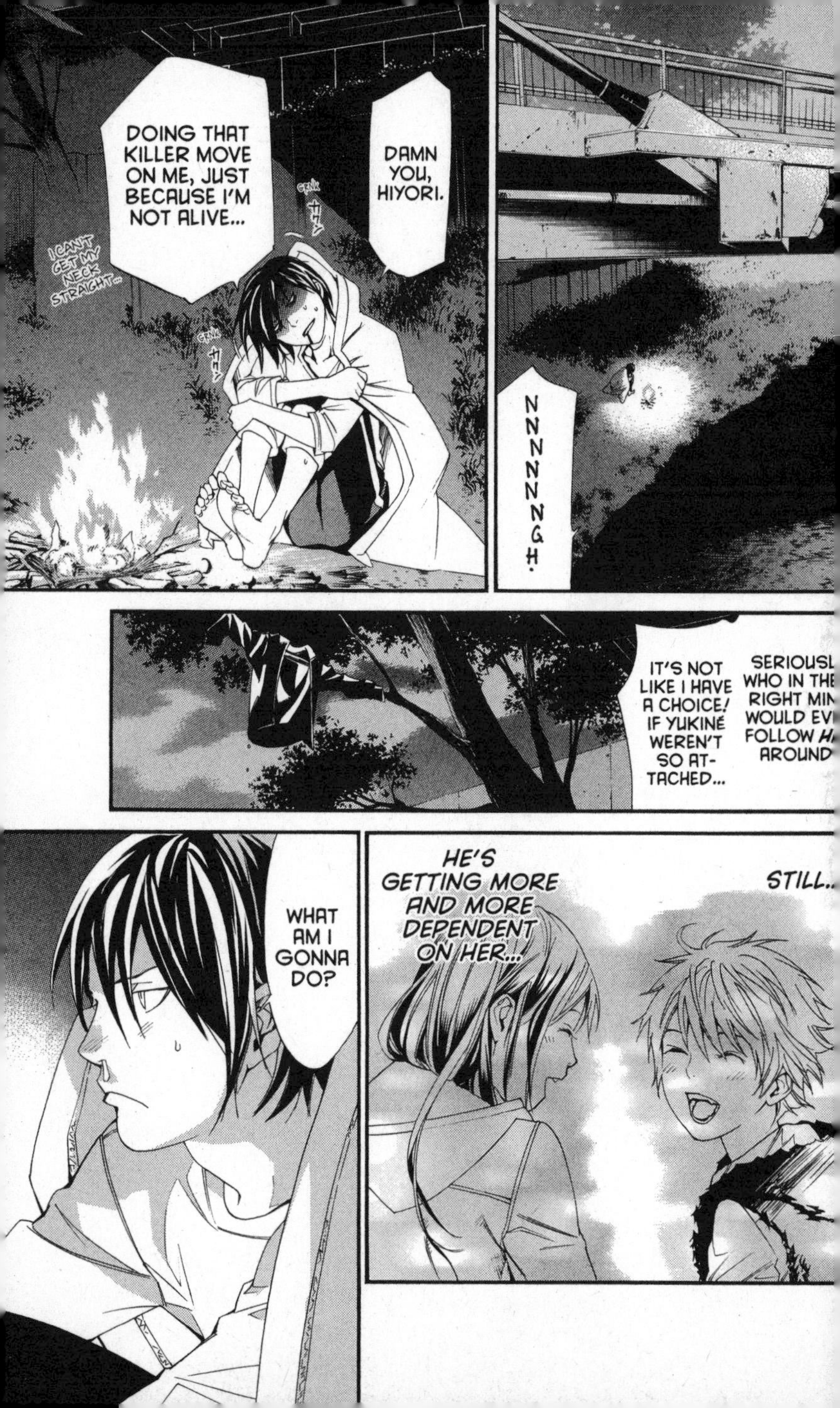
NNNNNNGH.
DAMN YOU, HIYORI.
GRNK
DOING THAT KILLER MOVE ON ME, JUST BECAUSE I'M NOT ALIVE...
I CAN'T GET MY NECK STRAIGHT...
GRNK
SERIOUSL WHO IN THE RIGHT MIN WOULD EV FOLLOW H AROUND
IT'S NOT LIKE I HAVE A CHOICE! IF YUKINE WEREN'T SO AT-TACHED...
STILL...
HE'S GETTING MORE AND MORE DEPENDENT ON HER...
WHAT AM I GONNA DO?

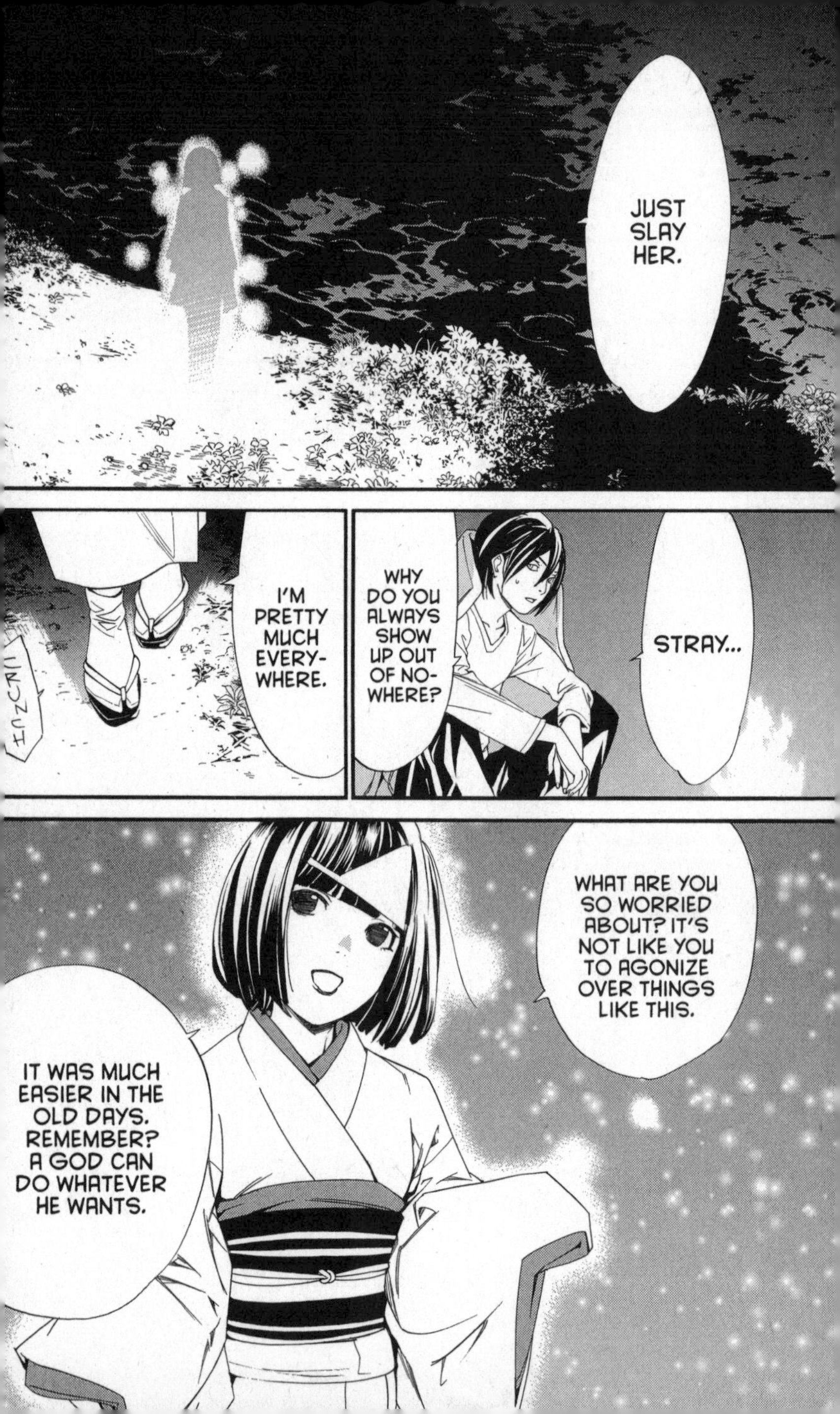
JUST SLAY HER.
STRAY...
WHY DO YOU ALWAYS SHOW UP OUT OF NO-WHERE?
I'M PRETTY MUCH EVERY-WHERE.
WHAT ARE YOU SO WORRIED ABOUT? IT'S NOT LIKE YOU TO AGONIZE OVER THINGS LIKE THIS.
IT WAS MUCH EASIER IN THE OLD DAYS. REMEMBER? A GOD CAN DO WHATEVER HE WANTS.

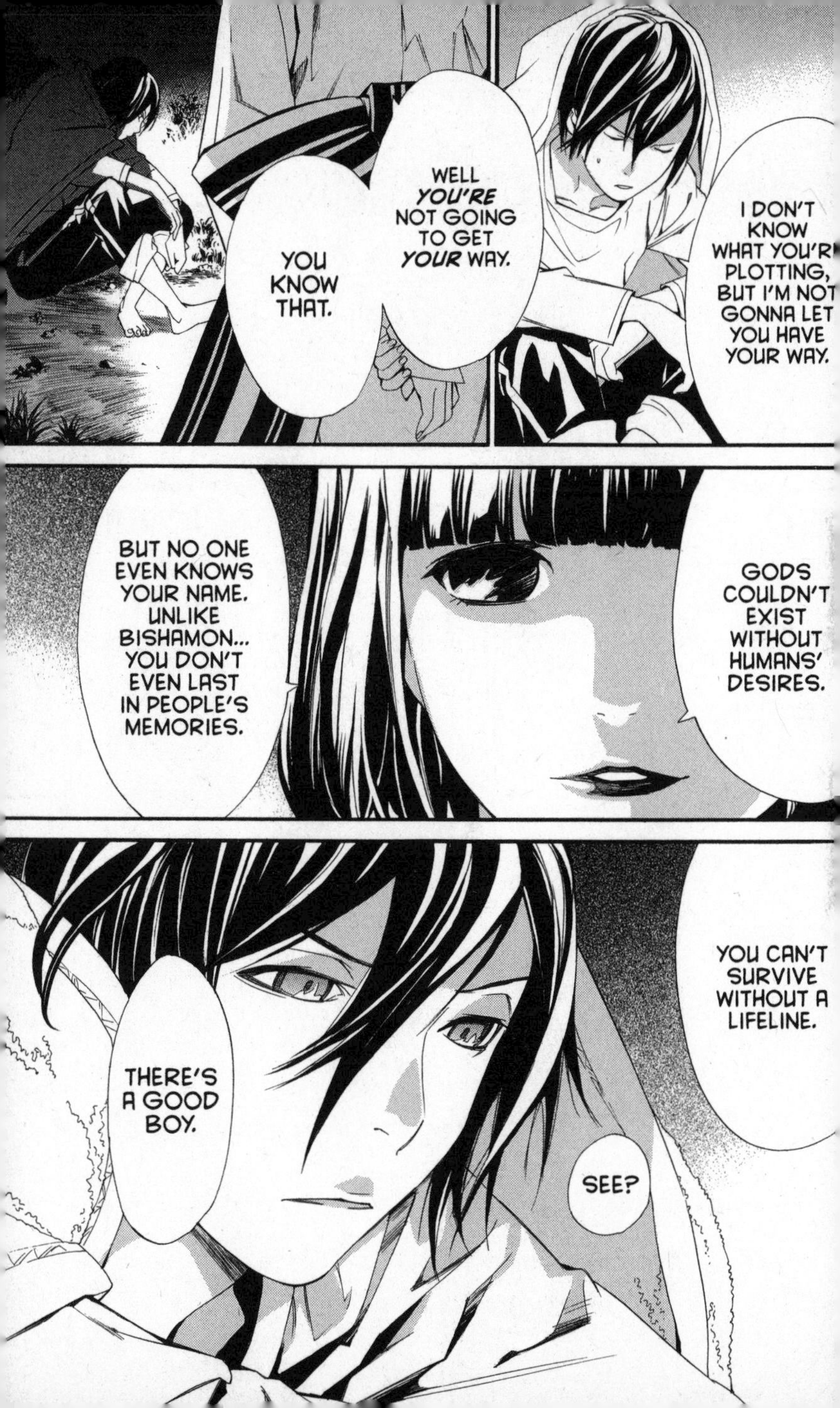
I DON'T KNOW WHAT YOU'R PLOTTING, BUT I'M NOT GONNA LET YOU HAVE YOUR WAY.
WELL *YOU'RE* NOT GOING TO GET *YOUR* WAY.
YOU KNOW THAT.
GODS COULDN'T EXIST WITHOUT HUMANS' DESIRES.
BUT NO ONE EVEN KNOWS YOUR NAME. UNLIKE BISHAMON... YOU DON'T EVEN LAST IN PEOPLE'S MEMORIES.
YOU CAN'T SURVIVE WITHOUT A LIFELINE.
SEE?
THERE'S A GOOD BOY.

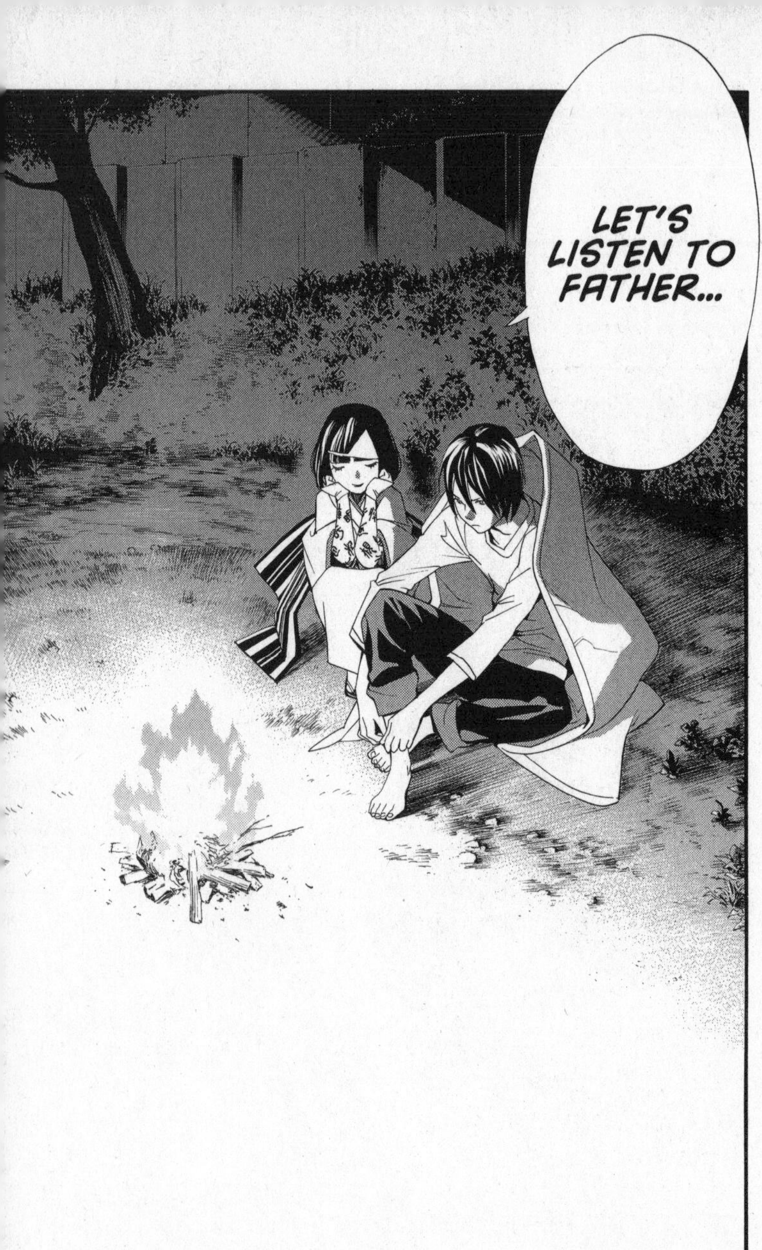
LET'S LISTEN TO FATHER...

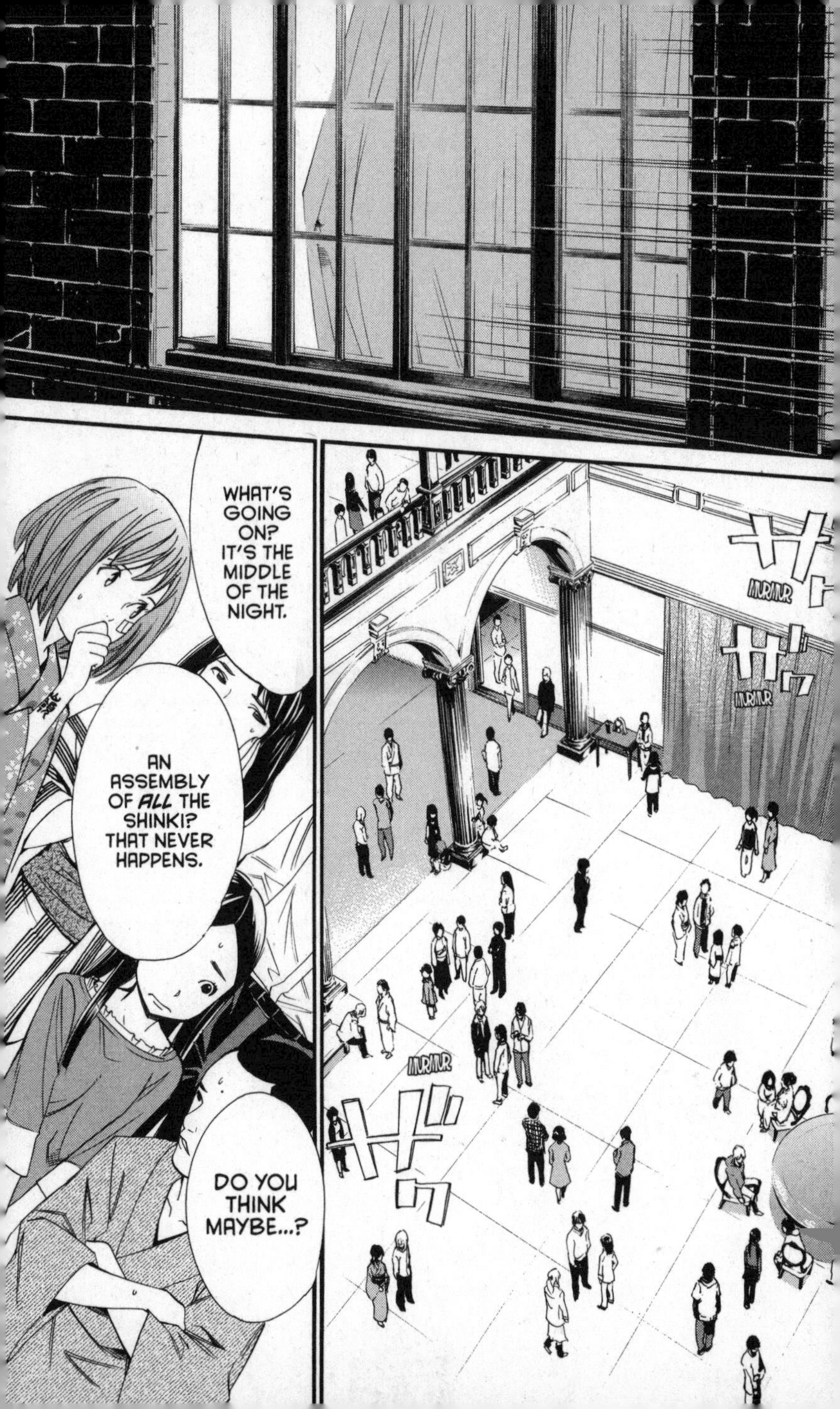
MURMUR
MURMUR
MURMUR
WHAT'S GOING ON? IT'S THE MIDDLE OF THE NIGHT.
AN ASSEMBLY OF *ALL* THE SHINKI? THAT NEVER HAPPENS.
DO YOU THINK MAYBE...?

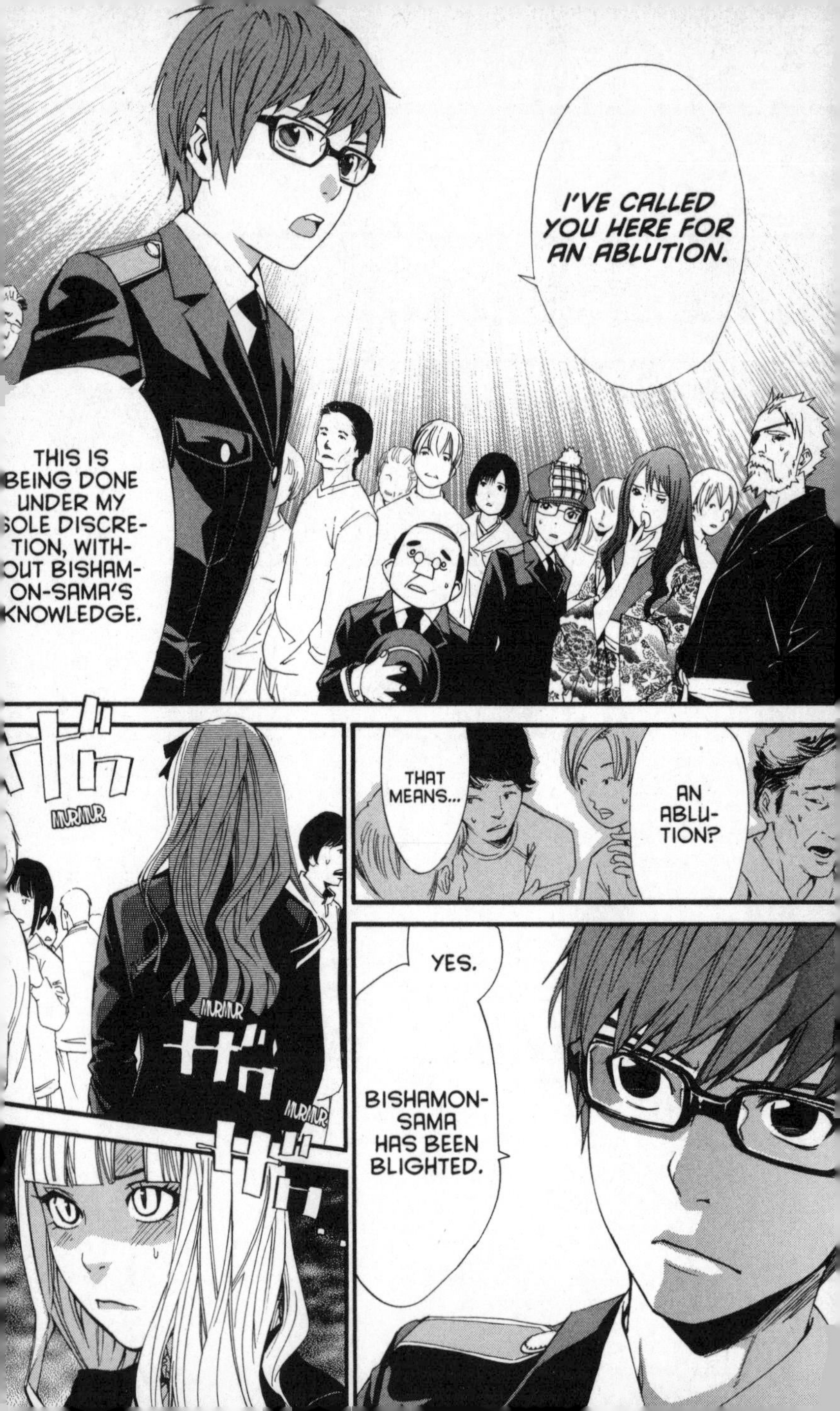
I'VE CALLED YOU HERE FOR AN ABLUTION.
THIS IS BEING DONE UNDER MY SOLE DISCRETION, WITHOUT BISHAMON-SAMA'S KNOWLEDGE.
AN ABLUTION?
THAT MEANS...
YES.
BISHAMON-SAMA HAS BEEN BLIGHTED.
MURMUR
MURMUR
MURMUR

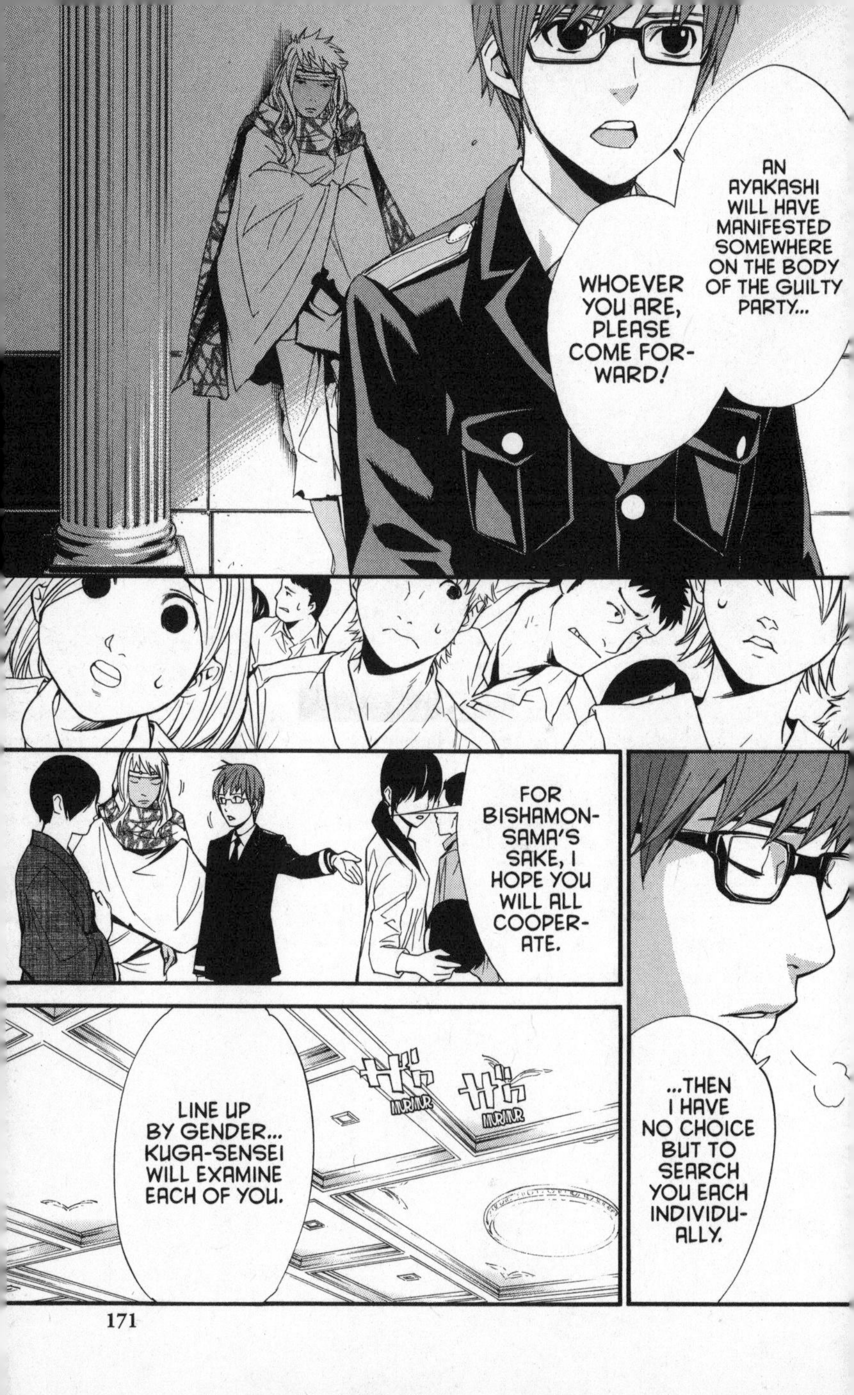
AN AYAKASHI WILL HAVE MANIFESTED SOMEWHERE ON THE BODY OF THE GUILTY PARTY...
WHOEVER YOU ARE, PLEASE COME FOR-WARD!
...THEN I HAVE NO CHOICE BUT TO SEARCH YOU EACH INDIVIDU-ALLY.
FOR BISHAMON-SAMA'S SAKE, I HOPE YOU WILL ALL COOPER-ATE.
MURMUR
MURMUR
LINE UP BY GENDER... KUGA-SENSEI WILL EXAMINE EACH OF YOU.

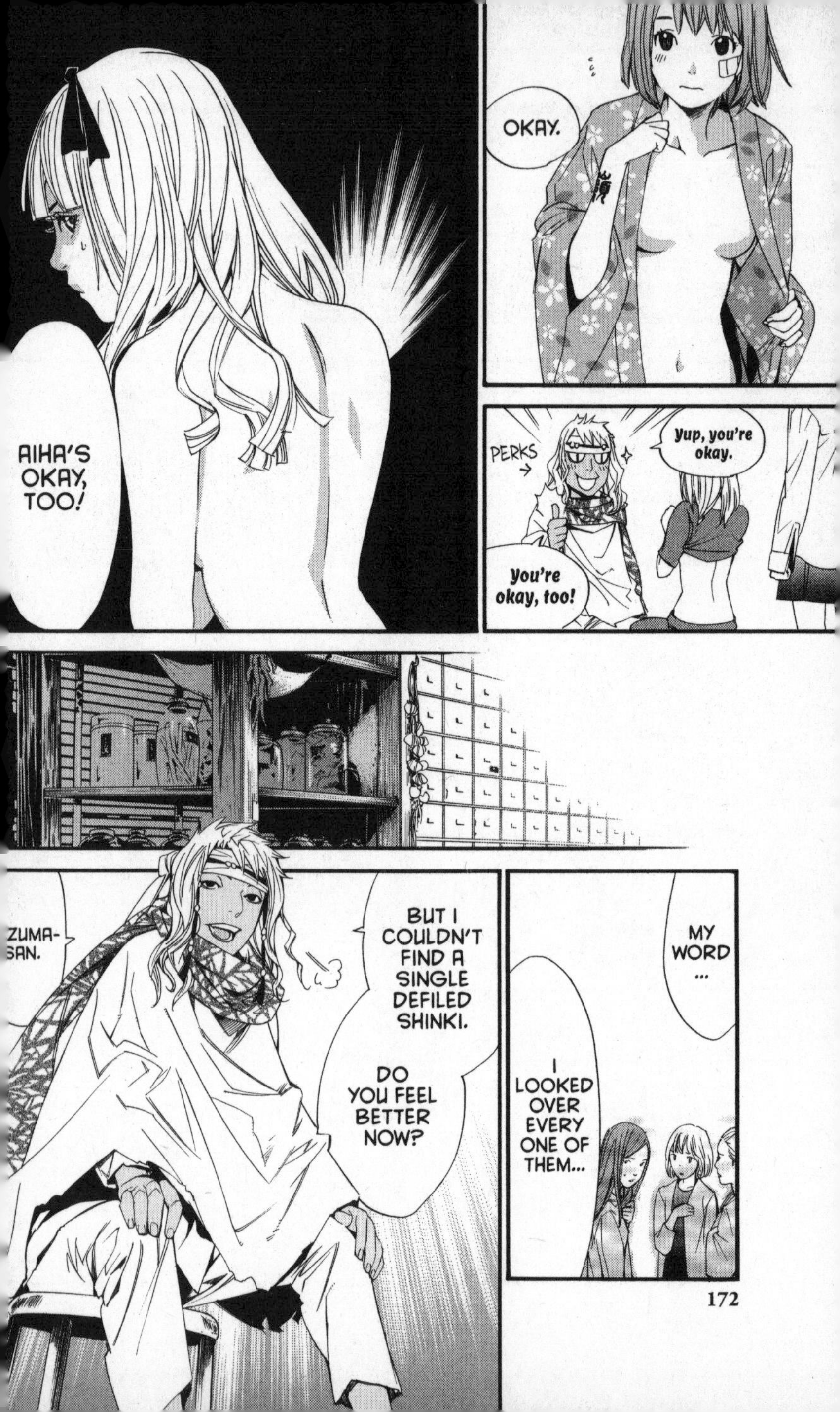
OKAY.
PERKS
Yup, you're okay.
You're okay, too!
AIHA'S OKAY, TOO!
MY WORD...
I LOOKED OVER EVERY ONE OF THEM...
BUT I COULDN'T FIND A SINGLE DEFILED SHINKI.
ZUMA-SAN.
DO YOU FEEL BETTER NOW?

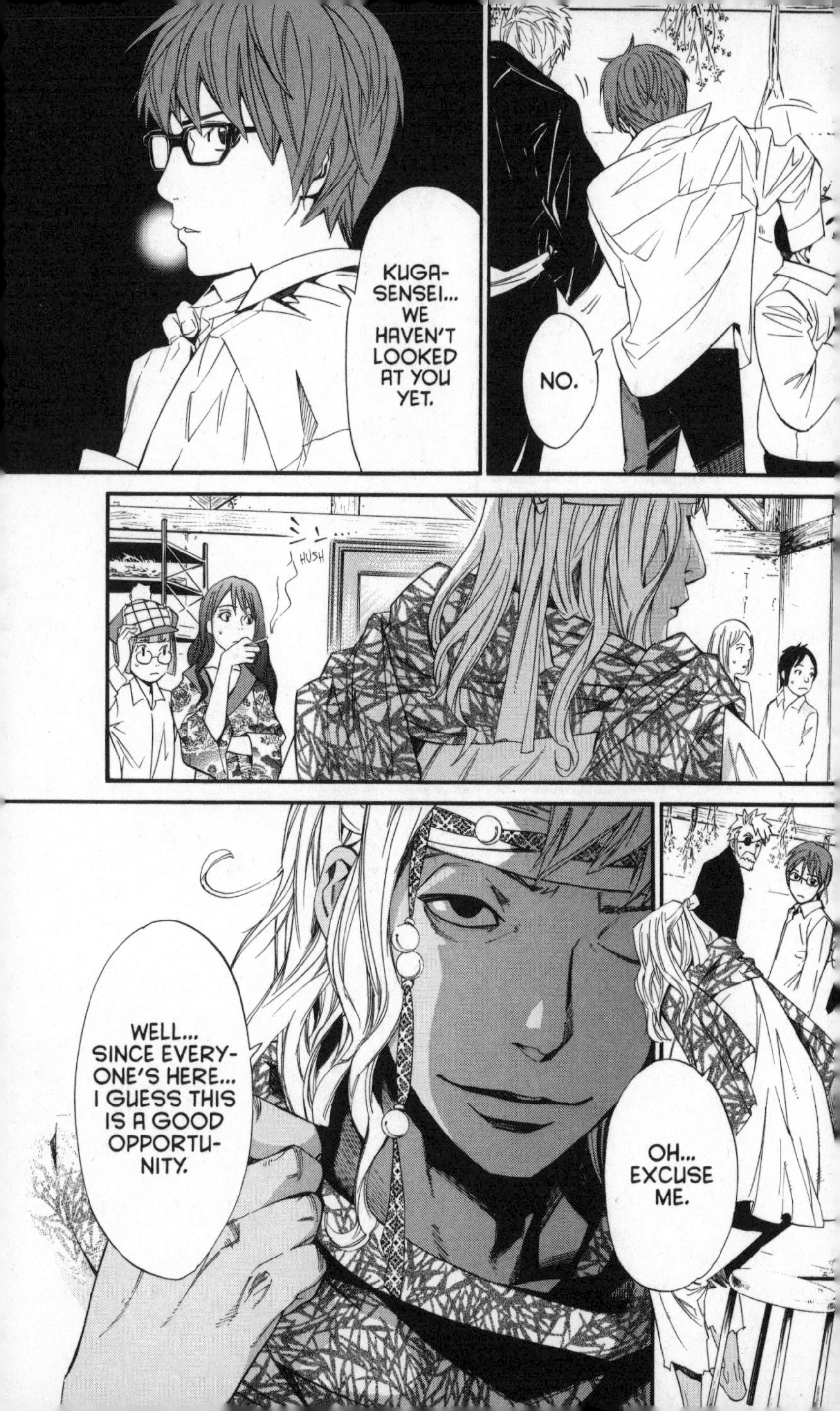
NO.
KUGA-SENSEI... WE HAVEN'T LOOKED AT YOU YET.
HUSH
OH... EXCUSE ME.
WELL... SINCE EVERYONE'S HERE... I GUESS THIS IS A GOOD OPPORTUNITY.

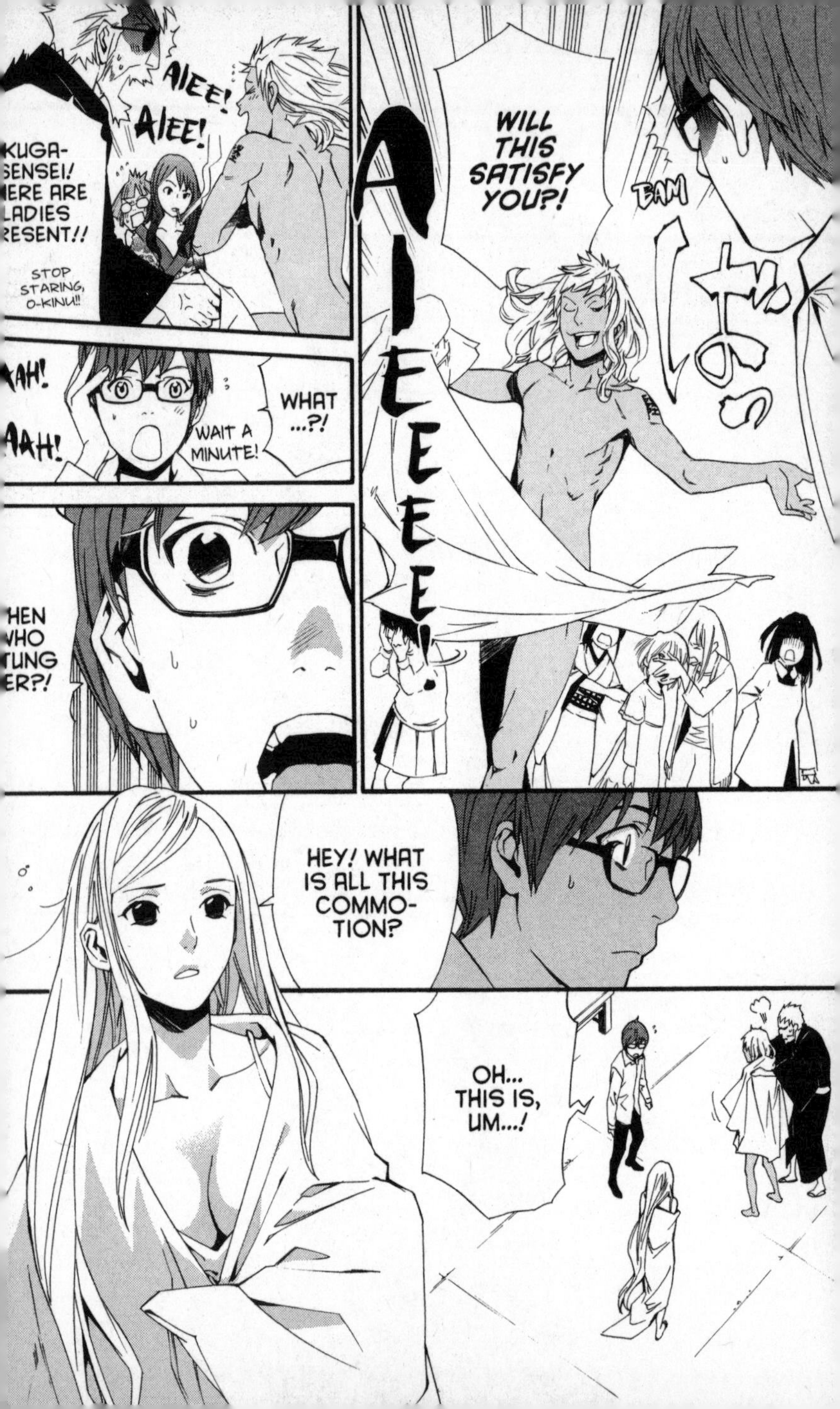
BAM
WILL THIS SATISFY YOU?!
AIEEEE!
AIEE!
AIEE!
KUGA-SENSEI! ERE ARE LADIES RESENT!!
STOP STARING, O-KINU!!
WHAT ...?!
WAIT A MINUTE!
AAH!
AAH!
HEN WHO TUNG ER?!
HEY! WHAT IS ALL THIS COMMOTION?
OH... THIS IS, UM...!

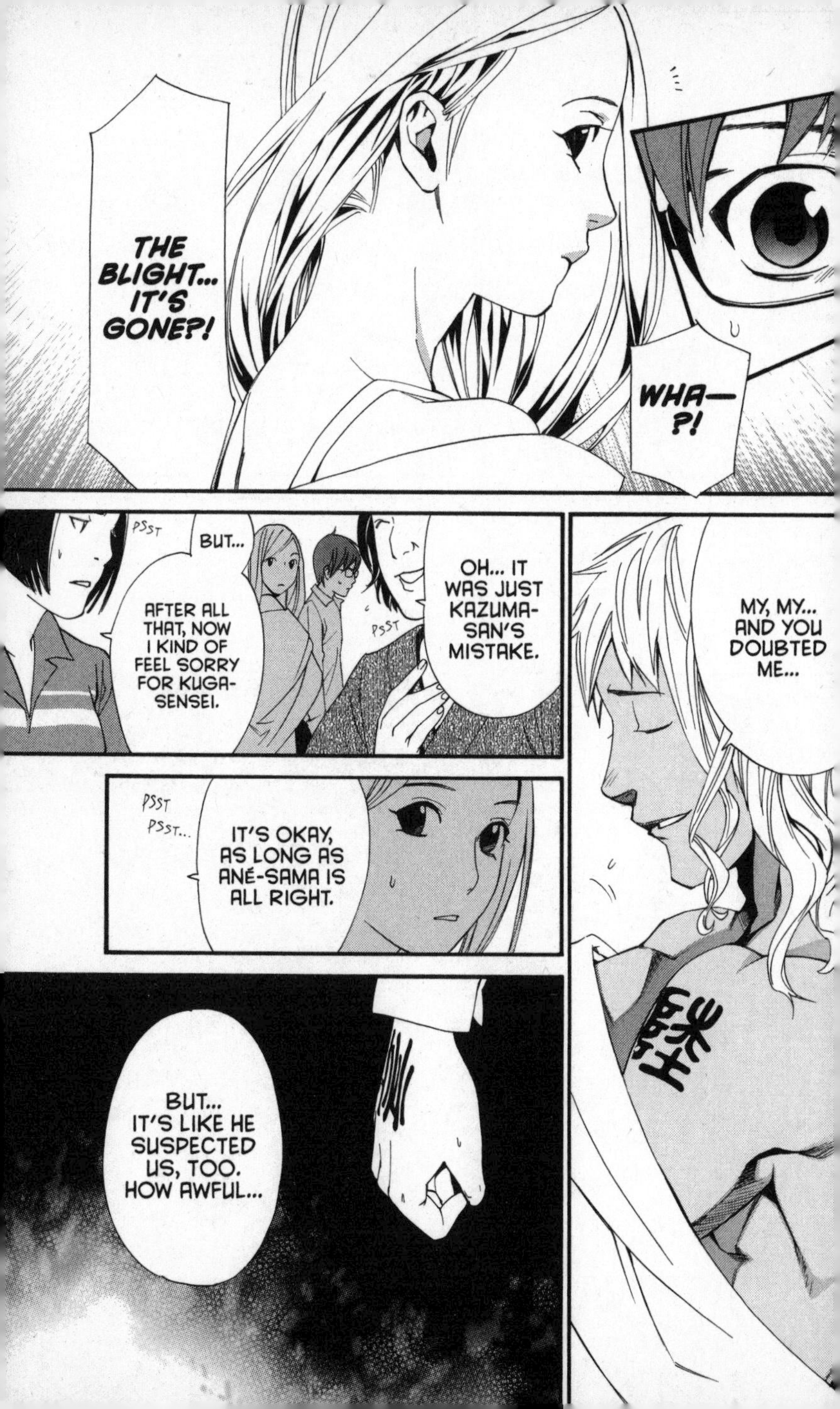
WHA—?!
THE BLIGHT... IT'S GONE?!
MY, MY... AND YOU DOUBTED ME...
PSST
OH... IT WAS JUST KAZUMA-SAN'S MISTAKE.
PSST
BUT...
AFTER ALL THAT, NOW I KIND OF FEEL SORRY FOR KUGA-SENSEI.
PSST
PSST...
IT'S OKAY, AS LONG AS ANÉ-SAMA IS ALL RIGHT.
BUT... IT'S LIKE HE SUSPECTED US, TOO. HOW AWFUL...

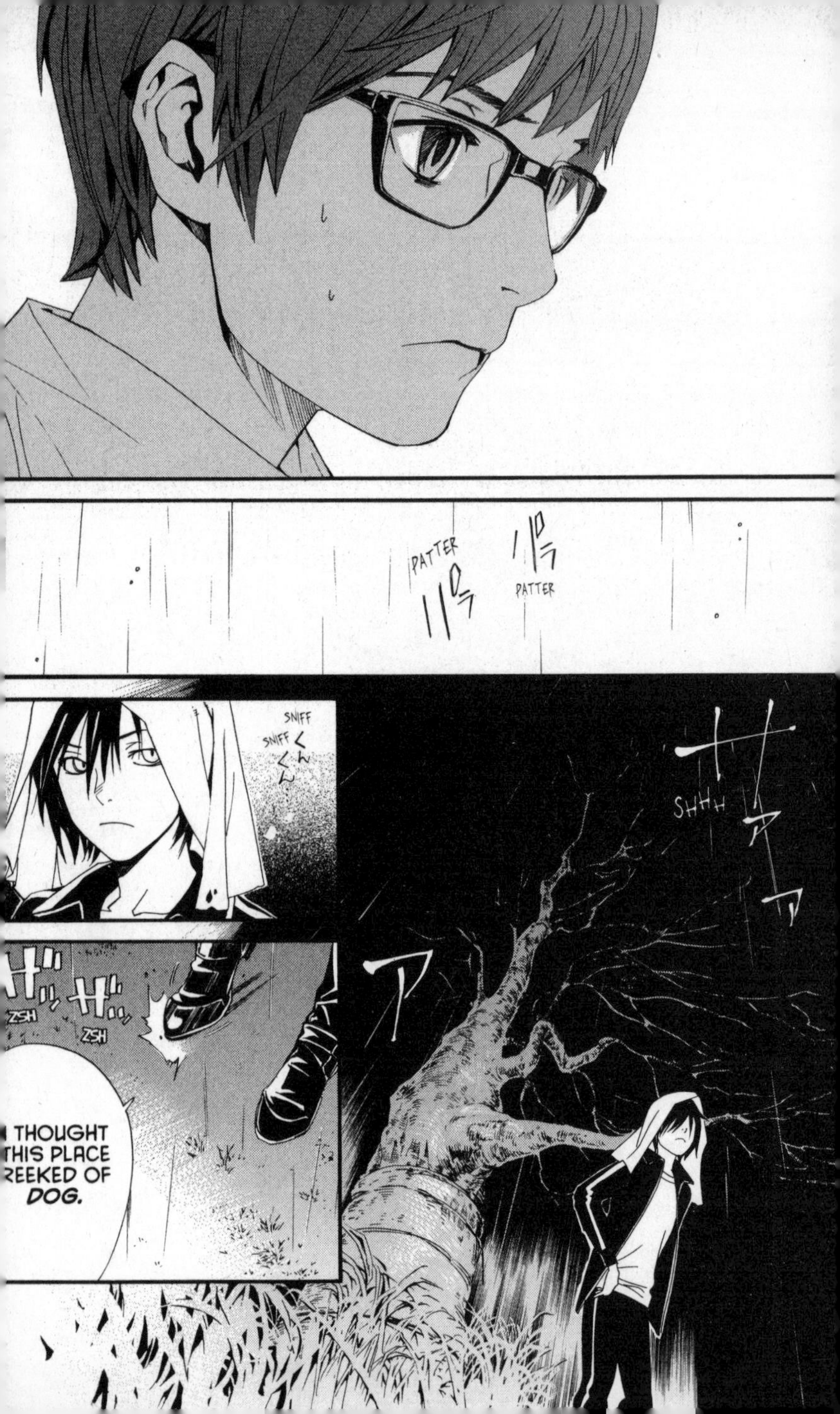
PATTER
PATTER
SHHH
SNIFF
SNIFF
ZSH
ZSH
I THOUGHT THIS PLACE REEKED OF *DOG.*

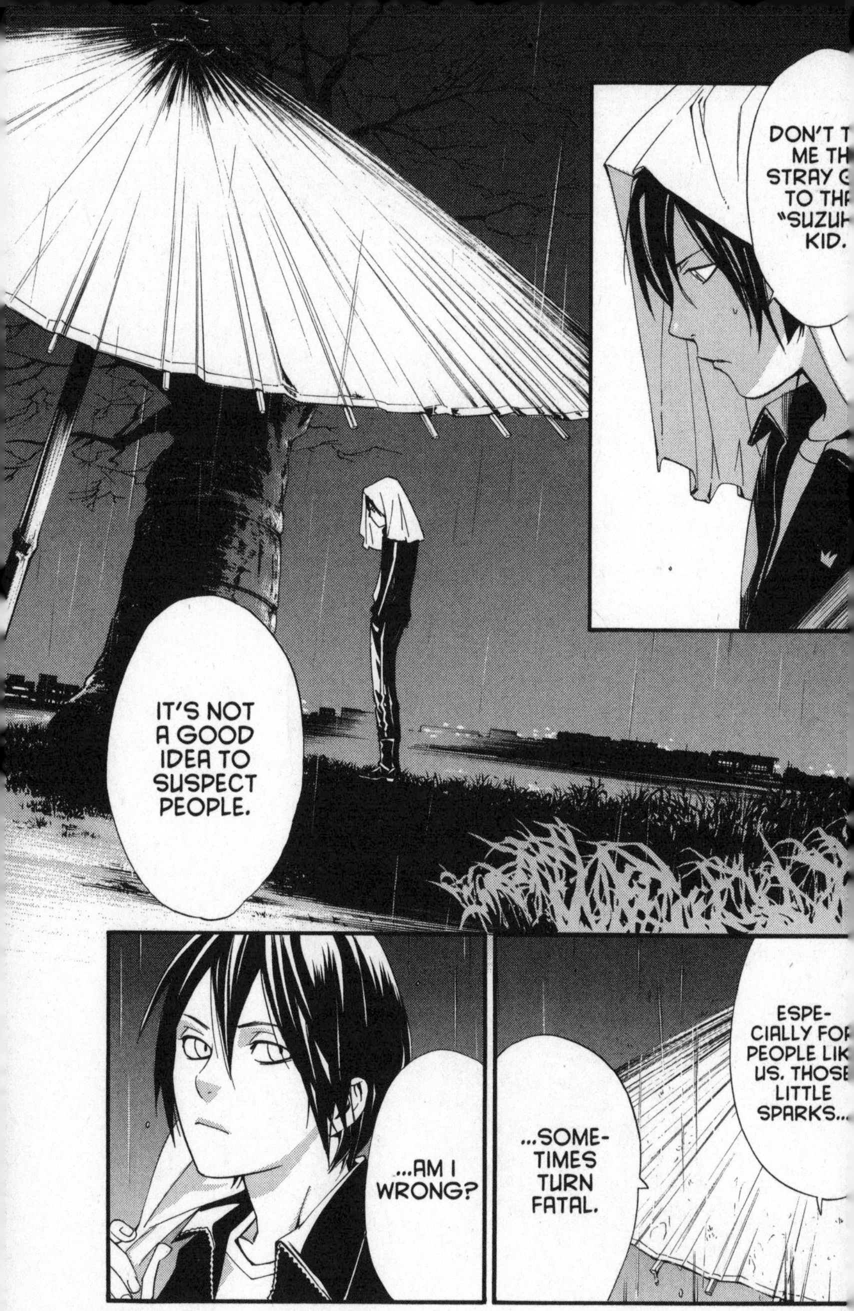
DON'T T ME TH STRAY G TO THA "SUZUH KID.
IT'S NOT A GOOD IDEA TO SUSPECT PEOPLE.
ESPE-CIALLY FOR PEOPLE LIK US. THOSE LITTLE SPARKS...
...SOME-TIMES TURN FATAL.
...AM I WRONG?

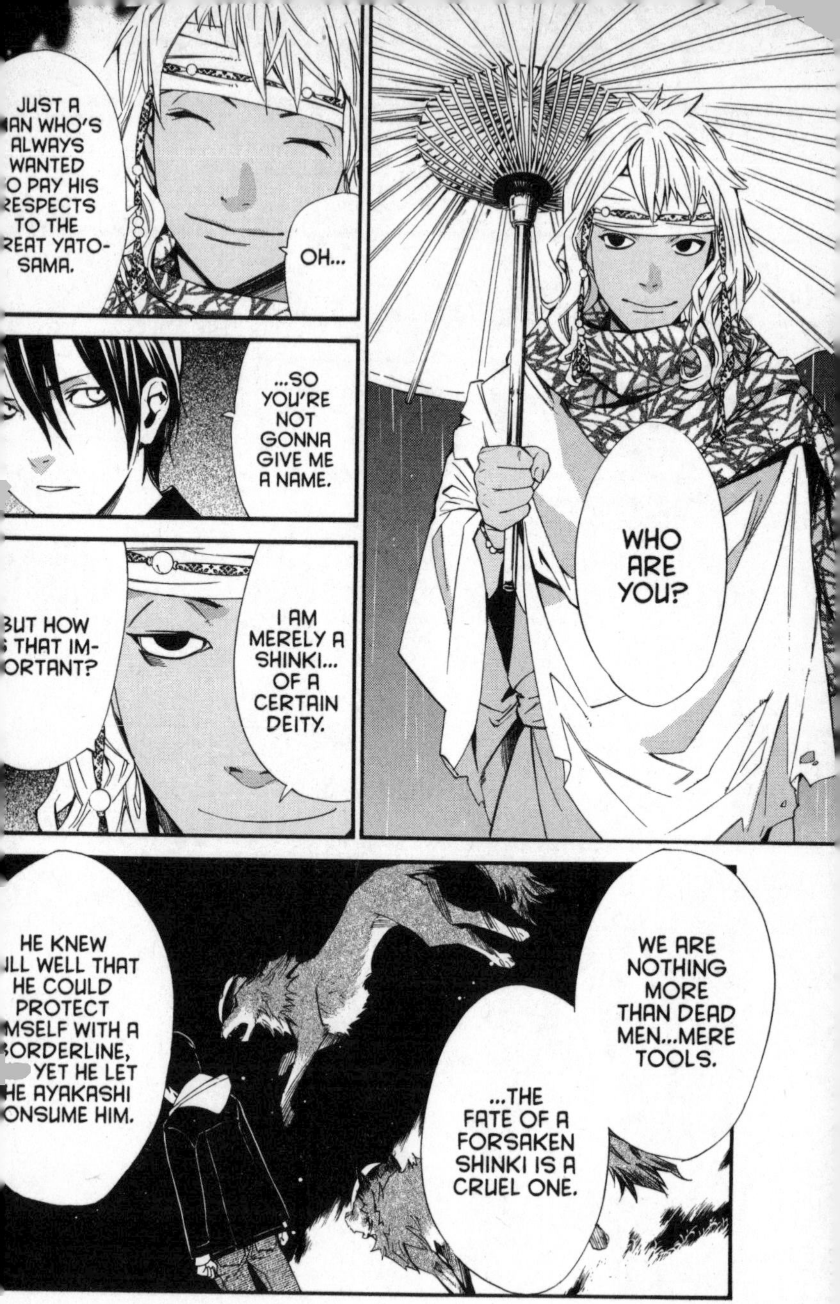
WHO ARE YOU?
JUST A IAN WHO'S ALWAYS WANTED O PAY HIS RESPECTS TO THE REAT YATO-SAMA.
OH...
...SO YOU'RE NOT GONNA GIVE ME A NAME.
I AM MERELY A SHINKI... OF A CERTAIN DEITY.
UT HOW THAT IM-ORTANT?
WE ARE NOTHING MORE THAN DEAD MEN...MERE TOOLS.
...THE FATE OF A FORSAKEN SHINKI IS A CRUEL ONE.
HE KNEW ILL WELL THAT HE COULD PROTECT MSELF WITH A ORDERLINE, YET HE LET HE AYAKASHI ONSUME HIM.

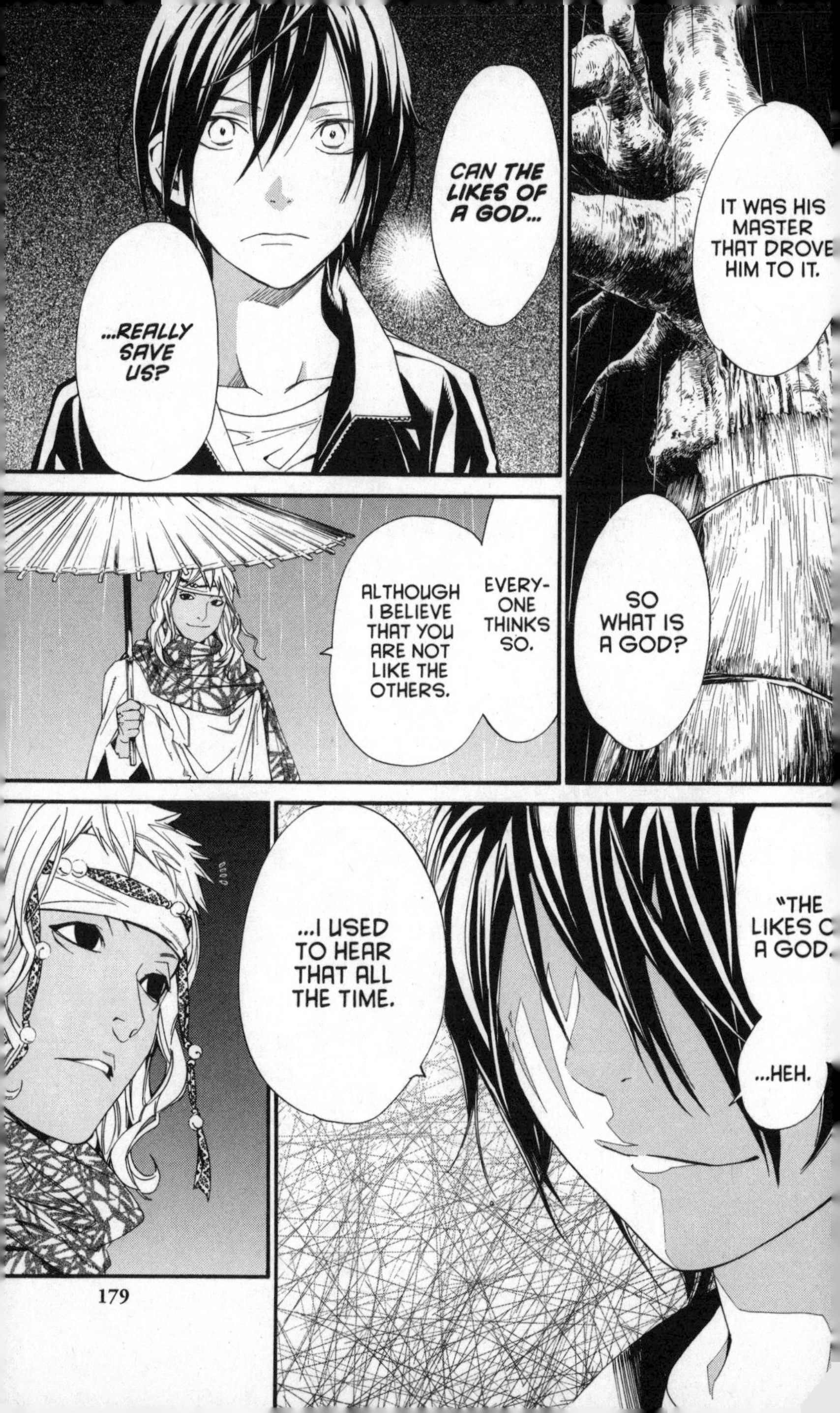
IT WAS HIS MASTER THAT DROVE HIM TO IT.
SO WHAT IS A GOD?
CAN THE LIKES OF A GOD...
...REALLY SAVE US?
EVERY-ONE THINKS SO.
ALTHOUGH I BELIEVE THAT YOU ARE NOT LIKE THE OTHERS.
"THE LIKES O A GOD.
...HEH.
...I USED TO HEAR THAT ALL THE TIME.

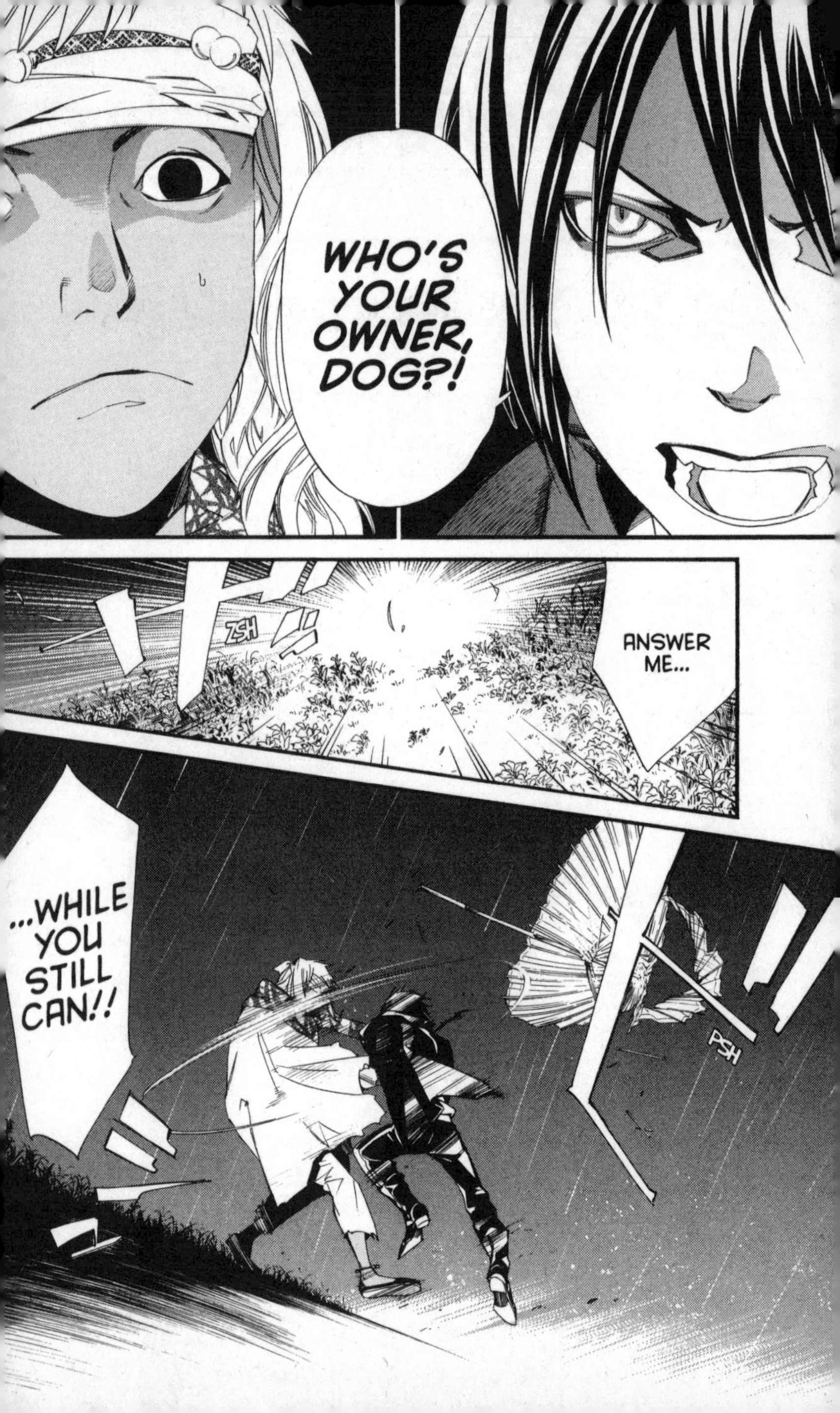
WHO'S YOUR OWNER, DOG?!
ANSWER ME...
ZSH
...WHILE YOU STILL CAN!!
PSH

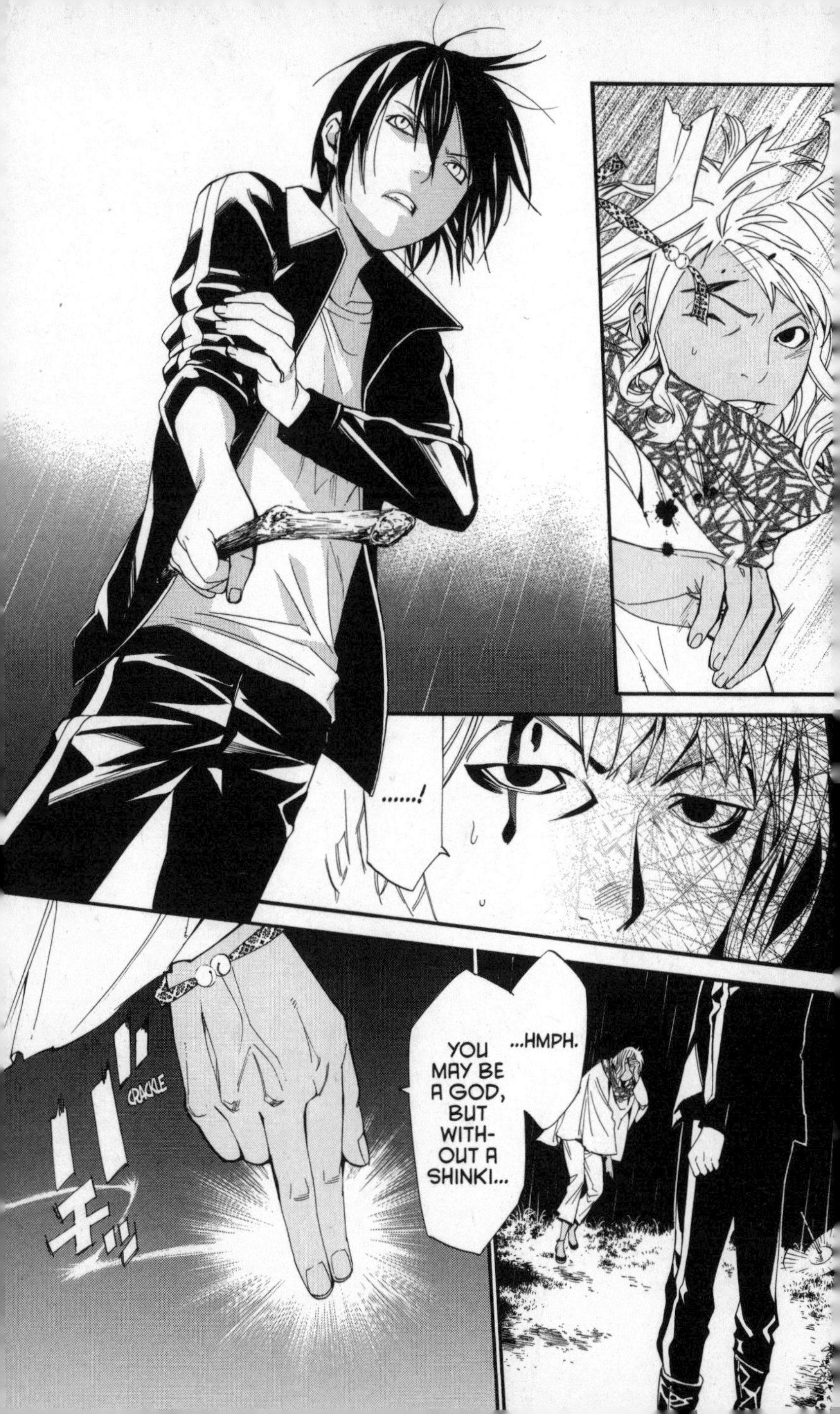

......!
...HMPH.
YOU MAY BE A GOD, BUT WITH-OUT A SHINKI...
CRACKLE

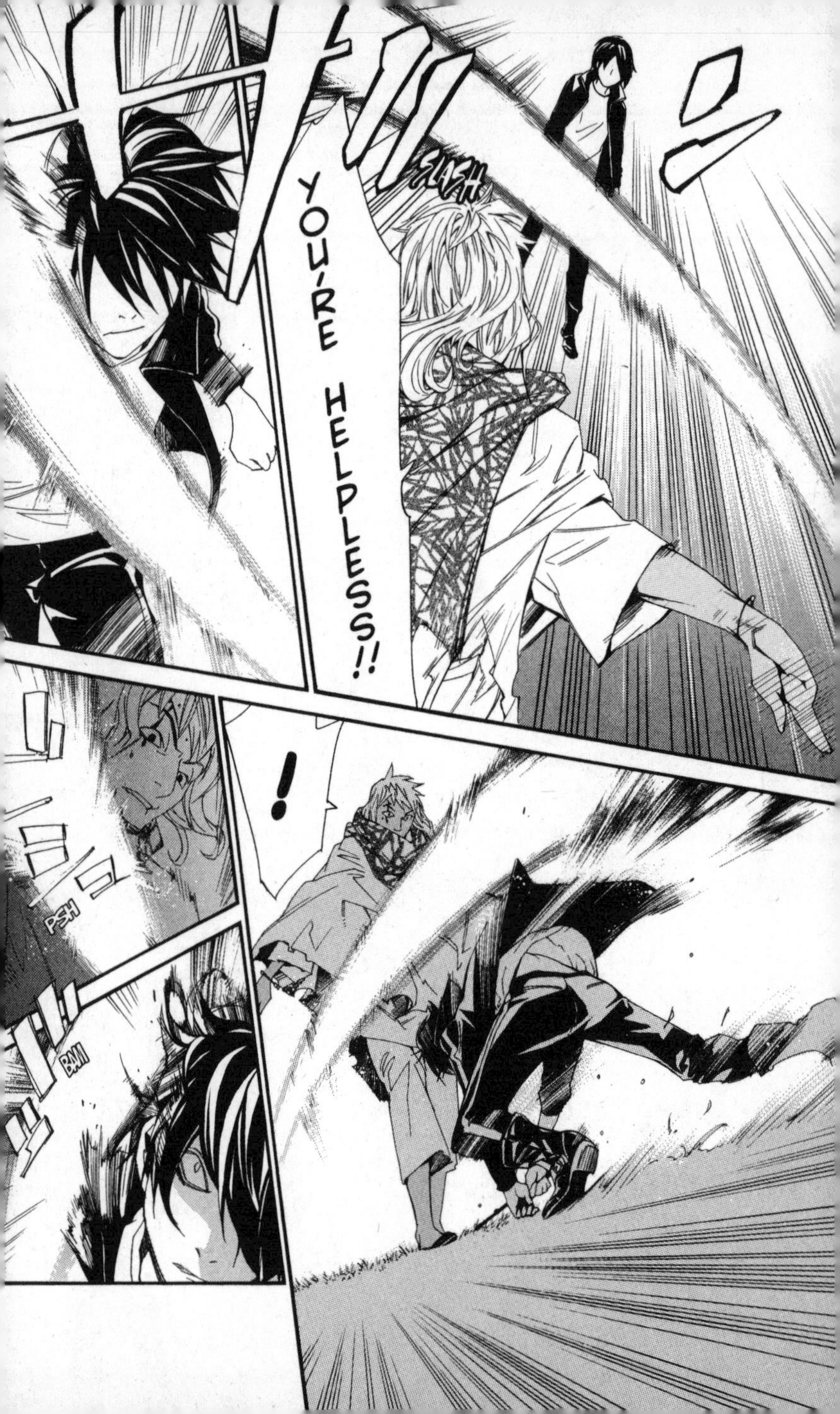

SLASH
YOU'RE HELPLESS!!
!
PSH
BAM

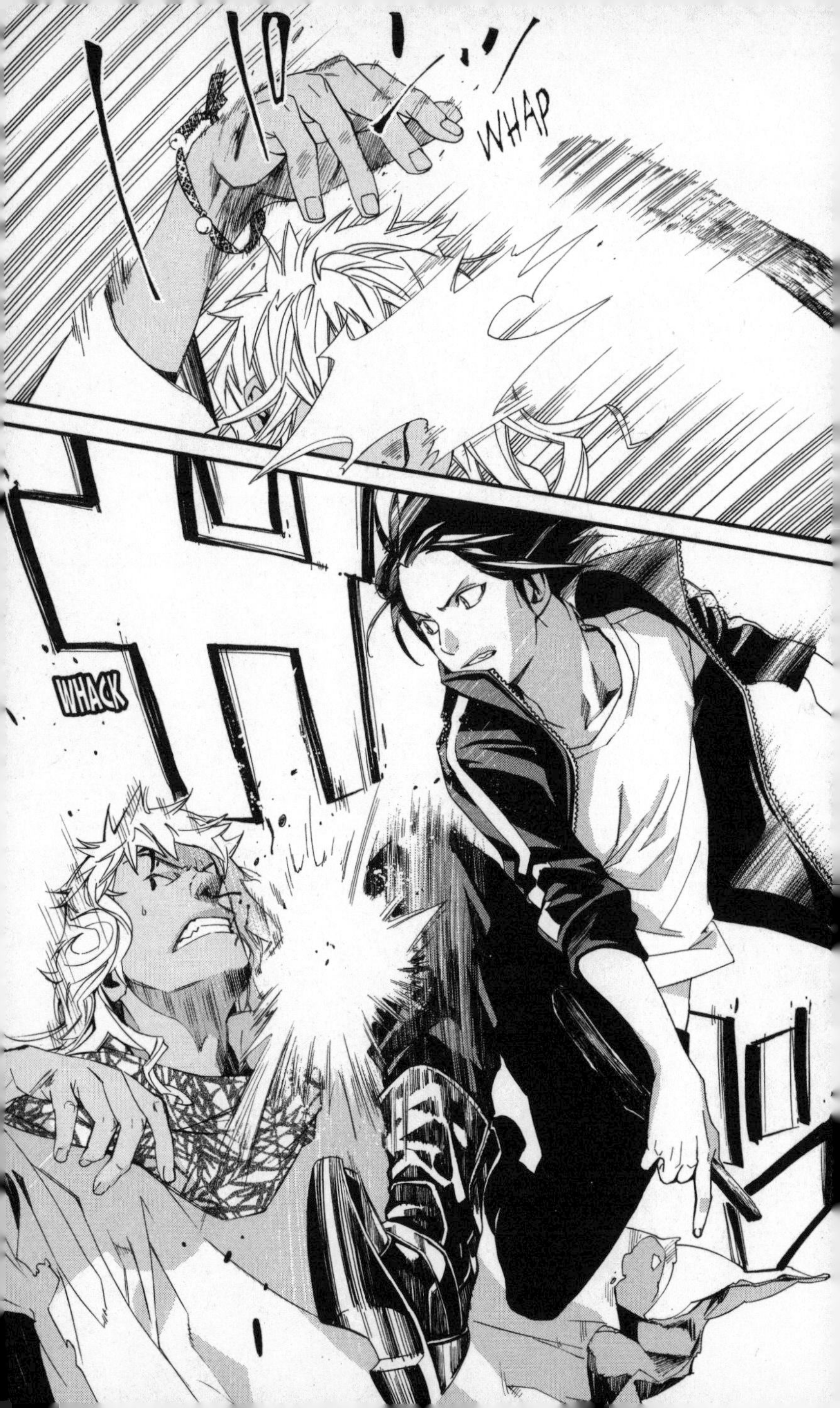
WHAP
WHACK

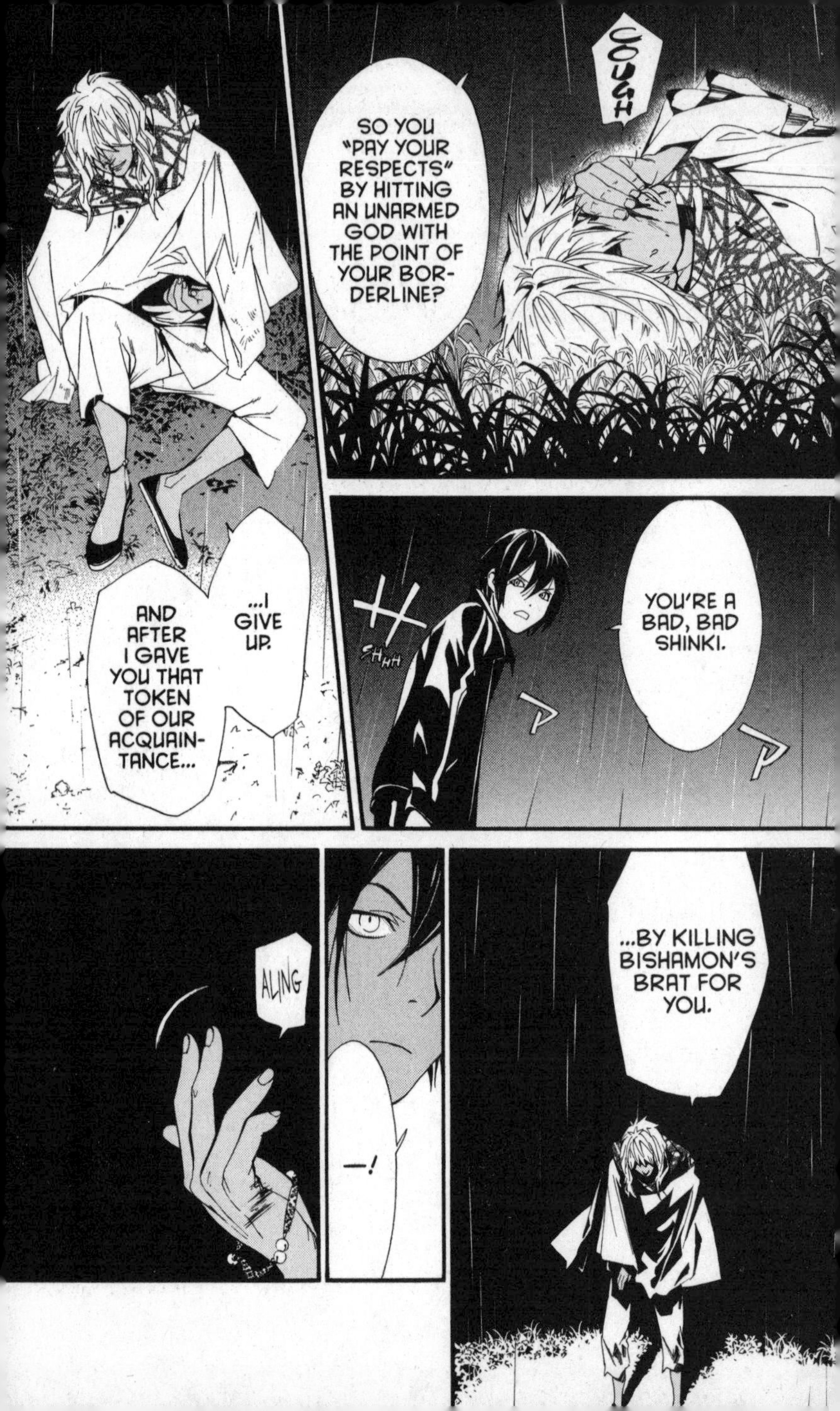
COUGH
SO YOU "PAY YOUR RESPECTS" BY HITTING AN UNARMED GOD WITH THE POINT OF YOUR BOR-DERLINE?
SHHH
YOU'RE A BAD, BAD SHINKI.
...I GIVE UP.
AND AFTER I GAVE YOU THAT TOKEN OF OUR ACQUAIN-TANCE...
...BY KILLING BISHAMON'S BRAT FOR YOU.
—!
ALING

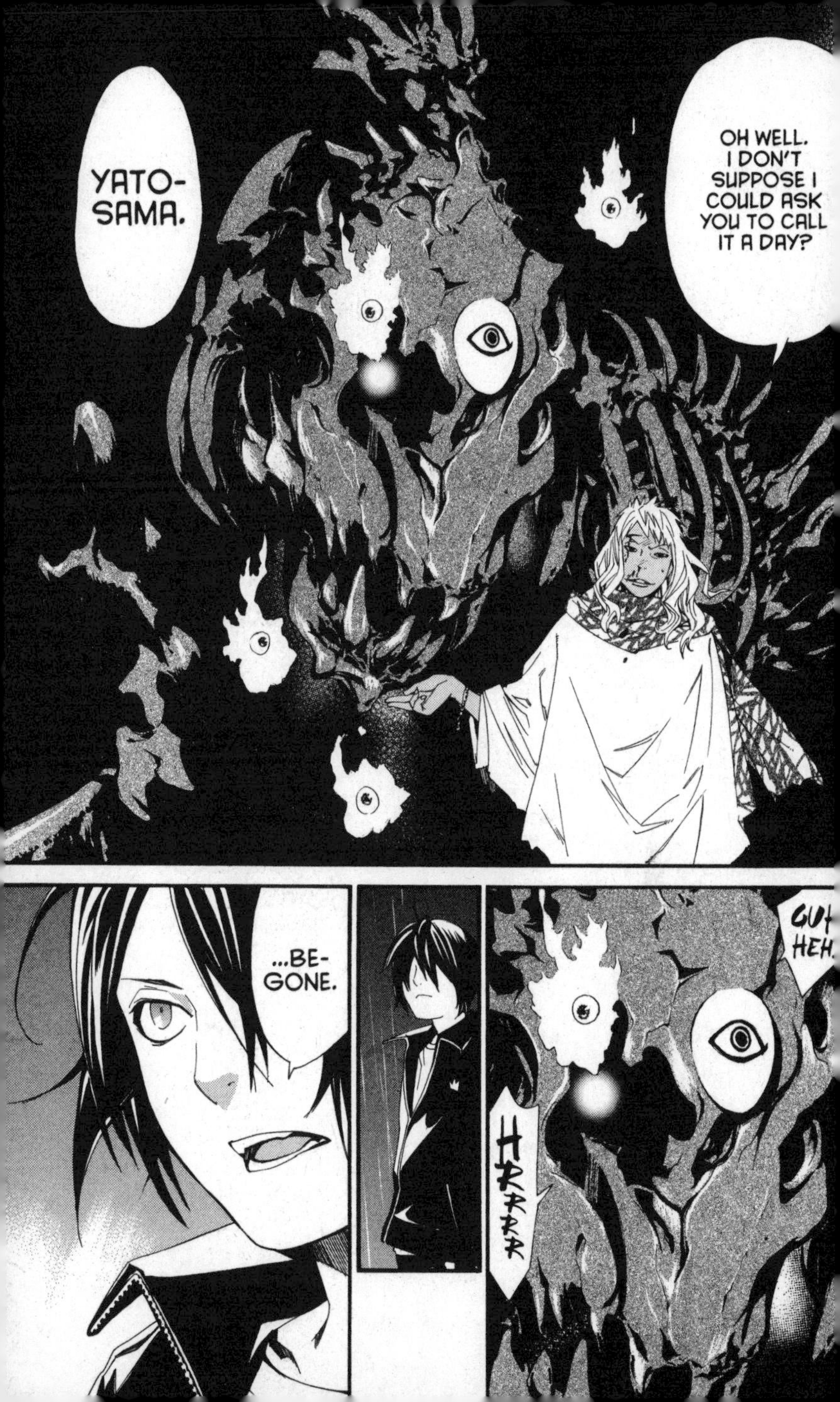
OH WELL. I DON'T SUPPOSE I COULD ASK YOU TO CALL IT A DAY?
YATO-SAMA.
GUH HEH.
HRRRR
...BE-GONE.

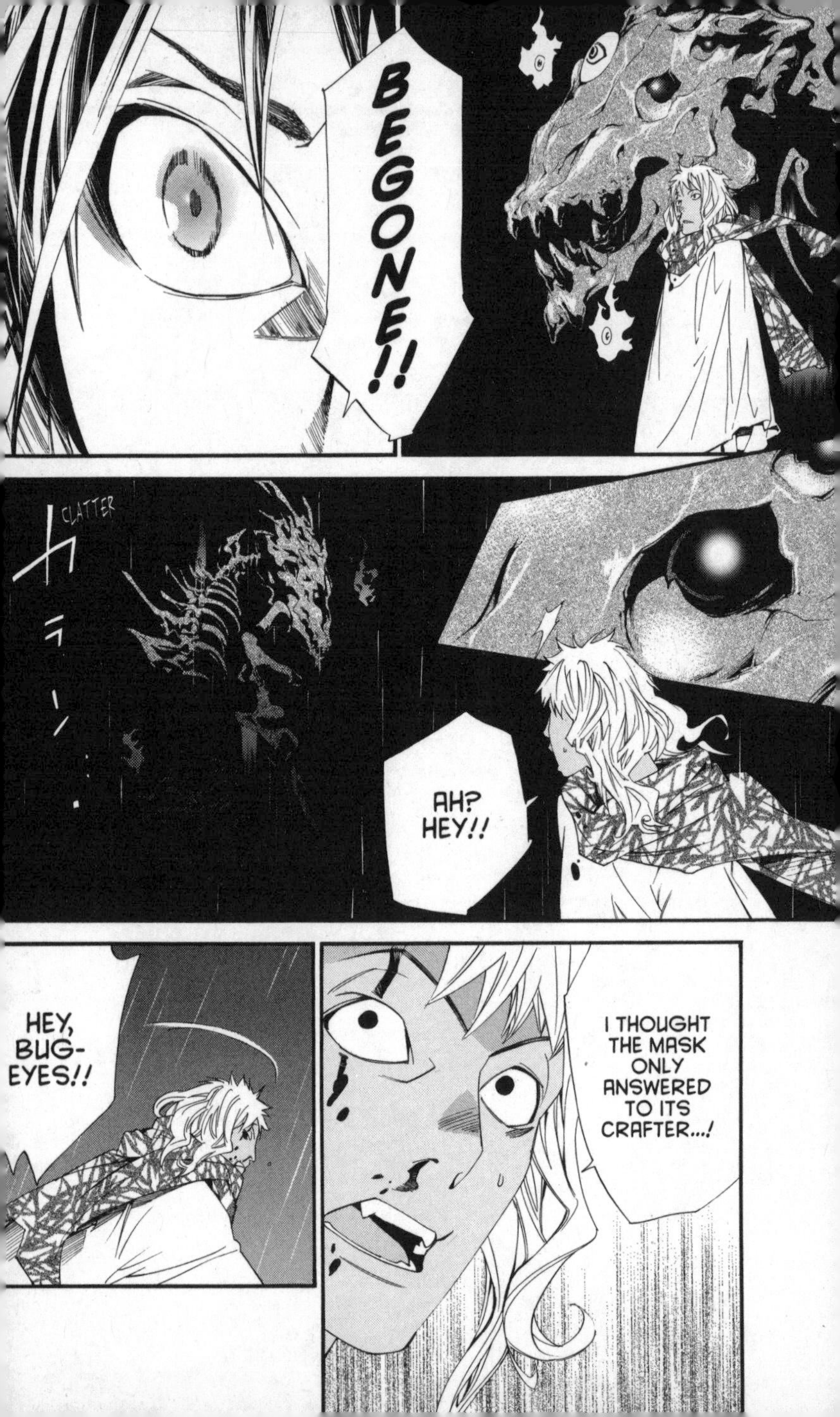
BEGONE!!
AH? HEY!!
CLATTER
I THOUGHT THE MASK ONLY ANSWERED TO ITS CRAFTER...!
HEY, BUG-EYES!!

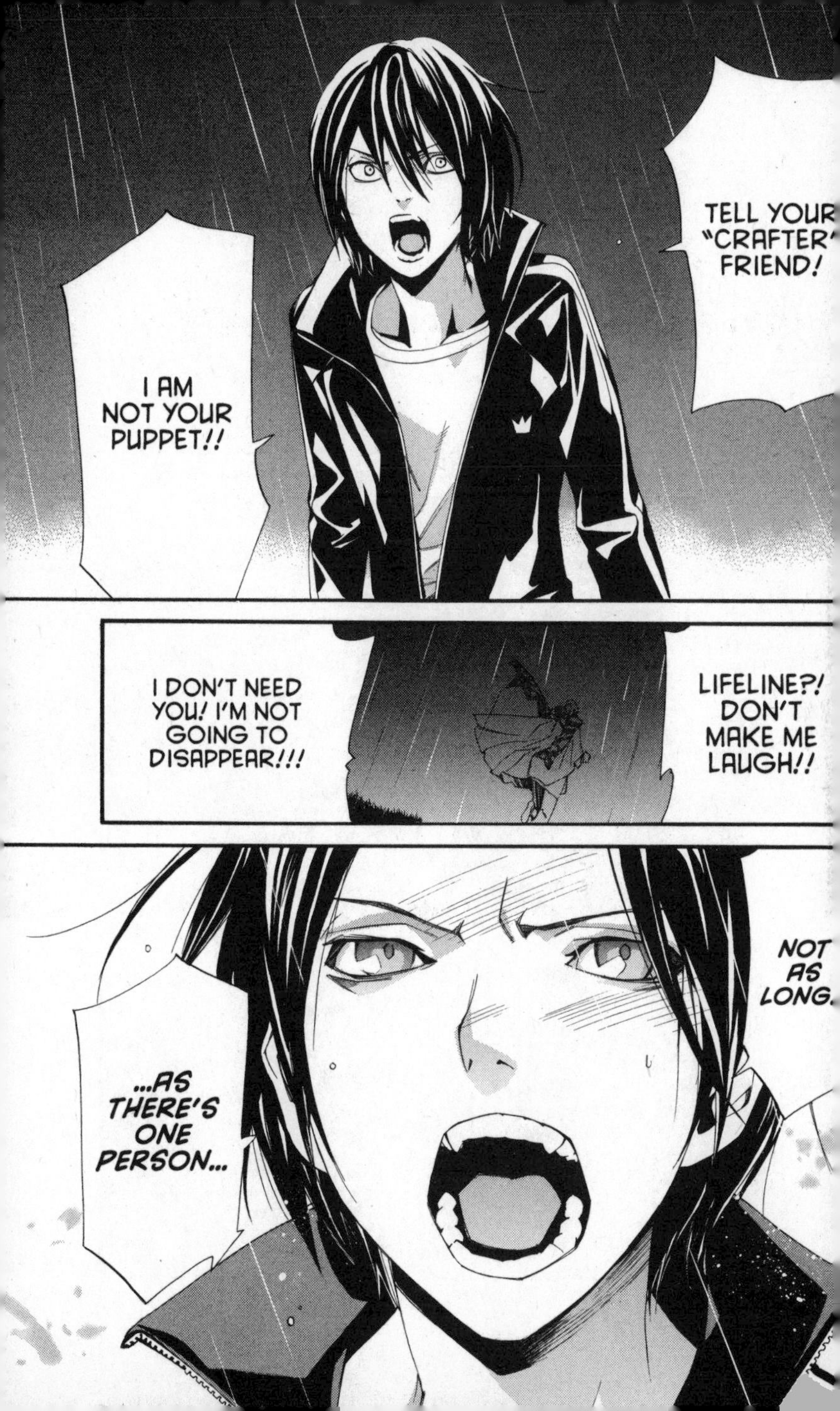
TELL YOUR "CRAFTER" FRIEND!
I AM NOT YOUR PUPPET!!
LIFELINE?! DON'T MAKE ME LAUGH!!
I DON'T NEED YOU! I'M NOT GOING TO DISAPPEAR!!!
NOT AS LONG.
...AS THERE'S ONE PERSON...

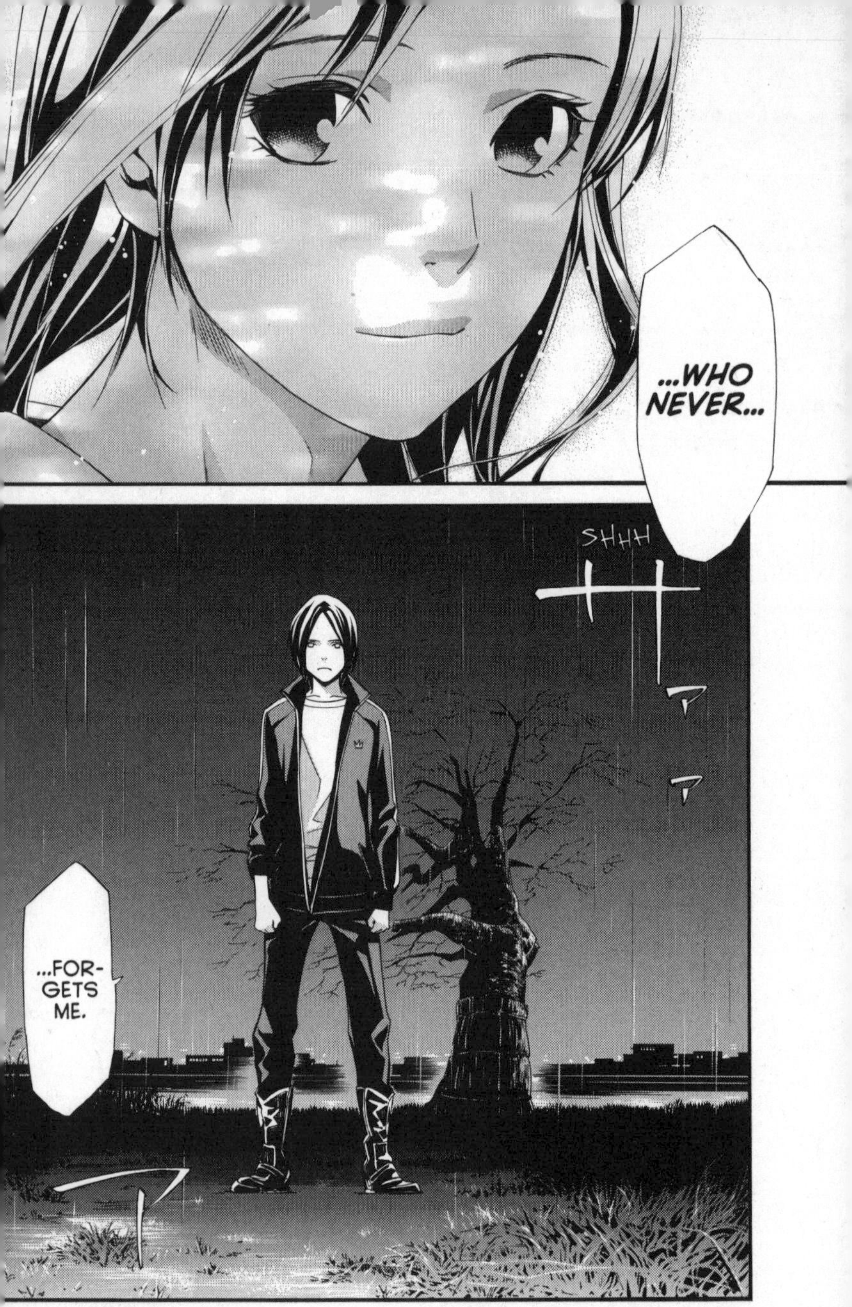
...WHO NEVER...
SHHH
...FOR-GETS ME.

ORAGAMI / TO BE CONTINUED

野

覺

禅

ATROCIOUS MANGA

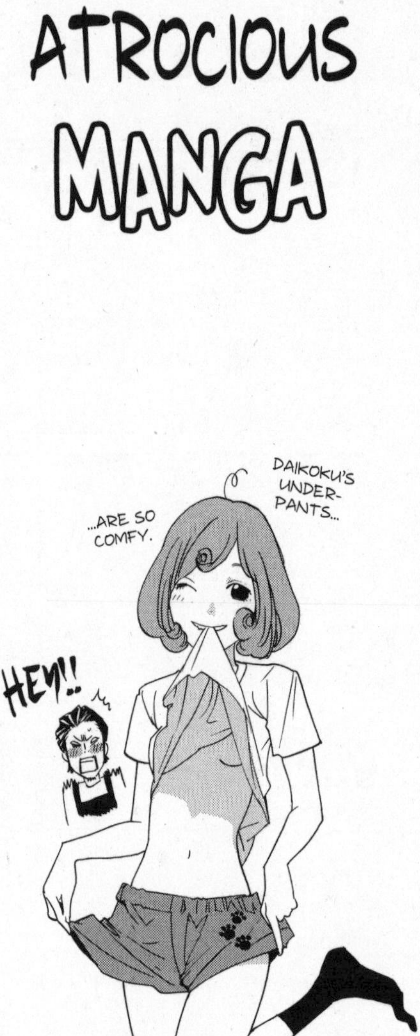
DAIKOKU'S UNDER-PANTS...
...ARE SO COMFY.
HEY!!

MARKETING 101

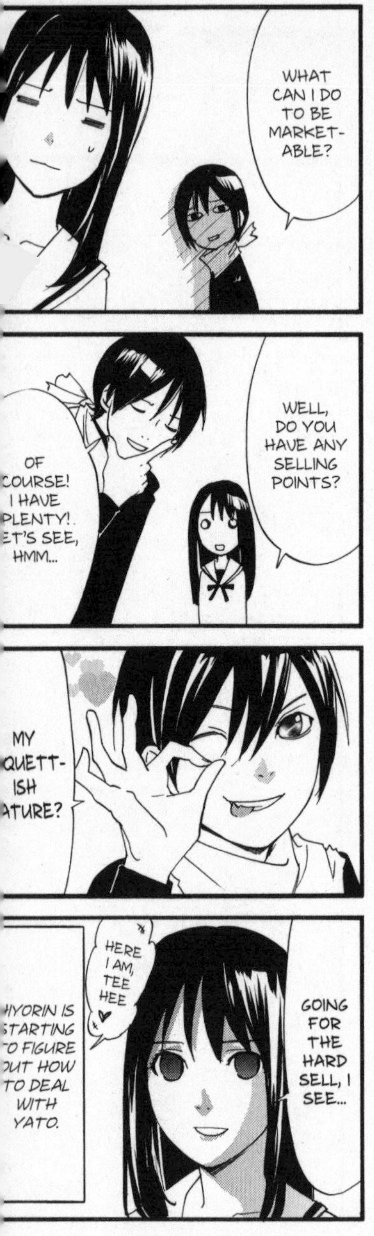
WHAT CAN I DO TO BE MARKET-ABLE?
WELL, DO YOU HAVE ANY SELLING POINTS?
OF COURSE! I HAVE PLENTY! ET'S SEE, HMM...
MY QUETT-ISH ATURE?
GOING FOR THE HARD SELL, I SEE...
HERE I AM, TEE HEE ♥
HIYORIN IS STARTING TO FIGURE OUT HOW TO DEAL WITH YATO.

HIYORIN WORKS PART TIME

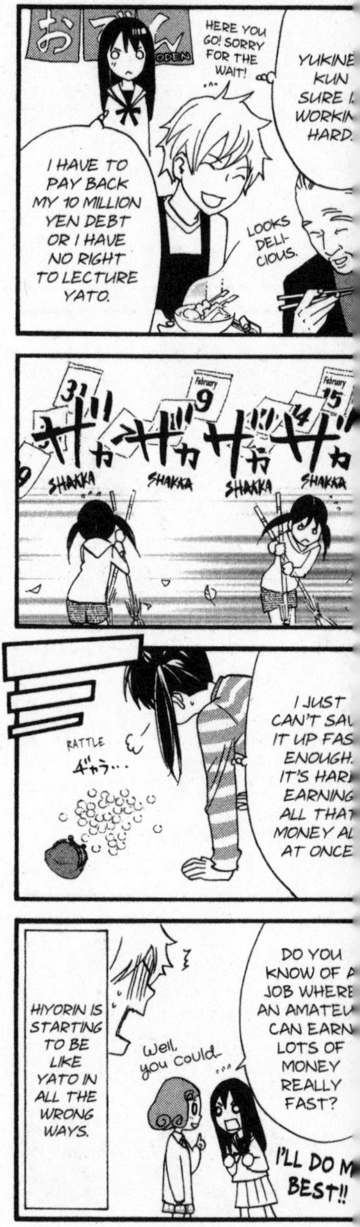
ODEN
YUKINE KUN SURE I WORKIN HARD.
HERE YOU GO! SORRY FOR THE WAIT!
LOOKS DELI- CIOUS.
I HAVE TO PAY BACK MY 10 MILLION YEN DEBT OR I HAVE NO RIGHT TO LECTURE YATO.
February 15
14
February 9
31
SHAKKA
SHAKKA
SHAKKA
SHAKKA
I JUST CAN'T SAV IT UP FAS ENOUGH. IT'S HAR EARNING ALL THA MONEY AL AT ONCE
RATTLE
DO YOU KNOW OF A JOB WHERE AN AMATEU CAN EARN LOTS OF MONEY REALLY FAST?
Well, you could...
HIYORIN IS STARTING TO BE LIKE YATO IN ALL THE WRONG WAYS.
I'LL DO M BEST!!

MARKETING 102

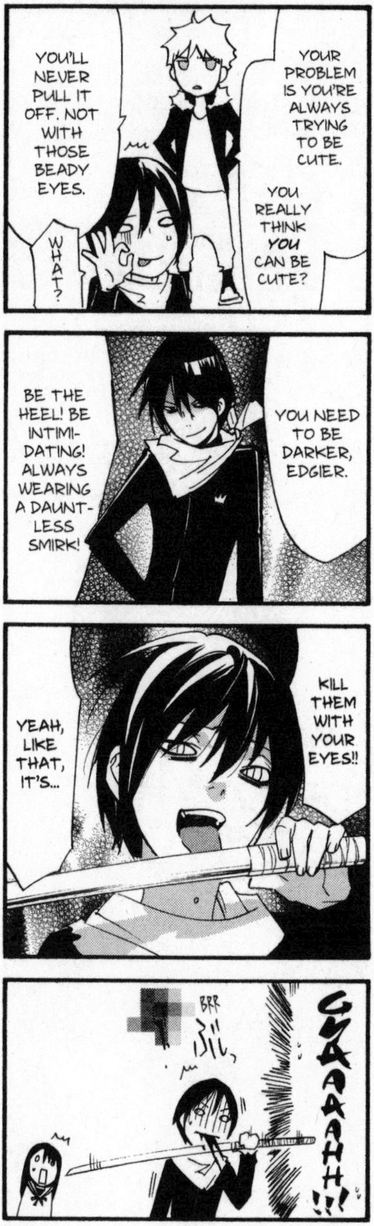
YOUR PROBLEM IS YOU'RE ALWAYS TRYING TO BE CUTE.
YOU'LL NEVER PULL IT OFF. NOT WITH THOSE BEADY EYES.
YOU REALLY THINK YOU CAN BE CUTE?
WHAT?
YOU NEED TO BE DARKER, EDGIER.
BE THE HEEL! BE INTIMI- DATING! ALWAYS WEARING A DAUNT- LESS SMIRK!
KILL THEM WITH YOUR EYES!!
YEAH, LIKE THAT, IT'S...
GYAAAAAHH!!!
BRR

THE GUIDE'S ULTIMATE GOAL

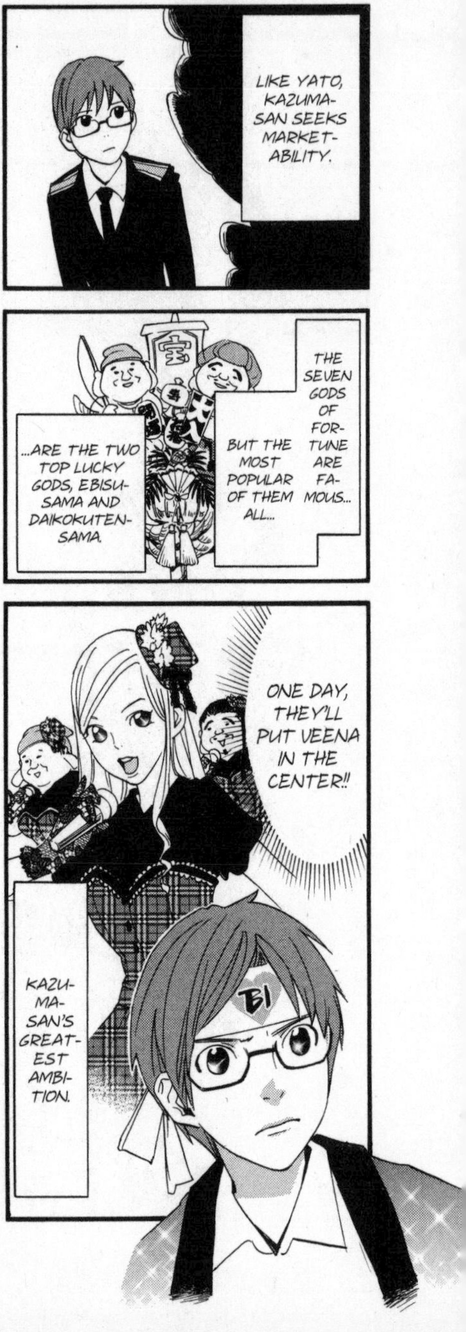
LIKE YATO, KAZUMA-SAN SEEKS MARKET-ABILITY.
THE SEVEN GODS OF FORTUNE ARE FAMOUS...
BUT THE MOST POPULAR OF THEM ALL...
...ARE THE TWO TOP LUCKY GODS, EBISU-SAMA AND DAIKOKUTEN-SAMA.
ONE DAY, THEY'LL PUT VEENA IN THE CENTER!!
KAZUMA-SAN'S GREATEST AMBITION.
BI

DRUNKARD

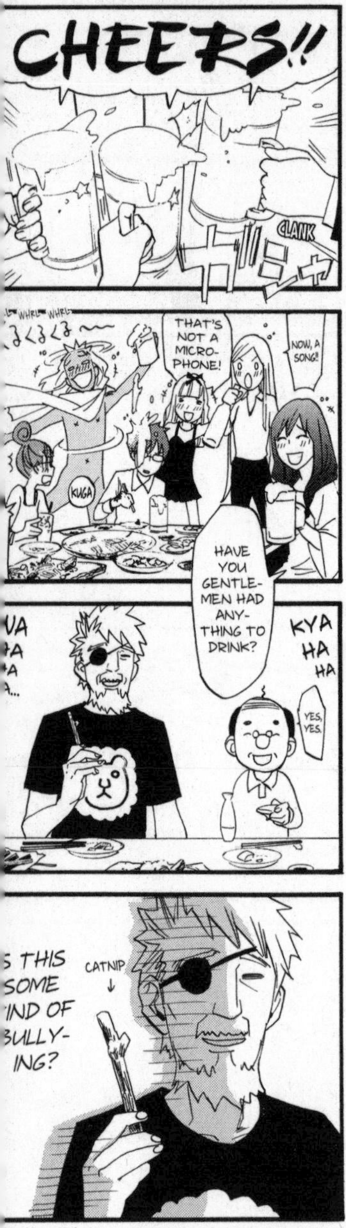
CHEERS!!
CLANK
WHRL WHRL
NOW, A SONG!!
THAT'S NOT A MICROPHONE!
KUGA
HAVE YOU GENTLEMEN HAD ANYTHING TO DRINK?
KYA HA HA
YES, YES.
CATNIP
S THIS SOME IND OF ULLY-ING?

KOFUKU'S THANK-YOU VISIT

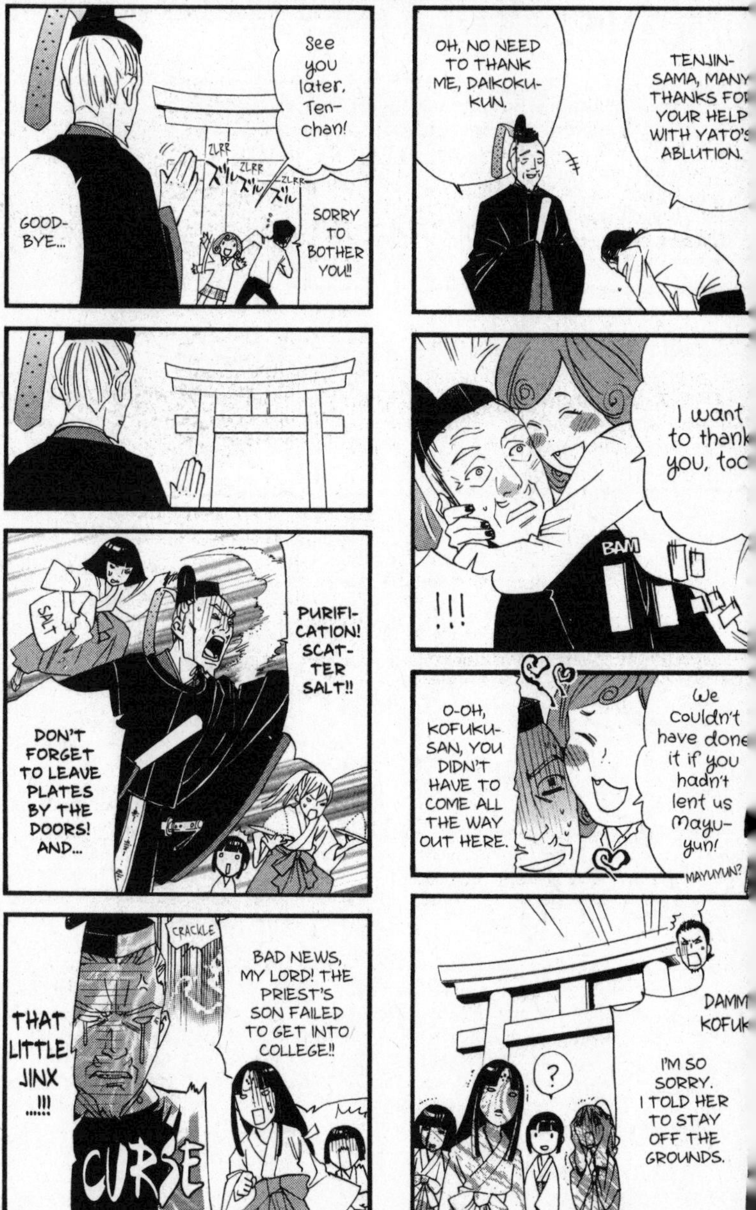

TENJIN-SAMA, MANY THANKS FOR YOUR HELP WITH YATO'S ABLUTION.
OH, NO NEED TO THANK ME, DAIKOKU-KUN.
I want to thank you, too
BAM
!!!
We couldn't have done it if you hadn't lent us Mayu-yun!
O-OH, KOFUKU-SAN, YOU DIDN'T HAVE TO COME ALL THE WAY OUT HERE.
MAYUYUN?
DAMM KOFUK
?
I'M SO SORRY. I TOLD HER TO STAY OFF THE GROUNDS.
See you later, Ten-chan!
ZLRR
ズル ZLRR
ズル ZLRR
ズル
SORRY TO BOTHER YOU!!
GOOD-BYE...
PURIFI-CATION! SCAT-TER SALT!!
SALT
DON'T FORGET TO LEAVE PLATES BY THE DOORS! AND...
CRACKLE
BAD NEWS, MY LORD! THE PRIEST'S SON FAILED TO GET INTO COLLEGE!!
THAT LITTLE JINX ......!!!
CURSE

THANK YOU TO EVERYONE WHO READ THIS FAR!!

TRANSLATION NOTES

Japanese is a tricky language for most Westerners, and translation is often more art than science. For your edification and reading pleasure, here are notes on some of the places where we could have gone in a different direction in our translation of the work, or where a Japanese cultural reference is used.

What federation is she with?, page 11

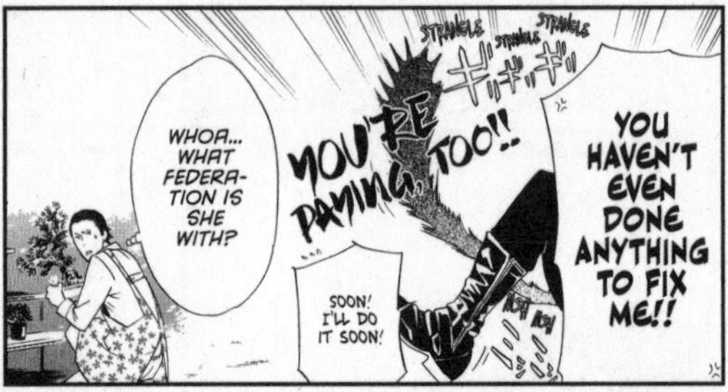
STRANGLE STRANGLE STRANGLE
YOU HAVEN'T EVEN DONE ANYTHING TO FIX ME!!
YOU'RE PAYING, TOO!!
WHOA... WHAT FEDERATION IS SHE WITH?
SOON! I'LL DO IT SOON!

For readers who, like the translators, are not familiar with professional wrestling, "federation" refers specifically to a professional wrestling promotion—a company that organizes wrestling events. In the original Japanese, Daikoku uses the word *dantai*, which means simply "group," but it is the specific word for group that is used in reference to pro wrestling organizations. Most likely, Daikoku sees the moves Hiyori is using on Yato and is wondering where she learned them, or he thinks she's good enough to be a professional.

Tomoné's 3D experience, page 12

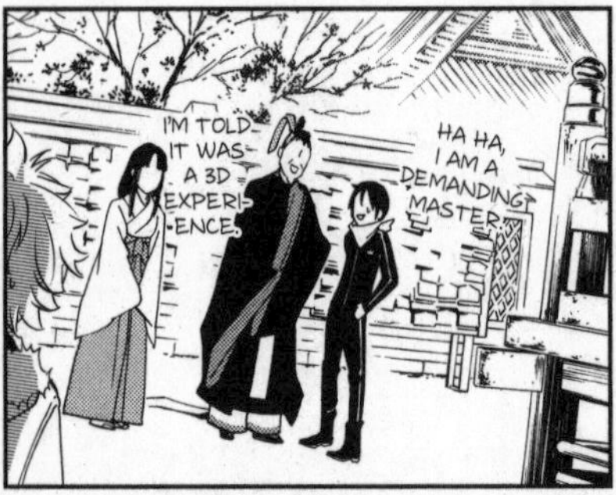
HA HA, I AM A DEMANDING MASTER.
I'M TOLD IT WAS A 3D EXPERIENCE.

As you may have guessed, 3D doesn't normally stand for "drippy, dirty, and destitute." It usually stands for "dirty, dangerous, and demeaning," which are the three Ds used to describe certain kinds of blue-collar work. There are variations in which the third D stands for "demanding" or "difficult," which could be because the 3Ds come from the Japanese concept of 3K (*kitanai, kiken, kitsui*), where the third K (*kitsui*) could be translated to demeaning, demanding, or difficult. When Mayu described her experience as Tomoné to Tenjin, she replaced *kiken* and *kitsui* with two of her own, *kusai* and *kasegi-nai*, which mean respectively "stinky" and "not earning any money." Because Yato's stink comes from the sweat that's constantly dripping from his hands, the translators (who had a very difficult time finding a synonym for "stinky" that begins with D) felt it would not be inappropriate to render *kusai* as "drippy," as in "dripping with sweat."

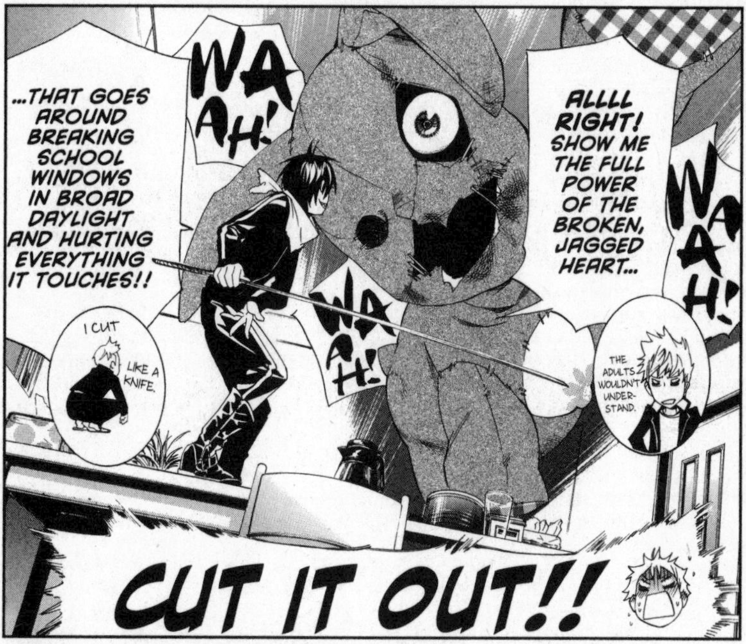
ALLLL RIGHT! SHOW ME THE FULL POWER OF THE BROKEN, JAGGED HEART...
WAAAH!
THE ADULTS WOULDN'T UNDERSTAND.
WAAH!
...THAT GOES AROUND BREAKING SCHOOL WINDOWS IN BROAD DAYLIGHT AND HURTING EVERYTHING IT TOUCHES!!
WAAH!
I CUT
LIKE A KNIFE.
CUT IT OUT!!

Yukiné's broken, jagged heart, page 34

Shame from Yato bringing up a past he'd probably rather forget is only one of the reasons Yukiné may find this speech annoying. Yato is also referencing a song from 1983 by the Checkers, called "*Giza-Giza Heart no Komoriuta*," or "The Lullaby of a Broken, Jagged Heart." (The lines that Yato's imaginary punk Yukiné supplies are also references to the lyrics, although the song says, "I won't ask you to understand," instead of, "The adults wouldn't understand.") This song may have a special place in Yato's heart, because when it originally debuted it didn't sell very well, but when the Checkers' second single became a hit, "*Giza-Giza Heart*" became much more marketable as well.

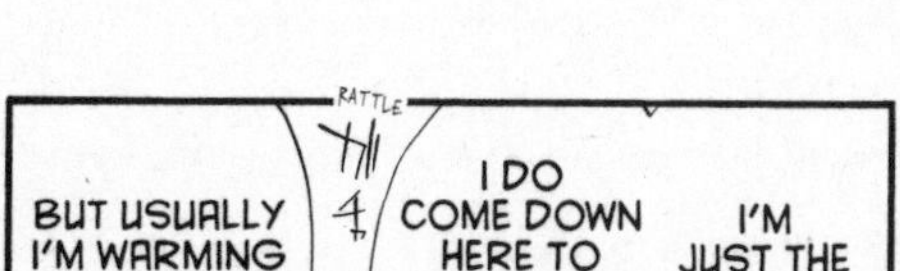
I'M JUST THE FAITHFUL MEDICINE MAN.
I DO COME DOWN HERE TO NAKATSU-KUNI FROM TIME TO TIME.
RATTLE
RATTLE
BUT USUALLY I'M WARMING THE BENCH UP IN TAKAMA-GA-HARA.

Nakatsukuni and Takama-ga-hara, page 56

In Shinto, Nakatsukuni is the name for Japan, or the earth. It means "the middle kingdom," referring to the fact that it's between Yomi (the land of the dead) and Takama-ga-hara, or the Plain of High Heaven (where the highest gods live). As one of the more respectable gods, Bishamon lives in Takama-ga-hara, and most of her shinki live at her estate there.

March 3 and March 6, page 59

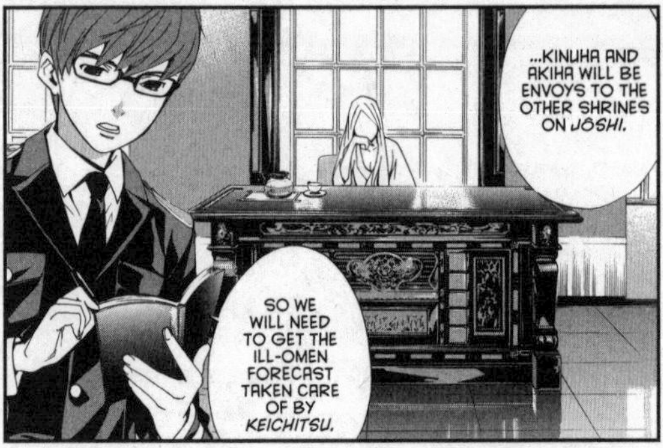
...KINUHA AND AKIHA WILL BE ENVOYS TO THE OTHER SHRINES ON *JŌSHI*.
SO WE WILL NEED TO GET THE ILL-OMEN FORECAST TAKEN CARE OF BY *KEICHITSU*.

Because Kazuma and Bishamon have been around for a long time—since before Japan adopted the Western calendar—they use older Japanese terms to refer to specific dates. *Jōshi* is March 3rd. The word means roughly "early snake," referring to the ancient eastern calendar based on the Chinese zodiac—it was a festival day originally observed on the first Day of the Snake in the third month of the year. In about the third century AD, the festival day was fixed as the third day of the third month. In modern Japan, it is celebrated as the Doll Festival, or Girls' Day.

Keichitsu refers to approximately March 6th. In the ancient Japanese calendar, the year was divided into 24 periods (called *sekku*). The third of these periods is *Keichitsu*, which means "awakening of (hibernating) insects" and begins roughly on that date.

O-Kinu-san, page 71

You may be wondering why Akiha calls Kinuha "O-Kinu-san" instead of "Kinuha-san." Based on Bishamon's shinki naming style, it's safe to assume that her true name is represented by a character which is usually pronounced *kinu*. Up until around World War II, it was a common practice to take the main part of a woman's name and add the honorific prefix O- to it, thus turning Kinuha into O-Kinu.

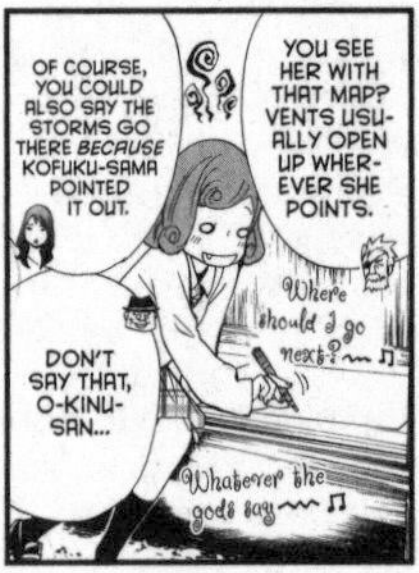
YOU SEE HER WITH THAT MAP? VENTS USUALLY OPEN UP WHEREVER SHE POINTS.
OF COURSE, YOU COULD ALSO SAY THE STORMS GO THERE *BECAUSE* KOFUKU-SAMA POINTED IT OUT.
Where should I go next?~♫
DON'T SAY THAT, O-KINU-SAN...
Whatever the gods say~♫

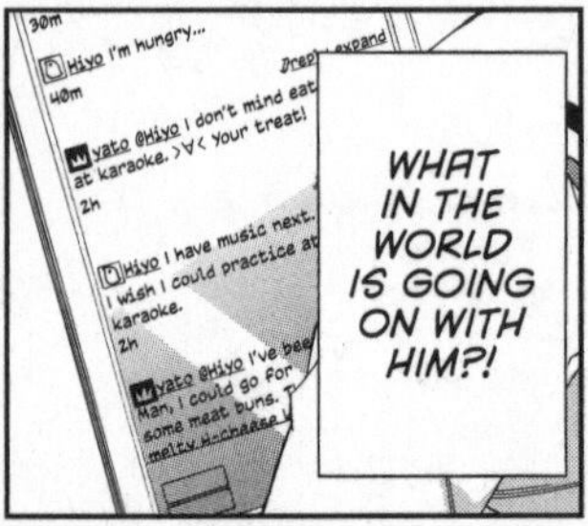
Hiyo I'm hungry...
WHAT IN THE WORLD IS GOING ON WITH HIM?!

Three sugar mommas, page 101

In the original Japanese, Yato expressed a desire for three hair-dressing wives. In Japanese, the term "hairdresser's husband" refers to a man who lives off of his wife's income. This comes from a *rakugo* (a form of comedic story-telling) tale called "*Umayakaji* (Fire at the Stable)." In the story, a hairdresser who is constantly fighting with her younger husband wants to know if he really loves her. She gets advice from a matchmaker who tells her a story about Confucius, whose disciples clumsily caused a fire which resulted in the loss of his best horse. Because Confucius was more worried about the safety of his disciples than the loss of his horse, their relationship and trust grew stronger. So the hairdresser recreates the scenario in this story, and when the stable burns, her husband truly is concerned for her safety. But the punchline is that if the hairdresser died, the husband would have no money for his lavish lifestyle.

Tomoko and Suzuha, page 113
The type of graffiti seen on this tree is called an *aiai-gasa*, which means "sharing an umbrella." The triangle with the vertical line through it represents an umbrella, and the names underneath represent the couple sharing it. It's a way of showing how close the two of them are, sort of like drawing a heart with the two names in it.

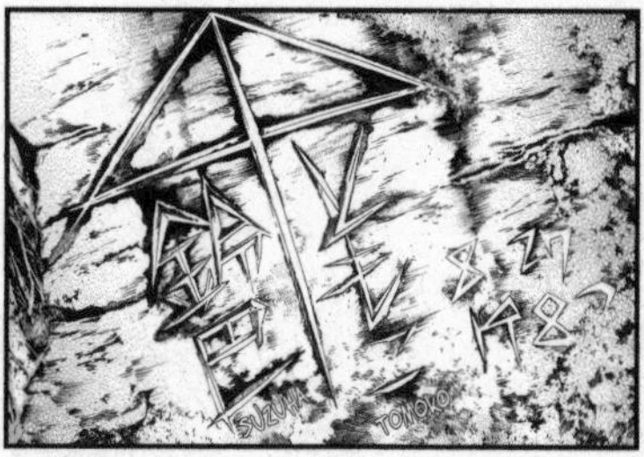
SUZUHA
TOMOKO

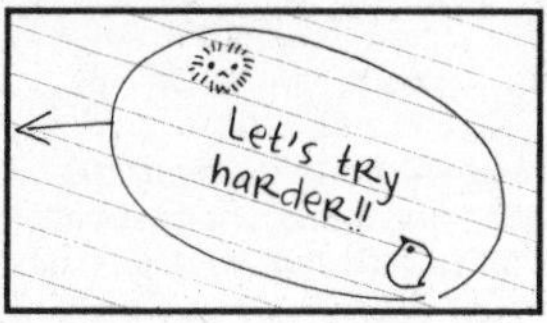
Let's try harder!!

Hiyori's mascot, page 123
Readers may have noticed that Hiyori tends to represent herself with a picture of a chick (as seen here and in her Twitter icon). This is because *hiyo* can be short for *hiyoko*, which means "baby bird."

Cherry blossom picnic, page 130
In Japan, the cherry blossoms are in bloom from the end of March to early May, and everyone goes out to enjoy their beauty. This outing is called *hanami*, or flower-viewing, and usually involves a picnic under the cherry trees.

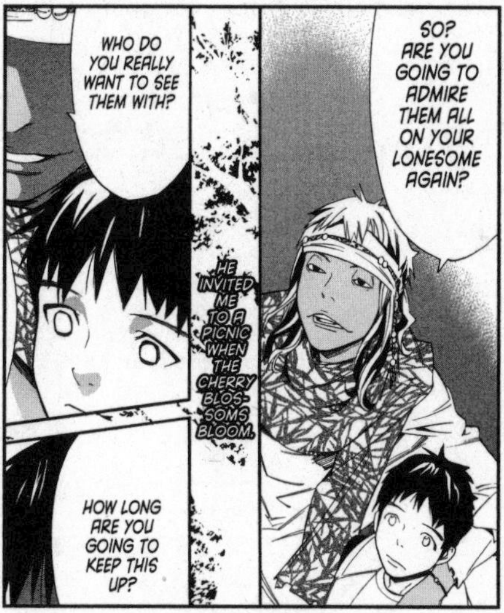
SO? ARE YOU GOING TO ADMIRE THEM ALL ON YOUR LONESOME AGAIN?
HE INVITED ME TO A PICNIC WHEN THE CHERRY BLOSSOMS BLOOM.
WHO DO YOU REALLY WANT TO SEE THEM WITH?
HOW LONG ARE YOU GOING TO KEEP THIS UP?

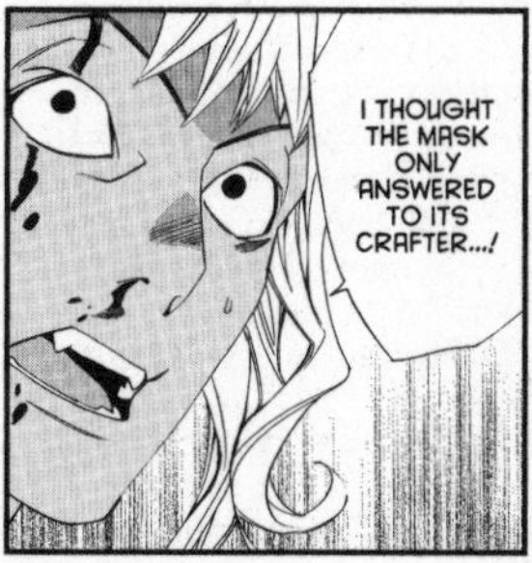
I THOUGHT THE MASK ONLY ANSWERED TO ITS CRAFTER...!

Caster, page 186
The word Kugaha uses here is *jutsushi*, which means "user of technique." It usually refers to someone using some kind of magic, be it spells, conjuring, summoning, etc. Because the translators do not yet know what specific kind of technique is being used, they chose the generic "crafter," as in "spellcrafter," because the *jutsushi* likely crafted the masks as well as the spell that was placed on them.

Going for the hard sell, page 190

MY COQUETT-ISH NATURE?
GOING FOR THE HARD SELL, I SEE...
HERE I AM, TEE HEE
HIYORIN IS STARTING TO FIGURE OUT HOW TO DEAL WITH YATO.

The translators admit that they changed the joke here, because it involves a Japanese idiom that doesn't (as far as they know) have an English equivalent. So let us explain the idiom, and then we'll tell the joke again, and maybe it will be funnier than the final English version. In Japan, the expression "to sell oil" means "to slack off." It comes from the Edo Era, when salesmen would sell hair oil to women, a practice that tended to result in more sitting and chatting with clients than real work getting done. So anyone who is "selling oil" is basically wasting time instead of being productive. Now here's the joke again: Hiyori asks Yato if he has any selling points, and Yato says, "I have plenty. Like my coquettish nature!" Hiyori responds, "You're a good oil salesman, too." Ah, ha, ha...

Be the heel, page 191

Again, for readers unfamiliar with the pro-wrestling world, the "heel" is the "bad guy" in wrestling promotions.

YOU NEED TO BE DARKER, EDGIER.
BE THE HEEL! BE INTIMI-DATING! ALWAYS WEARING A DAUNT-LESS SMIRK!

Spreading salt, page 193

PURIFI-CATION! SCAT-TER SALT!!
SALT
DON'T FORGET TO LEAVE PLATES BY THE DOORS! AND...

In Shinto, salt is used for purification. It is scattered on people and places to cast out impurities and ward off evil or unlucky spirits. Plates with piles of salt, called *mori-shio*, are placed outside doors so people can be purified as they pass through them, although the origins of this practice may have more to do with attracting important visitors by luring the oxen pulling their carriages to the door with salt. The point is, now that the goddess of misfortune has visited Tenjin's shrine, it is of utmost importance to purify her influence as quickly as possible.

NORAGAMI

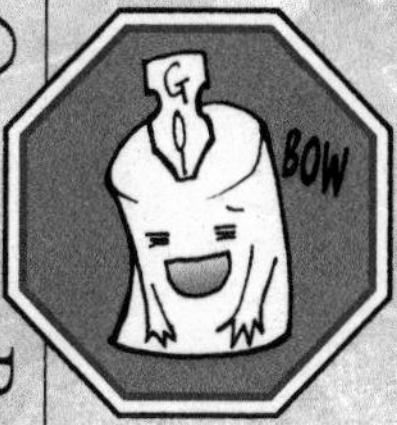
BOW

Hypothetically speaking.
If I were a shinki, I would want to be Bishamon's shinki and lie around all day.

Adachitoka

Kodansha Comics Trade Paperback Original.

Noragami: Stray God volume 4 copyright © 2012 Adachitoka
English translation copyright © 2015 Adachitoka

Published in the United States by Kodansha Comics, an imprint of Kodansha USA Publishing, LLC, New York.

Publication rights for this English edition arranged through Kodansha Ltd., Tokyo.

First published in Japan in 2012 by Kodansha Ltd., Tokyo.

ISBN 978-1-61262-994-0

Printed in the United States of America.

www.kodanshacomics.com

8 7 6 5 4 3 2

Translator: Alethea Nibley & Athena Nibley
Lettering: Lys Blakeslee